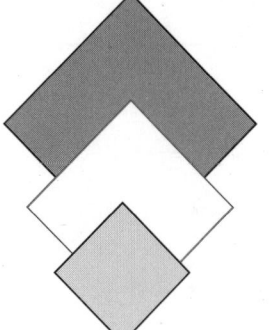

Perspectives on the Hospitality Industry

An Introduction to Hospitality Management

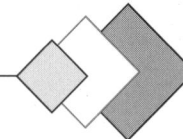

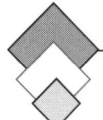

Carl P. Borchgrevink, *Editor*

KENDALL/HUNT PUBLISHING COMPANY
4050 Westmark Drive   Dubuque, Iowa 52002

Cover Photo Credits

Photo of cruise ship courtesy of Corel.

Photos of restaurant, airline ticket counter, airplane, doorman, and
   Eiffel Tower courtesy of PhotoDisc.

Photo of Luxor Hotel courtesy of the Las Vegas News Bureau.

Photo of sight-seeing couple and tour guide courtesy of the State of New Jersey
   Department of Commerce and Economic Development.

Printed in the United States of America
10 9 8 7 6 5 4 3 2 1

CONTENTS

Introduction *v*

About the Authors *vii*

CHAPTER

INTRODUCTION

This book is intended to provide a framework for an introductory hospitality course. The intent is to have the student read the text and use the text as a foundation in further study, either self-directed or under the guidance of an instructor. The introductory hospitality course is seen as a vehicle for introducing the students to the hospitality industry and its career options. Each chapter will contain learning objectives and sample questions as well as World Wide Web-based activities as appropriate. These questions and activities will require the students to discover and describe a variety of hospitality companies; while considering the available career options within said companies. The instructor is encouraged to assign the questions and activities that are most appropriate given the instructors approach. As the text is seen as foundational in terms of career planning, the first chapter starts with self-exploration and career exploration activities. These activities are not seen as exclusive to the first chapter. Rather, it is anticipated that the student will refer back to Chapter One activities and assignments throughout the reading of this text in an effort to maximize their learning and improve their understanding of the plethora of career options available in hospitality and related industries.

ABOUT THE AUTHORS

Clayton W. Barrows, Ed.D. is an Associate Professor of Hotel, Restaurant, and Tourism Administration at the University of New Orleans. Prior to joining UNO, Dr. Barrows spent 10 years in the hospitality industry where he worked as a manager in a variety of operations. Dr. Barrrows has published extensively. His current research interests include food and beverage training in private clubs and the marketing of brewpubs.

Carl P. Borchgrevink, Ph.D., CFBE is an Assistant Professor in *The* School of Hospitality Business at Michigan State University, where he also directs the Michael L. Minor Master of Science in Foodservice Management. Areas of expertise include leader-member exchange, food and beverage management, production and service, and organizational communication.

Ronald F. Cichy, Ph.D., CHA, CHE, CFBE is the director of *The* School of Hospitality Business at Michigan State University. He is the author and co-author of several books, and he is a recognized authority and researcher on the leadership qualities of hospitality leaders. As a professor he teaches total quality management in the hospitality industry. He serves on numerous industry and association boards of directors.

Linda K. Enghagen, J.D. is an attorney and Associate Professor at the University of Massachusetts at Amherst. In the field of hospitality, her teaching and research interests are in the areas of law and applied ethics. In addition to her appointment in the Department of Hotel, Restaurant, and Travel Administration, she holds an appointment in the Department of Mechanical and Industrial Engineering where she teaches Engineering Law and Ethics through a Distance Education Program. Professor Enghagen also writes and lectures on intellectual property issues for educators.

Jerry L. Fournier is Executive Vice President of HDS Services. HDS Services specializes in foodservice and hospitality management and consulting. Areas of expertise include hospitals and medical centers, long term care facilities, upscale retirement communities, corporate, education, commercial and private clubs.

Perry Hobson, M.S. is Senior Lecturer in Marketing at the School of Tourism and Hospitality Management, Southern Cross University, NSW, Australia. He has published extensively in both hospitality and tourism journals, and is on the editorial boards of *Tourism Management,* the *Journal of Hospitality and Tourism Research* and the *Journal of Vacation Marketing.* He has written a number of external study guides for distance learning. His areas of research include youth tourism, hotel and tourism development in Asia-Pacific, leisure shopping and tourism, and consumer behavior.

Michael L. Kasavana, Ph.D., CHTP is a Professor in *The* School of Hospitality Business at Michigan State University. He is an expert in information technology and continues research into the current and near future developments of property management and transaction processing technology. He has also created a series of instructional software products and on-line software. He is a sought after industry consultant and serves on many industry advisory boards.

Bonnie J. Knutson, Ph.D. is widely known as an authority on emerging lifestyle trends and creative marketing strategies. Her work has been featured in publications such as *The Wall Street Journal, USA Today,* and on CNN. She has had articles appear in numerous hospitality publications, and is editor of *The Journal of Hospitality and Leisure Marketing.* She was named an Advertising Education Foundation Teacher-Scholar, and she is a frequent speaker at industry meetings and serves on several industry advisory boards.

Jerry A. McVety is President of McVety & Associates—A Division of HDS Services. The division provides consulting services for and has extensive background in many aspects of the foodservice, retail, and club industries.

Jack D. Ninemeier, Ph.D., CHA is a Professor in *The* School of Hospitality Business at Michigan State University. He serves on the Foundation Board of the Dietary Managers Association and on the Academic Council of the Club Managers Association of America (CMAA). A prolific writer, he has penned more than 25 books that are utilized both in industry and classrooms throughout the world. His expertise includes planning and control for food and beverage operations.

Raymond S. Schmidgall, Ph.D., CPA is a Professor in *The* School of Hospitality Business at Michigan State University. He is the Hilton Hotels Professor of Hospitality Financial Management. He has authored the highly acclaimed *Hospitality Industry Managerial Accounting* and *Financial Management for the Hospitality Industry* books used around the world by both the industry and educators. He is a very active researcher and serves on numerous hospitality industry and educational association boards.

Michael P. Sciarini, Ph.D. is an Assistant Professor in *The* School of Hospitality Business at Michigan State University. His expertise is focused on career development, career paths, succession planning, and other human resources issues. He teaches lodging operations, strategic planning, and human resource.

A. J. Singh is a Ph.D. candidate and Visiting Professor in *The* School of Hospitality Business at Michigan State University. He has several years of Lodging Industry experience in India and the U.S. as an executive with companies such as Oberoi Hotels, Stouffer Hotels, and Hyatt Hotels. His doctoral research at Michigan State University includes an analysis of structural changes in U.S. Lodging Industry.

Alex M. Susskind, Ph.D. is an Assistant Professor of Food and Beverage Management in the School of Hotel Administration at Cornell University, where he teaches courses in food and beverage management and operations. Professor Susskind's research primarily examines the behavior and attitudes of guest service employees focusing upon issues such as: (a) the influence organizational downsizing, (b) the organizational climate of service-based organizations, (c) team-based interaction, and (d) recruitment and hiring processes. He has published articles in the *Journal of Hospitality and Tourism Research*, the *Hospitality and Tourism Educator*, *Communication Research*, the *International Journal of Hospitality Management*, the *Journal Hospitality and Leisure Marketing*, and The *FIU Review*.

John M. Tarras, J.D., CPA, CHA is an Associate Professor in *The* School of Hospitality Business at Michigan State University. Professor Tarras specializes in legal, finance, taxation, and strategic management issues facing the hospitality industry. In addition he has assumed a leadership role in gaming management.

Robert A. Willis is Vice President of Operations for HDS Services. HDS Services specializes in foodservice and hospitality management and consulting. Areas of expertise include hospitals and medical centers, long term care facilities, upscale retirement communities, corporate, education, commercial and private clubs.

Robert H. Woods, Ph.D. is Professor and Director, Center for the Study of Lodging Operations, Restaurant, Hotel, Institutional and Tourism Management, Purdue University, West Lafayette, Indiana. Current research interests include human resources and strategic planning issues.

The Career Perspective

Michael P. Sciarini, *The School of Hospitality Business*, MICHIGAN STATE UNIVERSITY

ABSTRACT

This chapter provides a framework for career exploration and planning for those interested in the hospitality industry. The central themes are: (1) the efficacy of continuous self assessment, (2) the necessity for continued career focused research, (3) the on-going challenge of finding and maintaining a "career fit," and (4) the need for and value of targeted self-marketing and promotion. Underlying these central themes is the notion that each of us must accept responsibility for our own career development.

OBJECTIVES

At the end of this chapter the student should be able to:

1. Take stock of his/her current interests, values, strengths and weaknesses and describe current ideal occupation.

2. Effectively conduct career related research through an array of resources including people, technology, and organizations.

3. Compare her/his *ideal* occupation characteristics with *real* characteristics for specific hospitality occupations and understand how to determine if a "career fit" exists.

4. Understand basic self-marketing concepts and self-promotion strategies; develop effective self-marketing tools (i.e., resumes, cover letters) and prepare to interview effectively.

Introduction

The world, regional, and national economies have historically been subject to peaks and valleys—that is, things go very well at times and not-so-well at others. The hospitality sector of the economy is no different. In fact, as this is being written, the financial performance of the U.S. hospitality sector has been relatively strong for a period of time, and there are those who forecast continued prosperity and significant growth. However, many of us can surely remember days (not very far-gone) when the economic picture on a macro and micro (hospitality) scale was not so bright. Mark Twain is quoted as having said that "history doesn't repeat itself . . . but it rhymes." The wisdom of this quote reminds us that while the current state of financial health for the majority of the hospitality world may be quite positive, it is not unreasonable to expect that it will not always stay so. The future (however distant) likely holds a downturn and potential stagnation or decline in employment opportunities. The intent of this chapter and the exploration and planning process outlined herein is to provide you with a perspective and a planning framework such that the state of the economy when you graduate becomes an essentially irrelevant consideration. In other words, if you will take ownership of the career exploration and planning process, it will not much matter what the state of the economy is before, as, or after you enter the full-time job market. If you will: (1) assess yourself honestly and accurately, (2) explore your options and determine where you best fit, and then (3) market yourself strategically, you may find career fulfillment even during "tough" economic times.

Start with Your Interests

In the more than twenty years that I have been working in or teaching and learning about the hospitality industry, I have been directly involved with researching what college students need to learn/know for management success. I have also consumed others research about how employers decide who to hire and specifically what employers are seeking in new managers (the references at the end of the chapter include over 30 articles written since 1985 on these and related topics). In addition to the formal research of these and related issues, I have engaged in numerous and lengthy discussions with many hospitality industry professionals and recruiters from a wide variety of companies and organizations on the aforementioned topics. Given the levels of formal and anecdotal research completed to date, I offer the following answers to the question, "What do hospitality employers value when making hiring decisions?"

Strong service orientation
  Clearly

Problem solving/decision making skills
  Yes

Relevant work experiences and "technical skills" (i.e., accounting, operations, supervisory)
  Absolutely

Strong academic performance as measured by GPA?
  Usually, but hardly ever exclusively

Communication and interpersonal skills?
  Certainly

Study abroad experience and/or second language capabilities?
  Sure

Extracurricular involvement (i.e. clubs, associations, Greek system)?
  Almost always

Willingness to relocate?
  Chain operators of all sorts still place value here, but there seems to be more company flexibility in recent years

But what is it that they **really** want? What single factor can compensate for nearly anything lacking from the above (certainly not exhaustive) list? Simply put, it is *PASSION*. Pure, unadulterated passion for their business and/or company will likely persuade more recruiters than any other single attribute (and may even be more powerful than combinations of other attributes). Some employers call "it" different things, such as, "having a fire in your gut" or intellectual curiosity. No matter what choice of words they use, employers love it when you love the business they are in especially their particular company and its mission, etc. Possessing all or most of the rest of the attributes previously

Photo © 1998 PhotoDisc, Inc.

Hospitality employers want to hire people who have strong service skills.

listed certainly helps, but all else being equal, the candidate with passion will get the offer—every time!

Before moving on to a discussion of self-assessment and the value of clarifying your interests and passions, it is useful to briefly describe how employers determine or detect your passions. If it were as simple as just "talking a good game" in the job interview, anyone could speak passionately and end up with a job offer. They are, however, unlikely to keep the job long if they are only acting—the hospitality business seems to have a way of sorting out those that lack interest and passion in their work. Savvy employers find the passion of a candidate in the quality and length of her/his industry and related experiences, and in the candidate's ability to show (through references) and tell (through effective interviewing preparation and skills) about the times they enhanced guest satisfaction, solved employee and/or guest problems, and ultimately helped their business earn higher profits. Passionate candidates also do their interviewing "homework"—that is, they target the organization(s) they are interested in joining and learn *all* about them (i.e., their history, mission, financial performance, who their leaders are, who they compete against, what their strategic plans are, etc.). Passionate candidates have targeted and carefully considered questions for their potential employers and express their desire to learn and contribute! They know themselves well enough to feel confident of their ability to learn, grow, and "add value" to an organization which possesses a culture conducive to nurturing the candidate's passion and desire to succeed.

Given the current state of the hospitality industry and the projected continued growth in opportunities for managerial and other positions, it is possible for many people to obtain employment in the industry and lack passion for their work. While it is (arguably) unfair to work for an employer while lacking passion for the job, more importantly, it is probably not fair to yourself to behave in this way. Don't you owe it to yourself (and those who matter to you) to get involved in an occupation and a career for which you have a passion and a genuine desire to succeed? While it is important to acknowledge the need to find balance between life roles (e.g., career, family, leisure, community/civic), I firmly believe that to whatever degree one decides to pursue a career (or any other life role—parenting, for example), one is more likely to achieve balance and reasonable contentment if the chosen career/life role is selected (in great part) because one has a passion to do well at it.

It has been my experience and observation that the most "successful" people in any given field—those who are among the best at whatever it is that they *do*—are generally so interested in and passionate about what they do that they would do it even if they didn't get paid (much) for it.

Self Assessment

Some of us are more aware of our interests and passions than others. The fact that you are reading this book and may be enrolled in a college course or major related to hospitality and tourism clearly speaks to your interests in this exciting field. Because the world of hospitality and tourism is rich with career options, you will be well served to invest time and energy in clarifying not only your interests but also your values, strengths, and weaknesses. Armed with this knowledge, you are well prepared to make sense of your "ideal" work environment and then research more narrow industry segments, specific organizations, and actual occupations. By comparing the qualities of your ideal work environment with the work-world realities revealed by your research, you may begin to identify the overlap—that is, those industry segments, organizations, and occupations, which hold the best opportunity for a balanced "next step" in your career/life.

Learn about your dream career from your role model.

There are a variety of formal and informal means to better understanding one's strengths, weaknesses, interests, and values. For purposes of this text, we will restrict our discussion to less formal assessment methods. For those readers interested in more formal self-assessment, we recommend a visit to your institution's career services or counseling offices.

A simple yet effective way to better understand your strengths is to make a list of *ALL* of your personal accomplishments. Leave nothing off—from work, school, extracurricular, church, or any other aspect of your life. Input from family, co-workers and friends may prove beneficial as you create the list. The next step is to analyze your list to "drill down" to the underlying personal attribute that contributed to each accomplishment. In the process of analyzing your accomplishments and underlying strengths, don't overlook your weaknesses—that is, personal attributes you may want to improve upon. Some of these may be apparent when comparing your strengths with the earlier noted list of attributes valued by hospitality employers. If hospitality employers value an attribute that is not on your strengths list, it may be a "weakness" or an area you would be wise to target with a specific plan for improvement.

A thorough understanding of your strengths and weaknesses is necessary but not sufficient. It is possible that your current strengths and weaknesses do not reflect your current interests. Perhaps your attributes in any given area are more the result of previous interests that are not closely linked to your current interests. Don't overlook the obvious but sometimes ignored sources for surfacing or clarifying interests such as, childhood dreams, favorite summer work experiences, role models—that is, people you greatly admire—and even your favorite academic courses and the teachers/professors who taught them.

Your current interests should be carefully balanced against the economic realities and public perceptions associated with pursing careers connected with these interests. Cases of individuals who were "talked out" of pursing hospitality (and other) careers are not uncommon. These sorts of situations result from well intentioned directives or advice (often from parents), and often include statements like "you'll never get rich doing that" or "no son or daughter of mine is going to clean hotel rooms/flip burgers for a living," or "I've paid $XXX in tuition so you can go work at (insert your favorite restaurant chain)?" Be careful of these sorts of comments and advice (and associated pressure); the world is filled with individuals who overcame this sort of influence to go on to achieve great things (both inside and outside the hospitality business). Likewise, there are many people who blindly accepted these directives and advice and now suffer, "stuck" in careers and occupations for which they lack passion and interest.

Your value system and your answers to the question, "what really matters to me?" are at the heart of dealing with the issue of pursing your interests versus the advice or directives of other interested parties. It is usually difficult to identify a career that simply provides everything you (and those who love and care about

Your career may change through the years as your personal life changes.

you) desire. There are always short- and long-term ramifications of any choice—and the trade-off associated with each choice are often more compelling and complicated as life goes on, when marriage, children, and other deep relationships may occur or intensify.

Your Ideal Occupation

Having gained perspective and greater knowledge of your strengths, weaknesses, interests, and values, it is now appropriate to shed greater light on your general and specific occupational preferences. In other words, before moving ahead with exploration of the realities of the hospitality industry and its many and varied occupations, it is time to think more about your ideal occupation.

Considering all that you know about yourself, picture your ideal occupation. Describe it as vividly as possible by answering the following questions:

❖ What does the physical environment look like?
❖ How large (or small) is the organization?
❖ Why does the organization exist?

❖ Is it your own business?
❖ Where are you located (domestic, international, regional)?
❖ What is the climate like?
❖ Is the area urban? Suburban? Rural?
❖ What are your tasks and responsibilities? (For whom do you do what?)
❖ What is a typical day like?
❖ What skills are you using?
❖ What do you wear to work?
❖ Are you working with people? How much?
❖ Are you working with equipment/ technology? How much?
❖ Are you working with information/data? How much?
❖ Are you in charge? On a team? A planner? A doer?
❖ Who and how many are you working with?
❖ What are your co-workers like?

Answering these questions is intended to extend your thinking about the occupational possibilities which exist (or may be created). It is pragmatic to note that most people do not have everything they could ideally desire in their occupation. Still, the better you are able to identify what you want, the more likely you are to achieve something close to your ideal.

Career Related Research

All of the self assessment work completed to this point provides the framework for making meaningful comparisons to the real occupations, organizations, and industry segments that exist (or might be created based on a new idea or concept you come up with). As you gather information about occupations and organizations, compare the information to what really matters to you. A bit later in the chapter you will be provided with a tool to assist you in your analysis. Use the following sources for conducting your career related research: people, technology, and organizations.

People

One of the best methods for determining the realities associated with any given occupation is to talk with someone currently doing the work or supervising those who do the work. This process is known as information interviewing because the goal is not a job offer but rather to learn about a particular occupation. In addition to yielding information about a particular line of work, information interviews allow you to expand your network of personal contacts and acquaintances, which can be very useful later, when you are actually ready to pursue employment opportunities directly. The following two web sites are focussed on informational interviewing:

http://danenet.wicip.org/jets/jet-9407-p.html

http://www.jobtrak.com/jobmanual/inform.html

To get started on information interviewing, begin with people you

know—family, friends, teachers, professors, neighbors—do any of them have jobs that seem to match with your ideal occupational characteristics? If none of the people you know seem to match up (which is usually *not* the case), ask them for recommendations. Friends of your family, friends, and neighbors are usually easier to approach than complete strangers. Graduates of your high school or the institution you are attending (or graduated from) are usually a good source for information interviews as well. If, after asking others for referrals, you still come up "empty," you have at least recruited others into the process and they may come up with a suggestion later.

It is important to be courteous and professional when seeking information interviews, especially when approaching individuals you have not yet met. Write a letter to ask for an appointment, thanking them in advance for their consideration and briefly explaining your purpose. After an interview takes place be certain to send a personal note of thanks, and add the individual you interviewed to your list of personal contacts—your employment network database for future consideration.

Photo © 1998 PhotoDisc, Inc.

Talk to someone who does the work to find out if this is the job for you.

Library

In addition to conducting information interviews with professionals in the field, the other key person to contact, for assistance with occupational and organizational research, is your school or local librarian. He/she can show and tell you about:

General Career Resources such as the *Occupational Outlook Handbook* and other government generated resources.

Organization-specific Sources including on-line database, electronic indexes, and company annual reports and financial statements.

Technology

In addition to your institution's librarian, there are many other resources to help you learn about data gathering via the World Wide Web. One of the best new resources is *CareerXRoads*, the 1998 directory to the 500 best job, resume, and career management sites on the World Wide Web. The authors, Gerry Crispin and Mark Mehler maintain a website (http://www.careerXroads.com/), which includes an archive of updates to their list of best sites.

Organizations

Trade and professional associations exist to promote their members' trade or profession, protect the trade/profession via governmental relations' activities, etc., and to educate their members. As such, associations are often great sources for career exploration information. Examples of hospitality web sites you may choose to explore are:

American Culinary Federation
http://www.it-ch.com/partners/acf

American Hotel & Motel Association
http://www.ei-ahma.org/webs/ahma/ahmahome.htm

Club Managers Association of America
http://www.cmaa.org

Council on Hotel, Restaurant and Institutional Education
http://www.inndirect.com/inndirect/yp/chrie.html

Hospitality Sales and Marketing International Association
http://www.inndirect.com/inndirect/yp/hospitalitysales.html

Meeting Professionals International
http://www.mpiweb.org

National Restaurant Association
http://www.restaurant.org

Society for Foodservice Management
http://www.sfm-online.org

Reality Check: Ideal vs. Real

After completing research on your choice(s) of specific hospitality occupations, you may then compare the realities you uncovered with the IDEAL occupation you described earlier.

Self Marketing

A visit to the library, local bookstore, or World Wide Web can yield scores of self-marketing resources. You can, for example, find information on how to write resumes and cover letters that will "knock 'em dead!" to how to overcome "sweaty palms" when interviewing (and even practice interviewing on-line), and finally how to negotiate the best deal when you get that job offer. The volume of resources available is testimony to the anxiety many of us feel when it comes to the self-marketing/job search process. From my perspective, too many people spend too much time worrying about the fine details (i.e., the color and weight of paper to use for their resume, font size, placement of bold and italicized words) and forget/ignore the "big picture" of self marketing. Rather than repackaging all of the fine strategies and excellent advice currently available, keep

the following general ideas in mind and then check out the resources and links listed later in this chapter to polish your specific self-marketing strategies and tools:

❖ A great resume does not ensure a job offer but a poor/weak resume may prevent one. Your resume serves three primary purposes:
  1. Gets you interviews
  2. Positions you to feature your accomplishments, results, and talents once you interview
  3. Help those you interview with to remember you and "share" you with others involved in the employment decision.

Just like hospitality industry direct marketing documents (e.g., restaurant menus, hotel brochures, and web sites), the more targeted you can be, the more likely you are to obtain your objective.

❖ Research separates otherwise equal candidates—earlier in this chapter we noted passion as a key attribute and that passionate candidates invest in knowing the employer well. The more you know about an organization the better you can answer the question every employer wants answered, "Why should I hire you?"

❖ *THIS IS A PROCESS*—the results of an interview are not *permanent*. If you are "rejected" it does not mean forever and may not even have resulted because of any deficiency on your part. There may simply have been a limited number of openings for which there were better candidates, *this time*. Conversely, if you receive an employment offer, it is only the "next step"—if you fail to perform well or the employer has financial difficulty, etc., then you must start again. Either way (rejection or offer) you must persevere and move on!

The Hospitality Career Planning Portfolio

The "creation" of your personal career-planning portfolio is a component of this chapter and text. Most importantly, this is an opportunity for you to:

❖ learn more about yourself
❖ practice a step-by-step process by which you may plan for your career(s)
❖ identify and progress towards your current/next career goal(s)
❖ become familiar with some of the information resources which may be useful to you as you navigate along your career/life "voyage"
❖ collect and organize important career and work-related information

Because you (as an individual) and the world (especially the world of hospitality) are likely to experience major changes over time, the effort and resources you *invest now* in creating your portfolio have the potential to pay off for you in a variety of ways (and for the rest of your life). This is an opportunity where you may very well "get out of it *even more* than you put into it."

You may be asked to create your portfolio in "pieces" throughout the semester. If so, dates for rough drafts of these segments will be announced periodically by your instructor. The final version (i.e. the last one you'll do this semester but hopefully *not* the last revision over the course of your long life/career) is due at the end of the semester.

The directions on the pages which follow may ask you to fill in information or answer questions. For most parts, you are encouraged to use whatever methods suit you (legible handwriting, drawing, including photos, etc.) in creating your responses. However, there are portions of the portfolio which must be typed (for example, the cover letter and resume). All sections of the portfolio that require specific completion guidelines/techniques will be clearly identified. Requirements of this nature are not arbitrary and are not intended to stifle your creativity—they will be imposed based upon the standards of professionalism that prevail in the hospitality industry.

The Hospitality Career Planning Portfolio has been developed specifically with the introductory hospitality student in mind. Portions of this portfolio have been modified or reproduced (with written permission) based on materials included in the LIFE WORK PORTFOLIO, developed by the National Occupational Information Coordinating Committee (NOICC) in 1995.

If your class has a home page be sure to visit it. If not, or in any event, you are welcome to visit the home page I have developed to assist or support you. The URL is: http://www. bus.msu.edu/shb/hb200/index.htm. This home page will help you explore the Internet-based components of this book.

My Strengths

List and describe at least five strengths—what you're good at! Explain why you feel each is a strength by providing specific examples (or proof) that you could use to "market yourself" relative to a future job, graduate school, etc.

_____

_____

_____

_____

_____

_____

_____

_____

_____

_____

_____

_____

_____

_____

_____

_____

_____

_____

_____

_____

_____

_____

_____

My Weaknesses

List and describe at least five weaknesses—things about yourself you'd like to improve upon! For each weakness, include a plan to make improvements . . . again, be as detailed and specific as possible.

_____

_____

_____

_____

_____

_____

_____

_____

_____

_____

_____

_____

_____

_____

_____

_____

_____

_____

_____

_____

_____

_____

_____

_____

My Interests

Create your own "Top Ten List" in answer to the question "**What matters most to me?**"

10. _____
_____
_____

9. _____
_____
_____

8. _____
_____
_____

7. _____
_____
_____

6. _____
_____
_____

5. _____
_____
_____

4. _____
_____
_____

3. _____
_____
_____

2. _____
_____
_____

1. _____
_____
_____

When faced with something new, describe how you learn best. If you have been provided a learning style assessment in class, it can be helpful to include or consider your results from the learning style assessment to support your description of your learning style. Last, describe coping strategies you may employ if/ when the instructional style of the teacher is different from your learning preference.

_____

_____

_____

_____

_____

_____

_____

_____

_____

_____

_____

_____

_____

_____

_____

_____

_____

_____

_____

_____

_____

_____

_____

_____

Personal and/or Career Goals *(Three years)*

Within the next *three years*, I plan to accomplish the following five (or more) goals . . .

_____

_____

_____

_____

_____

_____

_____

_____

_____

_____

_____

_____

_____

_____

_____

_____

_____

_____

_____

_____

_____

_____

Personal and/or Career Goals *(Five years)*

Within the next *five years*, I plan to accomplish the following five (or more) goals . . .

_____

_____

_____

_____

_____

_____

_____

_____

_____

_____

_____

_____

_____

_____

_____

_____

_____

_____

_____

_____

_____

Ideal Job

Before you begin looking around for career options, take time to think about what **your ideal job** would be like. This would be the job you've always wanted—a job that would meet most of your needs. Describe every detail you can think of:

Your Co-Workers

_____

_____

_____

_____

_____

_____

Your Boss

_____

_____

_____

_____

_____

_____

_____

The Location

_____

_____

_____

_____

_____

_____

_____

The Work (tasks involved, etc.)

_____

_____

_____

_____

_____

_____

_____

Ideal Job *(continued)*

A Typical Day

_____

_____

_____

_____

_____

_____

The Pay/Benefits

_____

_____

_____

_____

_____

_____

_____

_____

The Hours

_____

_____

_____

_____

_____

_____

_____

_____

What You'd Wear

_____

_____

_____

_____

_____

_____

_____

_____

Information Interviewing and Networking

You already know many people. The people you know also know many people. These folks are part of your network. Use your network to learn more about interesting career options. Start with your family, then go to your friends. Don't forget to ask former or current employers or co-workers for help. Also talk with people you've met while volunteering in community activities or school organizations. Who do they know who might be able to help you explore other career areas?

Use the space on the next page to chart your network. Add more pages as needed. When you talk with someone about career options, ask them if they can recommend others who might help you. Collect business cards, flyers, and brochures from people and businesses that interest you. Add a pocket and store these materials in your portfolio if you want to.

Networking is one of the most effective strategies for getting a job. After information interviewing, you may then get back in touch with your network when you've made a decision on your (new) career direction. Then use your network to help you get hired.

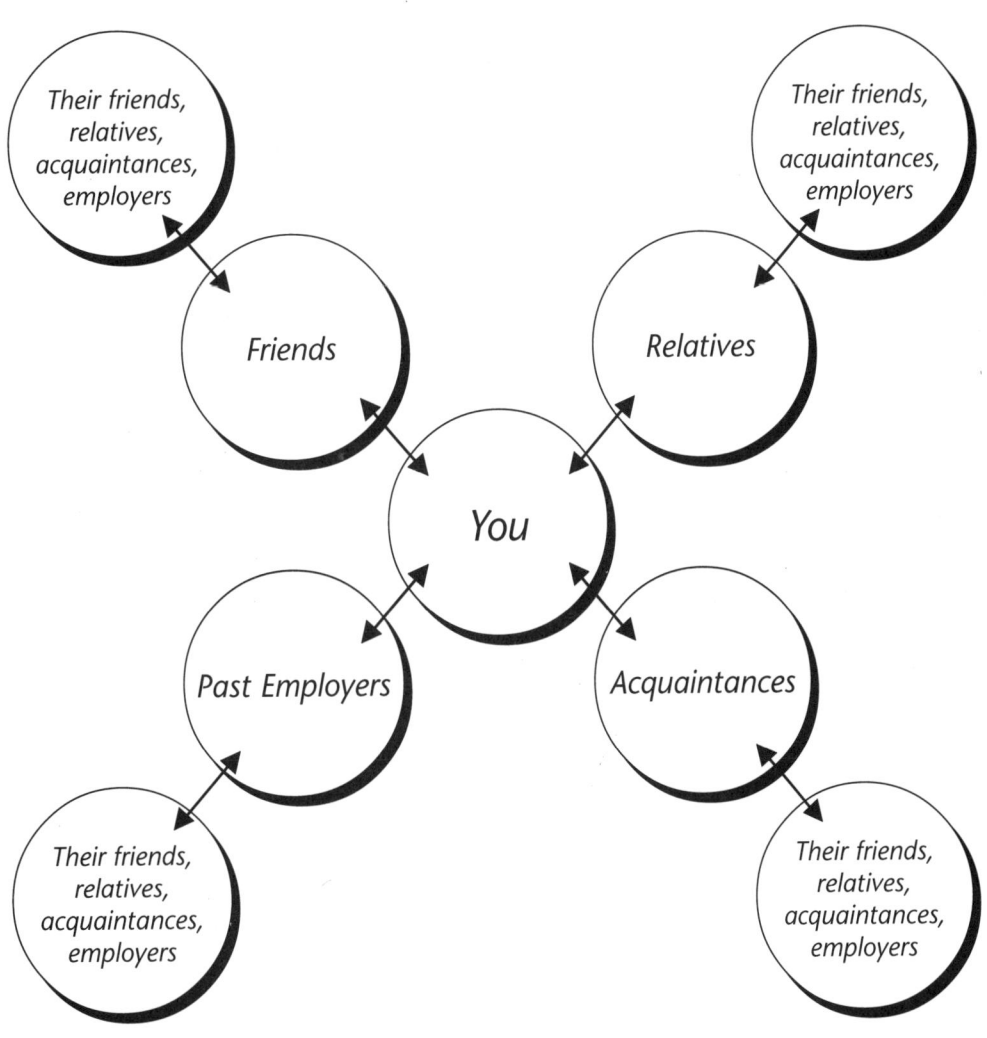

Information Interviewing

Based on your readings regarding informational interviewing, perform two information interviews with professionals currently working in a job/industry segment of interest to you. Summarize the interview results using the format(s) which follow.

INTERVIEW #1

Name of person interviewed _____

Title/occupation _____

Employer/organization name _____

Most important information learned _____

_____

_____

_____

Things that surprised me _____

_____

_____

Impact (positive and/or negative) of this interview on my thinking about this career/occupation

_____

_____

_____

_____

_____

_____

_____

_____

Other people in this occupation/career I could speak with _____

_____

Information Interviewing *(continued)*

INTERVIEW #2

Name of person interviewed _____

Title/occupation _____

Employer/organization name _____

Most important information learned _____

_____

_____

_____

_____

Things that surprised me _____

_____

_____

_____

Impact (positive and/or negative) of this interview on my thinking about this career/occupation

_____

_____

_____

_____

_____

_____

_____

_____

_____

Other people in this occupation/career I could speak with _____

_____

_____

Organization/Company Research

This form is to be used in researching organizations that you may be interested in doing an internship with and/or going to work for upon graduation. Use your library, the Web, your class's home page, and my home page, personal contacts, and anything or anyone else you may think of. Throughout the semester, you will use this form many times. Please make a copy as needed.

ORGANIZATION/COMPANY

_____

(name)

1. The organization's mission statement (i.e., for whom do they do what?)

_____

_____

_____

_____

_____

2. Provide a brief history of the organization (who started the organization, where, and when?)

_____

_____

_____

_____

_____

3. Determine "who" owns the company. Is it privately or publicly owned? If the organization is a chain, do they own and/or manage and/or franchise their operation(s)?

_____

_____

_____

_____

4. List the names and titles of at least three leaders of this organization you are researching (Chairperson, CEO, President, COO, VP of H.R., CFO, others as appropriate).

_____

_____

_____

_____

_____

ORGANIZATION/COMPANY

_____

(name)

5. Determine who the organization's competitors are and list three of them.

_____

_____

_____

_____

_____

6. Determine if the organization has a presence on the World Wide Web. What is the URL? Describe how the organization/company is using the Web as a strategic business tool (i.e. do they sell products or services directly? Do they recruit employees? Do they provide financial data for investors?). (Include a copy of the home page.)

_____

_____

_____

_____

_____

_____

_____

_____

_____

7. Check out the financial performance of your targeted organization for a minimum of the last three years. Have the net sales levels gone up or down? Why? Have net earnings (profits) gone up or down? Why?

_____

_____

_____

_____

_____

_____

_____

_____

ORGANIZATION/COMPANY

(name)

8. Create a list of sources (minimum of three unique sources) of published materials (i.e., articles from trade journals, national and regional publications, etc.) which relate to the policies, procedures, accomplishments, or objectives of your target organization. These materials should be written about the company by someone outside the company and published after January of last year. *Prepare a copy* of each of your three articles to hand in.

_____

_____

_____

_____

9. Identify the principal long-term objectives of this organization, including plans for expansion/ contraction of properties and/or concepts. Pay particular attention to plans for region(s) you prefer. Highlighted copies of annual reports may be included (if available). If you choose to quote directly from a source (i.e., an annual report) you must properly cite the source.

_____

_____

_____

_____

_____

10. Prepare a list of questions (minimum of five) that you intend to ask a recruiter from this organization. At least *four* of the five questions must relate to an issue *specific to this organization*. (For example: When talking to a recruiter from World Class Hotels, you might ask, "I was impressed to learn about the program your company has for victims of natural disasters, how was that program established? What sort of response is it getting from those in need?")

_____

_____

_____

_____

_____

_____

_____

_____

_____

Working for Myself

One choice for you as you look at work options is to be your own boss and start your own business. In the checklist below are some indicators that you might do well working for yourself. Check the statements that apply to you.

_____ I have a great idea for a new product or service . . . which is _____

_____

_____

_____

_____ I don't mind taking financial risks.

_____ I like to work hard on a project I believe in.

_____ I like being in charge of things and taking all the responsibility for success and failure.

_____ I am creative, flexible, and open to new ideas.

_____ I am a self-starter with a lot of self-discipline.

_____ I can commit myself 100% to meeting deadlines.

_____ I like working alone.

_____ I can do whatever it takes to get the job done.

_____ I have financial management skills.

_____ I like setting my own schedule.

_____ I am good at setting work priorities and keeping them.

_____ I am able to motivate myself and others when I believe in what I am doing.

_____ I work well with others even if I have just met them.

_____ I am able to convince others about my point of view.

If you are interested in starting your own business, visit the U.S. Small Business Administration Web site (http://www.sba.gov) for more information—including FREE software!

Club/Association Research

Collect information on (a minimum of) two different professional or trade associations (or clubs) that you may join to advance your professional/career development. One club/association must be located on-campus and one off-campus. Summarize what you learned below:

#1 ON-CAMPUS *CLUB/ASSOCIATION*

Name of organization _____

Address _____

Phone _____

e-mail _____

Why you chose this organization _____

_____

_____

Two examples of major activities that the organization plans/supports

_____

_____

_____

_____

Describe any continuing education and certification programs administered by this organization (include eligibility requirements, continuing education requirements, etc.)

_____

_____

_____

_____

_____

_____

_____

_____

Club/Association Research *(continued)*

#2 OFF-CAMPUS *CLUB/ASSOCIATION*

Name of organization _____

Address _____

Phone _____

e-mail _____

Why you chose this organization _____

_____

_____

_____

Two examples of major activities that the organization plans/supports

_____

_____

_____

_____

Describe any continuing education and certification programs administered by this organization (include eligibility requirements, continuing education requirements, etc.)

_____

_____

_____

_____

_____

_____

_____

_____

_____

_____

Where Do I Best Fit? *(Career Options Grid)*

In Section I, What Do I Know about Myself, you discovered many things about your . . .

- ❖ strengths
- ❖ weaknesses
- ❖ interests
- ❖ values
- ❖ learning style
- ❖ life roles
- ❖ future plans

In Section II, What Do I Know about Hospitality Careers, you discovered information about . . .

- ❖ your ideal job
- ❖ industry segments and occupations that interest you
- ❖ the skills they require
- ❖ their work schedules and environment
- ❖ their earnings and employment outlook
- ❖ sources of information
- ❖ going into business for yourself

The career options grid (on the following page) is a place for you to compare the information on the options you have been researching and what you know about yourself.

http://www.bus.msu.edu/shb/hb200/hbmenu.htm **includes links to sites where you may check your "fit" for various careers.**

Career Options Grid

Across the top of the grid are categories from the exploration section and the self-assessment section of the Portfolio. Under "Option," write in the names of options you have explored, a minimum of two. After you've listed your options, put an "X" in the first box if the option matches very closely with your ideal job. Put a "/" if the option is only partly compatible. Leave the space blank if the option doesn't fit at all. Continue to ask yourself, "Does this career option match what I want in my next job?"

Option 1:	Option 2:	Ideal:	
		X	**Skills and Responsibilities**
		X	**Interests**
		X	**Values**
		X	**Learning Style**
		X	**Work Schedule**
		X	**Work Environment**
		X	**Earnings**
		X	**Employment Outlook**
		X	**Life Roles**
		X	**Future Plans**
		X	**Other**
		X	**Other**
		X	**Other**
X	/	X	**Example**

Reviewing the Career Options Grid

When you've finished rating your options, carefully consider how they "measure up." Consider what might happen if you were to choose each option. Could you live with the potential positive and negative consequences of your decision? After thinking this over, complete the rest of this page.

Having given it a lot of thought, and having looked at my completed career options grid,

my option #1 _____ , is a _____
(perfect—terrible or something in between)

choice for me—because of the following (positive and negative) consequences of this choice . . .

_____

_____

_____

_____

_____

_____

_____

_____

_____

_____

_____

_____

my option #2 _____ , is a _____
(perfect—terrible or something in between)

choice for me—because of the following (positive and negative) consequences of this choice . . .

_____

_____

_____

_____

_____

_____

_____

_____

_____

_____

_____

Self Marketing Requirements *(Typewritten)*

A. Prepare a properly formatted business letter for use in contacting someone you may want to work for/with. Contact is not required, although encouraged if appropriate. The nature of your letter depends on your current goals. For example, you may desire an information interview or may be seeking an employment interview. *Type* (and include in your portfolio) a letter which is appropriate for your current stage in the career exploration/planning process. Don't forget to check your resources as you prepare your letter.

B. Prepare a resume designed to catch the attention of a potential employer. A one page chronological format is recommended. Again, take advantage of the available resources (web pages, library, the course text) to assist you as you create/modify your resume. Prepare this document as if you were submitting it for a real employment opportunity (i.e., type it and include a copy in your portfolio). If you lack "real life" experience, make this your "graduation day" resume.

Conclusion

Your life, like the portfolio, is a "work-in-process." Update and revise your portfolio as you live and learn, and reach/revise your goals. You can use this process (i.e., asking and answering the four major portfolio questions) to help establish new goals and develop new plans throughout your life. Ideally, your portfolio should be a sort of "tool kit" from which you pull resources/tools to update your resume, prepare for performance evaluations, negotiate raises, and sell your capabilities. Continuously revise your portfolio as you have new life/career experiences. As you face job changes, promotions, and other career related challenges and opportunities, you will have your portfolio to help you!

In the chapters that follow, you will come to better understand the menu of career opportunities available in the hospitality industry. The career menu is vast and exciting and yet it is important to recall the underlying premise/notion for this chapter: each of us must accept responsibility for our own career development. By utilizing the process described in this chapter, you may successfully navigate your way on an exciting occupational journey—one which is not ultimately sustained or controlled solely by the state of the economy or job market. By planning, modifying, and executing the strategies discussed in this chapter, you will empower yourself to succeed in developing a balanced and fulfilling career of whatever duration you choose!

Questions and Assignments

1. Explain how taking ownership of the career exploration and planning process may mitigate the potential impact of the general economy.

2. Discuss the role "passion" should play in your career choice.

3. List some of the critical issues that recruiters consider in the recruitment process. List them in order of importance to the recruiters. Discuss this list with your classmates or team.

4. How does "target marketing" apply to the job search?

5. Ask your classmates or teammates to develop a list of your perceived strengths. How does it compare to your own list? Discuss the implications.

6. Discuss how you should go about contacting an individual you have yet to meet or speak with to arrange for an informational interview.

7. What sort of career information is available to you at your library? Check with your librarian and develop a list of sources that you found most useful. Discuss how they were useful/relevant to you.

8. How important is the color and weight of the resume to the job search and placement process?

9. Discuss how you would respond to a rejection letter from a company that you are most interested in.

10. Explore at least three of following web sites and copy articles/pages relevant to hospitality careers for sharing and discussing with your classmates or team:

    http://www.hotel-online.com/Neo (Hotel OnLine)

    http://www.hospitalitynet.nl (Hospitality Net)

    http://www.restaurant.org (National Restaurant Association)

    http://www.sfm-online.org (Society for Foodservice Management)

    http://www.sfgate.com/~jlockley (Chef's Professional Agency)

    http://www.globalserve.on.ca/~nsbrud/foodlines.html (Food Lines)

    http://www.foodwine.com (Foodwine.com; Electronic Gourmet Guide)

    http://www.nrn.com (Nations Restaurant News)

    http://www.restaurantreport.com (Restaurant Report)

    http://www.chefnet.com (The Culinary Network)

    http://www.vtopia.com/inndirect (Inn Direct)

Bibliography and Suggested Readings

Antil, F. H. (1989). More Amps for Hospitality's Bright Lights: Given the Growing Internationalism and Corporate Dominance of the Hospitality Industry, Today's Aspiring Leaders Have an Increasing Need to Develop Advanced-Management Skills and a Generalist's Broad Perspective. *Cornell Hotel & Rest Admin Quarterly*, 30(2), 64–69.

Brewer, K. P. & Hurley, R. E. (1990). Managing Life Care Communities: New Integration of Skills for Hospitality Managers. *Hospitality Research Journal*, 14(2), 285–294.

Casado, M. A. (1993). Corporate Recruiters and Alumni: Perceptions of Professional Courses. *FIU Hospitality Review*, 11(1), 79–86.

Casado, M. A. (1992). Educators' Forum: Student Expectations of Hospitality Jobs. *Cornell Hotel & Rest Admin Quarterly*, 33(4), 80–82. (This study identifies some of the basic expectations of students before being recruited by hospitality companies.)

Dienhart, J. R. (1996). Research Skills Ranked Lowest. *Hospitality & Tourism Educator*, 8(4), 57–58.

Durocher, J. F. & Goodman, R. J. (1991). Training-Program Expectations: A Conundrum. *Cornell Hotel & Rest Admin Quarterly*, 32(2), 76–79. (This simple study reveals significant differences between students' perceptions of the industry's training programs and what's actually out there, to job dissatisfaction, discontented new managers, and unnecessary turnover.)

Farkas, D. (1997). Hiring Smarter: Ideas, Tips, and Suggestions for Recruiting Talented Managers. *Restaurant Hospitality*, 81(4), 47.

Foley, R. T. (1997). Human Resources: The Face of the Future; Control the Factors That Affect Your Employee Base. *Lodging*, 22(10), 33.

Izzolo, A. (1985). Profiling the Campus Recruiter at a Four-Year Hospitality Program. *FIU Hospitality Review*, 3, 71.

Johns, N. & McKechnie, M. (1995). Career Demands and Learning Perceptions of Hotel and Catering Graduates—Ten Years On: Courses Should Aim to Integrate the Teaching of Skills and Knowledge in a Way That Is More Relevant to the Workplace. *International Journal of Contemporary Hospitality Management*, 7(5), 9–12.

Jones, T. I., Alfred, W. C. & David J. (1993). Campus Recruitment: A Four-Year Program Profile, *FIU Hospitality Review*, 11(2), 73–80.

Knutson, B. J. & Patton, M. E. (1992). How Prepared Am I to Succeed in the Hospitality Industry? What the Students Are Telling Us. *Hospitality & Tourism Educator*, 4(3), 38–48.

Knutson, B. J. (1990). A Survey of HRIM Alumni: Were Their Expectations Met? *Hospitality Education & Research Journal*, 13(3), 463–468.

Knutson, B. J. (1989). Expectations of Hospitality Juniors and Seniors: Wave II. *Hospitality Education & Research Journal*, 13(3), 193–201.

O'Halloran, R. M. (1991). Ethics in Hospitality and Tourism Education: The New Managers. *Hospitality & Tourism Educator*, 3(3), 33.

Olsen, M. D. (1991). Structural Changes: The International Hospitality Industry and Firm: Unit Managers and Corporate Managers Both Face New Challenges in Addressing the Structural Changes Necessary to Remain Internationally Competitive. *International Journal of Contemporary Hospitality Management*, 3(4), 21–24.

Okeiyi, E. F., Postel, D. & Tindall, R. (1994). Topic Papers: Food and Beverage Management Competencies: Educator, Industry, and Student Perspectives: Hospitality Educators and Students Must Keep Abreast of Industry Expectations and Incorporate Them into Hospitality Management Curricula. *Hospitality & Tourism Educator*, 6(4), 37–40.

Parsons, D. (1991). The Making of Managers: Lessons from an International Review of Tourism Management Education Programmes. *Tourism Management*, 12(3), 197–207.

Sciarini, M. P., Woods, R. H. & Gardner, P. (1995). A Comparison of Faculty, Recruiter, and Student Perceptions of Important Employment Pre-Screening Characteristics. *Hospitality & Tourism Educator*, 7(1), 21–24.

Sciarini, M. P. & Gardner, P. (1994). Prescreening of Hospitality School Graduates: A Study of Hospitality Recruiter Decision Strategies. *Hospitality Research Journal*, 18(2), 97–114.

Sciarini, M. P. & Woods, R. H. (1997). Selecting That First Job: How Students Develop Perceptions about Potential Employers. *Cornell Hotel & Rest Admin Quarterly*, 38(4), 76–81.

Sciarini, M. P. (1996). Targeted Selection: An Industry—Academic Partnership That Works [ARAMARK]. *Hospitality & Tourism Educator*, 8(2/3), 115.

Sciarini, M. P. & Fourcar-Szocki, R. (1994). Top Ten List: How to Develop Your Network. *Hosteur*, 3(2), 5.

Sciarini, M. P. & Foucar-Szocki, R. (1994). Top Ten List: Ways to Take Charge of Your Career. *Hosteur*, 4(1), 3.

Sim, J. (1994). Relationships Among Students' Self-Perceived Competency, Knowledge- and Performance-Based Competencies in Foodservice Management. *Journal of Restaurant & Foodservice Marketing*, 1(2), 1–12.

Tas, R. F., Labrecque, S. V. & Clayton, H. R. (1996). Property-Management Competencies for Management Trainees. *Cornell Hotel & Rest Administration Quarterly*, 37(4) 90–96.

Umbreit, W. T. (1993). Essential Skills: What Graduates Need to Succeed: In Search of Hospitality Curriculum Relevance for the 1990s. *Hosteur*, 3(1), 10–12.

Umbreit, W. T. & Smith, D. I. (1990). A Study of Opinions and Practices of Successful Multi-Unit Fast Service Restaurant Managers. *Hospitality Research Journal*, 14(2), 451–458.

Williams, A. G. & Morrow, D. (1994). An Interview with a Hospitality Recruiter: Martin G. McDonough, Marriot International. *Hosteur*, 3(2), 6–8.

Woods, R. H. & Sciarini, M. P. (1997). Where Hospitality Students Want to Work: 1995–1996, *Journal of Hospitality & Tourism Education*, 9(2), 6–9.

The Historical Perspective

Carl P. Borchgrevink, *The School of Hospitality Business*, MICHIGAN STATE UNIVERSITY

ABSTRACT

This chapter takes a slice of history and describes the hospitality industry from the earliest known hospitality establishments through various developments over time to existing establishments. The chapter will establish that the hospitality industry is subject to the political and economic environment and the subsequent impetus to travel and engage in commerce. We will discuss the early taverns, coffeehouses and inns, the first restaurant, the first menu, the first dining and sleeping cars, as well as early hospitality pioneers. The visions and lives of a few of the pioneers will be discussed to show the necessary passion, determination, and will for success in hospitality.

OBJECTIVES

At the end of this chapter the student should be able to:

1. Understand how societal influences impact the hospitality industry.

2. Discover that hospitality is an ancient industry.

3. Learn of the negative connotation associated with the hospitality industry in the past.

4. Discover the origins of many things taken for granted in hospitality today.

5. Understand the wide ranging influences that a few people have had on the hospitality industry.

6. Appreciate that success in hospitality in the past, as today, takes much work, passion, and a will to succeed.

Introduction

Knowledge of the past does not guarantee success. Just as you get a better understanding of yourself by knowing your roots, your understanding of the hospitality industry will be improved by becoming familiar with the roots of hospitality. Knowledge about the past is a tool you can use in understanding the present and charting the future. At a minimum, knowledge about the history of hospitality will allow you to converse in intelligent and meaningful ways with your guests when they inquire about the past. Many guests are curious, and they may ask you for your insights as a hospitality professional.

This chapter takes the historical perspective and will discuss the impetus to travel, early lodging, and early offerings of food for consumption away from home. We will discuss the first restaurants and the first hotels, and we will consider some of the early influences on commercial food preparation and the emergence of quick service establishments. Moreover, we will visit some of hospitality's pioneers and visionaries. This chapter on the hospitality's historical perspective may appear to be Eurocentric, and to an extent this is correct, although I do not purposely exclude other influences. Such influences will be incorporated as best as possible. The reason for this is straightforward. Hospitality as we know it today, worldwide, is heavily influenced by the European hotels and restaurants.

Societal Influences

Any discussion of the history of hospitality will show that the hospitality industry is closely tied to society at large in that commercial provisions of food and lodging was a response to needs in society. The more people traveled, the more they were in need of food and lodging. Early hospitality entrepreneurs responded by meeting such needs.

People have always traveled. Our history books tell us that prior to settling and farming the land, we were

Photo courtesy Nik Wheeler/Corbis.

Hospitality as we know it today, worldwide, is heavily influenced by European hotels and restaurants.

hunter/gatherers that often led a nomadic existence pursuing food wherever it happened to be. Although nomadic tribes exist to this day, this is no longer a primary reason for travel. Multiple other reasons have developed over the years. These reasons include the desire to spread religious, ideological or political views, the need to escape persecution, overpopulation, to fight wars, explore new areas, expanding fiefdoms, kingdoms or empires, to engage in commerce, to participate in a religious activity such as a pilgrimage, to obtain an education, such as through an apprenticeship,[1] to improve health as in visiting a spa,[2] to connect with family and friends, and most recently for purely recreational reasons.

Travel and economic progress are clearly linked, as are travel and hospitality. For travel, and thus hos-

---

[1]The apprentice of the past would travel from master to master to learn his trade, and he was, upon completion, considered a journeyman, that is one who had fully completed his trade and was ready for employment by others.

[2]The word "spa," taken from the name of the famous mineral springs in Spa, Belgium, has become a common noun denoting any place with a medicinal or mineral spring.

pitality, to flourish beyond a small scale a common measure of exchange had to be developed. Precious metals, stones, jewelry, furs, shells, spices, nuts, oils and other foods, as well as services were often exchanged, or used as an exchange medium. You can imagine that it was somewhat cumbersome to carry such objects for trade purposes, furthermore, their value were not always commonly agreed upon. When coins of precious metals were pressed or molded and a somewhat standardized value stamped on them, trade flourished over larger regions. For example, the Vikings of Scandinavia engaged in a great deal of art, craft, and commerce, and readily accepted Arabic, Byzantine, and Frankish coins.

Commercial Hospitality's Beginnings

Trade, travel, and commerce, and thus the need for hospitality did not start with the Vikings. It is believed that early hospitality establishments were built in Sumer, a region of ancient southern Mesopotamia in present-day southern Iraq, which is believed to have existed as early as 5000 B.C. and flourished by 3000 B.C. The Sumerians gradually exerted power over the surrounding area. These are believed to have been the first people to develop trade in the modern sense of the word, and thus to be in need of hospitality services. The Sumerians were among the first to brew beer, and they had taverns where beer was offered for sale to local residents as well as travelers. The taverns were primarily beverage and perhaps food outlets, but some of them also had rooms for rent. Although these rooms were not intended for travelers, but for anyone frequenting the tavern who needed a bed, it is likely that they were, on occasion, rented for the night by traveling tradesmen. Among the foods that they might have served, we know from the story of Gilgamesh that the Sumerians would eat caper buds, wild cucumbers, ripe figs, grapes, several edible leaves and stems, honey, meat seasoned with herbs, and a flatbread made of barley, sesame seed flour, and onions.

We know that these taverns and inns persisted, as they are discussed in Babylonian history as well. Babylon had subsumed Sumer, and Hammurabi, king of Babylon (1792–1750 B.C.) developed a code of laws, which mentioned the taverns. The code was inscribed on a stone column in Susa. One of the tenets of this code was that tavern keepers were to report any criminal activities to the authorities. Furthermore, the code established that tavern keepers were not to dilute drinks or to pour the wrong measure of drinks. If the tavern keeper failed to keep the code, they did not lose their license, rather they lost their life. Penalties were rather strict in those days. Another early mention of lodging can be found in Joshua 2:1, which is believed to have been written in the 14th century B.C. Although most translations mention a harlot's house, it is important to note that in early records, inns and brothels were known by the same word. Apparently, there was no need to distinguish between the two. This may be one of the reasons hospitality establishments and those working in them were often considered disreputable.

As trade developed, the need for hospitality services increased. The response to this need in the Middle East was known as the *caravanserai*. An early inn, the caravanserai provided both food and shelter. A caravanserai was an inn built around a large courtyard designed to accommodate caravans at night. The term has Persian roots with *kārāvan* meaning "caravan" and *sarāy* meaning "camp" or "palace." They would not last as hospitality establishments today, as they were most often dirty and infested, and our authorities would shut them down for health violations. As late as the 19th century, descriptions of caravanserai suggest that travelers needed to shake fleas out of their mats every ten minutes or so. Fleas

were so abundant that they could be heard in addition to making their presence known by biting. Sanitation and hygiene were not common concerns until more recently; besides there were few caravanserai to chose from, so travelers had to accept that which was available to them.

It has been suggested that the ancient Egyptians were the first tourists in that they traveled for a variety of reasons beyond trade, such as sightseeing, attending festivals and religious ceremonies, and on behalf of the government. According to Egyptologist Gaston Maspero, Egypt, as early as 1300 B.C. had inns that provided for the needs of the traveler.

Hospitality in the Classical Age

In early Greece, commercial hospitality establishments were unknown, as every traveler had the right of sanctuary and asylum, and would receive hospitality free of charge from the local populace when traveling. This custom of providing and receiving hospitality occurs in many other cultures too, such as ancient Nordic culture. In any event, by the time of Homer hospitality establishments were known. In the 18th book of *The Odyssey* (approximately 850 B.C.) Homer makes reference to a tavern or place of common resort in which one could find a bench to sleep on. Herodotus, a Greek historian from the 5th century B.C., suggested that it was in Lydia that the first inns and taverns were established. Today we know they existed earlier. His work, however, establishes that inns and taverns were common in Lydia, a country of west central Asia Minor on the Aegean Sea, in what is today western Turkey. It is believed that Greece, by the 5th century, had a variety of inns and taverns. These taverns were of variable quality, and most often of ill repute. For example, Aristophanes (448–388 B.C.) provides references to lodging houses, and bed bugs, in his play *The Frogs*, while Petronius, who died about 66 A.D., quotes the Greek

philosopher Socrates (469–399 B.C.) as boasting that he never even looked into a tavern!

Rome, according to Roman mythology, was founded by Romulus and Remus. It was at first ruled by the Etruscans, who were overthrown about 500 B.C. The Roman Republic gradually extended its territory and expanded its influence, giving way to the Roman Empire during the reign of Augustus (27 B.C.–14 A.D.). The traditional date for the end of the empire is 476 A.D. Nonetheless, during this period, travel was considered to be reasonably safe within the empire, which provided an impetus for the growth of hospitality establishments. A wide range of inns and taverns developed. Some were of the highest quality and luxurious in their offerings, while others were again of ill repute. For those who were wealthy or influential, the Romans built exclusive inns along their roads. In order to enter and make use of such an establishment, you needed to have a special permit, the *diplomata tractatorium*. Such permits were for the few. The typical inns or taverns were of poor quality and repute. Indeed, although the citizens of Rome had quite a few recognized rights, if a citizen was an innkeeper, or married to one, many of the rights were forfeited. They were, for example, not allowed to bring legal actions in the Roman courts, and the wife or mistress of an inn or tavern keeper was exempt from the laws regarding adultery! Other hospitality establishments that existed during the Roman Empire include the *Cabarets*, shops that sold alcoholic beverages. According to Lucius Seneca, (4 B.C.–65 A.D.) eating houses displayed food attractively in order to lure customers in, only to provide a product of poor quality upon entry. Lucius Seneca also made note of the many street vendors and eating-house keepers loudly calling out their offerings. The excavation of Pompeii revealed several eating-houses, confirming their existence.

In terms of buying *food on the run*

for immediate consumption, we know that as early as during Nebuchadnezzar's time (605–562 B.C.), people often did not prepare food at home. They chose, rather, to purchase foods ready to eat in the market place. There are records of purchases of such things as forcemeatballs (an early precursor of the hamburger, sans the bun?) roast mutton, fish fritter, pancakes and almond paste sweets. Considering that the practice of buying food for immediate consumption was an Arabic tradition, has led some to believe that it was the Arabs who introduced the practice to Europe. The Arabs attempted to conquer much of Europe, and had a dominant presence in Spain and Italy from the 8th century to late 11th century A.D. At its peak the Arab Empire extended from the Atlantic Ocean across North Africa and the Middle East to central Asia, influencing the cultures and cuisine along the way.

Hospitality During the Dark and Middle Ages

The Dark Ages, a period of repression and unenlightenment, followed the decline of the Roman Empire. Travel became unsafe and infrequent. During the Dark Ages, and the early part of the Middle Ages, Christianity became the unifying force of culture, and the monasteries were the institutions that took the role of providing hospitality for those who ventured to travel. This was a period of feudalism and the manorial system. In its simplest form, the system consisted of the division of land into self-sufficient estates, each held by a lay or ecclesiastical lord, who lent it to peasants for farming. The peasants in return provided services, dues or taxes, and an oath of fealty. The only safe places for travelers during this time were the monasteries, and as they were self-sufficient entities, they were well suited to meet the needs of the traveler. The monasteries did not charge for their services, but expected to receive a donation from the trav-

eler upon departure. The size of the donation would vary depending upon the travelers' relative wealth.

The middle class and subsequently commerce declined during Middle Ages. As a result hospitality establishments declined in number; however, it is noted that some establishments did persist. For example, a decree by King Ethelbert (approximately 616 A.D.), who ruled all of England south of the river Humber, required order at the inns. The *Church House Inn* at Rattery in South Devon has been dated to 1026. Furthermore, we also know that public cook shops opened in London about 1200. These shops offered customers pre-cooked food to take home with them. Some are likely to have consumed the food on the run. King Louis IV of France decreed in 1254 that innkeepers should only provide lodging to transients or to those who have no home in the town. Apparently, too many were finding the accommodations at the tavern *more accommodating* than those at home! Finally, it is known from a Scottish statute of 1425 that commercial lodging facilities were available. The statute decreed that it was illegal, and punishable by a fine of forty shillings, to take up abode with friends if an inn was available. The only exception being for

Photo courtesy Corbis-Bettmann.

Queen Isabella is credited with inventing the menu.

noblemen who could stay where they pleased, although their servants and horses had to make use of the commercial establishments.

Not So Dark in Asia

While there was little commerce in Europe and the old Roman roads of Europe were rather empty during

It is apparently during this period that the menu first surfaced. The invention of the menu as "a document" has been credited to Queen Isabella of Bayern who was married to the King of France, Karl VI (1386–1422). According to legend, she became tired of answering questions from her fellow nobles and their guests as to what they were eating, or were about to eat. The custom in those days would be for the host to announce, or have announced, the dishes that were being served. Often the dishes were not served as distinct courses, but simply put on the table as they were done—whole roasts and all. Those eating would simply help themselves as needed. The diners would use the same plate and cutlery throughout, and hands were frequently used. Knife and spoon were prevalent, but the fork had barely started to make its breakthrough. In any event, the Queen apparently sought some order, and started to have the various components of the meal written down on individual pieces of paper. The idea became very popular among the French royalty, and spread rapidly to the other courts of Europe. For centuries, the menu was known as l'escriteau, which is French for "the written."

the Dark Ages, the situation was different in Asia. We know from the writings of Marco Polo, the Venetian traveler who explored Asia from 1271 to 1295, that the roads of Asia were well developed and that much travel and commerce took place. From his writings it appeared that travelers could find hospitality for a price in private homes, as well as in "houses of public resort" and caravanserai. For the Great Khan and those traveling with him, as well as for government officials, ambassadors, and others of high esteem, the Great Khan built official posting houses every twenty-five to thirty miles along the road. These houses were to provide every "article required," in addition to food and lodging, and fresh horses. The posting houses are described as having as many as 400 horses. As such, the Great Khans appear to have outdone the Emperors of Rome.

Hospitality Grows During the Renaissance

The Middle Ages in Europe were followed by the Renaissance, which is French for "re-birth." This was an era of emerging nation-states and exploration, the beginning of a revolution in trade, and scholarly pursuits beyond the purview of the church. In Italy, the Renaissance emerged by the 14th century and reached its height in the 15th and 16th centuries; elsewhere in Europe it may be dated from the 15th to the mid-17th century. As the nation-states emerged, travel and subsequent trade again became relatively safe activities. The need for hospitality establishments was again on the rise. During this period the monasteries still provided hospitality for the needy and the wealthy, but was less apt to respond to the needs of the growing middle class. Apparently the church felt that the middle class could afford to pay for services, and may have directed them to commercial hospitality establishments. In addition, as travel increased, and the need for hospitality grew, it is likely

that the monasteries were not able to handle the potential volume, and felt a need to choose which market niche to serve. As ecclesiastics, it was their clear role to tend to the needs of the poor, which they did. In terms of the other travelers, the wealthy had larger donations to offer the monasteries than the middle class did. Furthermore, the wealthy were not likely to want to mingle with the growing middle class. As such, there were monetary benefits to excluding the middle class from hospitality service. The poor, who were also at the monasteries, were not likely to share shelter with the wealthy, and would be relegated to the kitchens and less desirable parts of the monasteries. Some establishments such as the Tewkesbury Abbey in England, built houses for the poor outside of the main compounds. Thus we can see that the church influenced the growth of hospitality establishments. In addition, the Reformation, which came near the end of the Renaissance also, influenced hospitality. Many church practices, and thus practices that took place at the monasteries were considered offensive. For example, Henry VIII, King of England (1509–1547) closed the monasteries and gave the land to his supporters.[3] As a consequence, all travelers had to search elsewhere for accommodations. This was a boon for the development of hospitality establishments in England.

The Coffeehouse

Prior to the development of restaurants proper, it was at an inn, tavern, or coffeehouse that one could purchase nourishment. We turn now to coffee and coffeehouses. Coffee has long played an important role in hospitality; according to legend it was initially discovered by an Arab

---

[3]It is believed that one of the reasons Henry VIII closed the monasteries and religious hospices was in response to Pope Clement denying him a divorce from his first wife Catherine.

goatherd called Kaidi, who discovered that his goats became frisky when they ate the berries of a certain shrub. Initially a wine-like beverage was made from the entire fruit of the coffee shrub. It was not until the late 13th century that the Arabs started roasting and grinding the seed of the fruit, known today as a coffee bean. From a hospitality establishment perspective, the year 1475 is important. This is when the world's first coffeehouse opened. It was called Kiva Han, and opened in Constantinople, where coffee as a product had been introduced in 1453. The origin of the word coffee is debated. Some believe it originates from the name of the region Kaffa in Ethiopia, where coffee is believed to have been discovered. Others suggest that the name stems from qahveh, an Ottoman Turkish pronunciation of the Arabic term for coffee, viz., qahwah. The first time the word "coffee" appears in the English language is in 1601 in William Parry's account of a Persian expedition. The first coffeehouse in England is said to have been opened in 1651 by "one Jew called Jacob [sic]" in a room at the Angel Inn on High Street, followed the next year by the coffeehouse of apothecary Arthur Tillyard. Coffee was initially believed to be a cure for a wide range of ailments, as such it is reasonable that an apothecary, i.e., a pharmacist, would offer the beverage. The first coffeehouse to open in London was opened in 1652 under Armenian management in St. Michael's Alley, Cornhill. The first coffeehouses came to Paris twenty years later, and after an initial period of success, failed. By 1754, however, Paris had 56 coffeehouses, which they called cafés.

Coffeehouses, or cafés, soon became popular meeting places where clubs and societies met, poetry was read, and business conducted. More importantly, they were seen as a place where rank and social standing were *ignored*. It should be noted, however, that they were considered meeting places for *men of letters*, poets, artists, celebrities, and more. To the best of our knowledge, the first café to provide newspapers free of charge to regular customers was Madame Fournier, who ran a café on Rue Saint-Antoine. In England, the printing act, which regulated papers, was not renewed in 1695, and the paper trade started to flourish. In 1720, a group of coffeehouse proprietors were concerned with the cost of having to provide free papers to their guests and attempted to print their own paper. The literati responded by suggesting that proprietors of coffeehouses lacked the intelligence needed to run a newspaper! Soon cafés and coffeehouses offered billiards, cards, chess, and more, a tradition often maintained to this day.

In Oxford the city council and the university officials became alarmed at the popularity of coffeehouses, and encouraged restraint. In 1679 the mayor of Oxford outlawed the selling of coffee on Sundays, while in 1772 the university issued a proclamation instructing the owners of taverns, coffee- and alehouses, and victuallers,[4] not to allow students to incur debts exceeding 5 shillings and not to open at unauthorized hours. To the annoyance of the tavern and alehouse owners, the coffeehouses were also given permission to sell wine. In 1740 thirteen wine licenses were issued in Oxford alone. However, considering that Oxford during that period of time had three hundred alehouses and one hundred inns and public houses, the threat to their businesses was minimal. In Scotland, Marie Stuart informs us, the "coffee houses" sold ale as early as 1665. It was also typical for coffeehouses to serve some food as well.

In France, during the Revolution, the cafés played an important role as meeting places of secret committees of members of the National Convention and as a tribune for orators.

_____
[4] A victualler was an innkeeper.

However, by the mid-18th century coffeehouses started to lose their popularity in both England and France. The primary reason for this is believed to be a shift in economic trends, in that trade that favored tea rather than coffee had become more prevalent. As a consequence tea dropped in price and coffee increased. Many coffeehouses turned to the sale of food and non-alcoholic drinks to survive, while others became richly decorated, elegant establishments that offered an expanded repertoire of products. Sidewalk cafés and elegant grand cafés exist to this day, not only in Paris, but around the world as well. In the Colonies, later to be called the United States, coffee remained a popular beverage due to the tax on tea by King George III, which led to the Boston Tea Party in 1773. From then on, coffee was seen as the colonists' preferred, and patriotic, beverage. Coffee has been part of all "American" soldiers' rations ever since. In parts of Europe beyond Britain and France, such as Austria, coffee remained a popular beverage for a longer period of time. Vienna had 15,000 coffeehouses in 1842. By 1925, however, only 1,250 remained. It should be noted that cafés existed early in places such as Berlin and Venice.

The Traveling Son

From the 16th century onwards, wealthy British families started the _Grand Tour_, which is seen as leading to the "Golden Age of Travel." The Grand Tour was considered an essential finishing of a young person's education. The young persons were sent to Europe to explore and learn for a number of years. They would often visit Italy, the birthplace of the Renaissance, considered a hub of art and culture. France, particularly Paris with its culture, was also considered an important destination. The route of the Grand Tour would depend on the perceived needs and desires of the young Briton or Englishman. As

such, much of Europe may have been visited. This form of travel was at its height during the latter part of the 18th century, and is seen as providing an impetus for the growth of hospitality throughout Europe.

Early Individuals' Influences

As noted earlier in our discussion of Queen Isabella, influences in hospitality often came from the courts, the opinion leaders of yore. During the 16th and 17th centuries we find that royalty continued to influence the foundations of French hospitality. The first mention of this is by Catherine de' Medici (1519–1589). She was the daughter of Lorenzo de' Medici of Florence, Duke of Urbina. In 1533, at the age of 14 she was married to another 14-year old, Henri of Valois, duc d'Orléans, later Henri II of France. As was the custom in those days, Catherine de' Medici brought with her an entourage that included many Italian chefs. She is credited by many historians with introducing more refined cookery and dining to France.

Another important royal who influenced cuisine and hospitality was Anne of Austria (1601–1666), daughter of Philip III of Spain, and a member of the Spanish branch of the Habsburg royal family. In 1615 she married the French king Louis XIII. Her retinue included Spanish chefs who introduced the use of _Roux_ (flour and fat, cooked over low heat) as a thickener for sauces. Until that point the French had used substances such as ground almonds for thickening, if thickening was done at all. Through Anne of Austria, _Sauce Espagnole_, a foundational sauce in French cuisine was introduced.

Thirdly, we have Louis XIV (1638–1715), alternatively known as _Louis the Great_ and the _Sun King_. He was king of France from 1643–1715. A magnificent court and the expansion of French influence in Europe characterized his reign, the longest in French history. Among those influ-

Louis XIV made dining a State Occasion.

ences was the stimulation of large-scale dining affairs.[5] He made dining a *State Occasion*, an event of importance. He would stage elaborate banquets with enormous quantities of food and drink. It was not unheard of to serve twenty or more courses at such banquets![6]

---

[5]In a roundabout way, Louis XIV can be seen as having had additional hospitality influences. He may have impacted the prevalence of coffee as the beverage of choice in America. Dutch mariners smuggled coffee plants out of the Arab port of Mocha in 1690. They planted some in their Java colony and sent others to the botanical gardens at Amsterdam. In 1713 Louis XIV received a coffee bush from the Amsterdam greenhouses. It was subsequently stolen from the French Royal Gardens and transported to Martinique by French naval officer Gabriel Mathieu de Cheu, who planted the seedling. This seedling is seen as the start of the American coffee industries!

[6]The term *banquet* is today a well-established hospitality term for a large, often festive, hospitality food event. This was not always the case. The Old French word *banquet*, the likely source of our word, is derived from Old French *banc*, "bench," ultimately of Germanic origin. The meaning of the term appears to have developed over time from "little bench" in Old French to "a meal taken on the family workbench," to "feast." The English use of the word *banquet* is first recorded in a work possibly composed before 1475 with reference to a feast held by the god Apollo. The word appears to have been used from the 15th to the 18th century to refer to the feasts of the powerful and the wealthy. Today one needs not be powerful or wealthy to take part in a banquet.

The Stagecoach

Arthur White has suggested that nothing has had more of an impact on inns, particularly English inns, than the stagecoach. The exact date that the first stagecoach set off is not known. We do know, however, that a stagecoach left Chester to travel to London in 1657. From this period onward for about two hundred years until the train was invented, the stagecoach was the preferred mode of travel. Traveling by stagecoach proved to be much more economical than earlier travel singularly on horseback. This is particularly evident considering that road maps, not to mention directional signs, usually did not exist, and a traveler would often have to hire a local guide. As the stagecoach became popular regular routes were established, and along these routes coaching inns were subsequently built. The coaching inns provided fresh horses for the coachmen and rest and food for the passengers. Travel by stagecoach was most uncomfortable, slow,[7] and at times dangerous, but for many it was the only alternative available. It was not uncommon for travelers to find themselves on the coach for a week or two. Yet coach travel became popular, but remained a risky venture. White mentions a newspaper report from Bath in 1812 that matter-of-factly mentions that when the coach arrived they found two passengers frozen to death and one passenger dying among those on the coach. It has been suggested that one of the reasons the inns were so popular is that their rela-

---

[7]Louis XIV, whom we discussed above, set out from Versailles to travel to Bourbon l'Archambault in April, 1681. For weeks the roads had been specially prepared for his travel across them, yet they were only able to maintain an average speed of 16 miles per day. It is only after the roads received hard surfaces of compact broken stones (started by road surveyor Macadam in 1815), that some measure of speed was obtained. A Lord Campbell is noted as discussing the marvelous speed of seven miles per hour!

tive comfort stood in stark contrast to the discomforts of travel. Some have suggested that when a traveler reached an inn after being on the road for days, they were often reluctant to set out traveling again, and would extend their stay at the inn.

Discrimination or Levels of Distinction?

Just as we today have different quality levels, different levels existed in the early inns as well. This distinction, however, was not based on the travelers' choice or willingness to pay, but on their social status. In the cities where multiple inns might exist, if a person had his own horse and carriage, or could afford to ride on horseback, he could stay at the better inns. These inns often posted "No Coaches." If people were traveling in a stagecoach, they would stay at a "stage coach inn," which would not accommodate those traveling in open wagons. If a person were so poor he/she had to travel on foot, it would be virtually impossible to find an inn, and that person would be lucky to find a stable loft with clean hay. Along the stagecoach route, where one inn had to accommodate all, distinctions were still made, but within the establishment. Those of good social standing ate in the dining room, while those who were not so fortunate were relegated to the kitchen. Separate dining rooms were available for the truly wealthy. While the wealthy would have separate rooms and separate beds, it was not uncommon to simply sleep on mattresses spread around the floor, or to have communal beds at the inns. William Shakespeare (1564–1616), among others, makes mention of the *Great Bed of Ware*, which slept as many as sixty-eight people. This was likely an oddity, but other large beds have also been mentioned, such as the bed at Scole Inn,[8] designed to hold fifteen to twenty couples.

---

[8]White sites J. Larwood for this reference.

STUYVESANT BUS LINE

As the stagecoach became popular, regular routes were established, and along those, inns were built.

Early North America

In North America, the first accommodations available for a fee appear to have been made available in Quebec in 1608 as part of a fort-like settlement built by Samuel de Champlain. The first proper hospitality establishment that we have record of is an inn that was built in Jamestown about 1610. Unlike their European counterparts, the innkeepers in North America were not concerned with social status, but were willing to serve all who had money and were willing to pay. G.W. Lattin has suggested that this open-minded spirit, combined with aggressive expansion and willingness to take calculated risks, led to the rapid growth of hospitality enterprises in America: By 1800 the United States had become the world leader in hospitality.

Exactly when the first few taverns were built in North America is uncertain. There are references to a public house in Boston called *Coles*[9] in 1634.

In what was later to become New York, the first few public houses were built 1642–1643, and by 1649 Broadway was recorded as having seventeen "tap houses." The *Pennsylvania Magazine of History and Biography* mentions a *Blue Anchor Tavern* on Front Street in Philadelphia in 1671. In New England taverns were referred to as "ordinaries." They spread very rapidly as even the New England Puritans took it for granted that every settlement needed a tavern. White, in his discussion of ordinaries in Gloucester, Massachusetts, established that the five selectmen in 1774 were each given a salary of $5.00, but allowed to charge at the local ordinary as needed. Their combined charge totaled $150.00. The following year they were paid $25.00 each, and apparently told to meet their own needs. The first revoked license we are familiar with occurred with Corporal John who was the licensee at the White Horse of Ipswich, Massachusetts. It was revoked in 1658 due to keeping his bar open past 9 p.m., and encouraging young men to drink.

In terms of accommodation for the night, many taverns had rooms and beds for rent. It was not uncommon, however, in the poorer taverns simply to stretch out on the floor on your bundle of skins after eating and drinking. If you had secured a room, it was furthermore not uncommon to room with others, even of the opposite sex. Sometimes even beds were communal, as we know from the *Diary of Mme Knight*, which describes her traveling alone from Boston to New York in 1704. Apparently segregation of the sexes was not an issue in early America either. The rate for the bed or room in these early days was often left up to "a reasonable raconing" (reckoning) by the traveler, and in Virginia there was for a period a law that forbid innkeepers to charge a specified fee. They were simply to accept whatever was offered.

Although many of the inns and ordinaries were rather primitive, we know of a few high quality establishments as well. There are records of lavish meals and accommodations at *Gregories* (the *Tontine Coffee House*) in Albany, which was built in 1750. In Bethlehem, Pennsylvania the *Sun Inn* was built around 1758, and is described as having been built solely with the ease, comfort, and convenience of the traveler in mind. It could accommodate 160 guests, which made it a very large inn. Prior to 1794 most lodging properties in America were converted homes, but in that year the *City Hotel* was built in New York City. It had 73 rooms, a large number in those days.

Impact of Industrial Developments

As in Europe, hospitality establishments grew rapidly in America after the introduction of the stagecoach. The first regular route was established between Boston and Hartford, Connecticut in 1783. Although the stagecoach is seen as having a dramatic impact on hospitality, the Industrial Revolution (1750–1850) and the introduction of the railroad and rail travel, 1825 in England and

---

[9]The public house was initially known as Coles, due to the landlord being a Samuel Cole. Later when a portrait of John Hancock was hung outside of the tavern upon his election as Governor of Massachusetts, it became known as Hancock's Tavern.

1828[10]–1830 in America, had a greater impact. The Industrial Revolution led to greater prosperity, increased trade, and an increased need for travel and commerce, which rail travel made possible. A wide range of hospitality establishments would open at or near train stations, and wherever trade took place. Travel increased dramatically, and in the period from 1829 till the start of the Civil War in 1860, hotels opened at the fastest pace ever in American history until the 1920s. Europe also saw dramatic growth.

The First Restaurant?

The term "restaurant" is well known today, but it was not until the end of the 18th century that it became a common term. In Paris in 1765, Monsieur A. Boulanger, a seller of soups and broths, changed the world of hospitality by reinventing the eating house that had died out during the Dark Ages. Soups and broths were considered restoratives[11] in the sense that they provided sustenance that strengthened the hungry and weary. As one of many vendors of soups and broths, he was supposed to sell only that, but in 1765 he decided to offer to the general public a dish of sheep trotters in a white sauce. It is believed that he called the dish *le restaurant divin*, i.e., the divine restorative, and that he had a sign posted outside his shop inviting people to partake and become restored.

---

[10]The first rail travel in America used horse drawn carriages. It was not until after 1830 and the successful run of the Tom Thumb locomotive, built by Peter Cooper, that steam engines were used.

[11]Anthelme Brillat-Savarin (1755–1826) referred to chocolate, red meat, and consommè as restaurants. This meaning, restorative, survived until the late-19th century when it was adopted to refer to the establishment specializing in serving restorative foods. A. Brillat-Savarin was a French politician, gourmet and satirist. He is most known for writing the *Physiology of Taste or Meditations on Transcendent Gastronomy* in 1825, and coined the term "Tell me what you eat, and I will tell you what you are."

You may think that selling sheep's trotters in a white sauce is hardly a reason for the term restaurant to become widely used, and you are right. Monsieur Boulanger, in preparing and selling this dish to the public was seen as infringing upon a guild's monopoly. It was the *traiteurs*, the members of the catering guild, who were supposed to be the ones to prepare meat based dishes, and they claimed his dish of sheep trotters was within their domain, not within the domain of the *restauranteurs*, who were only to make simple broths and soups. The caterers' guild sued for infringement, and the case garnered a great deal of attention. The important point is that the courts found that he had not infringed upon their monopoly, and furthermore they issued a decree allowing both traiteurs and restauranteurs to prepare and sell such foods to the public at large. Indeed, they were even allowed to serve the food to guests within their own establishments. Subsequently several more such establishments opened up. Eating houses were again proliferating, soon to be known as restaurants.

Although Monsieur A. Boulanger is credited with opening the first restaurant, it has been claimed that his establishment was a far cry from anything we would today consider a restaurant. The first establishment considered worthy of the name as we know it today did not open for another twenty years. In 1782,[12] Monsieur Beauvilliers opened an elegant establishment called *La Grande Taverne de Londres* (The Great Tavern of London) at 26 Rue de Richelieu. His establishment was known for his superior kitchen, well-trained waiters, fine wine cellar, excellent recommendations, and the size of the bill. He was known to remember the faces and names of guests for twenty years, even if they only visited once or twice.

---

[12]Some suggest it may have opened in 1786. See Montagné.

The French Revolution and Hospitality

From 1789 through 1799 rapid growth in restaurants took place. Many consider this period the beginning of "modern foodservice." Monsieur Boulanger's case is part of the reason this growth could take place, but the primary impetus was political. This is a period of political unrest and upheaval, which led to the French Revolution. How is it that the French Revolution impacted hospitality? This is not immediately evident, particularly since the Revolution was a revolt against the ruling nobles and clergy. The French Revolution led to the beheading and exiling of many of the upper classes, nobility, and royalty. As the upper classes fled the country, or were beheaded, chefs found themselves without employment, as it was this segment of society that had been their primary source of employers. Some of the chefs were employed by the remaining upper classes, while many that could not find employment used the opportunity to open their own hospitality establishments. In addition, the French Revolution abolished the guilds and their restrictive and repressive guild rules, which made it easier to open eating establishments.

Continental Europe Influences America

The French Revolution also influenced food in America, in that many

It seems slightly ironic that one of the first "real" restaurants in Paris recognizes London, England. Beauvilliers must have had a keen interest in British food. In his 1824 book L'Art du Cuisinier *you can find dishes such as* woiches rabettes, plombpoutingue, *and* machepotetesse.

refugees from France arrived, and with them came their knowledge of and preference for French cuisine and culture. Combined with the fact that English influences were disfavored following the American Revolution (1775–1783), hospitality in America increasingly developed a Continental European influence. It is believed that many of the French chefs that fled abroad may have fled to Louisiana, which was still French territory at the time. What we do know, however, is that the first French restaurant, *Juliens Restarator*, was opened in Boston in 1794, and at about 1800 the refuge Francis Guerin opened a French restaurant in New York.

The Delmonico brothers from Switzerland were also important for American hospitality. They opened a pastry and coffee shop in New York in 1827, which over time grew to national and international fame. The most famous Delmonico, however, was their nephew Lorenzo (1813–1881) whom they brought over in 1932. They were the restaurateurs that were credited with popularizing European cuisine in New York, and making Delmonico's a symbol of fine dining in America. Delmonico's is considered to be the first truly continental restaurant to open in America, being the first to offer a la carte din-

While some believe the earliest appearance of a written menu in America occurred at the *Tremont* hotel in Boston, which opened in 1829; others suggest menus were first printed at Delmonico's in New York in 1836. Nonetheless, by 1838 fresh menus were printed daily at the *Astor House* in New York. All first class hotels, with the exception of the *Astor House*, offered French influenced cuisine and had French language menus in 1852. The *Astor House* preferred giving English names to all menu items that could be translated.

ing in the style of classical cuisine. Delmonico's was also the restaurant at which the first internationally renowned American chef presided. He was Charles Ranhofer (1836–1899) and authored *The Epicurean* in 1894. The Epicurean is an American culinary encyclopedia that covers all aspects of culinary art and table service. The book also includes a selection of copies of Delmonico's menus from 1862 through 1894.

The Influences of Two Chefs

Another important influence in this period of time is a man called Marie-Antoine (Antonin) Carême (1784–1833). He is considered the founder of what we know today as Classical (or Grand) Cuisine. Carême was a famous French chef who started off as a 12-year-old in a simple cook shop. He came from a large poor family, and at the age of twelve his father kicked him out of the home to fend for himself. Carême worked under many French masters and worked as chef to many kings, heads of state, and wealthy families. He is, for example, known for preparing a dinner for 1,200 guests at the Louvre in 1815 during a celebration of the restoration of the French Monarchy. He became quite famous as creator of very elaborate food displays, the forerunner of our wedding cakes, and sugar and tallow sculptures. More important for hospitality, though, is the fact that he revised and systematized culinary techniques, recipes, and menu planning, publishing several books on those topics. Carême has been referred to as the *Chef of Kings-King of Chefs*. He had a major impact on Escoffier's work.

George Auguste Escoffier (1847–1935) is often referred to as the father of modern (20th century) cooking. He is by far the most famous of all chefs, and has had a significant impact on modern foodservice. In general terms he rejected what he called the *general confusion* of the old menus and kitchens where mere quantity was para-

Photo courtesy UPI/Corbis-Bettman.

George Auguste Escoffier is by far the most famous of all chefs.

mount. He called for order in the kitchen and order, diversity, and relative simplicity on the menu. He has had at least three major impacts.

First, he simplified the reigning cuisine and developed the classical menu, which consists of 12 courses in a specified ordered sequence. It may be hard to imagine that twelve courses are a simplification. Remember, though, that for centuries quantity was consistent with opulence and display of wealth, and dish after dish would appear, often in random fashion. Although we seldom serve 12 course meals today, we still refer to Escoffier's classical menu in defining the proper sequence of courses.

Secondly, he reorganized the kitchen into a more streamlined workplace by introducing the kitchen brigade system with specified stations for a specific range of tasks and general lines of authority. For example, it is Escoffier who first assigned specialist status, such as *Rotisseur* (roast cook), *Saucier* (sauce cook) and *Poissonier* (fish cook). Variations of this system are still in use today, particularly at large hotels and full-

The term "menu" as we understand it today was apparently first used in the English language in 1837. The term can be traced back to its Latin root *minutus*, which has two potential meanings. One of which is reduction, reduced, small in size, amount or degree. Some believe that when guesthouses and inns in Europe started to post an abbreviated listing of what they had to offer outside their establishments, it was initially referred to as *minutus* or Old French *menut*, and eventually menu. This tradition of posting the menu outside of a hospitality establishment is a common European practice even today. The other meaning of the term *minutus* is that of possessing or involving minute knowledge, in which *menut* evolved into meaning "a detailed list." As such the term *menu de repas*, meaning a detailed list of the meal came into use. Eventually "de repas" was dropped from common usage.

service restaurants. In large American kitchens today, however, we are more likely to find fry cooks and broiler cooks than a poissonier.

Thirdly, Escoffier wrote several books, such as *Le Guide Culinaire* in 1903, which is still a widely used reference book on classical cuisine and the codification of classical cuisine. The codification established which culinary techniques and ingredients were associated with a specific culinary term or name (code). For example, using the garnishing term *Lyonnaise* would require use of onions, while the term *Forestière* implies mushrooms.

The 19th Century

Chicago's First Tavern

On December 8, 1828 the commissioners of Peoria County granted an Archibald Caldwell a license to run a tavern. The first tavern in Chicago was a small log tavern, and apparently business was initially slow, so Archibald Caldwell transferred his lease to the Wentworth's from Maine in 1829, who had stopped their westward journey due to poor weather. The flow of travelers increased and by 1835 Chicago had several taverns and a brick hotel.

The Tremont

Some suggest that the *Tremont* Hotel in Boston was the first hotel ever established. That will depend on the

definition used for a hotel. What is certain is that the *Tremont* was the first grand hotel built in America, and that it has characteristics much more similar to our hotels today than it does to the hotels and inns that preceded it. The *Tremont*, with 170 rooms, opened October 16, 1829. The proprietors were the Boyden family. It was the first hotel in which the explicit expectation was that the guests would have their own bed, and if traveling alone, their own room. It was considered a marvel that the individual guests would have their own room and their own key. If travelers chose the *Tremont* they would no longer be expected to share their

room and bed with strangers, nor would they have to sleep three and four to a bed in "spoon fashion." Up until this time it was still common for men and women who were not traveling together to share a room.

To the best of our knowledge, the "rack rate" at the *Tremont* in 1829 was $2.00 per day. This would provide, in addition to the room and bed, four meals per day and a bar of soap. The bar of soap, which may be the first amenity offered for free, was for the guests use in one of the eight "bathing rooms" provided. In your room you were provided your own wash basin and a pitcher of water. The eight "bathing rooms" along with a block of eight water closets were considered luxuries, despite the fact that they were located in the basement. The *Tremont* was only three stories high, and no one yet knew how to bring piped water above the ground floor! No hotels had private baths until 1853. The *Tremont* was also the first hotel to offer indoor toilets—the outhouse was still the norm.

The world's first hotel architect, Isaiah Rogers, designed the *Tremont*. He would influence hotels for half a century. The hotel was styled after Greek classicism, with high ceilings, floors of black and white marble

The Tremont Hotel in Boston was the first grand hotel built in America.

squares or fully carpeted and American-carved walnut furniture. The hotel had "good curtaining," French decorating, and gaslights[13] throughout. The dining room could seat 200 guests, and they had a dozen public rooms, which was unheard of until then. The *Tremont* provided a *reading room*, stocked with newspapers from all over America and Europe. This was also considered unique and a luxury, as there were no public libraries then.[14] Guests had free access, and the public could enter for a fee. The reading room is another innovation adopted by many subsequent hotels. Other innovations and luxuries at the *Tremont* included:

❖ An electro-magnetic annunciator, a device that allowed guests to push a button in their room and have a bell ring in the office, and a disc drop to show which room needed service. The number or rings would indicate the type of service required.

❖ Room service, which was made expedient by the annunciator.

❖ Bellboys

❖ Front desk clerks, i.e., employees whose responsibilities were limited to the front desk

❖ No sign outside. In those days, New England law required inns to post signs to assist illiterate travelers, informing them of the inn's whereabouts. The *Tremont* was not looking for illiterate travelers, and posted no signs.

The Astor House

It has been suggested that the German-born American business tycoon

COLONEL U. S. A.
Born July 13th, 1866.
Who at the commencement of the war with Spain, raised and equipped a Battery of Artillery for the government, and proved himself a brave soldier. When in Cuba he was on the staff of Major-General Shafter.

John Jacob Astor built his own version of the Tremont in New York—The Astor House.

John Jacob Astor (1763–1848), the wealthiest man of his time noted the success of the *Tremont*, and thought that if Boston could support such a luxurious hotel, New York, his home town, could do "one better." He hired the same architect Isaiah Rogers and contracted with the Boyden family to run the property. In essence the *Astor House* became a larger improved version of the *Tremont*. Using the same architect and management allowed John Astor to incorporate all lessons learned at the *Tremont*.

The *Astor House* opened in 1836, and was described by the *New Yorker* as being ". . . fitted up and furnished in a style of ostentatious richness and severe simplicity, . . ." The *Astor House* had 309 guest rooms, seventeen bathing rooms and two showers in the basement, and larger public rooms than the *Tremont*. The *Astor House* set a new standard for luxury, a standard that it held for about ten years. Many other grand hotels followed around the world. Among the more notable is *The St. Nicholas*,

recognized in 1852 for having spring mattresses and honeymoon suites, known as bridal chambers, and six stories of white marble. *The Fifth Avenue Hotel* in New York was known as the first to have a passenger elevator. *Holt's Inn* in New York, which failed in 1835, is the first hotel to have a steam-powered hoisting apparatus, but it was used only for luggage, not for people.[15]

A Second Tremont

Although we do not know with certainty that the hotel built in Chicago in 1835 was named the *Tremont House* in order to capitalize on the famous *Tremont* of Boston, this was likely the case. The hotel burned twice and was rebuilt each time. Despite the hotel's intended name, it became known as *Couch's Folly*. The brothers Ira and James Couch invested $75,000 in the third building of Chicago's *Tremont House*, which in 1849 provided a five-and-a-half-floor building described as being in "the highest style of art and in a princely class." Chicago at this time had about 28,000 inhabitants, and most Chicagoans of the day thought the Couchs' had grossly overbuilt and over-invested and would fail. Rather than fail, however, the growth in Chicago provided enough business to expand twice and reach 300 guestrooms by 1868. They were also known for having an "improved passenger elevator," and a "ten-thousand-dollar Ladies Parlor."

The current Tremont *in Chicago, which was built in 1923, is a small luxury property with 129 rooms. It was renovated and repositioned in 1978, and is considered one of the nation's first boutique hotels.*

---

[13]The use of gaslights as they spread is reported initially to be a problem. Apparently guests blew them out as they would blow out a candle, not realizing that gas would be escaping, and possibly asphyxiating them. Others were blown up as they attempted to relight the light with matches. Some hotels were known to have doors ". . . full of holes, where locks had been wrenched off in order to let the coroner in."

[14]Boston's first public library opened in 1852.

[15]Elevators for people did not become popular until E. G. Otis invented a safety device to avoid falling elevator cars in 1852.

Private Baths and Potato Chips

In 1853 we had two notable hospitality events. It is in this year that the first hotel opened that provided private baths to its guests; an innovation that had not been universally adopted even a century later. The hotel was the *Mount Vernon Hotel* at Cape May, NJ. Cape May is a peninsula off southern New Jersey between the Atlantic Ocean and Delaware Bay, a popular resort last century and a historic site today. In England the first private baths were not introduced until 1889, when the *Savoy Hotel* in London opened. In Dublin, Ireland, however, the *Shelbourne*, which opened in 1867 offered its guests fifteen private baths.

The other 1853 point of interest took place in Saratoga Springs, NY. Saratoga Springs is a city in the foothills of the Adirondacks north of Albany. Last century it was initially popular as a health resort due to its mineral springs, but became one of the country's most fashionable resorts late in the century with a casino and horse racing. The racetrack that opened in 1863 was the first major U.S. racetrack for flat racing, and became a horseracing center. The 1853 event relates to a significant food event, namely the invention of the potato chip. Chef George Crum of Moon's Lake House in Saratoga Springs received a complaint from one of his customers, suggesting that his french fries were too thick. Chef Crum's apparent response was to shave some potatoes paper thin prior to deep frying them. The customer, and many to follow, were delighted and ordered more! Chef George Crum opened his own restaurant in the area, and was as such an early American chef-proprietor. His restaurant was noted for a no-reservation policy, requiring rich and poor alike to stand in line.

Boston's Parker House

Boston hotelier Harvey D. Parker opened the first *Parker House* hotel

The term à la cârte is often used erroneously as a synonym for "cooked to order" or "prepared to order." This may be the case, but is not necessarily so. Many à la cârte items may be pre-made or partially pre-made.

on School Street in Boston[16] in 1855. The *Parker House* is, of course, known for the Parker House Roll, a folded soft roll. More importantly though, the *Parker House*, upon opening, became known for serving *à la cârte* meals at all hours throughout the day, rather than requiring people to arrive at specified meal times. The *Parker House* was considered to be far more fashionable and modern than the *Tremont* Hotel, and is believed to be one of the reasons the *Tremont* declined and closed.

Thomas Cook

The first travel agent was Thomas Cook, he had his beginnings in

---

[16]In 1925 a new Parker House opened on Tremont Street.

In a **true** *à la cârte* menu, each and every menu item or meal component is offered and priced separately. The guests get to choose exactly what they want and get that without any pre-arranged accompaniments. For example, if a guest ordered *Tournedos Rossini* and nothing else, they would receive the appropriate piece(s) of pan-fried beef tenderloin, set on a crouton, with a slice of *pâté de foie gras* (goose liver pâté), and black truffles on top, served with Madeira Sauce. No potatoes, no vegetables, no salad. . . . In other words, the guests get to compose their own dish, so to speak. *Semi-à la cârte* is much more common, and what we normally experience. In this approach the individual menu items or dishes have specified and pre-determined accompaniments such as a starch, vegetable, salad, etc. They are also priced as a complete dish or menu item.

1841 when he persuaded the Midland County Railroad in England, to reduce their fare on a stretch between Leicester to Loughborough. He was a temperance worker and printer trying to bring people to a meeting. The railroad agreed, and

The Parker House became known for serving à la cârte meals throughout the day.

rather than transport the typical 50 passengers, Thomas Cook provided 570 passengers during the same period of time. In 1864 his son joined his father, and Thomas Cook & Sons extended service to America. Also significant is the year 1866 when Thomas Cook initiated a system for providing hotel accommodations to his tour participants, wherever they traveled. This may have been the first hotel reservation system.

George Mortimer Pullman

Hospitality on rail can be seen to have its roots in the 1850's. Although rail travel had been introduced earlier in the century, it was not until the 1850's that the first practical sleeper car was introduced and subsequently impacted travel worldwide. In 1858 George M. Pullman, cabinetmaker, perfected the sleeper car for the Chicago & Alton Railroad. He designed a retractable upper berth that doubled the available sleeping capacity. In 1864 G. M. Pullman and Ben Field of Chicago patented a railway sleeping car with folding upper berths. The result was *The Pioneer*, which debuted in 1865. George M. Pullman and Andrew Carnegie founded the Pullman Palace Car Co. in 1867. The new company would build cars and operate them under contract for the various railway companies. In 1868 they put their first dining car into regularly scheduled service on the Chicago & Alton Rail-

In 1977 British Rail took over the cars and used them for first class travel between London, Brussels, and Paris. The service was closed October 31, 1980, as air travel had made the service obsolete.

road. The dining car was called *Delmonico*, after the famous New York restaurant.

The European engineer and founder George Nagelmaker traveled across America in Pullman cars, and as a result decided to bring sleeping cars to Europe. He started a company[17] for this purpose in 1876, and in 1879 started *Le Train Bleu* (The Blue Train) an all-sleeper express between Calais and Rome via Nice, that was scheduled three times a week. Subsequently (1883) Nagelmaker started *The Orient Express*, which is much more famous than *Le Train Bleu* due to it being featured in books and films. *Le Train Bleu* was the first deluxe sleeper car service in Europe, and lasted more than a century.

World's Largest

In 1875 two hotels opened that claimed to be the world's largest hotel. The *United States Hotel* opened in Saratoga Springs, NY, and was the world's largest in terms of number of rooms. It was, however, a seasonal hotel, which anyone from San Francisco would have been quick to point out. In San Francisco that year the *Palace Hotel* opened. The *Palace Hotel* was the world's largest city hotel, and

thus a year-round hotel. It is know to have had 755 rooms. Each room was twenty square feet and laid out in a hollow quadrangle. A crystal roof covered the ensuing interior court. The seven-story hotel was built using a wrought-iron-structure, had 437 baths, five elevators, and seven iron stairways. Fires were a major problem for hotels in those days, and every attempt was made to make the hotel fireproof. For example, the foundation was twelve feet thick, each of the seven staircases was a closed brick compartment, and on the roof of the hotel were seven tanks holding 130,000 gallons of water. Despite these efforts, the hotel burned down after the 1906 earthquake, but that was due to bureaucratic intervention. The municipal offices were threatened and the "city fathers" commandeered the water for their use. As a result the hotel *and* the municipal offices were destroyed.

Chicago's Palmer House

While Boston had its *Parker House*, Chicago had its *Palmer House*. In 1870, Potter Palmer, a successful merchant, built the first *Palmer House* in Chicago. It was advertised as the *only fireproof hotel in the world*. On

The current Palmer House opened in 1925 with 2,250 rooms at a cost of more than $20 million.

---

[17]Compagnie International des Wagons-Lits et des Grandes Express Européens

October 8, 1871, it burned down in the great Chicago fire! Following the fire, Potter Palmer built a more extravagant *Palmer House*. It was known for its mammoth barbershop with silver dollars embedded in the floor and for elegant and lavish dining. Their menu included buffalo, antelope, bear, mountain sheep, quail, partridge, and blackbird. The current *Palmer House* at State and Monroe Streets opened in 1925 with 2,250 rooms at a cost of more than $20 million. Purchased by Conrad Hilton in 1946 it remains a Hilton property today.

Fred Harvey

Frederick Henry Harvey came to the United States in 1850 and worked as a freight agent for the Burlington and Quincy Railroad owned by J. F. Joy of Chicago. He suggested to Joy that passengers would enjoy and support clean, well-run restaurants at the various train stations and junctions along the line, but Joy did not believe in the concept. The Santa Fe Railroad, on the other hand, was receptive to the idea, and let Harvey open a restaurant at the Topeka, Kansas railroad depot in 1876. The establishment was a success and soon other restaurants followed along the Santa Fe line and at other major railroad depots. Fred Harvey also started to operate hotels and in 1890 started a fleet of dining cars. In 1883 he owned 17 properties. By 1901 there were 47 Fred Harvey restaurants, 30 Fred Harvey dining cars, and 15 Fred Harvey hotels. Fred Harvey was the first hospitality chain operator. The Fred Harvey restaurants were known for well-trained *Harvey Girls* serving good food on Irish linen, to be eaten with Sheffield silverware. On tracks without dining cars, but with Fred Harvey restaurants at the stations, Harvey arranged for the railroad personnel to distribute menus to passengers, record their orders, and report the orders to the restaurants before the train reached the stations. Thus the food, which was cooked to order, was nearly done when the passenger-guests arrived, and the delays were kept to a minimum.

César Ritz: Host to the World

César Ritz was born in the little Swiss village at Niederwald in 1850. The family was large; César was the thirteenth child. His father was the mayor of Niederwald, a village of less than 200. They were poor, as was everyone else in Niederwald, but they were not lacking in the necessities of life, and they were well fed and clothed. The family had a house, built by César Ritz's grandfather in 1778, and some livestock. In the summer César Ritz would herd cattle at the edge of the forest. In the winter the roads would be deep with snow, and they would often find themselves snowed in for days. To get to the village school, the children would have to wade through deep snowdrifts carrying their books, and one log for the school stove, on their back in a basket.

César Ritz was a dreamer and was not content with life in Niederwald. He wished to explore and experience the world, but did not know what he wanted to do. His parents thought that he might become an artist and sent him, at age twelve, off to boarding school in Sion. Three years later the artist had not emerged, and his father arranged an apprenticeship for César at the *Hôtel des Trois Couronnes et Poste* in Brieg. In those days apprentices were not paid, but paid for the privilege of apprenticing. He was to become a wine-waiter, a sommelier, or so they thought. At the end of the year, César Ritz had still not found himself, and Mr. Escher, the proprietor of the hotel, thought poorly of him: "You'll never make anything of yourself in the hotel business. It takes a special knack, a special flair, and it is only right that I should tell you the truth—you haven't got it!" He was fired. Rather than return home, César took employment as an assistant waiter in the refectory of a

César Ritz was once told that he would never make anything of himself in the hotel business.

local Jesuit seminary. He was again fired from his hospitality job, but managed to hold on to his subsequent job as sacristan. He left for Paris in 1867, however, when he heard of the Great International Exposition.

César Ritz obtained work at *Hôtel de la Fidelité* on Boulevard de Prince Eugene, where he scrubbed and polished and ran errands as needed. He left shortly to work as a waiter at a local "blue collar" wine bar. A few months later he moved on to a "prix fixe" restaurant where the proprietors, Monsieur and Madame Chevalier, noted that César was a very fast waiter, but also very quick to break dishes! He left for *Gott's* restaurant at the corner of Rue Royale and Rue St. Honoré, where he worked hard to learn the trade and worked his way up from assistant waiter to restaurant manager.

Among the most fashionable restaurants in Paris in those days was the *Voisin*. César Ritz turned down a partnership with Gott in order to start at the bottom at *Voisin* to learn and earn under the guidance of the proprietor Bellenger. He learned quickly and was soon the waiter of choice for many of *Voisin's* guests.

While at *Voisin* the Franco-Prussian War broke out and the siege of Paris led to a drop in business. César Ritz took employment at *Brasserie*

Netzer, where he served many a beer. He left Paris and returned in 1872, when the war was over. Europe had started to feel the presence of a *new aristocracy*, rich Americans. César Ritz took employment at *Hôtel Spelendide*, one of the most luxurious hotels in Europe. He was soon promoted to *maître d'hôtel* in their restaurant, and became particularly adept at selling the best wines to American travelers who had enough money and were willing to spend it. The Americans were not wine connoisseurs, but apparently César Ritz persuaded them that the water was not safe and the wine was the perfect antidote. This was also when César Ritz started to develop a wide range of contacts and acquaintances.

Although César Ritz was successful in Paris he saw opportunity to learn more and expand his network of contacts when the International Exposition opened in Vienna. He took work as a waiter in the restaurant *Les Trois Frères Provençaux*, which was near Emperor Frans Josef's facilities. When the emperor entertained, he frequently borrowed staff from *Les Trois Frères Provençaux*, among them César Ritz. Thus he expanded his repertoire to include the needs of royalty, rulers, statesmen, and other members of the "international set."

The international set typically moved to southern France in the winters and to Switzerland during the summers. César Ritz decided it was beneficial to follow suit. He obtained a position as restaurant manager at the *Grand Hotel* in Nice during the winter and as *Oberkelner* at the *Rigi Kulm Hotel* in the Swiss Alps during the summer. He was in his mid-twenties. It was here that he truly established his reputation as an extraordinary hospitality professional, adept at organization and handling emergencies swiftly. It was late in the season and a storm had just passed through, the temperature was below freezing, much of the power was out, and the new central heating system failed. At this point the local Cook's travel office at Lucerne called the hotel and told them they should expect a luxury tour of forty American guests for lunch. The director of the hotel was in despair! What to do? The hotel was ice cold, as was the proposed menu. César Ritz sprung into action, he ordered forty bricks to be put in an oven, a table to be set in a small room rather than the large dining room, and called for the four large copper bowls used as the bases for palms in the foyer to be put in each corner of the room, and set about changing the menu. Out went every cold item; in came piping hot consommé and other warm items. The finale was crêpes flambées. The four pots were filled with methylated spirits and set ablaze. Each guest received a flannel wrapped brick for his/her feet. The guests never knew there had been a crisis. César Ritz's ingenuity and resourcefulness quickly spread within hospitality as he continued to build his reputation. By age thirty-three he was hired to run the *Monte Carlo Grand Hotel*, and he hired Chef Auguste Escoffier, who was by then thirty-seven. It has been suggested that prior to meeting and hiring Escoffier, César Ritz knew that he needed superb cuisine to claim his hotel was truly "de luxe," but had not been able to implement it, while Auguste Escoffier had not yet found anyone to fully appreciate his talents and allow him free reign to explore them. With their joint dedication to detail and excellence they were a perfect match.

A Couple of Firsts

Shortly after, in 1885, we find another development in hospitality, not a luxury establishment, but equally as important for hospitality. On September 5, 1885, *The New York Exchange Buffet* opened across from the New York Stock Exchange. It is considered the first self-service restaurant in that the guests would help themselves from the buffet.[18]

---

[18]In culinary terms *buffet* is a large, often tiered table set with various dishes, often reflecting the entire spectrum of the classical menu. Carême was known for his grand buffets.

In the 1870s in New England we find another development for the first time. Most restaurants in cities were too expensive for the average working American, yet they needed quick, affordable meals. The lunch wagon, often horse drawn, was developed in response offering sandwiches, pies, and beverages. By the 1880s these wagons became large enough for customers to come inside, and often they provided stools and counters to sit at. Some had tiny kitchens. These mobile lunch wagons eventually developed into what became known as "diners."

Grand Hotels

The Raffles

In 1886 in Singapore, what was later to become the *Singapore Raffles Hotel* was built. Initially it was built as a residence for British colonials with 123 rooms, but was later converted to a hotel. *The Raffles* is considered one of the last remaining "Grand Hotels" of the East, and is today carefully restored to reflect the early years of this century.

The world famous "Singapore Sling" drink was originally devised at the Raffles Long Bar.

Plank's Grand Hotel

The *Grand Hotel* on Mackinac Island, Michigan was built in 1887 as a vacation hotel to accommodate summer travelers who came by railroad. It was built on a high bluff with 262 rooms and a wide 660-foot long porch providing a view of the ships passing through the Straits of Mackinac. It was originally called *Plank's Grand Hotel* after the name of its first general manager John Oliver Plank, but was soon known simply as the *Grand Hotel*. It is one of the few remaining

Victorian hotels that have maintained the classical charm and luxury of a grand vacation hotel.

The Savoy Hotel in London

London's *Savoy Hotel* opened in August 1889. The *Savoy* is the first English hotel to have private baths. It offered seventy baths while another new hotel, *The Victoria*, had only four baths for 500 guests. Gilbert & Sullivan impresario Richard D'Oyly Carte of Savoy Theatre fame built the hotel on the site of the medieval palace of Count Peter of Savoy. The hotel was the first public building in the world to be fully lit by electricity. In fact, it had its own power station in the basement of the hotel, with generators that produced more power than the hotel could use. The hotel had seven floors, and installed six elevators, a rarity in 1889 Europe. This allowed the management to charge the same price for rooms at the upper levels as on the first floor, which was also unusual at that time. Although the *Savoy Hotel* claimed to be the first fireproof hotel in the world, it was surely the first in England; constructed of reinforced concrete on a steel frame. Wood was used primarily in window frames and doors.

D'Oyly Carte wished to have the best hotel possible and asked César Ritz to manage the property. César Ritz declined as he was not attracted to London, and was busy with his own ventures in Baden-Baden and Cannes. D'Oyly Carte was persistent and managed to persuade César Ritz to attend the opening of the Savoy. César Ritz, impressed by the social life in London, and noting that the Savoy had potential, agreed to come to London and manage the Savoy. He persuaded the best chef and the best maître d'hôtel at that time to join him.

Thus, Messrs. Ritz, Escoffier, and Echenard descended on London. At that point in time in London "dining out" for a couple or family meant going to someone's home for a meal and evening. It was not common to dine

London's Savoy Hotel opened in August 1889.

According to legend Chef August Escoffier created *Pêche Melba* [Peach Melba] at the *Savoy Hotel* to honor opera singer Madame Nellie Melba. The dish was inspired by the swan in Wagner's *Lohengrin* opera, and consists of a poached peach, vanilla ice cream, puréed and strained raspberries, toasted almond slivers, and whipped cream. *Melba Toast* was given its name by César Ritz to describe the super thin, crisp toast that was part of Madame Nellie Melba's diet while she stayed at the *Savoy Hotel* for a while.

at a hotel unless you were staying at one. Men had private clubs, where women were not allowed, and chop houses where "respectable ladies" would not set foot. This changed slowly. At the *Savoy Hotel*, two restaurants were planned: a dining room for those staying at the hotel and *The Savoy Restaurant* as an independent attraction for the public-at-large. The restaurant became known for exquisite food and service and for elegant after-theater suppers. The independence of the hotel restaurant and the theater suppers were innovations that, though slowly adopted by the public, were an important part of the *Savoy's* success.

Le Château Frontenac

In 1892 in Quebec City, the Canadian Pacific Railway president William Van Horne and a group of Canadians hired New York architect Bruce Price to build a hotel modeled on a Loire Valley chateau. *Le Château Frontenac* sits on top of the Cap Diamant Cliffs in the heart of walled-in Old Quebec as a stronghold landmark. The original hotel had 170 rooms and had an exterior built entirely of Glenboig bricks imported from Scotland. The hotel was expanded in 1924 and currently has more than 600 rooms and 24 suites with copper clad turrets and towers.

The Old Waldorf-Astoria

The original Waldorf-Astoria was built in two stages. In 1893 William Waldorf Astor built New York's *Waldorf Hotel* on Fifth Avenue and 33rd Street, where the residence of William B. Astor had stood. The 530-room, 13-floor hotel was designed by architect Henry Janeway Hardenburgh, and it was equipped with 350 private baths. A few years later, in 1897, John Jacob Astor IV decided to design and build a 17 story Astor house on the adjacent lot at 34th Street and Fifth Avenue and hired the same architect. They were combined into a 1000-room hotel with 765 private baths and was considered

The site of the original Waldorf-Astoria is where the Empire State Building was built, which opened April 30, 1931. As such, the original Waldorf-Astoria only stood for a relatively short period of time.

The original Waldorf-Astoria was built in two stages.

the most luxurious hotel in the world. Although the accommodations were excellent, the hotel was, for a period of time, better known for its superb food. This is due to the work of Chef Oscar Tschirky who became known worldwide as Oscar of the Waldorf.

The Waldorf Salad was created at the old Waldorf-Astoria before the turn of the century. Originally apples and celery were dressed with mayonnaise; chopped walnuts were added later.

It is at the original Waldorf that room service was introduced and that the practice of sending gifts of fruits, candies, flowers, and beverages to prominent guests with management's compliments was first started. Furthermore, the Waldorf introduced the practice of putting room clerks on all the floors. Moreover, the Waldorf was the first establishment to hire orchestras to play for the guests while they dined, and it was the first to allow men to smoke in the dining room.

The Ritz Hotel Syndicate

Part of the arrangements that were made to get César Ritz to come to London was that he was free to take interest in other hotels and restaurants outside of London as it suited him. This he did. He was involved in several projects and by 1896 started the Ritz Hotel Development Company, which initially sought suitable properties in Paris. César Ritz found that 15 Place de Vendome, a 17th-century townhouse with beautiful gardens, was for sale. It had originally belonged to Duc de Lauzun, who had led the French Cavalry at Yorktown in 1781. César Ritz envisioned a small, elegant, exclusive hotel, with all possible refinements in which he would cater to the needs of those who lived in palaces. Thus, he needed a property refined enough to interest them. Unfortunately, his backers in the Ritz Hotel Development Company saw it differently; they were expecting a larger property of different character, and were not willing to provide the needed backing. César Ritz then turned to the financiers among those he knew from his Monte Carlo days. Again he came away empty handed. He did, however, find the necessary initial support from Monsieur Marnier Lapostolle. Subsequently he got support from additional financial backers by promising an initial six percent annual return, which he provided. The Paris *Ritz Hotel* opened with 170 guestrooms in 1898. He left the *Savoy* in 1897, and his key colleagues there, including Escoffier, joined him at the Paris *Ritz Hotel*. The concept of "dining out" was in Paris as it had been in London, but Ritz was a key influence in changing that. The *Ritz Hotel* soon became "the place" to be and be seen.

Following the successful start of the Paris *Ritz*, César Ritz turned his attention to London again. This time to open the *Carlton*. Escoffier came along here as well. The *Carlton* was the first hotel ever to have a private bath to every room. The hotel was lavishly decorated and every attention was given to the interior. For example, César Ritz had a staircase

Monsieur Marnier Lapostolle was the inventor of Grand Marnier Liqueur and felt indebted to César Ritz for his assistance in naming it. Apparently Monsieur Lapostolle came into the Savoy one day and asked César Ritz to try his new liqueur, and asked him to suggest a name. His suggestion was Le Grand Marnier.

moved so that guests could make dramatic entrances to the dining room; indirect lighting was used so as to enhance the atmosphere and provide guests with the best possible apparent complexion. The hotel was an immediate success and provided a seven-percent dividend the first year. Although plans were made to build a London *Ritz* hotel, César Ritz never saw it completed. Unfortunately, César Ritz had a nervous breakdown in 1902 and never returned to work. He died in 1918. The London *Ritz* was opened in 1902. Although César Ritz himself never returned to work the company bearing his name carried on and continued to open *Ritz* hotels.

Twentieth Century

Ellsworth M. Statler: Caring for the Needs of the Business Traveler

His Early Years

The son of a reverend, E. M. Statler was born in 1863. He started work in a glass factory in Wheeling, West Virginia at the age of nine. The tallest building in Wheeling was the five-story *McLure House* hotel, and E. M. Statler apparently often claimed that someday he would be going there. He was interested and fascinated by the glamorous hotel built in 1852, and by some considered equal in quality to the *Tremont House* in Boston. At the age of thirteen E. M. Statler did go to the hotel in an attempt to obtain a job as a bellboy. His brother already worked there as a bellboy, and had told him that they might need more help. No such luck: he was turned away. Statler returned every day until they finally let him cover a shift for someone who was ill.

A bellboy's work consisted of carrying luggage, bringing ice water, hot water, coal and kindling, lighting fires in the guest rooms when needed, and just about any other task. He was hard working and handled all tasks enthusiastically, and was soon offered a permanent position. Statler was ambitious and set about to learn whatever he needed, always asking questions. He was known for persistently asking until he fully understood the issue of discussion. Some found him argumentative, but he saw himself as running a hotel later and felt that he needed to know. As he did not have much formal education, having left school at the age of nine, his language skills were not the best. He felt that a future hotelier must speak well, and he coaxed the bartender, a Mr. Tom Duffy, to teach him proper use of the English language. He became head bellboy in 1878.

In order to learn, Statler carried a small notebook with him in which he noted all he wished to learn, from rules of grammar through rules regarding hotel operations. One day, upon noticing that a guest checked out of the hotel after a disagreement with a waiter and a clerk, Mr. McLure noticed Statler writing in his notebook and asked to see it. He had written, "The guest is always right," and explained that one should never argue with a guest regardless of the problem, and that in this case it had led to the

In 1898 the idea for *Gideons International* took shape in Boscobel, Wisconsin. That year, two traveling salesmen, John H. Nicholson and Sam Hill shared a room at the *Central Hotel* and decided to start an organization of Christian businessmen (liquor traders not welcome!) to put bibles into the hands of the unconverted. Thus we find a bible in virtually every hotel room.

E.M. Statler believed that the guest is always right.

loss of a guest. Statler was shortly promoted to night clerk. As night clerk he offered to maintain the hotel's books, and used this as an opportunity to learn more about hotel operations. While night clerk he consistently questioned the owners, now the Norton brothers, as to the why and wherefore of room rates, departmental efficiency, restaurant food, and more. He even suggested that the owners eat in the dining room rather than in their private room, so that they could experience the food and service as the guests experienced it. He developed a reputation among the guests of the hotel as being very efficient and friendly.

After two years as night clerk, the hotel was closed for renovations and Statler was soon offered a position as day clerk in the *Butchel Hotel* in Akron, Ohio. They had heard rumors of his skill. He took the position, but when the *McLure House* opened again after six months, they asked him to come back. He did so under the condition they would lease him the billiard room in the hotel. Billiard rooms had poor reputations in those days and this particular room was really run-down. A frequent guest at the *McLure House*, George Meyers was a sales agent for the Brunswick Balke-Colender Company, manufacturers of billiard equipment. He arranged to

give Statler the equipment he needed, on credit, because he had seen him over the years, and he knew Statler was a hard worker whom he trusted. Statler soon turned the room around, improved its reputation and made it a popular place. By his early twenties, Statler became a most successful lessee of the McLure billiard room, while he also worked as day clerk at the *McLure*. He soon turned his attention to additional ventures and became a billiard impresario, a railroad ticket broker, an operator of a bowling alley with a pie shop were food and drink could be purchased.

The Ellicott Square Restaurant

In 1894 Statler passed through Buffalo, NY, and he noticed a large new office building was near completion. He saw a business opportunity and opened a 500 seat traditional restaurant in the building. Unfortunately, the Buffalo crowd was not used to "eating out" and the creditors were soon asking for their money. He declined to declare bankruptcy, as that was not the right thing to do, and persuaded his creditors to give him a year. Shortly after, during a Grand Army of the Republic convention, he installed turnstiles at the entry and exit doors, and charged his guests 25¢ to eat as much as they liked. The "one price all-you-can-eat" concept was very popular and he made both money and a name for himself. He soon persuaded business people, through advertising, that they could take care of more business if they stayed downtown for lunch rather than travel home, as was the custom. In addition, he discovered the value of merchandising and promotions. For example, word spread quickly when he had the chef wrap $5 gold pieces and insert them into ice cream servings as surprises; he would also give away free raffle tickets all throughout the weekend for a drawing that was held during the "new Sunday dinner" hour. Of course you had to be there to win. By 1901, Statler's restaurant was successful, and he was entirely out of debt.

The First Statler Hotel

His first hotel was built in response to the city of Buffalo putting on a World's Fair—The Pan-American Exposition in 1901. He built a temporary structure that was made to look substantial with plaster. He chose the temporary structure so that he could dismantle the property after the fair, and invest less money. Although the hotel was capable of accommodating 5,000 guests, the fair was not a big success, and he had, at the most, 1,500 guests staying at the hotel. He did turn a profit, however, as he had controlled his costs and investment carefully. Another reason he was profitable is that he decided to handle the problem of "skippers" head on. Skippers, those who left the hotel without paying the bill, were a major problem in those days. Statler simply required payment when they checked in rather than at checkout. Another innovation! When the fair was over, he dismantled the hotel. He was subsequently successful with a hotel at the Louisiana Purchase Exposition in 1904.

"A Room and a Bath for a Dollar and a Half."

Statler's first permanent hotel was built in Buffalo in 1907, and opened January 8, 1908. The *Buffalo Statler* was another milestone in hospitality's history. It is the first hotel to cater to the needs of the businessman. Statler was not interested in running a luxury establishment, rather he saw himself providing all the basic comforts and conveniences that the typical traveler needed, better food than most, and offering it at a price that ordinary people could afford.

The *Buffalo Statler* was the second hotel in the world to provide a bath with every guestroom, but the first to provide this in the United States, and the first to provide it to "ordinary folks." Additional innovations and conveniences at the *Buffalo Statler* included circulating ice water in every bathroom, telephones in every room, full-size lit closets in every room, mail chutes on every floor, light switches just inside the door, and keyholes above the door knobs. In addition, he provided every room with a free newspaper in the morning.

Statler stayed focused on identifying and meeting the needs of the increasing middle class, providing quick service and being innovative. He was, for example, the first to provide radios in every room of his hotel. When he died in 1928 he controlled more hotels than any other person, and had started what we today call a hotel chain.

The Automat

Although the first self-service restaurant opened in 1885, the ultimate in self-service was started in 1902 in Philadelphia. Called the *Automat*, it was an efficient, moneymaking idea started by Horn & Hardart's Baking Company. They purchased a mechanism from a German importer that had multiple glass-door compartments, each which could be opened by depositing a coin into a slot. The compartments held ready prepared food, and were filled by employees from behind the scenes. The establishments were sparkling places with glass, brass, marble, and oak. The first opened on Chestnut Street in Philadelphia, and soon became so popular that many more opened up in Philadelphia. Horn & Hardart's first New York *Automat* opened in 1912 on Broadway at Times Square.

The First Quick Service Hamburger Chain

The first *White Castle* restaurant, which opened in Wichita, Kansas in 1921, is believed to be the first store in the first quick service hamburger restaurant chain. The founders were Walter Anderson and E. W. Ingram. They offered ground beef, cooked on a grill, served in a roll sliced in two, with fresh onions. The concept became popular and they quickly found

The **Statler Service Code** was given to all employees who were required to memorize it and carry a copy with them. It read:

It is the business of a good hotel to cater to the public. It is the avowed business of the Hotel Statler to please the public better than any other hotel in the world.

Have everyone feel that for his money we want to give him more sincere service than he ever before received at any hotel.

Never be perky, pungent, or fresh. The guests pay your salary as well as mine. He is your immediate benefactor.

Hotel service, that is Hotel Statler Service, means the limit of courteous, efficient attention from each particular employee to each particular guest. It is the object of the Hotel Statler to sell its guest the best service in the world.

No employee of this hotel is allowed the privilege of arguing any point with a guest. He must adjust the matter at once to the guest's satisfaction or call his superior to adjust it. Wrangling has no place in Hotel Statler.

In all minor discussions between Statler employees and Statler guests, the employee is dead wrong, from the guest's point of view and from ours.

Any Statler employee who is wise and discreet enough to merit tips is wise and discreet enough to render a like service whether he is tipped or not.

Any Statler employee who fails to give service or who fails to thank the guest who gives him something, falls short of Statler standards.

It is not known when the first hamburger was made. What What we do know is that people in Hamburg, Germany, by the middle of the 19th century did enjoy pounded steak in various forms. German immigrants from that part of Germany likely brought this tradition to the United States. We also know that in 1836, when *Delmonico's Restaurant* printed its first menu, the menu included "Hamburg Steak," although we do not know how it was made. The first time that "Hamburg Steak" is found in the print media proper is in an 1884 issue of the *Boston Journal*. A Walla Walla, Washington newspaper used the term "Hamburger Steak" (emphasis added) in 1889. In 1900, Louis Lassen, of New Haven, Connecticut, ground lean beef, broiled it and served the patty between two pieces of toast without condiments to customers at his *Louis Lunch* establishment. Finally, German immigrants working the St. Louis Exposition in 1904 are known to have fried chopped beef and sold it for consumption at the fair.

that many, such as *White Tower* restaurants, tried to copy their success. U.S. courts, by the way, prohibited *White Tower*, in 1937, from operating in such a fashion as to be able to be mistaken for *White Castle*. The *White Castle* chain is still in existence today.

Hilton Hotels

One of the most famous hotel names is that of Conrad Hilton (1887–1979), the founder of the Hilton Hotel Corporation. He had his first taste of the lodging business in 1907 in San Antonio, New Mexico, when his family started to provide a room and a meal to travelers for $2.50 a day in the family's large adobe house facing the railroad station on a main line. If they had many guests for the night, the family members would sometimes relinquish their beds and

rooms to accommodate. At $2.50 they turned a profit. In addition to providing room and board the Hiltons had a general store, which also functioned as post office and telegraph. During his early years Conrad Hilton would help out in the store as needed, and spend his summers working there. By the age of twenty-one his father made him a partner in the store.

Hilton did not stay with the original family hotel or store, but ventured into politics; at age 25 he won a seat in the state legislature. Later that year, realizing that he did not want to be a politician, he decided to move into banking. In September of 1913 he had sold enough shares to charter a bank and the New Mexico State Bank of San Antonio opened. They struggled at first, but were successful. In 1916 when Hilton learned that Germany proposed to offer Mexico an alliance and the right to reclaim New Mexico, Texas, and Arizona, he decided to sell his bank and enlisted in the Army. He served for two years.

When Hilton returned, he left for Texas in search of new banking opportunities. In Cisco, Texas, he agreed to buy a bank, but the owner reneged on their agreement and demanded a higher price. Hilton refused the deal and crossed the street to

Photo courtesy Hulton-Deutsch Collection/Corbis.

One of the most famous hotel names is that of Conrad Hilton.

spend the night at *The Mobley Hotel*. The owner of the hotel was bit by the oil bug and wanted to sell. It was 1919 and Conrad Hilton purchased his first hotel. There were more oil prospectors and field workers than there were rooms. By 1929 he owned seven properties in the same area.

Soon the depression followed, and Hilton lost some of his properties, but recovered after the depression, and started to rebuild. In 1946, he formed the Hilton Hotels Corporation, in 1949 Hilton International[19] was formed, and in 1954 the Statler chain was purchased.

New York's Waldorf-Astoria Hotel opened October 1, 1931 on a full city block. It had twin 47-floor towers and 2,000 rooms, and lost money for 12 years. On October 12, 1949 Conrad Hilton bought the Waldorf-Astoria.

The Marriott Corporation

The hospitality beginnings of the Marriott Corporation took place in 1927 in Washington, DC, when J. Willard Marriott obtained an exclusive franchise to sell A&W Root Beer in Washington, Baltimore, and Richmond using syrup from Allen and Wright. In a team with his wife Alice they worked hard and saved and expanded as they could. In August of 1937, they opened *Hot Shoppe Number Eight*. This same year he arranged to prepare box lunches for Eastern Airlines crews, and thus began the first ventures into airline feeding. In 1957, the first Marriott hotel opened. It was the 370 room *Twin Bridges Motor Hotel* in Washington, DC. The initial nine-seat root beer stand has today grown into

[19]Later sold to Trans World Airways.

The first use of the term motel was on Route 101 in San Luis Obispo, a city northwest of Santa Barbara. In 1924 a Mr. James Vail focused on providing accommodations for motorists. He called his establishment a Motel Inn, *and advertised with an electric sign that had a blinking first letter, alternatively providing an "H" and an "M," for "Hotel" and "Motel."*

a worldwide empire of *Hot Shoppes, Big Boys, Roy Rogers, Farrell's,* numerous managed services operations, and Marriott lodging properties.

The Sheraton Corporation

The Sheraton Corporation had its beginnings in Cambridge, Massachusetts when two Harvard classmates, Ernest Henderson and Robert Lowell Moore, took over the *Continental Hotel* in 1933, which had opened the very day the stock market crashed in 1929. Throughout the depression the entrepreneurs, Henderson and Moore, bought up stock in Standard Investing Company at very good rates, and used the capital to finance their acquisitions. In 1937 they purchased the 200 room *Stonehaven* hotel in Springfield, often considered the first Sheraton hotel, although the small Boston residential hotel called the *Sheraton* was among three 1939 acquisitions. Subsequently they identified all their later hotel properties with the Sheraton name.

The Sheraton Corporation was the first hotel corporation listed on the New York Stock Exchange (1947), the first to use a telex system for room reservations (1948), and the first to develop an automatic electronic reservation system, the *Reservatron* (1958). In 1968 the Sheraton Corporation

became a wholly owned subsidiary of ITT Corporation, and in 1998 ITT Sheraton Corporation became a wholly owned subsidiary of Starwood Hotels & Resorts Worldwide, Inc.

Howard Johnson's

What is today known as Howard Johnson International had its start in 1925, when Howard Dearing Johnson purchased a small drug store in Quincy, Massachusetts. The store had a soda fountain and sold ice cream. Howard Johnson started to make his own ice cream, using a hand-cranked old-fashioned ice cream maker. He added food items such as frankfurters and hamburgers, thus starting the first Howard Johnson restaurant in a drug store. In 1929 he opened a restaurant with a broader menu, and he had visions of starting a chain offering "good food at sensible prices." Unfortunately, the great depression arrived in late 1929, and his expansions slowed.

By 1935, however, there were 25 Howard Johnson roadside ice-cream and sandwich stands in Massachusetts, and in 1936 he persuaded fellow businessman Reginald Sprague to open an eating place at Orleans on Cape Cod, which Howard Johnson would supply with food. The first Howard Johnson franchise took place in 1937 as a response to not getting bank financing for restaurant expansions. Also in 1937 he obtained a property which he leased to a Cambridge woman who invested in the building that Johnson built for her. He also hired and trained the employees, and retained the right to supply the needed food, equipment, and operational accouterments. He required no part of the profits, but charged a small fee for his services. Thus the first Howard Johnson franchise restaurant was started. In 1954 when Johnson ventured into the lodging end of hospitality, there were 400 *Howard Johnson* restaurants. The Howard Johnson lodging prop-

erties were also initially family oriented properties near highways; over the years the business traveler became increasingly important.

McDonald's

One of the most recognized restaurant companies worldwide, *McDonald's*, had its start in 1948 when the brothers Richard (Dick) and Maurice (Mac) McDonald converted a hamburger stand in San Bernardino, California into a quick service restaurant using assembly line principles to avoid having to depend on highly skilled employees. They were successful and later began to sell franchises.

In 1954 they placed a very large order for *Multimixers*, a milkshake machine for which Ray Kroc (1902–1984) was sole distributor. Kroc was interested in learning more, and set out to meet the McDonald brothers. He persuaded them to sell him franchise rights, and Ray Kroc opened his first *McDonald's* in 1955. By 1961, Ray Kroc had 200 *McDonald's* and bought the rights for *McDonald's* from the McDonald brothers. Today there are about 23,000 *McDonald's* restaurants in 109 countries.

Ray Kroc persuaded the McDonalds brothers to sell him franchise rights and opened his first restaurant in 1955.

Conclusion

The above is not a complete history of hospitality. That would take an entire volume or more. There are many hospitality companies that are not mentioned, some of which you may be familiar with. It was necessary to limit the coverage, and your favorite hotel or restaurant company or founder may not have been mentioned. In limiting the chapter, however, an attempt has been made to demonstrate some of hospitality's roots and important influences throughout the years.

Questions and Assignments

1. Discuss with your team or classmates why knowledge about the history of hospitality is relevant.

2. Establish and discuss the relationship between societal influences and the hospitality industry. Consider and list at least two current influences you are aware of. Discuss their impact.

3. Develop a list of reasons for which people travel and establish which of these groups of travelers you hope to serve in the future. It is helpful if you mention the capacity in which you hope to serve them.

4. Who are the first known people to have developed trade in the modern sense of the word? Discuss how this impacted hospitality practices and offerings.

5. What is Hammurabi, King of Babylon, known for in terms of early hospitality?

6. What is a *caravanserai*?

7. Why are the Egyptians considered to be the "first tourists"?

8. What is the *diplomata tractatorium*?

9. "Truth in advertising" is an important concept today. Was it a concern in historical times? Please justify your response.

10. Many eat "food on the run" today. What is the earliest known reference to this activity? Who might have introduced it in Europe?

11. Discuss the role(s) that monasteries played relative to hospitality.

12. Please discuss the origin of the use of menu, as best we know it.

13. What are the probable roots of the term "menu"?

14. Discuss the role that coffee and coffeehouses have played over time. Are they similar or different today?

15. Establish and discuss the impact that Catherine de' Medici, Anne of Austria, and Louis XIV had on hospitality.

16. Using your preferred web browser and preferred search engine, find some additional information regarding one of the three people mentioned in question 15. With your team or classmates, summarize what you found.

17. How is the stagecoach seen as impacting hospitality?

18. How was a stagecoach inn different from other lodging establishments?

19. What were the *ordinaries*?

20. Discuss the various sleeping arrangements that might be available at early taverns in America.

21. What is the story of the *first restaurant?* How does this *restaurant* compare to restaurants today?

22. How did the French Revolution impact hospitality in Europe and America?

23. Using your preferred web browser and preferred search engine, find if /how *Delmonico's* restaurant has left a *legacy of sorts* for hospitality today.

24. Establish and discuss the impact of Carême and Escoffier. The web or library should be consulted for additional information.

25. What key features of hotels do we take for granted today that were not common in early hotels?

26. In what way did hotels such as the *Tremont*, the *Astor* and the *Parker House* differentiate themselves from the existing hotels?

27. How was the potato chip invented?

28. Using your preferred web browser and preferred search engine, or library resources, find some information on the history of a food item of your choice. Bring your information to class to share with your team or classmates.

29. What does the term *à la cârte* mean?

30. Using your preferred web browser and preferred search engine, or library resources, find some additional information on Pullman, *Le Train Bleu*, or some other from of "hospitality on the go."

31. What is Fred Harvey known for?

32. How did diners evolve? Using your preferred web browser and preferred search engine, or library resources, find some historic information about existing or past diners. Share this information with your team or classmates.

33. Using your preferred web browser and preferred search engine, or library resources, find some information about existing or past Grand Hotels. Share this information with your team or classmates.

34. Discuss the *Statler Service Code* with your team or classmates. Is the code still relevant, or is it passé. Justify your answers.

35. Choose two of hospitality's founding pioneers. You need not limit yourself to those mentioned in this book. Discuss with your team or classmates the influences on their career and the influence they have had on hospitality. What lessons did you learn from their life and work in hospitality?

36. Choose a hospitality company or property mentioned in this text that still exists today. Perform an organization/company research as discussed in the first chapter of this text.

◈ Bibliography and Suggested Readings

Bartlett, J. (1996). *The Cook's Dictionary and Culinary Reference: A Comprehensive, Definitive Guide to Cooking and Food.* Chicago, IL: Contemporary Books.

Brillat-Savarin, J. A. (1825). *The Physiology of Taste* [Physiologie du Goût] Translated by F. Crowninshield (1926). New York, NY: Horace Liveright, Inc.

Bull, F., Eskeland, A. & Tandberg, E., eds. (1972). *Gyldendals Store Konversasjons Leksikon* [Gyldendal's Large Conversation Enyclopedia], 3rd ed. Oslo, Norway: Gyldendal Norsk Forlag.

Dittmer, P. R. & Griffin, G. R. (1993). *The Dimensions of the Hospitality Industry: An Introduction.* New York, NY: Van Nostrand Reinhold.

Dorf, M. E. (1992). *Restaurants That Work: Case Studies of the Best in the Industry.* New York, NY: Watson-Guptill Publications.

Firebaugh, W. C. (1928). *The Inns of Greece & Rome.* Chicago, IL: Pascal Covici, Publishers.

Gisslen, W. (1995). *Professional Cooking,* 3rd ed. New York, NY: John Wiley & Sons, Inc.

Hilton, C. N. (1957). *Be My Guest.* New York, NY: Prentice Hall Press.

Iverson, K. (1989). *Introduction to Hospitality Management.* New York, NY: Van Nostrand Reinhold.

Jarman, R. (1952). *A Bed for the Night: The Story of the Wheeling Bellboy E. M. Statler and His Remarkable Hotels.* New York, NY: Harper & Brothers, Publishers.

Lattin, G. W. (1995). *Introduction to the Hospitality Industry,* 3rd ed. East Lansing, MI: The Educational Institute of the American Hotel and Motel Association.

Microsoft (1995). *Bookshelf 1995*

Miller, F. (1968). *America's Extraordinary Hotelman: Statler.* New York, NY: The Statler Foundation.

Montagné, P. (1961). *Larousse Gastronomique: The Encyclopedia of Food Wine & Cookery.* New York, NY: Crown Publishers, Inc.

New Yorker, 3, 4th June 1836. New York: Greeley & Winchester.

O'Brien, R. (1977). *Marriott: The J. Willard Marriott Story.* Salt Lake City, UT: Deseret Book Company.

Palmer, D. W. (1992). *Hospitable Performances: Dramatic Genre and Cultural Practices in Early Modern England.* West Lafayette, IN: Purdue University Press.

Potter, N. A. & Bennett, A. (1987). Oxford Coffee Houses, 1651–1800. Oxford, England: Hampden Press.

Ritz, M. L. (1938). *César Ritz: Host to the World.* Philadelphia, PA: J. B. Lippincott Company.

Stuart, M. W. (1952). *Old Edinburgh Taverns.* London, England: Robert Hale Limited.

White, A. (1968). *Palaces of the People: A Social History of Commercial Hospitality.* New York, NY: Taplinger Publishing Company.

Understanding Tourism: A Destination Perspective

J. S. Perry Hobson, *School of Tourism and Hospitality Management,*
SOUTHERN CROSS UNIVERSITY, AUSTRALIA

ABSTRACT

This chapter will discuss tourism as it applies to tourism destinations. Relevant tourism terms and approaches will be defined and shared as basic concepts and theories are introduced. Also, important tourism models will be introduced and explained. Finally, the social and economic impacts of tourism will be established and discussed.

OBJECTIVES

At the end of this chapter the student should be able to:

1. Distinguish between a tourist and a non-tourist.

2. Explain the tourism system model.

3. Identify some of the factors that have caused changing leisure patterns.

4. Recognize the difference between primary and secondary tourism destinations.

5. Explain the Irridex model.

6. Understand the destination life-cycle model.

7. Recognize economic impacts of tourism.

8. Identify the positive impacts of tourism.

9. Identify the negative impacts of tourism.

10. Explain the issues relating to the development of tourism in a destination.

Introduction

Historians will record that one of the social hallmarks of the late-twentieth century is the vast increase in the temporary movement of people. Whereas in past decades and centuries the movement of people was related to war, famine, or permanent migration, this social movement has been entirely voluntary. It has been a movement without equal in history, and it is only recently that a field of study has been developed to help us understand it. Essentially, the academic study of tourism entails studying the behavior of people who have left their home for a temporary stay elsewhere. Considerations are: What motivated them to go where they went? What did they do when they got there? How long did they stay? How much money did they spend, and on what? Furthermore, what impacts—social, economic, cultural, and environmental did their stay have on the destination communities that they visited?

Tourism is still a relatively new field of study. Historically it has drawn heavily on academic theories from related fields, such as recreation, leisure studies, geography, sociology, psychology, and planning among others. As the field has rapidly matured, it has developed its own literature base, theories and concepts from which it is now possible to have a better understanding of the phenomenon. The purpose of this chapter is to introduce the basic concepts and theories that have been developed.

A Focus on the Destination

Hospitality facilities, such as hotels, are all physically located somewhere. Such facilities are rarely destinations in their own right. In other words, people generally do not just travel somewhere just to visit a hotel—though in some unique resorts this may be the case. The vast majority of leisure travelers choose to travel to a destination for a set of reasons. Only when that choice has been made, do they consider what sort of hospitality facility they want to use. Of course, the fact that a destination has a certain hospitality facility (attraction), such as a casino, may be integral to the choice of the destination. In looking at tourism from a hospitality perspective, the focus taken in this chapter will be that of the destination. This is a recognized approach from which to examine tourism (Westlake & Cooper, 1988). For it is to the destination tourists travel, and this is where they will spend most of their time and money. It is the place where facilities such as hotels, resorts, restaurants, or convention centers are built.

The high cost of developing the hospitality industry means that once a decision to build, or buy, has been made, then a company becomes locked into the destination. Such facilities cannot be readily or simply moved elsewhere. So, the hospitality industry becomes part of the destination and enters into a symbiotic relationship with the community, the local environment, and with other businesses located at the destination. Initially, the role played by the hospitality industry may be as developer and investor of new facilities. This role may evolve into being a marketer and promoter of the destination. Finally, the hospitality industry may play the role of historical preserver of the culture—as with renovated landmark hotels such as *Raffles* in Singapore. Needless to say, hospitality facilities should recognize that they have a vested interest in the well being of any destination of which it becomes part. This means being in tune with not only how tourists view the destination, but also how the local community sees the destination developing. If the environmental planning and development of a destination are badly managed, or if rampant over development occurs, the very essence of what made the destination desirable can be lost. As a result, tourists may go elsewhere, residents can be faced with a spoiled environment and a divided community, and investors can be left with empty hotel rooms.

What Is Tourism and Who Are Tourists?

Over the years the various terms relating to tourism have been defined in a number of different ways. There is no single set of all encompassing definitions that are globally used. In addition to the term tourism, other terms such as "tourist," "visitor," "excursionist" and "day tripper" are all commonly used to describe people that visit an area away from their home communities.

Tourism has been defined by McIntosh & Goeldnor (1988, p.4) as "the sum of the phenomena and relationships arising from the interactions of tourists, business suppliers, host governments, and host communities in the process of attracting and hosting these tourists and other visitors." In regards to the other terms listed, a number of definitions have been developed by the World Tourism Organization (WTO), an agency of the United Nations (UN). The principle terms are:

Visitor—any person visiting a country (area) other than that in which he has his usual place of residence for any reason other than following an occupation remunerated from within the country (area) visited.

The definition covers:

International Tourists—a temporary visitor staying at least 24 hours in the country (area) visited for the purpose of:

(a) Leisure, e.g., recreation, health, study, and sports.
(b) Businesses, family, mission meeting.

Excursionist—a temporary visitor staying less than 24 hours in the country visited, including passengers in cruise ships.

(*Source:* WTO various publications)

In fact, most tourism flows are domestic (within a country), and not international. Statistics on these movements are compiled and kept by various national or state agencies. Such statistics may not be as reliable, as it is often more difficult to collect data on domestic tourists because they do not have to pass through immigration points. A further complication is that many different definitions are used. For example, in the U.S. there are over twenty different definitions used by the fifty states. **In regards to domestic tourism (within a country), often the term *"trip"* is used as the unit of measurement.** This is usually defined as either:

(a) A person that is travelling 100 miles or more away from home, or

(b) A person that is staying away from home longer than 24 hours.

Types of Tourists

One common misconception about tourism is that all tourism is for leisure purposes. As the WTO definitions show us, not all tourism is in fact leisure travel. In many destinations, business travel may be a more important sector. There are two broad types of tourists: (a) Business travelers, and (b) Leisure travelers, though some people may make trips that combine both types of activities. Often these categories are further specified for statistical purposes. For example, the State of Illinois (U.S.) uses the following four categories to identify its tourists:

1. Business/Convention
2. Visiting Friends and Relatives (VFR)
3. Other Pleasure
4. Other purposes

The Business Traveler

Looking at this category in more detail, it is clear that there are many different types of business travelers. They can be broken down into

Many travelers are business rather than leisure travelers.

several typical categories as shown below.

1. Corporate staff—such as those in sales employed by large multinational companies.
2. Entrepreneurs—owners of small companies elsewhere on a business trip.
3. Trade show—to visit or display at an exhibition.
4. Meeting—to attend a company or association meeting.
5. Incentive—a fully paid reward trip for an employee (e.g., for meeting a sales target).

The Leisure Traveler

As with business travelers, the market for leisure travelers is also composed of a number of heterogeneous groupings. This market can also be segmented in a number of ways. For example, some are budget travelers; others are on a once in a lifetime honeymoon trip. As has already been outlined, leisure travelers often travel for very different reasons. The largest category is that of visiting friends and relatives (VFR). In terms of international travel, leisure travelers are broken down in to two groupings. Those that are:

1. Independent tourists (IT); tourists who make their own travel arrangements, and
2. Group inclusive tourists (GIT); tourists who come as part of an organized package trip.

Conceptualizing Tourism

In terms of some conceptual frameworks to help understand the tourism phenomenon, a number have been developed. One of the most commonly used is Neil Leiper's (1979) "Tourism System Model," though other models such as Mathieson & Wall's (1982) "Conceptual Framework of Tourism" are also widely used. Leiper's (1979) diagrammatic summary of the tourism system was a major step forward in helping academics to view the tourism phenomenon, and is shown in Figure 1.

The purpose of such a model is to enable academics, researchers, and students to look at the whole tourism system. As can be seen, the system model consists of five specific elements that operate within a broader macro-environment. In looking at the model, consider the recent trip of a fictitious Mr. Fred Bloggs from the U.K. to the U.S. He leaves his home

Figure 1. Tourism System Model.

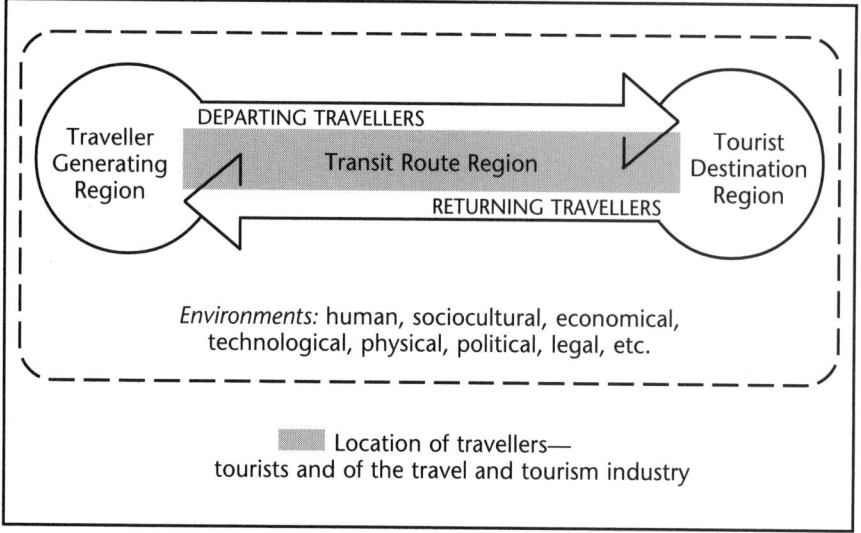

Source: Leiper (1995)

in Sheffield, U.K. (the tourist generating region) and stays overnight in London (a transit route region) before catching a flight to Los Angeles, U.S. (the tourist destination region) where he visits his long lost cousin John Doe. This simple example shows how the tourist moves from one part of the model to another. But, such information is purely descriptive. There is also a whole range of other information that those working in the tourism industry might like to know about Fred Bloggs' trip—such as what motivated him to travel when he did, what factors in the macro-environment affected his trip, and so forth. In discussing each key element of the model, such points will become more apparent.

A. Key Elements of the Systems Model:

1. **Travelers**—these are the people who travel from their normal place of residence to another place.

   Information we might want to know here is demographic information (e.g., how much do they earn, what are their occupations, etc.), or some socio-psychological information about them as individuals (e.g., what has motivated each of them to travel to the destination?)

2. **Generating region**—this is the place of residence that tourists come from.

   Not only is additional demographic information needed relating to which cities, states, and countries the tourists originate from, but so is information relating to access, booking patterns, structure of the outbound industry, and so forth. Clearly, there are cultural influences that have impacted the tourists from the region in regards to how they travel. For example, one feature of the outbound Japanese market is that a very high percentage of Japanese tourists still travel as GIT and not IT. This can be seen as a reflection of their group culture.

3. **Destination region**—here we look at the impacts of tourists on the destination.

   Such impacts may include economic impacts, social impacts on residents who live in the community, and impacts on development of the built and natural environments. These impacts may be positive (e.g., increasing numbers of jobs for residents), or negative (e.g., pollution of local beaches).

4. **Transit routes**—this part of the model considers the transit areas or routes that connect the generating and destination region.

Some transit regions benefit substantially from travelers passing though, whereas others may benefit little. For example, there is considerable impact on the eastern seaboard states of the U.S. caused by the traffic of Canadians driving from the provinces of Quebec and Ontario on their way to Florida for the winter. Certain other destinations benefit from being stopover points for airline travel, such as Dubai (in the Middle East) and Singapore (in the Far East). Travelers often stop over to shop. In other cases though, travelers may bring substantial problems to the transit regions—for example, by producing extra traffic, pollution and noise problems.

5. **The travel and tourism industries**—cover the various industries that make up the wider tourism industry.

   These industries are diverse, and rather than talk about "a tourism industry" as one industry, it is often better to consider the tourism industry as an umbrella term for a number of interrelated collection of industries serving the needs of the traveler. Such a term would include discrete and identifiable industries—such as the hotel industry, the airline industry, the gaming industry, the convention industry and so forth.

B. The Macro-Environment:

All industries and businesses operate within a macro-environment. This consists of factors such as the sociocultural, economic, legal, political, and technological environments among others. Within the macro-environment, there are a host of factors that can impact the tourism industries:

1. **Sociocultural**—Individuals and their travel desires are influenced by the changing norms of society (culture, social classes, etc.) of which they are part. As tourism is learned behavior it is impacted by

a variety of sociocultural influences. As Kotler, Bowen & Makens (1996, p.181) point out, "Culture is an integral part of the hospitality and tourism business. It determines what we eat, how we travel, where we travel and where we stay."

2. **Economic**—Tourism is impacted by changes in the economic cycle. For example, people often have different travel patterns during boom and recessionary times. During a recession people may decide to travel domestically, rather than take a more expensive international trips.

3. **Legal**—The industries can be impacted by a whole range of domestic and international legislation, such as bilateral airline treaties between countries. Such regulations can substantially influence the accessibility and costs of getting to a destination.

4. **Political**—There may be political considerations that impact the industries. For example, the U.S. government has bans on travel to certain countries, such as Cuba. This means that U.S. airlines are prohibited from flying there. In another example, the government of China (P.R.C.) has specified only seven approved foreign countries for its tourists to visit without a special permit.

5. **Technological changes**—the increasing use of a range of technologies is continuing to affect the travel industries. For example, computer reservation systems (CRS) revolutionized the way airlines and travel agencies did business in the 1980s. The Internet, particularly the World Wide Web (WWW), may further impact the tourism system once potential tourists use it extensively to make their travel arrangements. Other emerging technologies, such as new high-speed planes that can enter the lower orbits of space, may reduce travel times dramatically. Long-haul travel could be revolutionized. For example,

journey times from London (U.K.) to Sydney (Australia), could be reduced from the current twenty-two hours flying time, to less than three hours.

Sectors in the Travel and Tourism Industries

Industries supplying services to tourists comprise a range of different organizations. These vary from small, local, privately owned businesses (e.g., a souvenir shop), to multi-national corporations (e.g., *Hilton Hotels*), to government owned organizations (e.g., national parks). A commonly applied theory describes these industries as industrial "sectors" rather than describing everything as industries. The number of sectors is arbitrary and can range from three to thirty. From a destination point of view, a simple three-sector model would include attractions, accommodation, and amenities. However, in a fully developed form, industries function in all the geographic parts of the whole tourism system. This occurs if tourists use services pre-trip, in transit, and at the destination. Leiper (1995) has identified seven major sectors, as shown in the model above:

1. **The marketing specialist sector**—those involved in the marketing of tourism services, such as travel agencies and tour wholesalers. They tend to be located in the tourist generating regions, where they can be close to potential customers and their decision making process.

2. **Carrier sector**—includes public transport specialists such as airlines, bus companies, and cruise lines. These are located along the transit route part of the model, but also extend operations into the generating and destination regions of the model.

3. **Accommodation sector**—includes all those businesses involved in providing lodging and related services to tourists. While most

of them will be at the destination, many of them (e.g., motels and roadside restaurants) may be located in the transit region of the model. Typical businesses here would include hotels, resorts, camping grounds, bed and breakfast operations, as well as restaurants.

4. **Attractions sector**—includes those organizations that provide the tourist with a leisure experience. Typical examples would include organizations operating theme parks, sports events, fairs, casinos, zoos, national parks, and the like.

5. **Tour operators sector**—includes organizations that assemble or conduct pre-packaged travel arrangement for tourists, such as transport, accommodation and attractions. In the generating region they are known as "outbound operators," and in the transit route and destination region are known as "inbound operators."

6. **Coordination sector**—includes government departments of tourism, which attempt to coordinate operations. Organizations here would include the IATA (International Airline Transport Association), WTO (World Tourism Organization), and state and national government tourism authorities.

7. **Miscellaneous sector**—in this category a whole number of related businesses can be placed. It can include souvenir and duty free shops, foreign exchange units in banks that deal with traveler's checks and currency exchange, as well as insurance companies.

Types of Systems

Given the size and the competitive nature of many of the tourism industries, it is not surprising to find that many organizations within it choose to focus their activities. Organizations cannot be "all things to all people" and have looked at ways of building up their core competence, which means limiting the scope of their activities. Thus we may find a French tour operator that just focuses its activities on developing tours for the inbound Japanese market—ignoring other markets such as other foreign inbound markets, the domestic French market, or outbound domestic markets. Consequently, countries can have three sorts of tourism systems:

1. Domestic tourism systems—that cater to residents of a country who travel within their own country
2. Outbound tourism systems—that cater to residents going abroad
3. Inbound tourism systems—that cater to nationals of a foreign country who are coming to visit a country.

The Marketing of Destinations

Most countries, and states/regions of a country, have government run tourism organizations that are responsible for promoting the country as a destination to overseas tourists. For example, Singapore has the Singapore Tourism Bureau (STB), New Zealand has the New Zealand Tourist Board (NZTB), and the U.K. has the British Tourism Authority (BTA). Although the U.S. is one of the largest destination regions in the world, the crossover of state and federal responsibilities means that the U.S. has a relatively weak national tourism promotion agency. Most international promotion is currently undertaken by individual states (e.g., California) or from private sector attractions (e.g., Disneyland). Consequently, it is hard to say just how much some countries, such as the U.S., actually spend on their international tourism promotion. The nationally funded promotional budgets for countries vary enormously, and they can be broken down in a number of different ways. This is illustrated in Box 1.

Countries can have anything from one to four levels of tourism organizations that are responsible for promotion. For example, Australia has the

Australian Tourism Commission (ATC) that is responsible for promoting Australia overseas. Each state and territory also has a tourism promotion agency (e.g., Tourism New South Wales), which promotes the state domestically, but it may also be involved in some international promotion. Within the state, many regions also have additional agencies (e.g., Tropical NSW), which is responsible for promotion of the region to people within the state and to people in some other states. Furthermore, destinations within a region may also have their own tourism information bureau (e.g., Bryon Bay tourism information center) that is responsible for handling specific information and inquiries.

Example: Hong Kong (SAR), China (PRC)

The Hong Kong Tourist Association (HKTA) was set up by the Hong Kong government back in 1957 to develop the tourism industry. The HKTA has six broad objectives. They are:

❖ Increase the number of visitors to Hong Kong
❖ Develop the territory as a travel destination
❖ Promote the improvement of visitor facilities
❖ Secure overseas publicity of the territory's attractions
❖ Coordinate activities of the travel industry
❖ Make recommendations and advise the government of tourism matters

In 1959, the HKTA had 105 member organizations, whereas today it has over 2,000. It now has 318 staff members of whom 63 are stationed in the 15 overseas offices. The HKTA produces most of the research data on tourism in this Special Administrative Region (SAR) of China.

The main international organization responsible for tourism is the

World Tourism Organization (WTO). It is an office of the United Nations based in Madrid, Spain. It monitors international travel patterns and offers development help, particularly to third world countries.

Growth of the Tourism Industries

As has been noted in Chapter 2, people have been travelling for thousands of years, though initially it was for trade and not leisure. Other reasons were to visit religious shrines. The recognized father of modern tourism is Thomas Cook, who still has a chain of travel agencies and a tour company named after him. Back in 1841 he organized the first inclusive day trip by train from Leicester to Loughborough (U.K.). Mass tourism, on the scale we known it today, began after World War II, and increased more with the arrival of the jet plane in the 1960's. Such technological advances made it economical to carry more people over greater distances. New mass tourism destinations such as Orlando (U.S.), and Costa del Sol (Spain) were developed in the 1970s to service the growing demand for "getaway" holidays in the sun. As the planes became larger and could fly further at lower costs, destinations further away from the industrialized countries of Northern Europe and North America became places to visit. Cities in Asia, such as Hong Kong and Bangkok (Thailand), became within easy reach and resorts in places such as Cancun (Mexico), and Bali (Indonesia) were developed.

The Relationship Between Leisure and Tourism

There are two fundamental prerequisites that underpin the ability of people to be tourists. The first is that people have to have enough disposable income so that they can afford to travel, and the second is that they have sufficient leisure time, which

More Money Needed for Tourism Promotion

Countries are spending more money on tourism promotion, but it is still not enough and is often misdirected according to a report released by the World Tourism Organization (WTO) (see Luhrman, 1997). The WTO study, "Budgets of National Tourism Administrations," shows that global spending on tourism promotion by national governments reached US$1.2 billion in 1995, an increase of seven percent over the previous year. "The impact of this increase is evident in 1996 tourism results, which were up 4.5 percent in terms of international arrivals and 7.6 percent in receipts," said Enzo Paci, WTO chief of statistics and market research. "However, the total amount is still ridiculously small. For most countries, it is not nearly enough to cope with the fierce competition that destinations are facing" he said.

Australia heads the list of biggest spenders on tourism promotion at US$88 million, followed by Spain and the U.K. at US$79 million each, France at US$73 million, and Singapore US$54 million.

Tourism revenues earned for each US$1 spent on promotion vary widely. France received US$375 for each dollar spent and Spain received US$319 million. Australia, on the other hand, earned just US$78 for each dollar spent on promotion.

The WTO survey shows that promotional spending makes up 56 percent of the budgets of the National Tourism Administrations (NTA). The NTA with the largest overall budget was Israel at US$203 million, followed by Spain at US$135 million and Thailand US$92 million. Eighteen countries surveyed had budgets of US$40 million or more and eight countries topped US$70 million.

The NTA for France, which is the world's most popular destination country for foreign tourists, received the fifth biggest budget at US$84 million. While the United States, which is the world's number one earner from international tourism and second in arrivals, allocated just US$15 million in 1995.

The United States and many other countries are currently seeking non-government funding for tourism promotion, but three of the top ten promotion budgets in the world—Spain, Thailand, and Singapore—are still wholly government funded. Among the top spenders, only the Netherlands and the United Kingdom have been able to generate more than half of their financing from the private sector. "Although private sector funding is growing, it still represents a fairly modest share in most countries. For the majority of NTAs the private sector contribution does not come as easily as one might imagine," said Mr. Paci.

Apart from earmarking more money for promotion, countries should also better target their resources, the report says. "It appears that the budget allocated to certain countries usually does not bear any relation to that market's importance as a source of tourists or revenue for the destination country," said the WTO statistics chief.

In three of world's biggest tourism generating markets—Germany, Japan, and the United Kingdom—promotional spending by other destinations dropped sharply in 1995. Among the top ten tourism-generating countries, the only places where more promotion was targeted were the United States, Spain, and the Netherlands.

Top Tourism Promotion Budgets in 1996 (×US$1,000)

1. Australia	87,949
2. United Kingdom	78,710
3. Spain	78,647
4. France	72,928
5. Singapore	53,595
6. Thailand	51,198
7. Netherlands	49,700
8. Austria	47,254
9. Ireland	37,811
10. Portugal	37,271

Source: World Tourism Organization (see Luhrman, 1997).

Promotional Performance

Country	Promotional spending per tourist arrival	Promotional spending per US$1,000 in revenues	Revenues per US$1 spent on tourism promotion
Australia	23.32	12.80	78
United Kingdom	3.47	4.50	222
Spain	1.74	3.10	319
France	1.20	2.70	375
Singapore	8.35	7.10	141
Thailand	7.42	8.80	148
Netherlands	7.88	8.20	122
Ireland	8.60	21.00	48
Portugal	3.92	8.30	121
Israel	15.97	13.00	77

Source: World Tourism Organization (see Luhrman, 1997).

allows them to be able to travel. Consequently, tourism should be viewed as one of many leisure pursuits people may have. The tourist activities undertaken are part of people's recreation. In this context, the term "leisure" usually refers to time of unpaid work, whereas the term "recreation" refers to activities people involve themselves in during this free time. Recreational activities are usually undertaken in leisure time.

A little over one hundred years ago, the average work week, in today's industrialized countries, was six days, and 70 working hours with no paid vacation or work related benefits. As standards of living have risen, and productivity has grown, the populations of industrialized countries have generally demanded longer vacation times and shorter working weeks. However, all countries have differing average work weeks and amounts of paid vacation time. This is a reflection of the differing importance that nations place on leisure time, the power of unions to negotiate for lower working hours, and the legal minimums that have been established. For comparison purposes, the average vacation time of employees of major industrialized countries, is:

Comparison of Average International Vacation Time

Country	Average Vacation + National Holidays
USA	26
UK	33
Germany	40
Sweden	41

Germans, with one of the highest per capita amounts of leisure time and income, have traditionally spent the longest amount of time on vacation. Americans by contrast, have had one of the lowest national averages of number of days off work. From the tourism perspective, we need not only know how much leisure time people have, but also how it is distributed. For example, lowering the average workweek by one hour is unlikely to affect people's vacation patterns. But, if employees were allowed to save up that one hour a week, and then take all 52 hours (or six and half working days) at the same time, then that could have a very significant impact on people's travel patterns. It was predicted back in the 1960s, that by the end of the 20th century the industrialized societies would be in the "age of leisure." But since the late 1970s, it appears that working hours have actually increased in many countries. Taking the U.S. as an example:

Average U.S. Working Week and Leisure Time

	Working Week	Leisure Time
1975	43.1 hours	24.0 hours
1985	47.3 hours	18.1 hours
1995	38.9 hours	not available

Americans are working more hours, not less.

It should be pointed out that data in this area is difficult to accumulate and is sometimes contradictory (see for example Burns, 1997; Robinson & Godbey, 1997). However, what is apparent is that the predicted arrival of the "age of leisure" has yet to appear. There are a number of reasons for this. One of the underlying causes, has been the shift of industrialized economies from a primarily manufacturing industry base, to a service industry base. This has impacted individuals, as service jobs are often more demanding in terms of number of hours worked. In order to be competitive in the service industry, businesses have to be open and accessible. This often precludes individuals from taking extended periods of time off work especially where individuals have clients (e.g., hair dressers, lawyers etc.) or handle specific and timely information (e.g., stock brokers). In addition, some economists point out that many of the newer service industry jobs have been part-time or have been lower paid than the manufacturing jobs that they have replaced. Consequently, an increasing number of people (particularly in the USA) are finding that they are working two part-time jobs to make ends meet.

Changes in people's work arrangements affect their leisure patterns. In the 1980s and 1990s one clearly dis-

cernible trend was the move away from one annual long vacation to people taking numerous breaks of shorter duration. This would seem to be tied in to the employment and economic shifts already discussed. Short breaks have been seen as preferable because:

1. Long periods of time do not have to be taken away from work.
2. It is easier for dual income couples to co-ordinate getting away for short periods of time.
3. It provides the individual with more frequent periods of relaxation from the mentally stressful work environment.

What Motivates People to Travel to a Destination?

Clearly there are multitudes of reasons why people travel and become tourists. While a number of different ways can be used to categorize tourism, six broad categories have been identified by Smith (1977), see Box 2.

However, it has always been much easier to answer the who, when, where, and how questions of tourism, than the why. In other words, what motivates people to leave home and

Categories of Tourism

Valene Smith (1977) identified six broad categories of tourism:

1. **Ethnic tourism**—which is travelling for the purpose of observing the cultural lifestyle of another people, often to meet and deal closely with the culture.

2. **Cultural tourism**—to experience and see aspects of a culture, but not to get too closely involved with people of that culture. The tourist might visit staged shows, such as those at the China Cultural Village in Shenzhen (China, PRC).

3. **Historical tourism**—to visit historical monuments and sites, such as those in St. Petersburg, Russia. The emphasis is on the built environment.

4. **Environmental tourism**—to visit new environments. For example, to see jungles, ice flows, or palm tree lined beaches. The emphasis here is on the natural environment.

5. **Recreational tourism**—to participate in, or watch, sporting events, gambling, sun bathing, shopping, etc.

6. **Business tourism**—to attend a convention or meeting.

travel to visit another place? Why do people choose to go to a certain destination? What attracts them to visit? As Smith & Turner (1973) asked, "Just what motivates people? What does Florence have over sitting in front of the television? Why are the Fjords of Norway preferred to a sunny beach? Why Bali—or Acapulco—or wherever? Even more interestingly, why do some people choose not to take holidays at all?"

Measuring what motivates people has been problematic and many researchers have examined different combinations of factors. Three studies will be looked at here.

A. Push and Pull Factors

Williams and Zelinsky (1970) identified two sets of factors—"push" factors and "pull" factors. They believed these explain the choices of tourists (see Box 3). The push factors are an individual's socio-psychological motives, the pull factors are motives aroused by the destination. Consequently, it has been seen that the push factors have been useful for explaining the desire to take a vacation/holiday, while pull factors have been thought useful for explaining the choice of destination.

While this work helps to identify and explain two basic categories of factors, they are an over simplification of a much more complex situation.

B. Plog's Psychographic Typologies

In looking at the movement of tourists, it became clear that certain types of people were being attracted to certain types of destinations. The question became what could explain this? Stanley Plog (1974) decided to look

Two Dimensions of Tourist Motivation

Push Factors
Desire to escape and get away
The need to experience something different
Ego-enhancement
Peer pressure to take a holiday

Pull Factors
Presence of attractions of interest
Image of the destination
Availability of activities that cannot be done at home

at how to classify people according to their psychographical types. He attempted to match them to the types of destinations that they were likely to travel to. First of all, he plotted the U.S. population along a psychographic continuum—ranging from psychographic to allocentric. The term "psychocentric" is derived from the Greek word "psyche" or self-centered. This term is used for people who were seen as being inward looking and not very adventurous, with safety being more of a concern. The term "allocentric" on the other hand, derives from the word "allo" meaning varied in form. An allocentric person is one whose patterns are focused on varied activities. This type of person tends to be outgoing and self-confident, and is more likely to want to explore and to experiment. Travel can be one way for them to do this.

Plog found that the U.S. population was normally distributed along a continuum between the two extreme types (see Figure 2), with mid-centrics being the dominant middle grouping. Plog also looked at income levels of the population, and discovered that there were more psychocentrics at the lower end of the income spectrum. Whereas at the upper end of the income spectrum, people were found to mostly found to be allocentric.

Plog then identified the travel preferences of psychocentric and allocentric travelers (see Box 4), and he was then able to superimpose a list of destinations along the population curve (see Figure 3). This suggests that allocentrics would travel to exotic destinations, such as Africa and the South Pacific. Mid-centrics would go to Hawaii, whereas psychocentrics would take a fully inclusive package vacation to Disneyland. He also saw that the first visitors to a new destination are allocentric personality types. Progressively as more people know the place, and as the tourism facilities begin to improve, more and more of the mid-centrics arrive. Once the destination has become developed, the psychocentric personality types (who

Figure 2. U.S. Population Distribution by Psychographic Type.

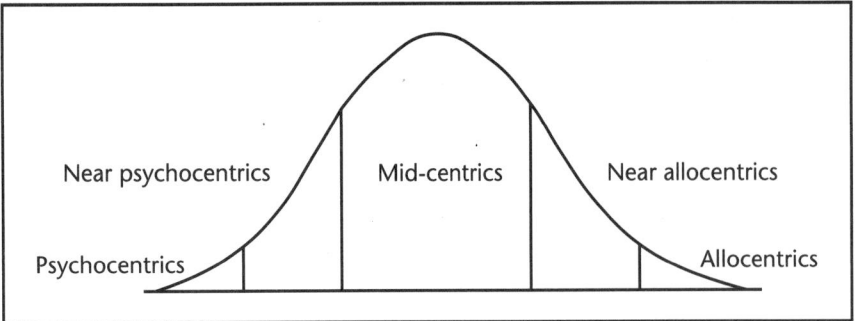

Source: Plog (1972)

Figure 3. Psychographic Positions of Destinations.

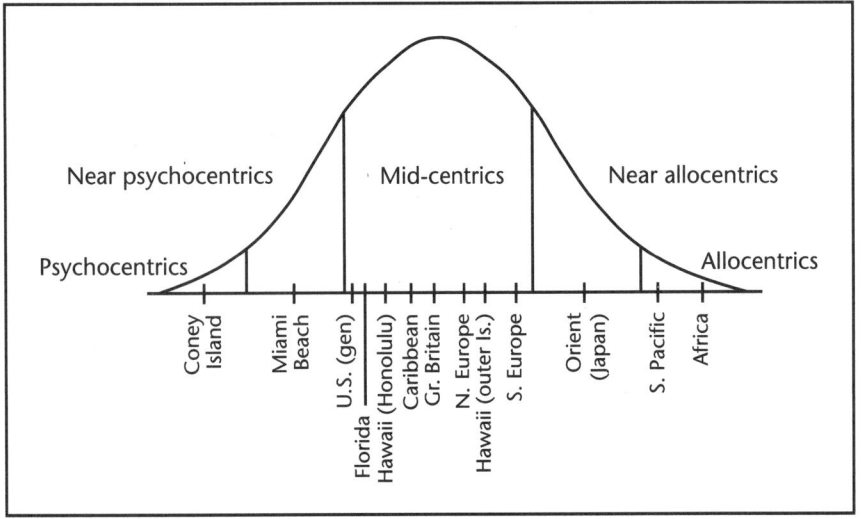

Source: Plog (1972)

Travel Preference Types

Allocentric Traits
Have a sense of discovery and are looking for new experiences
Are adventurous and like to explore alone
Seek out novelty and have high activity levels
Prefer areas that are not developed tourist destinations
Enjoy meeting and dealing with people from other cultures

Psychocentrics Traits
Prefer travelling to well-known destinations
Prefer taking a tour package
Seek familiarity—in regards to food, shops, and attractions
Are comfortable being with other travelers like themselves
Seek passive activities

are more concerned with familiarity, safety, and security) will be attracted.

Since Plog's work in the early 1970s, there have been a number of commentators and researchers who have examined Plog's findings. Clearly there are some obvious shortcomings. As McIntosh & Goeldner (1990, p. 144) point out, "Such a direct linkage between the classification of tourists and of destinations does not consider the important fact that people travel with different motivations on different occasions. A wealthy allocentric my indeed travel to Africa on an annual vacation, but may also take weekend trips to psychocentric destinations during other times of the year." In regards to income, it has also been pointed out that at lower levels of family income travel destinations may be determined by income constraints

rather than their psychological profile. Consequently, a poor allocentric college student who is currently unable to afford to go trekking across South America may instead travel to a nearby destination usually visited by psychocentrics. Other researchers have also doubted the very basis of this work. Smith (1990) tested Plog's allocentric/psychocentric theory in seven countries and has argued that Plog's findings are based on a flawed research process. Nevertheless, Plog's allocentric/psychocentric was a pioneering effort, and it still offers a way to examine travel motivations and destinations in current market conditions.

C. Crompton's Nine Factors

In furthering this research, John Crompton (1979) identified nine

factors that respondents identified as motives that influenced the selection of the type of vacation destination. Seven of these were classified as socio-psychological factors. The two remaining motives were classified as being in a category of cultural motives. In summarizing his findings he pointed out, that "the findings suggest that for some respondents, the destination itself was relatively unimportant. Respondents did not go to particular locations to seek cultural insights or artifacts; rather they went for socio-psychological reasons unrelated to any specific destination. The destination served merely as a medium through which these motives could be satisfied (Crompton, 1979, p. 415). Through this study he identified factors that motivated people to travel. The identified factors are:

Socio-Psychological Factors

The following seven motives are concerned with the social and psychological status rather than with the destination itself.

1. **Escape from a perceived mundane environment**—to be in and experience a different place and to escape from the daily routine.

2. **Exploration and evaluation of self**—a chance to re-evaluate one's life and discover more about oneself.

3. **Relaxation**—taking time to pursue activities of interest that would lead to mental relaxation.

4. **Prestige**—the ability to travel and the destination one could go to would impress others in their reference group at home.

5. **Regression**—the opportunity to do things that were inconceivable within the context of their current lifestyle and standing in the community, such as to do things that were reminiscent of adolescent behaviour.

6. **Enhancement of kinship relationships**—a chance to interact more with other family members, outside of the home and the usual set routines.

7. **Facilitation of social interaction**—the opportunity to meet new and different people. It was found that this motivation is people orientated, as opposed to being destination orientated.

Cultural Motives

The following two motives were concerned with specific factors a destination might offer, rather than the social and psychological status of the individual.

1. **Novelty**—a preference to see something new and to experience something different like going to a previously unvisited destination. Language and culture were found to be barriers.

2. **Education**—The ability to travel and learn about other cultures and places, for example, leisure travel positively influenced children's development towards a rounded individual.

Identification of tourist motivations has been the subject of much research and debate. Researchers have identified an extensive number of motivations. Thomas (1964) identifies 18 reasons that people travel and Lunberg (1972) identifies 20 reasons. Other researchers, such as Gray (1970), saw that only two factors, the desire for "wanderlust" and "sunlust," could be used to explain tourist motivation. But other researchers, such as Dann (1977), have seen that the need for leisure travel is essentially the consequence of the need for anonymity and ego-enhancement. Whereas Mannell and Iso-Ahola (1987) identified the motivations for leisure travel in terms of "escape" and "seeking" of personal and interpersonal rewards. In terms of measurement of such motivations, Fodness (1994) has identified a way of measuring them by using a behavioral segmentation model. But despite so much work being done in this area, many of the authors have highlighted the complexity of identifying an

Typology of International Tourist Roles

In looking at tourism from a sociological perspective, Cohen (1972) saw that a tourist experience combines a degree of novelty (new experiences), with a degree of familiarity (through food bought, use of brand names, type of activities, etc). However, what is experienced depends upon the type of trip that is taken, and the various tourism institutions that are used. He identified a continuum of possible combinations, and proposed that tourists fall into four different classifications. The first two classifications he referred to as the *institutionalized* tourist roles, and the second two as the *noninstitutionalized* tourist roles.

Organized mass tourist—they are the least adventurous and largely remain confined with their "environmental bubble" throughout the trip. The itinerary is entirely pre-paid and fixed ahead of time; the stops are well prepared and guided. Familiarity is at a maximum, novelty at a minimum. Example: A group inclusive tour (GIT) of three Asian countries, including all flights, hotel, transfers, and tours.

Individual mass tourist—Similar to the previous type, except that the tour is not entirely pre-planned, and the tourists have a certain amount of control over their time and are not bound to a group. However, all major arrangements are made through a travel agent. They only venture out slightly from the "environmental bubble." Familiarity is still dominant, but somewhat less so than the previous type. The experience of novelty is somewhat greater, though it is still often somewhat routine. Example: An independent package deal to a resort in Jamaica for a week. Flights, hotel, and transfers are all booked ahead of time.

Explorer—This type of tourists arrange the trip alone. They try to get off the beaten track as much as possible. Nevertheless they look for comfortable accommodation and reliable transport. Explorers dare to leave their "environmental bubble" much more than the previous types. Although novelty dominates, the tourists do not immerse themselves completely in the host society. Example: A self-organized self-drive holiday around the U.K. and Ireland. The tourists plan their own itinerary and stay in locally recommended Bed & Breakfast establishments.

Drifter—They seek to get away from the accustomed ways of life of home. They shun connection with the tourist establishments, are happy to live with the locals and try to live the way that locals live and speak their language. Drifters have no fixed itinerary and try to become totally immersed in the host culture. Novelty is at the highest and familiarity disappears. Example: A backpacker who tours around Australia and New Zealand. Stays in each place for a few weeks. Picks up jobs to earn some money picking fruit.

individual's real motives. Further-more, as Krippendorf (1987) has pointed out, many people have hidden agendas, which they may not necessarily be willing to admit to.

Two Types of Tourist Destinations

Mill and Morrison (1985) have classified destinations into being either *primary or touring destinations*, or *secondary or stopover destinations*. A primary destination is one that people are willing to travel a long distance to see. For example, people may travel specifically to see the Pyramids (Egypt), the Great Wall of China (P.R.C.), the Grand Canyon (U.S.) or Ayers Rock (Australia). A secondary destination is one that would not attract people from a long distance on its own. They draw people from nearby areas or induce people to "stop over" on their way to a primary destination. They can, for example be regional gambling centers or theme parks. This does not mean that a secondary destination gets fewer visitors than a primary attraction, some may even get more. As Powers (1988, p. 301) has pointed out, "Some secondary destinations may in fact get a higher number of visitors than primary destinations do. The Grand Canyon, for instance, attracts fewer than 3 million visitors a year, though they come from all over the world. In contrast, many regional theme parks draw many visitors, and Atlantic city, which is mainly a regional casino gambling center, attracts well over ten times that number."

The Destination Life-Cycle

In looking at the growth and history of the development of tourism in destinations, it became clear that certain destinations that were once booming have fallen in popularity. What could explain this? Richard Butler (1980) developed a model based on the concept of product life-cycle (PLC) taken

from the marketing literature and the concepts of carrying capacity from the natural resources literature. He wondered if a similar life-cycle concept could be used to explain how destinations develop. Whereas the PLC takes a product though the stages of introduction, growth, maturity, and decline, Butler also saw the notion of a life-cycle through which a destination will pass, but with six different stages (see Figure 4). He saw these could be plotted on a chart with an axis to plot the number of tourists and time.

The six stages Butler identified are:

1. **Exploration**—at this stage there are no specific facilities or developed attractions for visitors. Tourists stay with locals, and use local markets and shops. The attractions are only natural ones.
2. **Involvement**—in this stage the local community begins to offer services such as accommodation and food to tourists. The facilities are small scale and low-key and operated and owned by locals.
3. **Development**—in this stage local facilities are superseded by larger facilities with professional manage-

Photo courtesy New York Convention & Visitors Bureau.

People may travel specifically to see certain attractions, such as the sights of New York City.

ment being provided by outside sources. Natural attractions begin to be supplemented by man-made facilities. Planning is now needed, but the results may not be completely in keeping with local wishes.

4. **Consolidation**—by now large multinational corporations and franchises will have appeared. They dominate the tourism industry. Local control becomes removed, man-made facilities become more dominant.
5. **Stagnation**—The destination stagnates as the destination passes its optimum tourist carrying capacity. While it may still be well established it is no longer a *fashionable place* to visit. There is a high frequency of repeat visitors who seek familiarity in the surroundings. The economy is characterized by the frequent turnover in the ownership of tourist facilities as they struggle to make a profit.
6. **Rejuvenation or decline**—In this phase the destination either rejuvenates or declines to varying degrees. In the declining stages the visitor numbers drop away and the image changes from a vibrant destination to that of a has-been backwater. Rejuvenation is also possible if certain actions are taken. These include:

❖ The development of new attractions and facilities
❖ A diversification of the types and geographic base of visitors
❖ An environmental upgrade of the destination
❖ Heavy promotion to reposition the destination in the mind of potential visitors

The destination life-cycle has become a focus of much work by researchers. Since Butler's model was published it has been evaluated in a number of different locations, ranging from; Malta (Oglethorpe, 1984), to Canada's Northwest Territories (Keller, 1987), to Pattaya in Thailand

Figure 4. Butler's Model of the Hypothetical Evolution of a Tourist Area.

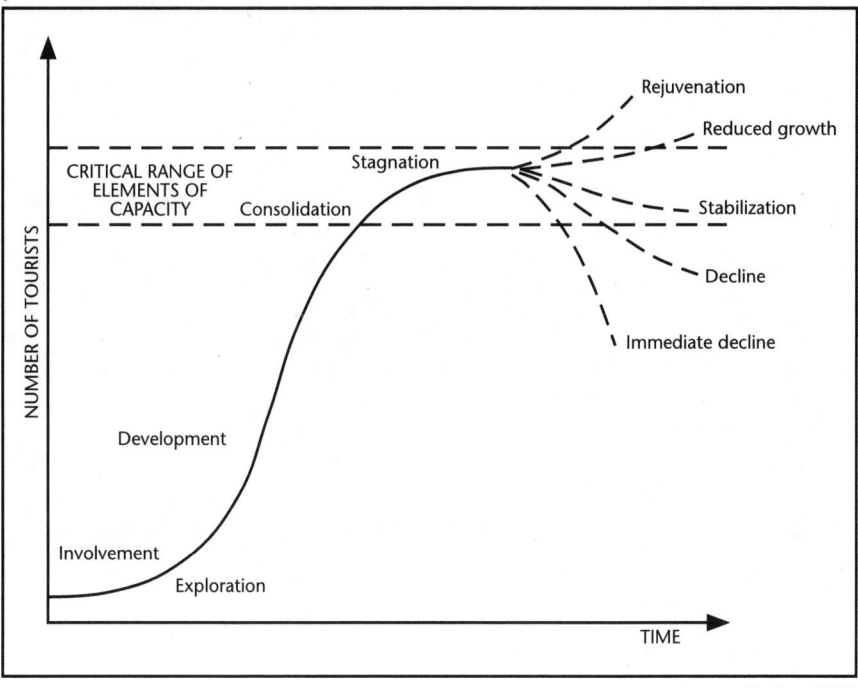

Source: (Butler, 1980)

(Smith, 1992), and to the Pacific Melanesian islands (Douglas, 1996). The model has also been the subject of a number of critiques. Prosser (1995) has pointed out that the critical arguments can be classified into five areas:

1. The feasibility of a single model of tourism development
2. Conceptual limitations of carrying capacity and the product life-cycle
3. Conceptual limitations of the life as it has been applied to various tourist destination areas
4. A lack of empirical support for the destination life-cycle concept
5. The limited practical utility of the life-cycle in tourism development planning.

Despite these shortcomings, Prosser (1995, p. 328) acknowledges that "the destination life-cycle continues to provide a useful framework for research seeking to enhance our understanding of tourism development processes, and their implications."

What Makes a Tourist Destination?

Given the destination life-cycle model, the question is what are the features and conditions that shape the evolution of a destination, making it become popular? Seven can be identified.

1. Attractions

The destination needs to have a feature or characteristic that makes it attractive to potential visitors. These attractions can be either natural or man-made.

Natural Environments

These are environments that have been created by nature. They can be scenery, climate, or wildlife related. Examples are:

❖ **Scenery related**—This is where tourists want to go and see a certain attraction that it is only possible to see in a certain area. Examples are:

 (a) Mountain areas—Rocky Mountains (North America)

 (b) Wilderness areas—Amazon Basin (Brazil)

 (c) Coastal areas—Great Barrier Reef (Australia)

 (d) Inland water areas—Mekong river (Indo-China)

❖ **Climate related**—This is where tourists temporarily move to an area for its climate. This is typically either:

 ◆ **Warmth related**—during the winter months the movement of people from the colder northern parts of the U.S. and Canada to destination such as Palm Springs (CA), or of Scandinavians to northern Africa, or

 ◆ **Sport related**—where people travel to an area at different times to engage in sporting activity that would otherwise not be possible. Examples are:

 (a) Skiing—in Austria during the winter months

 (b) Sailing—off Cape Cod (U.S.) in the summer months

❖ **Nature related**—This is where people travel to see, collect, or hunt a specific type of wildlife or plants. This may be done in a number of ways:

 (a) Urban park setting—such as the Botanical Gardens, Auckland (New Zealand)

 (b) Natural park settings—such as the Krueger National Park (South Africa)

 (c) In the wild—such as penguins in the Antarctic

Man-Made Environments

These are environments that have been created by mankind. Examples are:

(a) Urban areas—Berlin (Germany), Barcelona (Spain)

(b) Theme parks—Knott's Berry Farm (U.S.), Window on the World (China)

(c) Fairs, festivals, sporting events—Shakespeare festival (Canada), Wimbledon tennis (U.K.)

(d) Entertainment—casinos in Las Vegas (U.S.), theatre in London (U.K.)

(e) Shopping—Mall of America (U.S.), Hong Kong (China, P.R.C.).

Natural and Man-Made Environments

Some tourist destinations will encompass both categories of attractions For example, the Native American Indian remains at Mesa Verde, Orlando, (U.S.) while man-made, are in the natural environment of a park. Furthermore, scenic areas in many parts of the world (e.g., Cotswolds, U.K.) have had their landscape altered by hundreds of years of impact by man and farming. Even in natural areas where any form of mass tourism is found, there will have to be some form of human involvement in terms of providing facilities. Even remote sites now need facilities. The government of Nepal has announced that it would be installing toilets and a sewage disposal facility at the base of Mount Everest, due to the number of climbers who are now scaling the mountain.

2. Accessibility

Before large numbers of people can visit a destination it has to be accessible. Often this depends on factors such as; the availability of transit routes, such as roads and transportation; and the types of visa requirements and policies used.

Transit Routes and Passenger Transportation

In order to be a tourist one must travel. Tourists may travel by "common carriers"—airlines, ferry, coach companies, and railway or by their own personal form of transport. Transport is often the key to tourist development and growth. Inaccessi-

Cultural Attractions at a Destination

Ritchie & Zins (1978) identified twelve expressions of local culture that can attract tourists to a particular destination:

1. **Handicrafts**—such as leather goods, jewelry or pottery
2. **Language**—that a local dialect or other language is spoken in an area e.g., the Quebecois French dialect spoken in Quebec (Canada)
3. **Traditions**—to see and participate in such events as local festivals and celebrations e.g., Mardi Gras Carnival (Brazil)
4. **Gastronomy**—the unique types of food and drink available in an area, e.g., wine in the Barossa Valley (Australia)
5. **Art**—music, concerts, paintings, sculpture exhibitions, and performances, e.g., theatre on New York's Broadway (U.S.)
6. **History of a region and its visual reminders**—such as historic homes or battle fields, e.g., Gallipoli (Turkey)
7. **Resident labor**—the types of work engaged in by residents and the technology that is used, such as traditional farming methods, e.g., the Amish (North America)
8. **The architecture**—giving an area a distinctive appearance, e.g., Spanish colonial architecture in Merida (Mexico)
9. **Religion and its visible manifestations**—such as mosques, cathedrals and shrines, e.g., Lourdes (France)
10. **Education systems**—to learn about different education systems, e.g., Steiner Schools (Germany)
11. **Dress**—to see how people dress as an expression of their culture, e.g., native tribal villages or aboriginal people (Taiwan, ROC)
12. **Leisure activities and sports**—to be involved in a unique sport that only take place in certain places, e.g., Gaelic Football (Ireland)

bility—for example, poor road access or a small island not having the needed infrastructure, such as an airport—will preclude the growth of tourist development at that destination. The cost, availability and ease of transportation from the generating to destination region is vital and must not be overlooked.

Visa Policies

Accessibility also depends upon whether a destination has restrictive visa policies. Some countries (e.g., Australia) require that all tourists obtain a visa for entry prior to departure from the generating region. The need to apply for a visa and to send off passports to an embassy ahead of time can deter visitors from visiting a country. It can also make last minute trip planning impossible. Despite

concerns in waiving visa restrictions, the U.S. started to offer visas on arrival for a number of "safe" countries—such as the U.K., Japan, and Germany—in the early 1990s. Tourist arrivals soared as a result, and the overstay rate has been much lower than was predicted. A number of countries are now issuing electronic visas, and pre-clearance of immigration though travel agencies to cut down on congestion at airports.

3. Community Support

Local residents must be willing to accept visitors into their community and to support, or at least tolerate the development of facilities that allow for the development of the tourism industry. Of course, one key question is how many tourists and how much new development (and at what speed of development) are residents willing to accept before support wanes? In looking at this problem, the concept of a tourism related "carrying capacity" has been used (McCool, 1978). This scientific concept was initially used to measure how many animals an area can sustain in terms of space and food supply. Once too many animals are crowded into an area (for example deer in a wood), they will either fight amongst themselves to the death, or chase the weaker members of the herd away. This concept was first transferred into the field of recreation, and since then has been adopted by tourism researchers. In transferring the concept to tourism development, one of the questions becomes how many tourists can be put in a destination area before the local residents feel that it is too crowded? Once a threshold is reached what will be the reaction? Would residents become openly hostile to tourists? Such reactions will be discussed later in the chapter in the analysis of Doxey's (1975) "Irridex" model.

4. Security

A destination has to be able to offer an acceptable amount of security to its visitors. Various destinations, such as Florida (U.S.), Northern Ireland (U.K.), Lebanon, the former Yugoslavia, Egypt, and Cambodia have all had varying degrees of security problems, where tourists have felt that travelling and staying at the destination was simply not safe. When there is an option to visit the destination or not, it is very unlikely that tourists will be willing to take a risk with their lives. The risk may, of course, be statistically small. Nevertheless, the perception of risk can have a very devastating effect. For example, due to the perceived threat of terrorism in 1986 (by Libya), and again in 1991 (by Iraq), Americans perceived Europe to be unsafe. The U.K.'s tourism from the U.S. (its largest single market) declined by between a quarter and a half during these periods. Hotels were left with empty rooms and the airline profits were devastated.

5. Provision of Relevant Support Facilities

The continued growth and development of tourism destinations depends largely on the two following components. The more advanced the facility the greater their importance. These are:

(a) **Infrastructure**—this term refers to development on or under the ground. For example roads, rail, ski lifts, water and sewage lines, telephone lines, boat docks, and airport runways.
(b) **Superstructure**—this term refers to development built above the ground. It primarily refers to buildings. For example the runway at the airport is infrastructure; the buildings are superstructures. This term describes hotels, museums, attractions, restaurants, and the like.

Infrastructure is the key to the development of a tourist facility. Without basic access by road or air, or without water and sewage, it is not practical to develop the superstructure. Sometimes, the infrastructure for tourists is already in place. For example, if there was to be the development of a new hotel in Vienna (Austria), then roads, water, sewage systems, etc. are already present. But, if the development was to be a new ski resort in Siberia (Russia), then the infrastructure might have to be put in specifically to cater for the tourists. As such, new access roads, ski lifts etc. would have to be constructed.

6. Imagery, Marketing, and Channels of Distribution

Destinations have to bear in mind how potential tourists perceive them, and how easy or difficult it is for tourists to obtain information to make a booking.

Image and Marketing

The image that a destination projects can be a powerful tool in helping to communicate to the market just what it offers. But, in a world where an increasing number of destinations are attempting to communicate to the marketplace, establishing an accurate and clear image that differentiates one destination from another is becoming an increasing challenge. Sometimes destinations have developed an image independent of marketing departments of their tourism offices. These can be positive or negative. Paris (France) is renowned as being a city "for lovers," whereas Amsterdam (Holland) is often seen as a city where it's "easy to get drugs."

Image is clearly important for today's marketing, and over the years various researchers have looked at the problems of measurement of destination image (Hunt, 1975; Pearce 1982; Gartner, 1989). Several quite different approaches have been taken. For example, Embacher & Buttie (1989), using the case of Austria, used a grid analysis to assess and plot the image of that country as a summer vacation destination. Phelps (1986) developed a structured thirty-two attribute checklist to assess at pre- and post-travel images of Menorca (Spain). More recently, Echtner & Ritchie (1991; 1993) have developed a model that can be used to measure the image of a destination. In their work they found that the image of a destination is based on two key components:

1. Those that are attribute based (such as on climate, facilities, friendliness), and
2. Those that are holistic (presented through the mental pictures or imagery of the place)

Each of these components contains tangible functional characteristics (e.g., great surfing beaches), and components that have more abstract psychological characteristics (e.g., the feel of a place).

Images of destinations can also range from those based on "common" functional and psychological traits (e.g., a good swimming beach where you hang out with the "in crowd"), to those based on more distinctive, or even "unique" features or aura of a place (e.g., seeing a "must-see" sight such as the Sphinx in Egypt; or chanting with Tibetan monks in Lahasa, Tibet).

The conceptual framework that was developed is shown in Figure 5 and consists of three continuums:

1. Attribute—Holistic
2. Functional—Psychological
3. Common—Unique

An illustrative example, using the country of Nepal is given in Figure 6.

Increasingly, destinations are having to work hard to develop sophisticated marketing and promotional campaigns that are aimed at a specific targeted segment of the market. The marketing of existing destinations and attractions can be especially challenging. As Lewis, Chambers, & Chacko (1995) point out, "The essence of marketing is to design the product to fit the market. When the product exists, the situation is reversed. We

Figure 5. The Components of Destination Image.

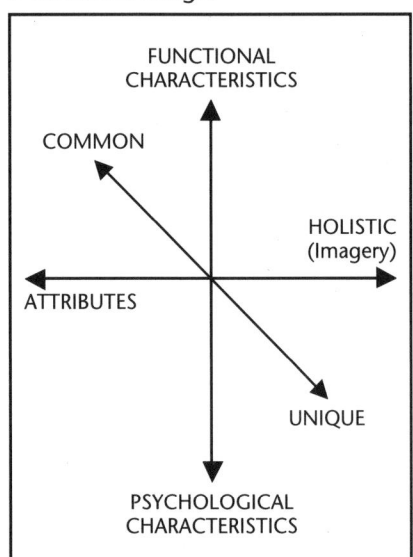

Note: This figure should be envisaged in three dimensions.

Source: Echtner, Charlotte and J.R. Brent Ritchie, *Journal of Travel Research,* Spring 1993, pp. 3–13. Copyright © 1993 by Sage Publications, Inc. Reprinted by permission of Sage Publications, Inc.

Figure 6. An Illustrative Example of Four Components of Destination Image (Nepal).

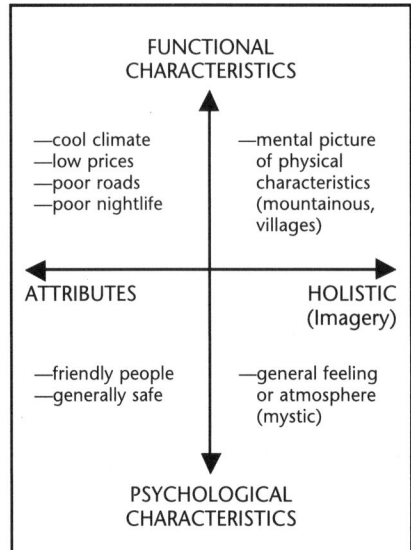

Source: Echtner, Charlotte and J.R. Brent Ritchie, *Journal of Travel Research,* Spring 1993, pp. 3–13. Copyright © 1993 by Sage Publications, Inc. Reprinted by permission of Sage Publications, Inc.

have to find the market that fits the product."

Channels of Distribution

In order to access a destination, the traveler often uses the services of an intermediary. Many operators in the tourism industries do not sell directly to the consumer (e.g., tour operators), or as with airlines, for example, they prefer to use intermediaries such as travel agencies. When potential tourists plan a trip, they typically go to a travel agent who will provide them with some information, give advice, and then book the trip for them. It should not be forgotten, that a considerable number of leisure travelers that go to a travel agent do so without having made a final decision on the choice of their destination. Consequently, travel agents can have enormous influence over what information and destinations are presented to potential travelers. This has been found to have an influence on consumers' perceptions and choices (Josiam & Hobson, 1995).

Travel agency bookings are, usually, done through a powerful computerized reservation system (CRS), and the travel agent takes a commission charge on the cost of what has been sold from the airline and the hotel. In the U.S., over three-quarters of all international air travel and international hotel reservations are typically sold through travel agencies. Alternatively, the travel agent may sell the client a package put together by a tour operator. This might include an airfare and accommodation at a destination for one inclusive price. Destinations that are difficult to get information about, or do not have easily available packages can face an extra challenge in getting bookings though travel agencies.

7. Relative Cost/Benefit Advantages

Costs, in terms of time and money, of getting to and visiting a destination can have a direct effect on its popularity. Inevitably persons make comparisons of financial cost when they travel on a limited budget, and they are contemplating trips with several alternative destinations in mind. This is often exacerbated when a tour operator packages similar types of destinations in the same brochure for easy comparison.

The underlying costs for some destinations may be lower, as a result of cheaper land prices, labor costs, foodstuffs, and the like. In addition, the fluctuations of international exchange rates (which can be dramatic) may give a cost and price advantage to various destinations at different times (see Box 7). Furthermore, in regards to mass tourism destinations, there are certain economies of scale that large tour operators and charter airlines may be able to achieve. This will allow them to lower the costs that they can pass onto the customer.

Eventually, consumers will have to weigh up in their own minds what are the various costs versus the perceived benefits that the destinations offer.

Example of the Fluctuating UK/USA Exchange Rate

YEAR	British pound		US$
1985	1.00	=	1.00
1987	1.00	=	1.50
1990	1.00	=	2.00
1993	1.00	=	1.60
1997	1.00	=	1.70

However, as has been mentioned earlier in this chapter, the influence of other factors, such as perceived image and prestige, may have more of an influence than straightforward cost.

The Economic Impacts of Tourism

Tourism has been found to bring significant economic impacts. The tourism sector of most economies has grown at a faster rate than the general rate of most economies over the last two decades. Many countries and communities have identified tourism as a force for increasing economic prosperity, and they have actively encouraged its development.

The reasons for this vary. For some areas, tourism has been the only viable alternative once traditional primary industries (such as farming), and secondary industries (such as manufacturing) have declined. For other areas, it has been seen as a way of creating an economic base where none existed before.

Once tourist arrivals increase, the impacts flow through the economy. The construction industry benefits from having to build new hotels. Restaurants, their suppliers, and farmers benefit from having to provide more food to the visitors. Shops and local handicrafts may benefit from tourists looking to buy souvenirs of their visit.

Tourism creates extra demand for services, and as a result creates employment. This flow of money into the economy is known as the "multiplier effect" (Laws, 1995) and is shown in Box 8. This method measures the "direct spending effects" of visitors in their initial spending round and (what it implies in employment) is amplified as the resident population spends some of the extra revenue earned as profit or income. This first "induced effect" further stimulates economic activity. However, not all the money may be spent in the local area and goods may need to be im-

ported specifically for tourists. Such money leaving the local economy is referred to as "leakage."

In the first round the tourist spends money directly with the tourism business such as the hotel, restaurant, or shop. The hotels, restaurants, and shops then have to pay their employees and the suppliers that provided them with the food and goods that were sold. The employees and

Photo © 1998 PhotoDisc, Inc.

Tourism creates a demand for services.

The Tourism Multiplier Effect on the Economy

ROUND 1

Direct effects:
DIRECT TOURIST SPENDING

Spending on tourist facilities such as hotels, restaurants, retail goods, tours, transport, museums, etc. Any sales taxes on these goods and services go straight to the national/local government.

ROUND 2

Induced secondary effects:
TOURISM INDUSTRY EXPENSES

Expenses such as the wages and salaries of employees, advertising expenditures, costs of food and beverage supplies, and any other costs to businesses that receive income from tourists in Round 1. Various additional taxes (national/local) will also be levied on the profits of these businesses.

ROUND 3

Induced tertiary effects:
INDIRECT BUSINESS BENEFICIARIES

Here the employees and businesses in Round 2 spend their income/profit on items such as food, drink, transport, housing costs, etc., or save it. Income taxes will be paid on the money earned by employees, and they may have to pay sales taxes on what they buy.

Figure 7. Tourism Multiplier—The Overall Effect.

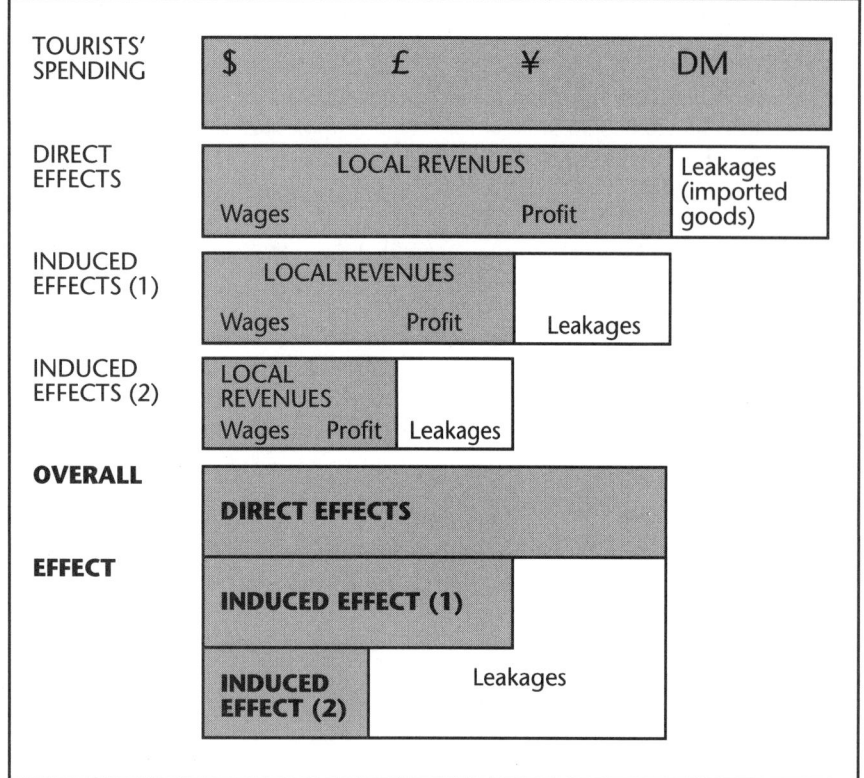

Source: Based on Laws, 1995

Figure 8. Magnitude of Tourism's Economic Impact.

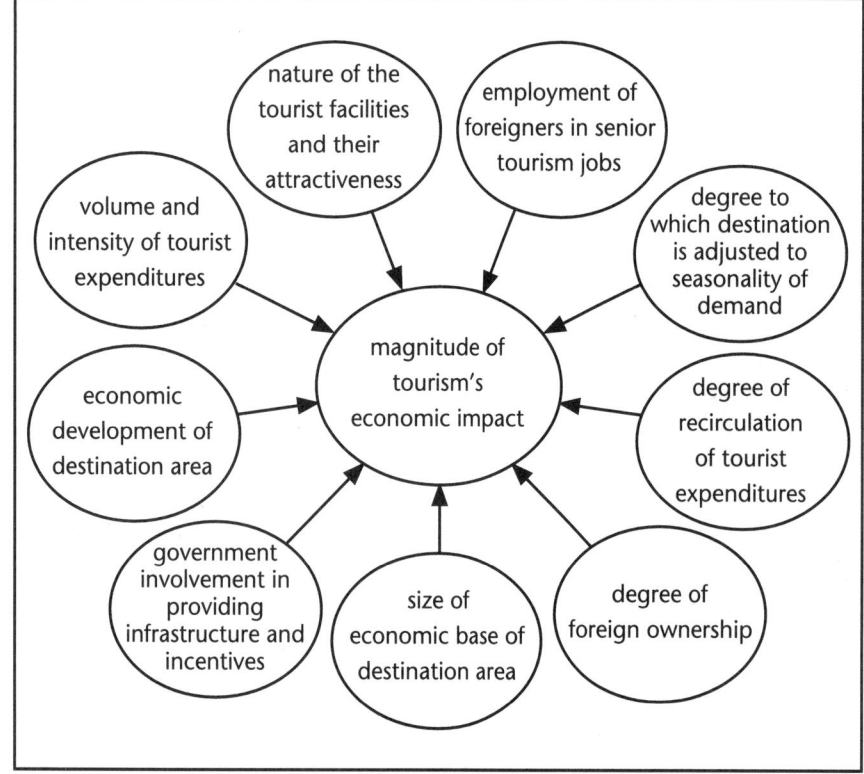

Source: Lea, 1988

suppliers in turn then spend that money. In the meantime, the government is collecting tax money (as direct sales taxes, income taxes, and taxes on business profits), and may be using them as general funds for such projects as local schools and upgrades of local infrastructure. This way the money a tourist spends keeps moving through the economy. It is only lost when goods and services from outside the economy are paid for, and it is then that the money may leak out. The magnitude of tourism's economic impacts will depend on a range of other factors such as the degree of foreign ownership, use of employment of foreigners in senior tourism jobs, type of tourism, and so forth (see Figure 8).

How the Residents of Destinations Respond to Tourism

The development of tourism in some tourism destinations has been shown to create social stress and negative attitudes towards tourists. Several resident-visitor social relationship models have been created to help explain this. One of the first of these was devised by Doxey (1975), who saw that the existence of local tolerance thresholds and hosts' resistance to further tourism development were based on a fear of losing community identity (see Figure 9). Based on studies in Niagara-on-the-Lake (Canada) and on the island of Barbados in the Caribbean, he developed the *Irridex* model to help explain the various stages a community can pass through. He saw that communities pass successively through stages of euphoria, apathy, irritation, and antagonism, to a final stage in which people forget what they have cherished and the environment is destroyed.

The level of irritation that arises between the residents and tourists is determined by the compatibility of each group. But, even with seemingly compatible groups, the sheer number of tourists may generate tensions. Further complicating factors identified were: differences between race, culture, economic status, and nationality of tourists and residents.

The IRRIDEX Levels— Index of Touristic Irritation

1. **Euphoria.** At this first level, residents are enthusiastic and excited by the new tourist related developments. They welcome strangers and investment into the community. There are new job opportunities and locals can participate.

2. **Apathy.** At this level, the industry becomes established, outside companies begin to move in, and residents begin to take the tourists for granted. The contacts between residents and tourists become more formal (commercial) and planning is mostly concerned with marketing and getting more tourists.

3. **Irritation.** This level occurs as the saturation point (carrying capacity) of the community is reached. Residents begin to have misgiving about the tourism industry and policy-makers attempt to find solutions via increasing infrastructure rather than seeking a limit to growth.

4. **Antagonism.** By the time the community reaches this level, irritations are being openly expressed. Residents see the tourists as a cause of their problems—whether they be pollution, increased taxes, or traffic congestion. Mutual politeness gives way to behavior that is antagonistic toward the tourist, and the tourist is seen as someone to "rip off." Planning is now remedial, and tries to find ways to fix the problems for residents. Meanwhile, promotion is often increased to offset a deteriorating reputation of the destination.

5. **Final level.** By the time the community reaches this level, it has forgotten what it cherished and what it was that drew tourists to the destination in the first place. Residents have to accept that their ecosystem has been destroyed. They may still be able to draw tourists, but will tend to draw a very different type of tourist than they welcomed in the initial stages of development.

Given the simplicity of the Irridex model, a number of problems have been pointed out. To begin with, it assumes a unidirectional sequence—where residents' attitudes and reactions will change over time within a predictable sequence. Various other researchers have identified that a more complex set of variables is at work here. Butler (1975) contends that a community's emerging attitude towards tourism is unlikely to be so straightforward, and it will be affected by varying degrees of contact and involvement its residents have with the industry and tourists. Murphy's (1983) analysis of community responses to local tourism growth revealed that significant differences can exist between how the residents, business sector, and administration view tourism development. Nevertheless, Doxey's *Irridex* model shows us that unplanned, unbridled tourism can cause a backlash against tourists by residents of some communities. There are many signs that this has happened, from the firebombing of hotels in the Caribbean in the 1970s, through the burning of second homes in Wales in the 1930s, to various "no growth" policies towards tourism in towns such as Carmel, California (U.S.) and the appearance of T-shirts with slogans such as "Tourists are terrorists" in the 1990s. These are all reminders that resident attitudes towards tourism development should not, and cannot, be ignored. A number of researchers have tried to identify how resident perceptions towards tourism can be measured (Ap, 1990; Johnson, Snepenger, & Akis, 1994). But, it has proven to be a difficult concept to measure. Furthermore, the residents of various communities appear to react and deal with the pressures of tourism development quite differently.

Tourism—A Solution for All Destinations?

Tourism offers many advantages, particularly economic ones, to a destination. But, one must also consider what disadvantages tourism can also bring to a destination. A brief analysis of the main advantages and disadvantages to tourism development includes:

Advantages Tourism Can Bring to a Destination

Tourism has many positive impacts on communities. The many benefits of tourism are often cited to include:

Figure 9. The IRRIDEX Model.

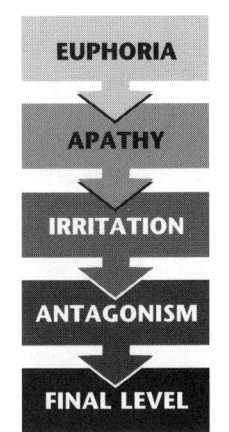

EUPHORIA — Initial phase of development, visitors and investors welcome, little planning or control mechanism.

APATHY — Visitors taken for granted, contacts between residents and outsiders more formal (commercial), planning concerned mostly with marketing.

IRRITATION — Saturation points approached, residents have misgivings about tourist industry, policy makers attempt solutions via increasing infrastructure rather than limiting growth.

ANTAGONISM — Irritations openly expressed, visitors seen as cause of all problems, planning now remedial but promotion increased to offset deteriorating reputation of destination.

FINAL LEVEL

Source: Doxey, 1976

1. Increases employment opportunities. The tourism industry is often labor intensive so it creates new jobs as the money flows through economy.

2. Increases government revenues. Taxes are generated from tourist expenditures and fees (such as airport and bed taxes). Such money usually goes into the local, regional, or national consolidated account for general government expenditures.

3. Creates increased gross domestic product. Tourism developments increase the economic activity of an area, or country, and increase the overall wealth.

4. Brings in foreign currency. Tourists have to exchange money when they buy tourism services in a foreign country. The money they exchange provides that country with foreign currency, which can then be used to pay for imported goods and services.

5. Increases demand for new infrastructure such as airport and roads that residents can also use. This can also stimulate local commerce and industry unrelated to tourism.

6. Rekindles residents' in their home communities or their own culture. The interest shown by tourists in a local culture can inspire residents to play a more active role in keeping traditions alive, and this can help to preserve them. Furthermore, residents may put on artistic events that they might not have bothered to do, just for the local community.

7. Justifies environmental protection of areas of natural beauty and wildlife. Tourism is also regarded as a relatively pollution free industry compared with many other industries.

8. Supports community activities that residents alone could not support. For example, most of the theatres in London and New York survive because tourists pay to come and see the plays. They could not all survive on local resident revenue alone.

Disadvantages Tourism Can Bring to a Destination

However, there are also several negative issues relating to the development of a tourism industry. The following section covers the negative issues of tourism in more detail. The drawbacks to tourism can be:

1. Overcrowding resulting in strained resident-tourist relationships. For example, during the summer at many popular destinations it is impossible to find parking or get a spot on the beach. This annoys local residents who see tourists as invading their home and disturbing their lives.

2. Tourists can bring pollution to a community in a number of different forms. It can come from:

   (a) **Air pollution**—for example, exhaust fumes from cars and tour buses, which add to the poor air quality.

   (b) **Water pollution**—for example, many cruise ships dump sewage overboard, polluting beaches.

   (c) **Noise pollution**—for example, noise from airports, nightclubs, and roads.

   (d) **Visual pollution**—from new multistory buildings which are not in keeping with traditional architecture and change the urban skyline.

3. Destruction of the environment—the sheer volume of tourists has caused erosion in many areas. Examples include; erosion of natural wilderness areas—due to the use of 4WD vehicles; erosion of buildings—such as the buildings along the canals in Venice (due to the increased boat traffic).

4. Undesirable social activities—when great numbers of people from outside of a community come to visit, they may also bring with them a number of customs and habits that local residents do not appreciate. Specific problems

that tourism has been seen to bring to communities include:

   (a) **Crime**—Tourists inevitably bring money with them, and often become easy targets for purse-snatchers and muggers. Other criminal activities such as drug taking and selling often involve tourists. In countries, which have had non-convertible currencies, such as Cambodia, an illegal black market in currency conversions (that are widely different from the official rate) may also occur and undermine the economic control of the country.

   (b) **Prostitution**—It is illegal in many countries but because it brings in tourist revenue, many governments may turn a blind eye to it. Alternatively, the revenues can also be used as bribes to make sure key people turn a blind eye. For example, in Thailand prostitution is technically illegal, however, "sex packaged trips" are commonly organized from Japan and Europe to Bangkok. Various horror stories of children being kidnapped from rural villages and being put on the streets in Bangkok have been well documented (Black, 1995).

   (c) **Begging**—Tourists are easy targets for beggars and in many counties there are thousands of people who can make more from panhandling for money from tourists than from working. Begging in many parts of the world was unknown until tourism developed. Tourists often feel they can help and are viewed as easy targets by the panhandlers. Often giving money to beggars only encourages more and more people to turn to begging. This is often the case where wages are extremely low.

Often a few coins from a tourist can be worth more than a day's labor in the fields.

5. Discrediting of local social and cultural values—tourists transport themselves from their home socio-cultural environment to a different one. Often tourists feel superior (they have the money), and the host is often treated as inferior. Furthermore, the tourist can inflict new socio-cultural values or practices on the communities they visit. For example, tipping in restaurants was unknown in many Southeast Asia countries before the arrival of American tourists. Now locals had better tip, or else they are rudely and poorly treated. In other cases, residents have changed dress patterns so that they can copy the tourists who come to visit them.

6. Creates economic leakages so that not all of the economic benefits stay in the destination area. There is often an increased tendency to import goods to satisfy tourists in many parts of the world, as the range of goods taken for granted in the industrialized countries is not normally available. Many tourists are not prepared to try local foods and drink, and this results in hotels and restaurants being forced to import items exclusively for the tourists. This distorts the balance of payments, and weakens the multiplier effect. Inevitably, it also means that the residents perceive imported goods to be better, and this causes them to desire goods that they may not be able to afford.

7. Adds to inflation and increased land values—often tourists are willing and can afford to pay much more for local produce and desirable residences than locals. Prices may rise as a result. For example, in Wales (U.K.) many coastal communities now have more than 50% of the houses owned by people who do not live there full-time. The houses are only briefly used as summer homes. The influx of such tourists has resulted in inflating the value of house prices, forcing many of the locals to leave these coastal communities. In turn, this has meant that community services such as schools, shops, and hospitals are being closed because of the lower year-round population base. In Wales, community frustration became so intense that a reactionary independence group began burning down holiday homes to get non-nationals to sell up and leave, and to dissuade others from buying.

8. Causes seasonality problems—as tourism is often only a seasonal activity. This means that tourism often does not provide steady year round employment and income. In summer it may be difficult to find a vacant spot on many of the beaches in southern France. On the other hand, in the winter you are lucky to find someone there. For operators this means difficulty in finding employees at peak times. Often they need to be brought in from other areas. This often distorts rental prices (e.g., Cape Cod, U.S.). Furthermore, locals who are there year-round are laid off during the winter months, and this ensures economic hardship for many families.

9. Increases demand on local public services—tourists also need and demand local services such as police, fire departments, or bus services. Often these services may only be of little extra benefit to the host communities. For example, the host community may have to provide lifeguards and rescue boats to watch over the influx of tourists. As these expense come from the local tax base, and many locals see that they are paying for the tourists' recreation activities.

10. Opportunity costs—similar to public services, there is often a large initial capital outlay needed to attract tourists to a city. For example, new sewage plants or roads may have to be built. Often the community has to gamble on the project, and finance it initially from the local tax base.

11. Leads to an over-dependence on tourism—Certain areas have become economically over-dependent on the tourism industry, and on specific tourist markets. For example, over 90% of all tourists to the Bahamas come from the U.S. What happens if the currency appreciates in value and American tourists decide it is too expensive and go elsewhere? All sorts of factors can affect the flow of tourists (natural disasters, terrorism, etc). Destinations that become too focused and dependent on tourism have no economic fallback if their tourism industry falters.

Case Study: Hawaii in 1998 (from German language newspaper *Die Welt*)

Tourism has been shown to be a two-edge sword. The following article highlights some of the problems that have been experienced in the well-known tourist destination of Hawaii (U.S.).

Asian crisis hits Hawaii

HONOLULU.—Recession is a phenomenon which at first glance does not seem to have any place in a holiday paradise such as Hawaii. But recession has found a place here.

It is 6pm. The day is just beginning in the George Livingstone Bar at the Regency Hotel on the island of Kauai. The loudspeaker blares out the message that it is 'time for a rendezvous with Iniki!'.

That is the most macabre invitation to a drink there is in Hawaii, but the guests come in droves. At five past six, there is not a spare seat in the place.

No guest to this part of the world has ever been as terrible as Iniki. Iniki was a hurricane which five years ago swept across the island and left behind a trail of death and destruction.

What remains is a nightmare for those who were there when it happened and an insatiable curiosity among those who have only heard about it.

And the curious go to the George Livingstone Bar to see the catastrophe on video.

But since that disaster, Hawaii has been plagued by a more persistent and pernicious phenomenon than a hurricane and one which has wrought more havoc.

While Iniki restricted its destruction mainly to Kauai, all of Hawaii's islands are plagued by the current problem. It is almost invisible, goes by the name of 'recession' and has caused 'Paradise Hawaii' to be given a variation on its monicker: Paradise Lost.

While in the other 49 States of the US, recession has been kept at bay since 1992 by an ongoing boom, it has somewhat enigmatically gained a toehold in the former paradise of Hawaii. And it has been holding on grimly.

As the rest of the United States has flourished over the past five years, Hawaii has wallowed in the shadow of crisis. And that shadow has never been darker than it is now.

The reason is that the fortunes of the State have for a long time risen and fallen not according to the forces of America but by those of Japan.

Hawaii became the 50th State of the United States in 1959 but for a

Image courtesy Corel.

decade and a half it has been carrying the distinct hallmarks of a Japanese colony.

And that is why the present bout of Asian flu plaguing the world's economies is causing outbreaks of coughing nowhere more intense on American soil than in Hawaii.

The change began in the early 1980s, the time of the great Japanese invasion.

The Japanese arrived with great dreams and still greater briefcases bursting at the seams.

One of the arrivals was Genshiro Kawamoto, a billionaire from Tokyo. In 1987, he allowed himself to be chauffeured along Kahala Avenue in Honolulu in a Rolls-Royce.

Kahala is the most expensive residential street in Hawaii and, as he was driven along it, Kawamoto bought 170 houses: he literally bought them as he was driven past.

Today, the property in another up-market street, Kalakaua Avenue—the boulevard at Waikiki Beach—is 90 per cent in Japanese hands.

The Japanese practically concreted the beach over and built skyscraper hotels. Cost per night: As much as $US500 ($A769).

The urge to buy was so irresist-

ible that even the Catholic Bishop Joseph Ferrario decided 10 years ago to sell St. Augustine's Church on Waikiki Beach for $US45 million (now $A69.2 million) to a Japanese real estate agent who wanted to build a hotel on the site.

The embarrassing deal was called off at the last minute by the Vatican.

Super-rich Japanese came and bought houses on the island of Oahu at double the going rate, immediately tore them down and replaced them with pompous marble villas.

When the initial hunger for luxury had worn off, the Japanese turned to recreational golf. Some of the country clubs they created were so exclusive that entry fees of $US1 million ($A1.54 million) were being demanded.

This was all made possible by an attempt in 1985 to cut the American balance of trade with Japan by devaluing the dollar.

Overnight, the Japanese in Hawaii saw their wealth double.

At the same time, Japanese tourists began arriving. Hawaii became the dream destination for Honeymooners. Hawaiians themselves liked these tourists because they stayed for only half as long as tourists from the US mainland but spent more than twice as much.

The result of the boom was that the population of Hawaii doubled from 632,000 in 1960 to 1.2 million in 1990. At the same time, the State, which once was a huge sugar cane and pineapple plantation, went through a change.

Today sugar and pineapples provide only 1 per cent of Hawaii's gross domestic product (GDP) while 40 per cent comes from tourism and 11 per cent from the Pentagon, which maintains 46 military bases on seven islands.

Today the boom is a thing of the past. The great awakening came, at the latest, with Iniki. Paradise is now even too expensive for the Japanese and too full of risks as they look again at the yen. The tourist tide is ebbing.

Many Japanese are instead looking at the much cheaper island of Guam, which is also in the Pacific but which can be reached even more quickly than Hawaii. And for many Americans, Las Vegas is suddenly more attractive and exciting than Hawaii.

The Hawaiian housing market is collapsing. The expensive golf courses are empty. The flight to the mainland has begun because nowhere in America is life as expensive as it is in Hawaii.

While the average price for a one-family house in the US is $US127,500 ($A196,000), it is $US310,000 ($A476,563) in Hawaii.

In addition, Hawaii has the highest tax rates of all 50 US States.

Unemployment rate across the US is 4.6 per cent but it is 6.3 per cent in Hawaii. In 1996, the number of people leaving Hawaii exceeded for the first time those arriving, by 4500.

The bitter irony is that the only business in the State with any future is the business with the past. Nothing reflects that as starkly as the battleship Arizona, whose crew of 1177 was consigned to a watery grave when it was sunk in Pearl Harbour on December 7 1941.

That was the day that World War II began for America. This year, the most dramatic military memorial of America is due to get an addition: the battleship Missouri is to be anchored just 300m away from the Arizona.

It will be a museum commemorating an American victory: It was on the Missouri that, on September 2 1945, Japan signed its surrender. That ended the war.

So is Hawaii a Paradise Lost? Perhaps. A milestone of history. Certainly—regardless of all booms, recessions and a nightmare by the name of Iniki.

Conclusion

We can ask whether tourism is a positive or negative force for a destination. Unfortunately, there is no simple answer to this question. The answer lies more in how well the tourism industry can be planned and managed. Good management strategies will be able to help maximize the identified advantages tourism can bring while minimizing the disadvantages.

It should be recognized that some destinations, such as Las Vegas, Nevada (U.S.), or Cancun (Mexico), have been planned from scratch. Others have simply evolved very haphazardly with little planning and management. New destinations have often had the luxury of developing tourism facilities from the ground up, and good planning has been able to make a major difference.

As we look into the 21st century, a number of challenges face established and emerging destination. Perhaps one of the greatest of these will be the continued acceptance of tourism developments by communities. On the one hand, the world can be seen to become increasingly globalized, while on the other hand, it is becoming increasingly localized. People are becoming more focused on local issues, where they want input and a say about what is going on in their communities. This may mean that the easy acceptance that new tourism developments have had in a number of destinations will end. Residents may seek to protect what is special about their home communities from an increasingly homogenized world.

Destination management strategies for dealing with the pressures of tourism are going to be crucial as we look to the future. Failure will mean further destruction of the natural environment, and the potential loss of the uniqueness of the world's cultures and communities. For an industry that is based and thrives on such resources, that could truly be a disaster.

1. Please discuss the concept of a tourism destination. Why is it relevant to discuss tourism from the destination perspective?

2. Establish the difference between an *international tourist* and *an excursionist*.

3. What are the two broad categories of tourists? How are they distinguished from one another? Is one more important than the other? Please justify your answer.

4. With your team or classmates, list the key components in Leiper's *Tourism System Model*. Define two of the components and discuss their relationship.

5. A number of macro-environmental factors that can impact tourism are mentioned above. Consider and discuss the impact of such a factor in your local environment.

6. Choose two of the travel and tourism industries sectors discussed in the text above and define them using examples local to you. Use your preferred web browser and preferred search engine or library resources, and find additional information on one entity within your chosen sectors. Bring your information to share with team or classmates.

7. Using your preferred web browser and preferred search engine or library resources, find information on a tourism organization that promotes a region of your choice. Share the materials with your team or classmates. Be prepared to highlight features of your destination and discuss why you chose that region.

8. Box 1 discusses the amount of money that is spent on tourism promotion. Using your preferred web browser and preferred search engine or library resources, find information in support of, or in conflict with, the main premise of Box 1. Discuss your findings with your team or classmates.

9. Using your preferred web browser and preferred search engine or library resources, find some information on a travel agency of your choice. Perform an organization/company research as discussed in the first chapter of this text.

10. Discuss the relationship between leisure and tourism.

11. Consider the relationship between leisure time and the workweek. Using your preferred web browser and preferred search engine or library resources, find some information that discusses the change over time of leisure time and the workweek. Discuss your findings with your team or classmates. What does your research tell you? Do you expect the "age of leisure" to come some time soon?

12. Choose and discuss your preferred travel/tourism motivation model. Apply it to travel you have done or wish to do.

13. Distinguish between primary/touring destinations and secondary/stopover destinations. Using your preferred web browser and preferred search engine or library resources, find some information on one of each. Discuss how (why) you classified them as primary/touring destinations and secondary/stopover destinations.

14. Consider the destination life-cycle. How could you avoid decline? Identify a destination that is in one of the stages of the model. Discuss how (why) you determined it is in that particular stage.

15. Outline the various components of a tourism destination.

16. Using your preferred web browser and preferred search engine or library resources, find some information on a man-made environment and a natural environment destination. Discuss the destinations in terms of the relevant components of a tourism destination.

17. Define accessibility as it relates to tourism.

18. Using your preferred web browser and preferred search engine or library resources, find some information on safety and security as it relates to tourism and travel. Discuss your findings with your team or classmates. What does your research tell you?

19. Consider image and tourism marketing. Using your preferred web browser and preferred search engine or library resources, find some destination marketing materials. Discuss the materials with your team or classmates. What aspects of the destination are they trying to promote? Refer to the model and discussion in the text when answering.

20. What role do you see travel agents playing when potential tourists are planning a trip? With this knowledge, what would you recommend hospitality managers do, if anything?

21. What potential role can the currency exchange rate play for a travel destination?

22. Establish and discuss the economic impacts of tourism. Using your preferred web browser and preferred search engine or library resources, find some information that supports your position(s).

23. Establish and discuss the social impacts of tourism. Using your preferred web browser and preferred search engine or library resources, find some information that supports your position(s).

24. Describe the IRRIDEX model.

25. Provide a brief summary of five advantages and five disadvantages of tourism.

Bibliography and Suggested Readings

Black, M. (1995). *In the Twilight Zone*. Geneva, Switzerland: ILO.

Burns, L. (1997). Time for life: The surprising ways Americans use their time. *Wilson Quarterly*, 21(3), 99–100.

Butler, R. (1975). Tourism as an agent of social change, in *Tourism as a Factor in National & Regional Development*. Occasional Paper 4, Peterborough, Ontario, Department of Geography, Trent University, 85–90.

Butler, R. W. (1980). The concept of a tourist area cycle of evolution: implications for management of resources. *Canadian Geographer*, 24, 5–12.

Cohen, E. (1972). Toward a sociology of international tourism. *Social Research*, 39(1), 164–182.

Crompton, J. (1979). Motivations for vacations. *Annals of Tourism Research*, 6, 408–424.

Dann, G. (1977). Anomie, ego enhancement and tourism. *Annals of Tourism Research*, 4, 184–194.

Doxey, G. (1975). A causation theory of visitor-resident irritants: Methodology and research inferences. *Proceedings of the Travel Research Association*, 6th Annual conference, San Diego, CA, 195–198.

Doxey, (1976). When enough's enough: The natives are restless in old Niagara, *Heritage Canada*, 2(2), 26–27.

Douglas, N. (1996). *They Came from Savages: A Hundred Years of Tourism in Melanesia*. Lismore, Australia: Southern Cross University Press.

Embacher, J. & Buttie, F. (1989). A reparatory grid analysis of Austria's image as a summer vacation destination. *Journal of Travel Research*, 27(3), 3–7.

Echtner, C. & Ritchie, J. (1993). The measurement of destination image: An empirical assessment. *Journal of Travel Research*, 31(4), 3–13.

Fodness, D. (1994). Measuring tourist motivation. *Annals of Tourism Research*, 21(3), 555–581.

Gray, H. (1970). *International Travel: International Trade*. Lexington, MA: Heath Lexington Books.

Gartner, W. (1989, Fall). Tourism image: Attribute measurement of state tourism products using multidimensional scaling techniques. *Journal of Travel Research*, 28, 16–20.

Hunt, J. D. (1975). Image as a factor in tourism development. *Journal of Travel Research*, 13, 1–7.

Johnson, J., Snepenger, D. & Akis, S. (1994). Residents perceptions of tourism development. *Annals of Tourism Research*, 21(3), 629–642.

Josiam, B. & Hobson, J. (1995). Consumer choice in context: The decoy effect in travel and tourism. *Journal of Travel Research*, 34(1), 45–50.

Keller, C. (1987). Stages of peripheral tourism development—Canada's Northwest Territories. *Tourism Management*, 8, 20–32.

Kotler, P., Bowen, J. & Makens, J. M. (1996). *Marketing for Hospitality and Tourism*. Upper Saddle River, NJ: Prentice Hall.

Krippendorf, J. (1987) *The Holidaymakers*. London, England: Heinemann.

Laws, E. (1995). *Tourism Destination Management*. London, England: Routledge.

Lea, J. (1988). *Tourism and Development in the Third World*. London, England: London, 45.

Leiper, N. (1979). The framework of tourism. *Annals of Tourism Research*, 6(4), 390–407.

Leiper, N. (1995). *Tourism Management*. Melbourne, Australia: TAFE Publications.

Lewis, R., Chambers, R. & Chacko, H. (1995). *Marketing Leadership in Hospitality: Foundations and Practices*: New York, NY: Van Nostrand Reinhold.

Lunberg, D. (1972). *The Tourist Business*, Boston, MA: Cahners.

Luhrman, D. (1997, 10/2). *More Money Needed for Tourism Promotion*. News from the World Tourism Organization, Madrid, Spain: WTO Press and Communications.

Mannell, R. & Iso-Ahola, S. (1987). Psychological nature of leisure and tourism experience. *Annals of Tourism Research*, 14, 314–331.

Mill, R. & Morrison, A. (1985). *The Tourism System*, Englewood Cliffs, NJ: Prentice Hall, Chp. 8.

Mathieson, A. & Wall, G. (1982). *Tourism: Economic, Physical and Social Impacts*. London, England: Longman Group, Ltd.

McIntosh, R. & Goeldner, C. (1990). *Tourism, Principles, Practices and Philosophies*, 6th edition, New York, NY: Wiley & Sons.

Murphy, P. (1983). Perceptions and attitudes of decision-making groups in tourism centres. *Journal of Travel Research*, 21(3), 8–12.

Oglethorpe, M. (1984). Tourism in Malta. *Leisure Studies*, 3, 147–162.

Pearce, P. (1982). Perceived changes in holiday destinations. *Annals of Tourism Research*, 9, 145–164.

Phelps, A. (1986). Holiday destination image—The problem of assessment: An example developed in Menorca. *Tourism Management*, 7, 168–80.

Powers, T. (1988). *Introduction to Management in the Hospitality Industry*, Chp. 11, 301.

Plog, S. (1974). Why destination areas rise and fall in popularity. *The Cornell Hotel & Restaurant Administration Quarterly*, 14(4), 55–58.

Prosser, G. (1995). Tourist destination life-cycles: Progress, problems and prospects. In Shaw, N. (ed.) *Proceedings of the National Tourism & Hospitality Conference*, Melbourne, Australia: CAUTHE, 318–328.

Robinson, J. P. & Godbey, G. (1997). *Time for Life: The Surprising Ways Americans Use Their Time*. University Park, PA: Pennsylvania State University Press.

Ritchie, J. & Zins, M. (1978). Culture as a determinant of the attractiveness of a tourist region. *Annals of Tourism Research*, 5, 252–267.

Smith, S. (1990, Spring) A test of Plog's Allocentric/Psychocentric model. Evidence from seven nations. *Journal of Travel Research*, 28, 40–43.

Smith, R. (1992). Beach resort evolution: Implications for planning. *Annals of Tourism Research*, 19, 304–322.

Smith, V. (1977). *Hosts and Guests*. Philadelphia, PA: University of Pennsylvania Press, 2–3.

Smith, M. & Turner, L. (1973). Some aspects of the sociology of tourism. *Society & Leisure*, 3, 55–71.

Thomas, J. (1964). What makes people travel? *Asia Travel News*, 64–65.

Westlake, J. & Cooper, C. (1988). The tourism destination as a focus of study. *Proceedings of "Teaching tourism into the 1990's—An international conference for tourism educators."* Guilford, England: University of Surrey.

Williams, A. & Zelinsky, W. (1970). On some patterns in international tourist flows. *Economic Geography*, 46(1), 549–567.

The Global Perspective

A. J. Singh, *The School of Hospitality Business*, MICHIGAN STATE UNIVERSITY

ABSTRACT

This chapter will discuss the lodging business from the global perspective, establishing that many hospitality companies are rather large and have a worldwide, or global, presence. The range in size of the companies that operate in the global arena will become apparent. The chapter will further discuss global growth rate as well as highlight regional differences. In doing so, some of the impetus for and approaches to growth and global expansion will be discussed.

OBJECTIVES

At the end of this chapter the student should:

1. Be able to establish and discuss the size of the global lodging market.

2. Be able to discuss the current global growth rates and acknowledge regional differences.

3. Have an understanding of the regional differences in performance and profitability.

4. Be familiar with the concept of a multinational hotel company.

5. Have knowledge of several of the multinational hotel companies.

6. Have specific knowledge of several lodging properties in the international marketplace.

7. Understand the various screening criteria that are considered when entering new foreign markets.

8. Know what an international hospitality executive is.

Introduction

The International Lodging Industry: An Overview

The international travel and tourism industry is one of the fastest growing sectors of the world economy. In order to support this growth, the lodging industry has had to grow accordingly, albeit faster in some regions of the world than others. The accommodations, lodging, or hotel industry, are some of the alternative terms used for this important subset of the international travel and tourism industry.

Any study of the international lodging industry is fascinating because of its size, complexity, and diversity of products. The industry includes 50 room "mom and pop" type motels in small cities and highways and 5,000 room behemoths in large cities like Las Vegas. Lodging products include bed and breakfast facilities, conference and convention hotels, casino hotels, all suite products, a wide range of resorts and spas, and themed hotels. Similarly, the range of the prices for accommodations also varies. Room rates at budget hotels may be as low as $25.00 per night, while luxury hotels may cost upwards of $400.00 per night.

A recent study by the World Travel and Tourism Council placed the international lodging industry at 11.3 million guest rooms at the end of 1995 (WTTC, 1995). Table 1 provides an overview of the size of the international hotel industry. As can be noted from the table, the majority of the world's supply of hotels is concentrated in two regions—Europe and North America. The former has over 55 percent of the world's hotels while the latter has nearly 22 percent. The third largest region is the Asia-Pacific region (Northeast Asia, Southeast Asia, South Asia, Australia Pacific) with about 12 percent of the world's hotels. Although not evident from the table, it is also the fastest growing region in the world. As recorded in the *Compendium of Tourism Statistics*, by the World Tourism Organization (1992), the growth rate in this region from 1981 to 1990 was 192 percent. By comparison, the growth rate of hotels in North America during the same period was 42 percent, and Western Europe was 7 percent.

It should further be noted that the average size of hotels in North America is much larger than their European counterparts (56 rooms vs. 28 rooms). This is indicative of the differences in the two lodging markets and the presence of more and larger hotel chains in North America. Furthermore, hotels in Northeast Asia with average size properties at 71 rooms, are the largest hotels of all the regions. This is indicative of the presence of large multinational hotel chains in this region.

Recently a study on the future of the lodging industry was conducted by New York University and Arthur Anderson Consulting. The survey sample included 4,000 hotel executives from various regions of the world. Table 2 is a part of the study that assesses the growth of hotels in various parts of the world. The actual question on the survey was "By the year 2000 how would you assess the pace of new construction?"

As is clear from Table 2, the respondents of this survey were very optimistic about growth prospects in all regions of the world. The majority of the responses were clustered in the "More" or "Much More" cat-

T1 Size of the International Hotel Industry

Region	Total Revenue (10⁹) US$	Number of Hotels	Percent of Total Hotels	Total Number of Rooms	Average Size of Hotel (rooms)	Total Number of Beds	Total Number of Employees
Africa	$ 6.3	10,769	3.5%	343,347	32	675,960	1,259,019
Caribbean	7.9	5,290	1.7	155,253	29	300,097	277,614
Central America	1.2	1,160	0.3	41,221	35	83,862	232,180
North America	62.1	66,943	21.7	3,738,977	56	6,725,390	2,268,256
South America	9.8	14,576	4.7	487,787	33	1,005,972	1,283,917
Northeast Asia	23.7	10,192	3.3	719,480	71	1,470,857	1,120,339
Southeast Asia	12.8	13,211	4.3	453,657	34	898,212	730,585
South Asia	3.1	3,663	1.1	159,417	44	223,519	472,092
Australia and Pacific Islands	6.6	10,082	3.2	229,319	23	567,346	539,286
Middle East	9.2	4,735	1.5	162,178	34	326,181	455,432
European Economic Area	87.5	151,945	49.4	4,242,193	28	8,108,983	1,873,772
Other Europe	22.5	19,178	6.2	676,631	35	1,421,265	805,230
Total	247.8	307,683	100.0*	11,333,199	37	21,540,267	11,194,418

Source: World Travel & Tourism Council, Madrid (1995)
*Totals may not add to 100.0 due to rounding.

Region	Mean	Much less 1	Less 2	No Change 3	More 4	Much more 5
North America	4.2	0.2%	0.2%	8.2%	47.6%	27.1%
South America	3.7	—	2.0	23.9	38.2	9.0
Asia-Pacific	3.9	—	2.6	20.3	39.4	14.9
Africa	3.6	—	3.8	32.7	27.3	8.6
Western Europe	4.0	0.2	0.4	14.3	43.8	18.9
Eastern Europe	3.9	0.2	3.8	18.1	36.1	17.5
Middle East	3.6	—	3.0	28.3	34.3	8.0

Source: Hospitality 2000: A view to the next millennium. Arthur Anderson and New York University. (1997). Question 13. N=498

ica was the rate leader in the economy segment. The profitability of luxury hotels in Asia was the highest ($20,476 per room) followed by African and Middle Eastern luxury hotels. On a worldwide basis, North American hotels were not the leaders in Revenue (REVPAR) or profitability. This is primarily a result of more competition in North America and a higher cost of operation.

History and Growth of Multinational Hotels

César Ritz of the *Ritz Hotel* fame can be credited as being the first multinational hotelier in the middle 1800s. As he became famous for operating luxury hotels, many owners paid him a retainer to appoint managers and operate them as *Ritz Hotels*. This he did all over Europe in partnership with famous chefs such as Auguste Escoffier. As such, the Ritz concept of operating hotels may be considered to be a precursor to the modern day management contract.

As the 19th century came to a close, the story of the hotel industry shifted to the United States. E. M. Statler is credited with developing the

egories. For a summary of this study see the section titled "FOCUS 1" on page 102.

Whereas Table 1 evaluated the size, scope, and geographical distribution of the international lodging industry, Table 3 evaluates the worldwide market composition of the hotel industry and source of business for the hotel industry in each of the regions.

As noted from Table 3, most of the regions of the world have an almost even split between domestic and foreign sources of business. The North American Hotel Industry, however, relies primarily on domestic travelers for more than 80 percent of its business. This is indicative of the size and scope of the domestic economy. In the case of Africa and the Middle East, it's exactly the opposite. They rely primarily (76 percent) on foreign tourist arrivals to support their hotels. Once again, this is indicative of the size and scope of the domestic economy, which in this case is not the primary source of business. It is expected, however, that in the case of the emerging economies, as the domestic size of these economies grows, domestic travelers will become an increasing source of their business.

Overwhelmingly, in every region of the world, business travelers and tourists make up the two largest segments of the lodging industry's market mix. Together, these segments make up over 60 percent of the total world-

wide market. Tour groups make up the third highest segment, in all regions except North America, where conference participants are the third largest segment.

Across all hotel categories, North American hotels enjoy the highest occupancies. The luxury segment of the market had an occupancy rate of 72.5 percent while the economy segment had 69.0 percent. However, the same is not true for average room rates. The highest average room rate for the luxury segment of the market was in Europe, whereas North Amer-

T3	Worldwide Market Composition					
	Total World	Africa and Middle East	Asia and Australia	Europe	Latin America and Caribbean	North America
SOURCE OF BUSINESS						
Domestic	49.2%	23.9%	45.3%	49.7%	52.9%	81.9%
Foreign	50.8	76.1	54.7	50.3	47.1	18.1
MARKET COMPOSITION						
Government Officials	3.9%	7.6%	6.0%	2.7%	2.9%	4.7%
Business	38.3	37.9	36.6	41.1	36.5	30.9
Tourists	22.3	15.8	21.9	21.7	24.0	28.7
Tour Groups	17.3	16.8	16.3	15.7	23.6	5.2
Conference	9.9	4.7	9.5	10.7	8.2	21.3
Other	8.3	17.2	9.7	8.1	4.8	9.2
Total	100.0%	100.0%	100.0%	100.0%	100.0%	100.0%

Source: Horwath International and Smith Travel Research (1995)

		Average Occupancy	Average Daily Rate	Revenue (REVPAR)*	Income before fixed charges (per room)
All Hotels		66.5%	$ 81.02	$35,661	$ 8,336
Africa and Middle East	Luxury	59.8	138.48	63,799	18,562
	First Class	63.6	82.61	44,265	15,853
	Mid-Price	58.9	54.50	21,795	5,215
	Economy	61.7	24.05	10,936	2,010
Asia and Australia	Luxury	72.0	136.76	77,524	20,476
	First Class	70.3	89.34	43,944	9,606
	Mid-Price	73.6	70.03	33,858	8,998
	Economy	65.2	44.83	19,220	3,445
Europe	Luxury	63.3	150.90	62,776	15,036
	First Class	61.8	90.85	39,692	8,457
	Mid-Price	63.3	69.78	33,574	8,771
	Economy	60.3	48.16	27,881	6,106
Latin America and the Caribbean	Luxury	63.9	119.21	49,317	7,448
	First Class	55.9	70.34	25,006	5,071
	Mid-Price	59.6	49.62	17,478	3,143
	Economy	61.6	25.28	12,428	1,226
North America	Luxury	72.5	105.37	46,001	12,071
	First Class	70.5	79.57	31,777	8,590
	Mid-Price	68.6	63.03	23,189	5,781
	Economy	69.0	50.62	20,209	4,301

Source: Horwath International and Smith Travel Research (1995)
*REVPAR = Revenue per available room

first modern chain of hotels beginning with the *Buffalo Statler* in 1908, (Lattin, 1993). He was followed by a second generation of hoteliers such as Conrad Hilton who started the *Hilton* chain of hotels in the 1920s, and Ernest Henderson who founded the *Sheraton* in 1937 (Rushmore, 1992). Until World War II these three chains, Statler, Hilton, and Sheraton grew primarily in the United States. However, after the war, a combination of factors spurred international growth. These included the desire of soldiers returning home to travel abroad, President Roosevelt's initiative to improve the economies of lesser developed countries, and the Marshall plan for reconstruction of Europe after the war (Gee, 1994).

The lead on this was taken by Pan American Airways, which formed Intercontinental Hotels Corporation (IHC), a wholly owned subsidiary.

They opened their first international hotel in Brazil and later expanded to countries in South America and the Caribbean Islands. Sheraton expanded internationally to Canada by acquiring two Canadian hotel chains in 1949. Hilton formed Hilton International in 1949, and opened its first international hotel, the Caribe Hilton in Puerto Rico.

Following the international expansion of the American chains, European hotel companies, led by Lord Charles Forte of the Forte chain of hotels, entered the international arena. His earliest venture into the

hotel industry was in 1958, which later grew into the Trust House Forte Company operating 41 hotels by 1970 (Gee, 1994).

Between 1945 and 1955, the first generation hotels expanded mainly by owning hotel real estate or by acquiring the right to manage the hotel via a management contract. In the late 1950s, Kemmons Wilson, the founder of Holiday Inns, was the first to start the concept of franchising in lodging. By standardizing the operating systems, and establishing a central reservation system, franchising became a quick and less capital intensive way to expand the presence of a chain in major markets. Starting from the 1960s and extending unto the current time, the two models of franchising and management contracts have been the methods of choice for multinational hotel chains.

The 1970s and 1980s saw an expansion of multinational chains from various continents. The next generation of international hotels included chains from North America, Europe, and the newest rivals, from the Asia-Pacific regions, entered the global arena. Some of the better known, later entrants into the international hotel race include, Hyatt Hotels, Marriott Hotels, Radisson Hotels, Choice Hotels International,

Photo courtesy UPI/Corbis-Bettmann.

Kemmons Wilson was the first to start the concept of franchising in lodging.

and HFS (now part of Cendent Corporation) from the United States; Club Med, Accor, Meridien, Kempinski, and Grupo Sol from Europe; The Taj group, Oberoi Hotels, and Welcome Hotels from India; New Otani, Nikko, Regent International, Mandarin Oriental, Peninsula, and Dusit Thani from the Asia-Pacific region.

A Profile of Multinational Hotel Companies

As recently as 30 years ago the international enterprise was quite a rare phenomenon, and the term multinational, or transnational, was not often heard. Today, every business textbook and business periodical has a section informing us of events impacting the global corporation. Experts have predicted that by the year 2000 global corporations will control approximately half of the world's assets, (Gee, 1994).

What is a global corporation? There are two terms that have been used interchangeably to define corporations that conduct business in territories outside their own, these are Transnational Corporations (TNC) and Multinational Corporation/Enterprise (MNC/MNE). A multinational corporation (MNC) is a firm owned and managed in one country, while the Transnational Corporation (TNC) is usually owned and managed by nationals in different countries (Go, 1995).

For the purposes of this chapter, we will use the term multinational hotel firm to mean hotel chains that have their corporate office in one country and operate, own, manage, or franchise hotels in more than one country. For example, Marriott International has their corporate office in the U.S., but operates hotels globally.

Many of these hotel chains from the United States and Western Europe have been drawn into the global arena because their own (home) markets have reached maturity, thereby reducing their rate of growth. In addition, these multinational firms, mainly from formerly industrialized

nations, have been attracted to growth opportunities in the fast growing nations especially in the Asia-Pacific region. The opportunities that have attracted these companies include, government incentives offered by many nations that want to attract investment to their countries. As Gee (1994) states in his book, "In the early years of tourism development, foreign governments assumed the financial risk of hotel projects by providing guarantees or equity participation, while the hotel company provided name recognition in addition to operational and marketing expertise. A brand name and expertise were essentially what countries wanted to buy."

Photo courtesy Morton Beebe—S.F./Corbis.

Marriott International has corporate offices in the United States, but operates hotels globally.

Furthermore, an improvement in the economies of these nations, resulting in greater buying power, the existence of specific resources (labor and material), and the increasing fungibility of capital markets, made these emerging nations attractive to the hotel chains from the West. In fact, the early entrants into these

markets (1960s and 1970s), such as the Hilton, Intercontinental, and Sheraton had a near monopoly and could, therefore, negotiate very favorable contracts for themselves.

The situation started to change in the 1980s. The increase in western chains entering the Asia-Pacific region led to the development of hotel chains based in Japan and Hong Kong that rivaled the western chains. These were chains such as the New Otani, Nikko, and ANA from Japan; Mandarin Oriental, New World Hotels, and Peninsula from Hong Kong; Dusit Thani from Thailand; and Oberoi Hotels and Taj Hotels from India. Many of these hotels first started as domestic, and later expanded into becoming regional multinational hotel chains. Today, many of these chains compete directly with western hotels not only in the Asia-Pacific region but also in Europe and North America.

Despite the growth of multinational hotel chains from various regions of the world, a few facts are important to keep in mind. As noted in Table 5 in terms of overall scope, the multinational hotel chains originating from the United States still maintain a leadership position. However, chains are increasingly challenging their market share from various parts of the world. One hundred and ten firms studied by Kundu, as part of his research on the globalization of the hotel industry, indicates that North America and Europe account for 80 percent of the multinational hotels, and Asian firms constitute 17 percent of the total rooms.

Another fact to note from Table 5 is that hotel firms originating in the United States are more widely dispersed than their European or Asian counterparts. The latter tend to concentrate their international expansion to their own region. For instance, 46 percent of the rooms operated by European multinationals are concentrated in Europe, and 44 percent of the rooms operated by Asian multinationals are in Asia, while hotel companies that originate in North America have only about 25 percent of their properties in North America.

The regions in which the multinational hotel firms are focused are led by Asia and Oceana with 31 percent of the total room concentration. They are followed by Europe, which has 29 percent of all rooms operated by multinationals, and finally North America has 21 percent of all multinational hotel firm rooms. It should be noted that of the almost 139,000 rooms in Asia are operated by multinational chains, approximately 73 percent are operated by multinationals from North America and Europe. On the other hand, only 22 percent of the total multinational hotels in the United States are operated by Asian multinational chains, and 5 percent in Europe. It is clear, that even though the tide is not as one sided as it was in the 1960s and 1970s, multinational chains still have a stronger presence in the East than the other way round.

However, what is not evident from the data in Table 5, is that even though a multinational chain may originate from a certain part of the world, they may be owned by an entity from another country. For example, Intercontinental Hotels was sold to Grand Metropolitan PLC from the U.K. in 1981, and then later pur-

T5 Universe of Multinational Hotel Firms

Source by Firms		Destination by Rooms Outside Home Country								
Source Country	Percentage By firm	North America	Europe	Middle East	Africa	Asia	Oceana	South America	Caribbean	Global Total rooms
NORTH AMERICA										
USA	22.7%	43,333	34,104	3,095	10,532	57,057	12,793	20,431	13,842	195,187
Canada	2.7	7,477	228	—	—	—	—	—	419	8,124
	25.46%	50,810	34,332	3,095	10,532	57,057	12,793	20,431	14,261	203,311 (37.6%)
EUROPE										
UK	21.8%	18,954	39,650	775	9,718	21,178	3,130	6,892	3,520	103,817
France	10.9	8,763	32,202	863	14,225	12,896	742	3,071	2,011	74,773
Germany	7.3	1,613	6,671	—	—	1,718	—	313	1,220	11,535
Italy	1.8	314	2,955	—	—	—	—	—	—	3,269
Spain	2.7	6,192	10,369	—	508	3,344	—	777	997	22,187
Sweden	2.7	1,241	12,166	—	—	900	—	—	—	14,307
Switzerland	2.7	2,640	3,530	—	956	4,432	—	—	—	11,558
Others	4.6	—	7,452	—	—	—	—	—	—	7,452
	54.56%	39,717	115,500	1,638	25,427	44,468	3,872	11,053	7,748	249,423 (46.0%)
OCEANA										
Australia	1.8%	—	—	—	—	873	4,558	—	—	5,431
		—	—	—	—	873	4,558	—	—	5,431 (1.0%)
ASIA										
Japan	4.6%	6,418	1,567	—	—	6,246	1,566	—	1,571	17,368
Hong Kong	7.3	16,405	6,461	125	171	24,496	1,951	395	2,805	52,809
Singapore	1.8	—	—	—	—	3,431	—	—	—	3,431
India	1.8	1,850	600	1,310	1,189	1,761	200	—	—	6,910
Malaysia	0.9	—	—	—	—	600	—	—	—	600
Others	0.9	164	—	—	—	—	—	—	918	1,082
	17.28%	24,837	8,628	1,435	1,360	36,534	3,717	395	5,294	82,200 (15.4%)
TOTALS	100.0%	115,364	158,460	6,168	37,339	138,912	24,940	31,879	27,303	540,365
		21.3%	29.3%	1.5%	6.9%	25.7%	4.6%	5.9%	5.1%	100.0%

Source: Doctoral Dissertation. "Explaining the Globalization of Service Industries: The case of Multinational Hotels." Sumit Kumar Kundu. Rutgers State University. Original source, International Hotels Group Directory, 1993.

chased by the Saison Group from Japan in 1988 (Gee, 1994). At the writing of this chapter, the company may be sold to Bass PLC from the U.K. (Hotel Business, March 1998, 7–20). In this manner, even though the strength of their own brands may not be strong enough with the older and easily recognized U.S. brands, they are entering the U.S. market by purchasing U.S. hotel chains. More recent mergers and acquisition of multinational hotel chains will be discussed later in the chapter (see section "Modes of Entry").

Tier 1: It is clear from Table 6, that the world's largest hotel chains are based in the U.S. The top ten hotels, ranging in room size from 490,000 (HFS) to 91,177 (Carlson Hospitality) are all U.S. based, with the exception of Accor, which is the fourth largest chain and based in France.

Tier 2: The tier 2 hotels ranking from the 11th to the 20th largest is almost evenly split between U.S. based chains and those from Europe, especially the U.K. and France. Grupo Sol, a chain based in Spain also is in the second tier. The range of rooms in this tier is from 80,598 (Hyatt Hotels) to 32,096 (La Quinta).

Tier 3: These hotels are an eclectic group; the Asian hotel chains make their first appearance in this tier. Countries represented in this tier include U.S., France, Japan, Hong Kong, and Spain. The range of rooms in Tier 3 is from 26,643 (Prince hotels, Japan) to 10,417 (Sholodge, U.S.).

Tier 4: In Tier 4 the hotels are an even more diverse group. Hotel chains in this group include those based in Poland, Canada, Germany, India, Mexico, Bahamas, Scotland, South Africa, Japan, Finland, Switzerland, Norway, Dominican Republic, and Sweden. The hotels in this tier range from 10,100 (Orbis, Poland) to 5,110 (Aston, U.S.).

T6	A Select Listing of the World's Largest Corporate Chains (Top 200 Corporate Chains)			
World Ranking 1996	Company	Headquarters Country	Total Rooms	Total Hotels
TIER 1				
1	HFS Inc	USA	490,000	5,300
2	Holiday Inn Worldwide	USA	386,323	2,260
3	Best Western International	USA	295,305	3,654
4	Accor	France	279,145	2,465
5	Choice Hotels	USA	271,812	3,197
6	Marriott International	USA	251,425	1,268
7	ITT Sheraton	USA	130,528	413
8	Promus CO's	USA	105,930	809
9	Hilton Hotels Corp	USA	101,000	245
10	Carlson Hospitality	USA	91,177	437
TIER 2				
11	Hyatt Hotels	USA	80,598	176
12	InterContinental Hotels	UK	69,632	193
13	Hilton International	UK	51,305	160
14	Grupo Sol Melia	Spain	47,371	203
15	Forte Hotels	UK	46,847	259
16	Double Tree Hotels	USA	43,555	166
17	Westin Hotels & Resorts	USA	42,897	97
18	Club Med	France	37,906	133
19	Societe du Louvre	France	36,059	567
20	La Quinta Inns	USA	32,096	249
TIER 3				
22	Prince Hotels Inc	Japan	26,643	86
25	Walt Disney Co	USA	19,415	18
26	Nikko Hotels International	Japan	18,632	49
29	Hotels & Compagnie	France	17,579	342
31	Shangri-La Hotels & Resorts	Hong Kong	16,985	34
32	Scandic Hotels	Sweden	16,000	98
33	Riu Hotels Group	Spain	15,896	63
34	Omni Hotels	USA	15,184	41
35	ANA Hotels	Japan	15,031	43
39	Thistle Hotels Group	UK	13,574	100
40	Dusit Thani/Kempinski	Thailand	13,208	55
42	Occidental Hotels	Spain	12,805	52
44	Queens Moat Houses	UK	11,626	91
48	Ritz Carlton Hotel	USA	10,682	33
50	Sholodge	USA	10,417	100
TIER 4				
53	Orbis Co	Poland	10,100	47
54	Delta Hotels	Canada	9,983	31
55	Treff Hotels	Germany	9,731	70
56	Steinberger Hotels	Germany	9,528	58
60	Taj Group of Hotels	India	8,900	60
61	Grupo Posadas de Mexico	Mexico	8,686	36
65	Sun International	Bahamas	8,031	37
68	Stakis Hotels & Resorts	Scotland	7,600	51
73	Protea Hospitality	South Africa	7,337	89
77	New Otani	Japan	7,132	23
78	Sokos Hotels	Finland	7,035	45
79	Grupo Situr	Mexico	6,983	29

(continued)

Table 6: A Select Listing of the World's Largest Corporate Chains
(Top 200 Corporate Chains)   *(continued)*

World Ranking 1996	Company	Headquarters Country	Total Rooms	Total Hotels
80	Movenpick Hotels & Resorts	Switzerland	6,945	34
85	Rihga Royal Hotels	Japan	6,172	20
87	Swissotel Ltd	Switzerland	5,718	16
88	Rica Hotels & Restaurants	Norway	5,700	47
89	Allegro Resorts Corp	Dominican Republic	5,690	22
91	Hunquest	Hungary	5,618	36
94	Oberoi Hotels	India	5,412	27
99	Sunwing	Sweden	5,202	17
100	Aston Hotels	USA	5,110	29
TIER 5				
101	US Franchise Systems, Inc	USA	5,094	47
104	SMI Hotels & Resorts	Singapore	4,975	12
106	Grecotel & Resorts	Greece	4,945	20
112	Mandarin Oriental Hotel Group	Hong Kong	4,555	12
113	Sonesta	USA	4,476	18
115	Rydges Hotel Group	Australia	4,420	27
125	Bristol Hotels	USA	3,759	12
126	Helnan Hotels	Denmark	3,721	17
129	Sahid Group of Hotels	Indonesia	3,494	21
130	Cubanacan	Cuba	3,486	34
131	Atahotels	Italy	3,477	10
132	Hesperia Hotels	Spain	3,474	22
138	Warwick International	France	3,400	22
140	Othon Hotels SA	Brazil	3,329	18
144	Southern Sun Hotels	South Africa	3,177	17
145	Pestana (GP) Hotels	Portugal	3,156	15
149	Auberges des Gourverneurs	Canada	3,028	14
151	Austria Trend Hotels	Austria	2,964	22
152	Imperial Hotels Group	Thailand	2,922	10
160	Raffles International	Singapore	2,657	4
164	Doral Hotels & Resorts	USA	2,550	8
167	Peninsula Group	Hong Kong	2,503	6
168	Sandals Resorts	USA	2,500	12
173	Dedeman A.S.	Turkey	2,290	9
174	Gloria International	China	2,277	8
178	Dan Hotels Corp	Israel	2,190	8
179	SuperClubs	Jamaica	2,180	9
186	Jurys Hotel Group PLC	Ireland	2,085	13
190	Rotana Hotels	UAE	2,045	14
193	Hotel Lotte Co. Ltd	Korea	2,000	3
195	Bayview International	Singapore	1,970	11
198	Carlton Group of Hotels	Australia	1,826	5
199	Central Group of Hotels	Thailand	1,792	8
200	Doyle Hotel Group	Ireland	1,736	10

Source: HOTELS Giants Survey 1997. Based on top 200 corporate chains.
Please note: The Tiers were introduced as an interpretation aide by the author.

Tier 5: Like the former group, this Tier includes a diverse grouping of countries. Additional countries in this group include Singapore, Greece, Hong Kong, Australia, Denmark, Indonesia, Cuba, Italy, Spain, Brazil, Portugal, Austria, Turkey, China, Israel, Jamaica, Ireland, UAE, and South Korea. The rooms in this tier range from 5,094 (U.S. Franchise Systems, U.S.) to 1,735 (Doyle Hotel Group, Ireland).

Table 7 provides a ranking of the top 200 corporate hotel chains by the countries in which their headquarters are based. It is evident that the largest chains are located in the U.S. France, Great Britain, Japan, and Spain are ranked from 2nd through 5th. It is also interesting to note that the average room size of U.S. based hotel chains (128 rooms) is smaller than the world average (137 rooms). The primary reason for this is the large presence of franchised properties in the U.S. Most franchised hotels are generally small and serve the midscale and economy markets. While countries such as Japan, Hong Kong, Singapore, Thailand, Switzerland, Mexico, China, and some of the countries in the Mediterranean have larger hotels. This is primarily because in many of these countries, the corporate chains primarily operate upscale properties, which are larger in size.

As noted from Table 8, Accor, a French hotel chain, has a presence in the largest number of countries (70). However, it is also interesting to note that there is not much difference in the global distribution of the top five multinational hotel chains. They have a presence ranging from 62 to 70 countries. This is indicative of the intense competition between the multinational hotels; when one chain opens a hotel in a particular country, another often follows suit.

International Corporate Hotel Chains Ranked by Country

Rank	Headquarter Country	Rooms	Hotels	Average Hotel Size (Rooms)
1	USA	2,643,899	20,715	128
2	France	387,980	3,621	107
3	Great Britain	237,310	1,267	187
4	Japan	152,109	613	248
5	Spain	135,462	805	168
6	Germany	80,151	660	121
7	Hong Kong	42,671	99	431
8	Canada	40,354	144	280
9	Sweden	26,485	150	177
10	Singapore	24,156	79	305
11	South Africa	22,834	179	128
12	India	21,196	137	155
13	Thailand	20,522	81	253
14	Australia	19,062	106	180
15	Switzerland	12,664	50	253
16	Italy	12,142	62	196
17	Finland	12,058	77	157
18	Hungary	11,618	73	159
19	Mexico	10,603	45	236
20	China	10,354	42	246
21	Poland	10,100	47	215
22	Bahamas	8,031	37	217
23	Norway	5,700	47	121
24	Dominican Republic	5,690	22	259
25	Greece	4,945	20	247
26	Syria	4,620	16	289
27	Tunisia	4,443	18	247
28	Cyprus	4,343	29	150
29	Ireland	3,821	23	166
30	Netherlands	3,788	28	135
31	Denmark	3,721	17	219
32	Indonesia	3,494	21	166
33	Cuba	3,486	34	102
34	Brazil	3,329	18	185
35	Portugal	3,156	15	210
36	Austria	2,964	22	135
37	Turkey	2,290	9	254
38	Israel	2,190	8	273
39	Jamaica	2,180	9	242
40	UAE	2,045	14	146
41	Korea	2,000	3	667
	Total	**4,034,635**	**29,461**	**137**

Source: Adapted from HOTELS Giants Survey 1997. Based on top 200 corporate chains.

Why Do Lodging Corporations Go Global?

During periods of increasing competition and shrinking market share, hotel chains have three strategic choices (Gee, 1994):

1. They can increase their markets in their home countries.
2. They can create new products and, therefore, a new market niche to penetrate.
3. Expand their operations into overseas markets.

Initially, U.S. hotel chains expanded into neighboring Canada, Mexico, and Cuba. After the Cuban revolution in 1959, tourism in Cuba came to a halt, and the growth of tourism took place in the other Caribbean Islands. Currently, U.S. hotel companies have expanded to most countries around the globe. As with the U.S. companies, European and Asian chains initially expanded within their regions, but later focused on North America as their brands gained more prominence and recognition. There are eight primary reasons why hotel companies expand internationally:

1. Expanding Their Markets

Mature lodging markets such as the U.S., do not provide many avenues to the hotel chains for rapid growth. Therefore, they seek countries that are growing at a rapid rate and do not have an adequate supply of world class hotels. This explains the focus of many U.S. based multinational hotel chains in newly industrialized countries (NICs) in the Asia-Pacific region.

2. Strategic Positioning of Brand

A major objective of large multinational hotel firms is to make their brand the most recognizable on a global basis. This usually means that if one of the competing brands has a presence in a region or country, they need to follow. Furthermore, many international hotel chains follow their domestic customers into a country. If IBM or General Motors opens a large facility in a particular country, and if these two corporations are a major source of revenue for a particular hotel company in the U.S., they would follow these companies into those markets.

3. Increasing Profits

An obvious lure of international expansion is the potential for high profits, especially in regions

Multinational Presence of the Largest Corporate Chains

Hotel Chain	Number of Countries
Accor	70
Best Western	69
InterContinental	69
Holiday Inn Worldwide	65
ITT Sheraton	62
Marriott International	51
Forte Hotels	50
Hilton International	49
Carlson Hospitality Worldwide	42
Choice Hotels International	40
Club Mediterranee	40
Hyatt Hotels	37
Grupo Sol	25
Westin Hotels & Resorts	23
Park Plaza International Hotels	20

Source: Weinstein, 1997

where competition is limited. Usually, there is a "first mover" advantage associated with the firms that are first to bring their products into the market.

4. Prestige and Identity

Some of the benefits of international expansion are less tangible. The image of an international company has a marketing and public relations value that may not be measurable. While no hotel company will decide to go global solely on the basis of this criterion, it is certainly an important determinant of their decision to expand into overseas markets.

5. Risk Reduction Through Diversification

A long-term objective for the company may be to reduce the risk of its total real estate portfolio. In order to do this, they may acquire hotels in various parts of the world. Political or economic crisis in India that reduces business or tourist travel to that country and consequently affects hotels located there, will not affect the company's hotel located in London.

6. Invitation of Host Government

Many countries, especially in developing parts of the world, are turning to tourism as a source of revenue. As they lack the basic technology related to developing world class hotels (to attract international tourists) they may provide incentives to multinational hotel companies to open hotels in their country. These incentives are generally associated with either reducing risk or providing favorable terms related to management contracts.

7. Invitation by Local Investor(s)

Investors seeking to develop hotels in their home country may look for a multinational partner. In this case, they would approach a hotel chain and try to interest them in their project. Many times the multinational uses this as an opportunity to gain entrance into a country.

8. First to Enter Opportunities

Due to ever-changing political and economic conditions globally, companies are presented with growth opportunities in various regions. The fall of communism and the creation of the commonwealth of independent states in the former Soviet Union, has created many "first to market" opportunities for multinational hotel companies. Other recent growth opportunities exist from the liberalization of foreign investment and repatriation rules in countries like India. Not all multinational companies move into these new markets as soon as they are open. Generally, there are some companies that take the additional risk by being the first to enter a country, but by the same token, also generate the highest profits if the venture is successful. In many cases, the government of the host country, which provides some incentives and guarantees to attract the hotel company mitigates the risk.

Modes of Entry

Once the decision has been made to expand overseas, a hotel company generally follows one of the three methods to gain entry into the host country.

1. Management Contract

Most hotel chains from the United States that expand overseas use a management contract as the primary means to enter the country. This reduces their overall financial risk associated with the venture. In a management contract, an agreement is formed between a hotel company and the owner of a specific hotel or group of hotels. The responsibility of the management company includes managing the day to day operation of the hotel. This includes all functions associated with marketing, lodging operations, personnel, accounting, finance, and other general management functions. In return, the management company is paid a fee, which is generally a percentage of the revenue it generates.

Not every region of the world relies equally on the management contract entry mode. Only 2 percent of the rooms in Europe are under man-

Hotel	Location	Buyer	Seller	Price (US$ MM)	Hotels/ Rooms
Hotel George	Paris	HRH Prince Alwaleed Bin Talal/Riyadh	Granada Group/London	$172.0	1/258
Hyde Park Hotel	London	Mandarin Oriental Group/Hong Kong	Granada Group/London	146.0	1/185
Forum Hotel	Budapest	Intercontinental Hotels/London	Budapest State Privatization Company	49.4	1/400
Double Tree Hotel	Salt Lake City	Wyndham Hotels/Dallas	City Hotels SA/Brussels	44.0	1/381
La Samanna Hotel	St. Martin	Orient Express/London	Frankel Estate/St. Martin	20.0	1/80
Westbury Hotel	London/ New York	Chelsfield PLC/London	Granada Group/London	146.7	2/472
Conrad International	Hong Kong	Sino Land Co./ Hong Kong	Hilton Hotels/Beverly Hills	112.0	1/513
J. W. Marriott	Hong Kong	Chisore Enterprise/ Hong Kong	Queensway Hotel Ltd/ Hong Kong	N/A	1/604
United Nations Plaza Hotels	New York	Regal Hotels/Hong Kong	City of New York	102.0	1/427
Ambassador Hotel	Monterrey (Mexico)	ITT Sheraton/Boston	Canavati family/Monterrey	15.0	1/239
Hotel De La Cite	Carcassone (France)	Subsidiary of Orient Express/London	Jean Michel Signoles/ Carcassone	N/A	1/26
The Balmoral Hotel	Edinburgh (Scotland)	RF Hotels/London	Bank of Scotland/Edinburgh	N/A	1/186
Lucayan Beach Resort/ Grand Bahama Beach Hotel, Clarion Atlantik	Freeport (Bahamas)	Hutchinson Whampoa/ Hong Kong	Hotel Corporation of Bahamas/Sun & Sea Estate Ltd/Freeport	100.0	3/922
Browns Hotel	London	Raffles Holdings PLC/ Singapore	Granada Group/London	74.9	1/118
Hotel Du Parc	Montreal	Mass Mutual Life Insurance/Springfield	Crowne Life Insurance/ Regina	12.3	1/364

Source: Hotels, Various issues

agement contract, while in regions such as Asia, Africa, and the Middle East, 60 to 75 percent of the properties are operated under a management contract (Gee, 1995). The specific terms and conditions of a management contract are complex and vary with the type of hotel and country. In the early days of international expansion, U.S. hotel chains literally "wrote" the contract, as many developing countries relied upon them for international exposure. However, now the atmosphere is much more competitive as chains from various parts of the world may bid for a contract.

2. Franchise Agreement

In a franchise agreement, a hotel franchise chain, known as the franchiser, forms an agreement with the owner of a hotel property, known as a franchisee. This agreement allows the franchisee to use the franchiser's name and standardized business operating systems. The greatest advantage of a franchise is the instant worldwide brand recognition and marketing of the property through the chain's central reservation system. An American tourist visiting Madagascar would have somewhat of a sense of assurance

if she saw a hotel with a Holiday Inn logo, versus one that reads "Sleep Easy Inn."

It should be noted, however, that the ease with which franchising has grown in the United States cannot be directly replicated in other parts of the world. As Tom Oliver, CEO of Holiday Inn states, " Here in the U.S. people buy every square inch of land around the interstate highway, in Europe (and other countries) government regulations sharply restrict the development of hotel properties. It is harder to find good franchisees who have good sites and good economics.

And then in some countries you don't even have the infrastructure" (Cruz, 1998).

The case for and against franchising internationally has proponents on both sides. Grupo Sol Melia, a worldwide chain of 230 properties, uses franchising as only an incidental part of its global expansion methods. Their philosophy is that a company first needs an operating history in a new country before creating a structure to support the franchisees. They feel that the brand quality is at risk without the operating history. On the other hand, U.S. chains like Cendent Corporation, are 100 percent franchised. A recent example is the opening of this brand into the Philippines, a testament to their philosophy that no corporate trailblazing was necessary before introducing a new brand in a new country (Cruz, 1998). Franchise fees generally include an up front fee for joining the franchise and on-going royalty and central reservation fees.

3. Investments

Overseas Hotel Investments can be accomplished by four types of investment methods:

(a) **Direct Foreign Investment (DFI)**—In a DFI a multinational corporation invests its own capital into a foreign country. The impact of this infusion of capital results in the construction of a property such as a hotel or resort. The evaluation of these investments is similar to those made in the home countries, with the addition of exchange rate, political risk, and cultural considerations (Butler, 1996).

Most hotel chains from developed countries avoid investing their own capital when expanding into under developed or emerging countries. Furthermore, some host countries have restrictions as to the amount (if any) of equity that foreign firms may have in their countries. Since the middle to late 1980s these protectionist policies have been relaxed in most countries. A study on international equity participation indicated that the number of overseas properties managed with equity participation prior to 1982 was 10 percent. This increased to 13 percent after 1982 (Eyster, 1988).

(b) **Foreign Acquisition**—There are generally two methods of cross border acquisitions. The acquisition may consist of direct acquisition of an existing real asset, such as an existing hotel or group of hotels. The second method is to buy equity interest in a foreign company. This is easily done for public companies in countries that have active stock markets.

(c) **Mergers**—In a cross border merger, two firms pool their assets and liabilities to form a new company. Stockholders of the old company trade their original shares for shares in the new company. Table 10 lists the top ten mergers of 1997, valued at a total of $9.4 billion. This is more than the 1996 total of $8.8 billion.

(d) **Joint Ventures**—In a joint venture, two or more entities pool their resources to achieve a well-defined mission. The entities are usually complementary, each one bringing a particular strength to the venture. Typically, joint ventures may be formed between a financing entity such as an investment firm and a hotel operating company, or between a government entity of the host country and a multinational hotel chain.

"When you joint venture, you're able to have quality control, and form a partnership that puts together the very best strengths of you and your local partner," says J. T. Kuhlman, COO of InterContinental Hotels & Resorts. They have used this method to expand into 79 different countries (Cruz, 1998).

Country Evaluation

All overseas hotel projects, whether they are direct investments or management contracts of franchise arrangements, involve varying degrees of risk. This risk arises from the differences in the political, social, and economic environment of the host country. Therefore, multinational companies that undertake international projects conduct a business environment analysis to help them decide on the suitability of the country or compare the environments of alternative countries. Generally,

Merger	Size of Merger
Promus-DoubleTree	$ 4.70 billion
Starwood-Westin	1.57 billion
Marriott-Renaissance	1.00 billion
Patriot American-Wyndham	763.00 million
Starwood-Flatley Co/Tara Hotels	470.00 million
Extended Stay America-Studio Plus	290.00 million
Patriot American-Carefree Resorts	210.00 million
Prime Hospitality-Homegate Hospitality	132.00 million
Wyndham-Clubhouse Hotels	130.00 million
Innkeepers USA Trust-Summerfield	127.00 million

T10 Top Ten Hotel Mergers of 1997

Source: Lodging (October 1997)

T11 Rating Scale for Screening National Environments

Screening Criteria	National Rating 1–10	+ Weight 1–10	= Combined Score
Political Stability			
Government Attitude			
Repatriation of Capital			
Repatriation of Earnings			
Investment incentives			
Ownership restrictions			
Controls on foreign managers			
Taxation provisions			
Exchange rate			
Per capita income			
GNP			
Prospect of economic growth			
Rate of inflation			
Size of market			
Tourist number growth			
Hotel occupancy rate			
Hotel industry legislation			
Hotel concentration			
Tour operator activities			
Attractions			
Availability of necessary supplies			
Cost of supplies			
Labor cost			
Combined Score			

Source: Decision criteria for transnational hotel expansion. Frank Go, Sung So Pyo, Muzaffer Uysal, and Brian J. Mihalik. *Tourism Management,* December 1990

this analysis is conducted using a format similar to the one identified below. Once a rating has been established, the company can decide whether they want to proceed or abandon the international project.

What Makes a Successful International Hotel Executive?

Students who graduate with a degree in hospitality management should consider themselves international hotel (or hospitality) executives. While it is true that most students will not have an opportunity to work on an overseas assignment as soon as they graduate, they are international executives from the first day they enter the hospitality indus-try. An international hotel executive is defined in a much broader sense than merely working at an international property. Here are the reasons why this is so:

1. You may work for a (foreign) multinational hotel company operating in your own country.

2. In many countries, such as the U.S., the work force has become increasingly international. Many of the workers are from Asia, Mexico, Cuba, or Canada.

3. Many of the larger hotels located in resorts or gateway cities cater to a large percentage of international tourists and business travelers.

4. Increasingly, associates (other managers) may originally be from another country.

5. Finally, as you are promoted to a senior management position in your hotel organization, you may have the opportunity to manage an overseas property or region within your firm.

Chuck Gee (1995) in his book on international hotels states, "Most studies show that American students, when compared with students from other nations place fairly low in their comprehension of foreign cultures. Europeans, on the other hand, tend to be fairly sophisticated in their knowledge of other cultures and languages." While you may never be completely prepared for an overseas assignment, there are certain skills and attitudes, which are important when companies select executives for these positions. Here is a list of some of the important traits and experiences that will position you as an international hotel executive.

1. An understanding and appreciation of different cultures.

2. The ability to communicate in more than one language.

3. An interest in international travel.

4. Internship or work experience overseas.

5. Study program or short courses attended overseas or with an international group.

6. Taking an international business course, or graduating with a minor in international business.

7. Work experience with a multinational hotel company

8. An understanding of the international hotel industry (The fact that you are reading this book means that you are on your way!)

Hospitality 2000: A View to the Next Millennium

A study of key issues facing the international hospitality
industry in the next millennium

■ *Roger S. Cline and Dr. Lalia Rach* ■

Arthur Anderson and New York University

As the 20th century draws to a close and new millennium approaches, it is important to consider how the international hospitality industry will adapt to meet the diverse and changing needs of its customers around the world. Beyond new reservation systems, on-line guest services, or the latest in guestroom design, the hospitality industry will face a broad array of new challenges as the current trend towards increasing globalization continues to change the profile and needs of customers around the world. Among the highlights of the Hospitality 2000's research findings are the following:

- Successful hotel organizations of the future will place their primary emphasis on the customer (the guest) rather than the physical asset (the hotel).
- Leisure travel is expected to grow significantly faster than business travel in all regions surveyed.
- Hotel industry marketing will continue to be dominated by sales and marketing function located at individual hotels. Word of mouth advertising will gain in importance as a communication channel influencing the customer's buying decision.
- Strategic alliances and joint ventures are expected to be the primary growth vehicles for international expansion.
- The human element involved in delivering quality service will not be replaced by technology, rather it will gain in importance.
- Food and beverage facilities will increasingly be leased to third parties and themed restaurant concepts will be introduced more frequently as entertainment becomes a greater factor in the guest experience.
- The development of new hotel brands will be driven by he need for large hospitality enterprises to increase market share and meet the evolving needs of the market as a result of changing lifestyles and demographics.
- Public financial markets will grow in importance to become the dominant source of capital for the industry.
- Global distribution systems, yield management, and service improvements will become the most important marketing strategies.
- Long range planning priorities will include chain expansion, upgrading of equipment, the application of technology and focus on the core "hospitality" business.
- The industry will be increasingly dominated by a few large hospitality enterprises relying on international growth for expansion.

Stages in the Development of a Nation's Hotel Industry
▬ Paul Slattery ▬

We developed a theory illustrated in the figure below to explain why domestic business demand for hotels in the U.K. (this can apply to any country) grew by 145 percent in the 1980s. It argues that the structure of an economy is a determinant of the extent and pattern of growth in domestic business demand for hotels.

In economies that are dominated by extractive and manufacturing industries (Phase I economies) business demand for hotels is relatively modest and cyclical.

When the free market services sector of an economy develops and chains of service businesses expand nationally (Phase II economies) there is an acceleration in business demand for hotels. In the U.K. this occurred between the mid-1970s and the end of the 1980s. In the U.S. it occurred between the mid-1950s and the mid-1980s.

When an economy becomes a full blown service economy (Phase III) the rate of growth in business demand for hotels slows and reverts to a cyclical pattern but at much higher volumes than Phase I.

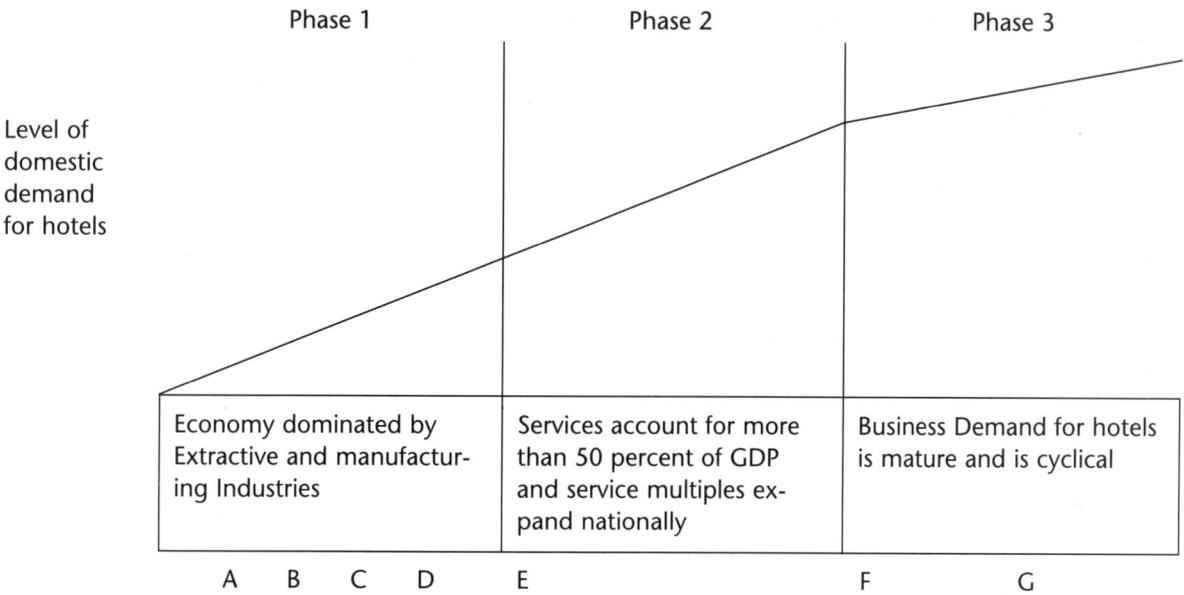

A = Eastern Europe, B = Africa, C = Latin America, D = Far East, E = Continental Europe, F = United Kingdom, G = USA

Source: International development of hotel chains. Paul Slattery (1996), in *The International Hospitality Business*, edited by Richard Kotas.

Operating and Ownership Structure of the International Lodging Industry

Country	Owned	Managed	Franchised	Leased
United Kingdom	80.4%	6.2%	4.1%	9.3%
W. Europe	31.9	31.9	23.3	12.9
E. Europe	4.9	38.2	55.9	1.0
Asia	9.7	74.8	14.9	0.6
USA	6.9	20.5	70.8	1.8

Source: International development of hotel chains. Paul Slattery (1996), in *The International Hospitality Business,* edited by Richard Kotas.

The structure of the international hotel industry is diverse. While in the U.K. the primary operating arrangement is that of ownership (>80%), the opposite is true in the United States, where a majority of the hotels exist in the franchise format (70%). The high percentage of management contracts (74.8 %) in Asia reflects the large presence of multinational hotels in those countries. Western Europe has an even split between hotels that are owner operated and those with management contracts. The franchise arrangement in Western Europe is becoming more popular. Eastern European hotels are almost all either under a management contract or franchised (94%). As in Asia, this reflects a large presence of multinational hotels, which almost never invest their own capital in newly opened economies. The leasing method of operating hotels is almost non-existent in the U.S., Asia, and Eastern Europe. The U.K. and Western Europe have a small percentage in the leased format.

Differences in the Cost of Operating International Hotels

(Ratio to Sales)

Category	Total World	Africa and Middle East	Asia and Australia	Europe	Latin America and Caribbean	North America
REVENUE						
Rooms	58.3%	49.9%	55.2%	51.6%	57.1%	64.9%
Food	22.6	27.3	24.0	25.8	19.6	20.4
Beverage	8.4	8.5	9.6	12.6	6.5	5.6
Other F&B	2.7	2.0	2.6	2.7	4.0	2.4
Telephone	3.1	5.7	3.6	2.8	4.6	2.6
Minor operated departments	3.0	4.0	2.7	2.6	4.9	2.7
Rentals and other income	1.9	2.6	2.3	1.9	3.3	1.4
Total Revenue	100.0%	100.0%	100.0%	100.0%	100.0%	100.0%
DEPARTMENTAL EXPENSES						
Rooms	28.5%	19.4%	25.3%	26.9%	33.0%	31.5%
Food & Beverage	82.4	71.2	84.8	79.4	88.2	83.0
Telephone	69.1	72.3	78.0	62.7	87.2	64.7
Other Departmental	2.1	2.2	2.0	1.9	3.1	1.9
Total Debt Expenses	48.6	42.9	49.4	52.5	52.5	44.6
TOTAL DEBT PROFIT	51.4%	57.1%	50.6%	47.5%	47.5%	55.4%
UNDISTRIBUTED OPERATING EXPENSES						
A&G	10.3%	11.9%	9.1%	9.7%	13.2%	9.8%
Marketing	5.0	2.9	5.1	3.9	4.2	6.2
Franchise Fees	0.6	0.2	0.3	0.3	0.2	1.1
Energy	4.6	4.7	5.0	3.6	5.7	4.9
POM	5.2	6.5	4.8	4.6	6.9	5.3
Total Undistributed Operating Expenses	25.7%	26.2%	24.3%	22.1%	30.2%	27.3%
GROSS OPERATING PROFIT	25.7%	30.9%	26.3%	25.4%	17.3%	28.1%
Management Fees	2.4	4.6	3.1	2.2	2.1	2.2
INCOME BEFORE FIXED CHARGES	23.3%	26.3%	23.2%	23.2%	15.2%	25.9%
Property Taxes	2.5	0.5	1.5	2.1	2.0	3.4
Insurance	0.8	1.0	0.6	0.7	0.9	0.9
Reserve for replacement	1.2	5.2	2.2	0.5	0.6	1.3
AMOUNT AVAILABLE FOR DEBT SERVICE AND OTHER FIXED CHARGES	18.8%	19.6%	18.9%	19.9%	11.7%	20.3%
TOTAL FIXED CHARGES	20.6%	13.2%	18.8%	21.5%	16.4%	22.2%
PRETAX INCOME (LOSS)	2.7%	13.1%	4.4%	1.7%	(1.2)%	3.7%

Source: Horwath Worldwide Hotel Industry (1995)

Questions and Assignments

1. Using the web browser and search engine of your choice, open The World Travel and Tourism Council web page at *http://www.wttc.org* and find some additional information relating to the global nature of hospitality. Alternatively, use your library resources. Bring the information you find to class for discussion with your team and classmates.

2. Using the web browser and search engine of your choice, open The World Tourism Organization web page at *http://www.world-tourism.org* and find some additional information relating to the global nature of hospitality. Alternatively, use your library resources. Bring the information you find to class for discussion with your team and classmates.

3. Establish the average size of hotels from two different regions. Discuss the underlying reasons for the size differential or lack of size differential.

4. What is the fastest growing region for lodging properties in the world? Using the web browser and search engine of your choice or the library resources, establish some reasons for this region's growth. What are the long-term prospects according to your research?

5. What role has Pan American played in hospitality?

6. Define multinational hotel firm.

7. Using the web browser and search engine of your choice or your library resources, choose one of the multinational lodging companies mentioned and perform a company/organization research on one of their properties abroad. Do not repeat a company you have already investigated. See Chapter One for details of research.

8. Which region of the world accounts for the majority of multinationals?

9. Establish and discuss the "universe" of multinational from the perspective of source and destination. See Table 5.

10. Consider Table 6. Choose two hotels or hotel companies from two different tiers. Can you establish a clear difference between them? Use your library resources or the web to support your discussion.

11. Establish and discuss the reasons why lodging companies (might) choose to expand internationally.

12. Using your favorite web browser visit http://www.hospitalitynet.nl and http://www.hotel-online.com/Neo and search for a news article discussing a current or recent management contract arrangement. If a web browser is not available, use your library resources.

13. The chapter discusses three modes of entry into a foreign market. Briefly discuss the three while establishing their similarities and differences.

14. Using your favorite web browser and search engine or your library resources, visit the home page of one of the companies listed in Table 9. Describe the property briefly. Can you establish who is the current owner of the establishment, and whom you would contact if you wished to inquire into employment with them? Does the home page discuss employment opportunities?

15. Refer to Table 11. Assume you are about to invest in a hotel abroad. Of the screening criteria that are listed, which are the five most important to you? Why are they the most important? Be prepared to discuss this with your team and classmates.

16. To what extent are all hospitality executives and managers international executives and managers? Justify your response.

17. Refer to Focus 1. Considering the content, what does this tell you about actions you could/should take now (curricularly as well as extracurricularly) and later in your career.

18. Refer to Focus 4. If any of the terms are unclear, have your instructor explain them. Consider the differences in cost across regions. What strikes you as interesting? If nothing strikes you as interesting, why do you think this is the case?

19. Choose a hotel chain (you may refer to Table 8 if desired). Using your favorite web browser and search engine or your library resources, try to establish the chain's *mission statement*. Bring the statement to class to compare with those brought by your team or classmates. Discuss how the various mission statements are similar or different. Does one of the mission statements strike you as particularly good or poor? How does this impact your interest in this company as a future employer or business contact?

20. Contact a hospitality executive that is either working abroad, or has worked abroad, and perform an informational interview as per Chapter One.

Bibliography and Suggested Readings

Arthur Anderson and New York University (1997). *Hospitality 2000: A View to the Next Millennium.*

Butler, K. C. (1996). *Multinational Finance.* Unpublished Text.

Cruz, T. D. (1998, February). Speed to market. *Hotels,* 32(2), 40–48.

Dunning, J. H. & McQueen, M. (1982). Multinational corporations in the international hotel industry. *Annals of Tourism Research,* 3, 69–90.

Eyster, J. J. (1988). *The Negotiation and Administration of Hotel and Restaurant Contracts.* Ithaca, NY: School of Hotel Adminstration Cornell University.

Gee, C. Y. (1994). *International Hotels Development and Management.* East Lansing, MI: Educational Institute of the American Hotel & Motel Association.

Go, F. M. & Pine, R. (1995). *Globalization Strategy in the Hotel Industry.* London, England: Routledge.

Go, F. M., Pyo, S. S., Uysal, M. & Mihalik, B. J. (1990, December). Decision criteria for transnational hotel expansion. *Tourism Management,* 11(4), 297–304.

International Hotel Association, Horwath International, Smith Travel Research. (1995). *Horwath Worldwide Hotel Industry.*

Kundu, S. K. (1993). Explaining globalization of service industries. (Doctoral Dissertation, Rutgers State University). *Dissertation Abstracts International, 55/04,* 1030. Oct 1994.

Lattin, G. W. (1993). *The Lodging and Food Service Industry.* East Lansing, MI: Educational Institute of the American Hotel & Motel Association.

New Briefs. (1998, March 7–20). *Hotel Business.*

Rushmore, S. (1992). *A Guide to Market Analysis, Investment Analysis and Valuations.* Chicago: Appraisal Institute.

Weinstein, J. (1997, July). Hotels giants survey. *Hotels.* 42–71.

World Travel & Tourism Council. (1995). *Measuring the Size, Scope of the Global Hotel Industry.* Madrid.

World Travel & Tourism Council (1995). *Travel & Tourism: A New Economic Perspective.*

World Tourism Organization. (1992). *Compendium of Tourism Statistics.* Tarrytown, NY: Pergamon Press, Elsevier Science, Inc.

Year of the Deal. (1997, October). *Lodging,* 23(2), 11.

5

The Real Estate and Franchising Perspective

John M. Tarras, *The School of Hospitality Business*, MICHIGAN STATE UNIVERSITY

ABSTRACT

This chapter will establish the important role that real estate plays in hospitality. Considerations relative to location, financing, ownership, and legal concerns will be discussed. Franchising is used extensively in hospitality, and this chapter will explain the franchising concept and approach. Franchising advantages and disadvantages relative to franchisors and franchisees, respectively, will be introduced and reviewed. The chapter ends with an introduction to franchise costs.

OBJECTIVES

At the end of this chapter the student should be able to:

1. Establish the importance of considering hospitality from a real estate perspective.

2. Describe the key issues to consider in locating and choosing hospitality sites.

3. Differentiate market area analysis, supply analysis, and demand generators.

4. Understand the importance of accurate revenue and cash flow forecasts.

5. Define equity financing and debt financing as they relate to hospitality real estate.

6. List and describe the various types of business entities hospitality companies may form.

7. Define franchising and discuss franchisor and franchisee advantages and disadvantages.

8. Understand the unique costs inherent in franchising.

Introduction

In hospitality education an often overlooked criteria for consideration of the hospitality industry is the real estate perspective. This is especially true in larger developments such as resorts and casinos. But real estate can be just as important in the consideration of restaurants, clubs, and any other hospitality developments where a physical structure needs to be constructed or leased.

During the 1980s, when the real estate market was booming, many hotel companies such as Hilton were supplementing their annual reports with schedules showing the fair market values of their hotels. Many hotel companies saw the underlying value of the real estate component grow at a much greater rate than their income from operations. Many hotel companies took advantage of the rapid increase in values to sell the appreciated properties at huge profits and take back management contracts to operate the properties.

Then in the late 1980s, the hotel market became saturated as money from financial institutions such as the Savings and Loan companies, tax preferred investment vehicles such as limited real estate partnerships, and government subsidies in the form of Urban Development Action Grants. This resulted in a major overbuilding of hotel properties, which led to the major recession for the industry. Many hotels failed, and construction of new hotels came to a screaming halt. Many of the larger hotel companies flirted with bankruptcy, and only through drastic cost cutting efforts were they able to avoid going under.

Today, the hotel market is once again a profitable industry, and in many areas there is an actual shortage of business class hotels. However, the financial institutions remember the overbuilding of the 1980s and are still wary of investing in new properties. Therefore, the capital market is not as generous as in the past in loaning money to the hotel industry. So today's developer needs to be much more creative in raising financing for any new project.

This chapter will focus on the main real estate considerations that a hotel developer will need to consider when developing a new project. The hotel is used as an example because it is the most complex real estate transaction within the hospitality industry. However, the concepts will apply to almost any type of hospitality development. Finally, there will be a discussion on franchising, which is prevalent in the hospitality industry.

Location of Property

Site Analysis

There is an over used description to describe the importance of picking a site. It states that there are three things to remember when choosing a real estate site and they are "location, location, and location." However, there is a lot of truth to that statement. So the first and foremost criteria in understanding any real estate deal is the process of picking a site.

Site analysis can be either informal or a formal process. Usually, what the developer is looking for is a site in which the traffic flow will be able to support the business. For instance, *McDonald's* spends a great deal of time and money in locating their restaurants because they rely on a large number of patrons who spend relatively little money on each meal. Therefore, you would never see a *McDonald's* restaurant located on a dead end street. There would not be enough traffic to support the business.

Another aspect of location is the physical suitability of the property for development. There are various government regulations, from zoning ordinances to environmental impact studies, that may be required before any development can begin. Then there is the suitability of the land itself. Can the property support the structure being planned? Here the developer needs to conduct survey studies, soil core studies, and perk tests, to name just a few, to determine if the property can even be physically built upon the site.

Access and visibility is another issue that faces the developer of a hospitality property. For instance, is there adequate parking nearby for guests at a lodging property being planned in a major city, or will the developer need to purchase a larger parcel to build his own parking structure? Adequate vis-

Location, location, location is what's important in real estate. New York's Central Park area is a great location for nearby hotels.

ibility is another consideration facing any hospitality firm. If you can not find the hotel, then how can you stay there? For example, in Chicago there is a sign for a chain hotel that states next exit. However, there are several turns that must be made to find the property making it a difficult task for someone not familiar with the area to find that particular hotel.

How close a hotel is to the demand generators is also a consideration. For instance, a businessperson will want to be as close as possible to his or her ultimate destination and will frequent hotels that will require the least amount of travel.

Market Area Analysis

The developer will want to study the overall market of an area to determine whether there is a need for another property. This is sometimes called a feasibility study. Within the feasibility study, the company will want to determine the extent of the market that it wishes to enter. This is called the market area analysis.

The market area analysis consist of analyzing economic trends such as: population age and distribution, retail sales, work force characteristics, major businesses and industries, office space, airport statistics, and any other relevant information that will enable the real estate developer to obtain an accurate economic outlook for the potential building site.

Much of the site analysis data requirements can be obtained from government agencies, chambers of commerce, and various industry trade associations. For example, Sales and Marketing Management has reports on specific areas of the country on population levels, age distribution, retail sales, eating and drinking place sites, and effective buying income.

After the developer collects the necessary data, the data needs to be put in a format that will aid analysis of the site. He often does this by comparing years and marking the increase and decrease in percentage

terms of key information that he has determined will be relevant in his decision making. (It is a very difficult process to try and predict the future with any accuracy.) The developer is basically making an educated guess as to the future, but at a minimum, wants to insure that the property has a reasonable chance to be a successful project.

Supply Analysis

Evaluation of competition is the next logical step in the development process. With so many hotel companies competing for a limited number of guests, it is important that the market will be able to absorb the extra rooms created by a new facility.

Competition is usually broken down into primary and secondary. Primary competition includes any facility that attempts to attract the same guest as the developer's property. Secondary competition generally consists of facilities that attract the same guests under special circumstances. For instance, a business traveler may normally stay at a first class hotel, but the budget hotel is much more convenient, and so the first class hotel losses that customer due to the budget's unique location.

In the lodging business, primary competition occurs among lodging facilities that are similar to the developer's property with respect to the following criteria: facilities offered, class, and image. Secondary lodging properties may share similar location characteristics, but they share few of the other major qualities of the developer's property, particularly class and image.

Another important consideration in the supply analysis is franchise affiliation. Franchise affiliation is becoming increasingly important in the hotel industry as frequent guest programs and centralized reservation systems have created a brand loyalty among many travelers. In many cases, guest will stay outside a given market

Franchise affiliation is increasingly important in the hotel industry.

area just to take advantage of the perks offered by a particular brand. So it becomes very important for the developer to consider whether his property is going to be affiliated with a particular franchise.

Also, a developer has to be aware in choosing a franchise brand that there may be other developers who are building under the same franchise within the market area to be served. This could dilute potential business as each property competes for guest through the central reservation system.

Finally, the developer needs to analyze any future development planned for the market and what impact that will have on his overall business. This is a very difficult process because hospitality firms do not need to disclose future site locations. Thus, a promising market can suddenly become overbuilt because several hospitality firms have decided to build properties at the same time.

Demand Generators

Demand generators differ from market analysis in that in market analysis the developer is looking at the overall market conditions that exist. In analyzing demand generators the developer is focusing on specific attractions that will attract guest to a particular hotel property. For example, demand generators could be amusement parks, casinos, colleges and universities, company headquarters, convention centers, office and industrial parks, resort areas, and tourist attractions. The developer will spend time trying to determine if the generators identified will justify his building of the property. Usually, the developer will conduct interviews and surveys to determine as exact as possible the demand generators in the chosen market.

Revenue and Expense Forecast

After the developer has conducted his detail market study, he is ready to forecast revenue based on the data collected and analyzed. This is, perhaps, the most important aspect of the site selection. If the property can not generate sufficient cash flow to support the property then the project will fail. For hotels, revenue forecast consists of calculating the occupancy rate and the average daily rate

(ADR) for the property. The average occupancy rate should be reasonable and realistic in the market selected. Many developers have overstated occupancy rates in the past and this has caused many projects to be built that should not have been. The ADR must be realistic within the given market and level of competition present.

The sales forecast is the key to determining the property's ability to be profitable. This is because the expense items forecasted are usually based on a percentage of the sales. Once the expenses have been deducted, the operating income or loss from operations is obtained. The hospitality owner then will need to calculate the real estate operating expense, such as real estate taxes and mortgage payments, in order to calculate the total profit and loss of the property.

In real estate the owner pays close attention to the cash flow that is generated by the operation of the property. It is the cash flow that pays the debt service and the expense. Therefore, analysis done in real estate to determine if a hotel is profitable is calculated on a modified cash flow basis.

Financing of Real Estate

Obtaining financing for a hospitality property (especially hotels) is the most difficult task facing most developers. There are literally thousands of developers with ideas of where to build a successful hotel, but they are often frustrated by their inability to obtain affordable financing. Generally, a small hospitality firm will contribute a down payment, which is the equity in the project, and borrow the remainder, which is the mortgage debt. Larger projects basically do the same but in a more sophisticated form. Owners of larger properties often obtain equity and financing from a variety of sources.

Equity Financing

Almost no lender is going to loan money to a hospitality project unless the owner(s) is willing to contribute a substantial amount of their own money to the project in the form of equity. The amount required can be as little as twenty percent in the case of hotel projects to sixty percent in the case of restaurants. The amount required is determined by the lender's determination of the risk of the operation.

In larger projects, equity is often raised by going to outside investors who will contribute money in exchange for a percentage of ownership of the project. Some popular means of raising equity contributions have been through Real Estate Investment Trusts, Limited Partnerships, Pension Funds, and Limited Liability Companies. These are sophisticated and complicated arrangements that require a great deal of experience on the part of the developer.

Debt Financing

There are a wide variety of mortgage loans that are used to finance hospitality projects. The most common is the permanent mortgage loan. This loan can range from five to 20 years

Photo courtesy New York Convention & Visitors Bureau.

Demand generators can be convention centers, such as New York's Javits Center.

in length and the interest rate can be either fixed or variable. On smaller projects, the owner is usually asked to personally guarantee the loan amount or have a relative guarantee the loan if the assets of the owner are inadequate from the lender's perspective. A guarantee occurs when the hospitality firm is in the form of a corporation, and the lender wants to make sure that there are sufficient assets to pay the loan off in case the business fails.

The key to obtaining a hospitality mortgage is to be prepared by putting together a loan package that will show excellent financial potential of the project with low investment risk. It must be presented to the lender in a highly professional manner so that the opportunity stands out from all the other submissions. Other types of mortgage financing for larger hotel projects can take many different forms. Some of the more common types of financing, besides permanent mortgages discussed above, include construction loans, mini-permanent loans, bullet loans, and zero coupon financing.

Generally, commercial banks are the first choice for most small firms applying for financing. However, larger projects can draw upon a wide variety of lenders. Examples of different sources of loans include, life insurance companies, private credit companies, pension funds, limited partnerships, blind pool syndicates, and Real Estate Investment Trusts.

Ownership Considerations

Another important consideration for anyone considering a hospitality operation is what type of business entity to operate the project under. Generally, in real estate the owner tries to protect himself as much as possible by structuring his business to avoid as much risk as possible. Therefore, he will give very serious consideration as to which type of operating structure to operate under. Most hospitality

businesses operate under one of the following types of business entity.

1. Individual ownership
2. Partnership (general and limited)
3. Regular corporation (C corporation)
4. S corporation
5. Limited Liability Company (LLC)
6. Trusts
7. Real Estate Investment Trust (REIT)

The two main considerations in choosing a business entity are tax considerations and legal considerations. Each form of business entity has its own tax consequences; therefore, it is important to study each entity's tax impact on the hospitality firm before deciding on a particular business entity. A brief discussion of the tax treatment for each type of ownership follows:

Individual ownership—Lumps income, gain, and loss from hotel properties together with the owner's other items of income, gain, and loss.

Partnerships—whether general or limited, are not taxable entities, but are merely tax conduits; taxable income, gain and loss is passed through directly to the individual partners, who then treat these items as though they were individual owners of the property.

Regular C corporations—are taxable entities separate from their shareholders: they report income, gain, and loss separately. Consequently, corporate income and gain is subject to a double tax, once on the corporate level and again on the shareholder level when the income or gain is distributed as dividends.

S corporations, LLCs, and REITs—are separate legal entities that distribute income and losses in a way similar to partnership forms. There are, however, very specific statute requirements in the Internal Revenue Code that must be met to qualify for these entities.

Trusts—are taxable entities separate from their beneficiaries and thus similar to regular C corporations.

Legal Considerations

It is important for the hospitality owner to look at the various business situations that he is likely to encounter and to determine, thereby, what form fits best. The wrong choice could mean missing a business opportunity that could cost the hospitality owner severely. Some of the more important non-tax considerations to review when choosing an entity are as follows:

❖ Cost of formation
❖ Number of people and type of management needed to run the property
❖ Degree of flexibility required to conduct the activities
❖ Extent of and probability of exposure to liability
❖ Ease of transferability of interest in the entity
❖ Estate planning of the owners
❖ Ease of transferability of hotel property
❖ Expected duration of the venture

Franchising

In the hospitality industry franchising is use extensively in both restaurants and hotels. Basically a franchise is an agreement between an owner of a concept (franchisor) and the party wishing to use the concept (franchisee). The franchisor allows the franchisee to make use of the chain's name and services (e.g., a central reservation system and defined operational procedures) in return for a fee, which the franchisee pays the franchisor. Under such an agreement, the franchisor has no ownership or financial interest in the franchisee's property and is not directly responsible for its economic success.

An owner usually will develop a concept and then open a few successful operations on his own. Over time, the franchisor will develop an image and a brand name that is proven successful in attracting customers. Specific operational procedures are established that produce a standardized method of doing business, which is proven to be financially profitable. Once the operations are proven successful then the concept is ready to be franchised.

Franchising in this country really began to take off in the 1950s. Some of the hotel chains that first offered franchises were *Holiday Inn*; *Howard Johnson's Motor Lodge*; and *Ramada Inn*. Some of the early restaurant franchise operations were *McDonalds*; *A&W Root Beer*; and *Dairy Queen*.

Hospitality franchising flourished during the 1960s and 1970s when consumers demanded known quality establishments. When the benefits of a chain affiliation became apparent to sophisticated business investors, then franchising was almost a requirement to obtain the necessary financing for a project.

Advantages for Franchisors

1. *Inexpensive, Rapid Expansion*

Hospitality firms that seek to become major chains often use franchising as a growth vehicle because doing so generally requires a relatively modest capital investment compared with developing or acquiring properties on their own. In addition, franchising does not require the extensive management structure that is needed to operate each property. The bulk of the expenses for a franchise company consist of the advertising and promotional efforts needed to sell franchises, and of obtaining the critical mass of franchisees required in order to have an economically viable chain.

Another cost-saving aspect of a franchise system is that the development responsibilities are shifted to individual franchisees. Because these parties of the franchise typically have first-hand knowledge of local real es-

tate and business markets, they are usually in a better position than the franchisor to acquire the best sites and to handle the overall developmental process.

The capital that makes a franchise organization grow comes from the owners of the individual hospitality properties in the form of fees and royalties. The franchisees assume the major portion of the financial risk associated with opening a property, but in return they receive most of the economic rewards.

2. *Profitable Source of Revenue*

The revenue generated by a hospitality franchise typically starts with initial fees, paid along with ongoing royalty fees by franchisees when they join the franchise system. In addition, some franchisors require additional payments for services that they provide such as marketing, advertising, reservations, frequent traveler programs, and training.

The expenses incurred by franchisors that are chargeable against

these fees are generally for services provided by the franchisor and are usually minimal. Many of the services provided by franchisors generate fixed fees (e.g., centralized reservation systems, chain directories, and various administrative functions), so a franchise chain must have a sufficient number of properties under contract in order to be profitable. Once the number of franchisees reaches this level, the franchise company typically becomes extremely profitable.

3. *Customer Recognition and Brand Loyalty*

Customer recognition is an important attribute for a hospitality firm. While recognition can be created through advertising and promotion, one of the best methods of developing a known hotel brand name is to have a product for people to see and use. The rapid growth potential offered by franchising accelerates the essential process of creating customer recognition. Once customers recognize a hospitality product and have been satisfied after using it, brand loyalty develops,

Howard Johnson's was an early franchised chain.

which results in repeat patronage along with positive word-of-mouth promotions.

Disadvantages for Franchisors

1. *Loss of Operational Control*

The operational responsibility for a franchised property lies with either the hospitality owner or the owner's agent (i.e., a management company). The franchisor exerts very little influence over the day-to-day operation of the property. Franchise chains attempt to control the quality and image of individual hospitality properties through the use of rules, regulations, and periodic inspections. However, the persistent fact that the franchisor does not really have basic control over an operation can sometimes result in lower standards of quality and service than the franchisor wishes to maintain. When this occurs, the guests who experience the substandard level of quality service can form an incorrect image of the entire chain, which can easily have a detrimental effect of repeat patronage or word-of-mouth promotions.

Franchise chains attempt to exert operational control by periodically inspecting each property to see that the facilities are well maintained and the hospitality firm is operating at the prescribed standards. Backing up these inspections are extensive operating requirements contained in the franchise agreement. Objective standards set by franchisors, such as how long french fries are to be cooked, hours of operation, and guestrooms having color television sets are relatively simply enforced. Subjective standards are more difficult to evaluate and enforce. For example, determining whether an operator complies with regulations stating that a hotel must, at all times, be clean and well maintained or that an operation must be "first-class" can be difficult.

The ultimate penalty franchisors can wield in order to enforce their various regulations and standards is the termination of the franchise. However, the time it takes to actually terminate a franchise, particularly if the franchisee is uncooperative, can range from several months to one or more years. The termination process becomes even more difficult if litigation is involved and dispute involves a subjective regulation.

2. *Liability Issues*

When a franchised property is involved in litigation, particularly in suits involving tort liability claims, the franchisor is often named as a defendant. Even though the hospitality chain is often found to have no control over the incident and therefore to bear no liability, the cost of legal defense can often be considerable. Occasionally, franchisors are found to be liable even though they do not have direct control over the operation of the property. This liability exposure can be, and generally is, limited through insurance, which in itself can represent a considerable expense.

3. *No Control Over Pricing*

Another element beyond the control of a franchisor is the establishment of uniform pricing structures throughout the chain. It is illegal for the franchisor to set prices on a uniform basis. Uneven pricing from one property to another can confuse customers and adversely affect the image of the entire chain.

4. *Costly Start-Up*

When a hospitality chain begins franchising, the company generally experiences a negative cash flow until the number of its properties reaches the necessary critical mass. Cash flow should improve when the critical mass is reached, but the franchisor must have sufficient funds set aside to provide the necessary services to the franchisee it has on board during the build-up period.

5. *Mandatory Disclosure Document*

Both the federal government and certain state agencies strictly regulate all forms of franchising. Aimed at protecting the small investors from risking life savings on fraudulent franchise schemes, these regulations require full disclosure of many of the important business aspects of a franchise investment. This level of disclosure eliminates the possibility of franchisors creating individual agreements for each potential franchisee and adjusting terms through negotiation. As a result, most terms of a franchise agreement are fixed and are not subject to alteration.

The Federal Trade Commission (FTC) is the primary governmental overseer of franchising in the United States. In order to offer (sell) a franchise, potential franchisors must first file with the FTC a disclosure document known as a Uniform Franchise Offering Circular (UFOC). While this document does not receive either an approval or disapproval from the FTC, it must be accurate and current.

The UFOC must be given to a prospective franchisee at the earlier of the first "personal meeting" or "the time for making disclosures." The FTC defines the "time for making disclosures" as ten business days prior to the earlier of (1) the execution by a prospective franchisee of any franchise agreement imposing a binding legal obligation, or (2) the payment by a prospective franchisee of any consideration in connection with the sale or proposed sale of a franchise. In addition to the FTC disclosure requirements, several states impose additional franchise regulations, some of which are more stringent than the federal rules.

The ultimate effect of this level of disclosure is to establish uniformity in franchise structures, requirements and fees, and thus eliminate any advantage a franchisor may have over a franchisee in terms of bargaining power.

Advantages for Franchisees

1. Instant Recognition and Shortened Start-Up Period

The primary benefit of a franchise affiliation for any owner is the name recognition that it provides. Customers often look for a hospitality facility with a recognizable name and image. They want to know that the quality of the accommodations and service at the hotel they choose will meet the expectations they have that are based on prior experience with the same product. Although an independent hospitality property without a chain identity may well develop its own reputation and patronage, the period of time needed to penetrate the market in this fashion may extend over many years.

2. Proven Method of Operation and Product Merchandising

Successful, established hospitality chains generally allow potential franchisees access to the manuals and training programs that they have developed as internal guidelines for their mode of operation and product merchandising. By reviewing these materials, a franchisee can be certain that the franchisor has tried and proven systems and procedures that will increase the chances of franchise success.

New franchise companies typically have several company-owned properties that serve as laboratories for developing systems and procedures. Prospective franchisees, lenders, and investors look at the operating results of these properties and use them as a means of confirming the ability of the franchisor to run viable, profitable properties.

Disadvantages for Franchisees

1. Excessive Cost if an Incorrect Franchise Is Chosen

The selection of a franchise is one of the most important decisions that an owner must make. Choosing the wrong franchise almost always adversely affects operating results. For example, an affiliation with a Mexican food restaurant when the market has already saturated with fine local Mexican-style restaurants can result in the franchise failing financially.

Franchisors typically have no financial interest in the properties they franchise and make no representation that a particular franchise will be an economic success. In fact, franchisors set operating standards that may, in themselves, be costly to the franchisee, such as requiring a hotel to upgrade its facilities even though such upgrades may not have a direct impact on the operating profitability of the hotel.

Even though franchise offerings are regulated by the FTC and state agencies, franchise salespeople have occasionally resorted to unethical practices in order to sell new franchises. The compensation received by many of these salespeople is based on the number of franchises they sell, so without strict supervisory control some salespeople may attempt to sell franchises either to unqualified owners or for projects that have no economic feasibility.

2. Nontransferable Franchises

Some hospitality franchisors do not allow existing owners to freely transfer a franchise to a new owner in the event of a sale. Some of the transfer restrictions typically imposed by franchisors include:

- ❖ Payment of a transfer fee
- ❖ Approval of new owner by the franchisor
- ❖ Application for an entirely new franchise
- ❖ Refurbishment of the property to meet current franchise standards
- ❖ Right of first refusal on transfer.

Ultimately, the risk posed to the seller by these transfer restrictions is that the franchise may not be renewed or that it can be renewed only at a steep price. For example, a transfer may require spending hundreds of thousands of dollars in order to bring a franchise up to current company standards. Anything that could inhibit the transfer of a valuable franchise could also adversely affect the market value of the property.

3. Short Term of Franchise

Franchisees and potential buyers face the risk that the reversionary value of an investment in a hospitality property will be discounted if its franchise cannot be renewed or extended. Since the economic lives of hospitality properties span often over forty year in some cases, and franchise terms typically range from ten to twenty years, continuation of a favorable franchise affiliation is important. A change of name and image midway along a hotel's economic life can also result in severe marketing and financial difficulties.

4. Little Control over Other Franchisor Affiliations

Most franchise agreements are not overly restrictive regarding the number of new properties in a market area with which the franchisor can be affiliated. Occasionally, a franchise will grant a property owner an exclusive area for a specific period of time. In most cases, however, a franchisor is free to add a new product to a market whether it is another franchised property or a property managed or owned by the franchise company.

5. Adherence to Chain-Wide Standards

The various regulations and standards developed by franchisors are designed to cover all the properties in a chain and ensure uniform mode of operation and image. Occasionally, these standards may be inappropriate for a specific property or unsatisfactory to a particular owner, but franchisors generally do not allow any deviation from their system. The chain-wide standard that can negatively affect individual properties include:

- Required year-round operation
- Set operating hours
- Minimum staffing level requirements
- Participation in chain advertising
- Required amenities (e.g., a swimming pool in the case of a hotel).

Property owners who would be adversely affected by these standards are sometimes able to work out exemptions with franchisors before signing an agreement.

6. Lack of Control over Chain Quality and Image

Individual franchises have little control over any of the operating policies of the franchisor that adversely affect the overall quality and image of the franchise chain, and so they are essentially at the financial mercy of the franchisor. An analysis of the hospitality organizations that started during the 1950s and the 1960s yields examples of chains that faded in popularity, and others that increased in strength because of their ability or inability to maintain efficient operating policies. Necessary policies for a franchise company include:

- Mechanisms for terminating franchises that do not maintain an appropriate level of quality and service
- Mechanisms for removing hospitality properties from the system that are not functionally up-to-date
- Periodic update of marketing strategies and chain-wide customer image
- Consistent product and unified image

Franchise Costs

1. Restaurant Franchise Costs

Many fees are associated with most franchise operations. It is important when evaluating a franchise opportunity to understand all of them.

For example, the cost of building the restaurant structure could be hundreds of thousands of dollars. That is why many restaurant franchisees rent rather than build. But even if the franchisee rents, he or she will probably have to spend several thousand dollars on leasehold improvements to bring the property up to the stands of the franchisor. In addition, the franchisee must purchase equipment for the restaurant, and this can easily run into thousands of dollars. The franchisee will also have to purchase an initial inventory supply, incur pre-opening expenses such as hiring and training, and provide sufficient working capital for the operation of the restaurant. Other non-operating costs of obtaining the franchise are:

- *Franchise fee.* This is the initial franchise fee that is charged to open each operation. This can range from free for a new franchise attempting to get off the ground to several thousand dollars. This fee may be refundable in part if the franchisee is unable to obtain financing. The franchise fee compensates the franchisor for the use of its name and trademarks and to defray the expenses the franchisor incurs in selling franchises, consultation, training, and assistance to franchisees before the opening of each restaurant.
- *Royalty fee.* After the restaurant is open, it pays a royalty fee based on a percentage of gross sales from the operation. This fee can vary significantly from franchise to franchise, but is usually in the single digits for most franchises. Established companies such as *McDonald's* can command double-digit royalty fees.
- *Advertising fee.* Most national franchisors charge a fee of usually one to four percent based on gross receipts. This fee is usually placed in a special fund that can only be used for advertising and public relations. Often the fran-

chisor contributes to this fund for company-owned stores.

- *Local advertising.* In addition to requiring the franchisee to pay a fee for national advertising, many franchisors also require the franchisee spend a minimum amount for local advertising, a fee that is usually based on a percentage of gross receipts.
- *Renewal fees.* Most franchisors charge a renewal fee when the franchise contract expires for the franchisee to retain the franchise.
- *Upgrade costs.* Most franchisors insist that the franchise be upgraded to remain competitive. Usually, the franchisee is responsible for the entire cost of renovation.
- *Transfer fee.* The franchisor charges a fee for the transfer of ownership of an approved franchise. Generally, the fee is lower if the transfer is to an existing franchisee.
- *Training costs.* Many franchisors provide the initial training for a small fee. Even if there is no charge for training, the franchisee is usually responsible for travel, lodging, and personal expense.
- *Other costs.* Other expenses may arise or are contingent upon certain events. For instance, many restaurant franchises require that new franchisees spend a certain amount on the "grand opening" of every store. Also, most franchisors require that if an audit of the books reveals that revenues were understated by more than certain percentage, the franchisee is required to pay for the audit as well as the royalty shortage.

Hotel Franchise Costs

Many expenses common to restaurants also apply to hotels. The single biggest difference, however, is that hotels are usually constructed, and thus renting property is not an option in most cases. This makes the hotel franchise a larger business investment.

Photo courtesy James Marshall/Corbis.

Established companies such as Burger King can command double-digit royalty fees.

Hotel and motel franchises usually require a minimum number of rooms for each property. The cost to build a hotel (including the land franchising, legal fees, site construction, furnishings, fixtures, and equipment) could amount to several thousand dollars per room for budget hotels to hundreds of thousands of dollars per room for luxury properties. The franchisors offer almost no help in financing the construction of these properties.

Other likely costs beside normal operating costs in obtaining a franchise are:

❖ **Franchise fee.** This initial fee is usually based on a dollar amount per room plus a minimum amount regardless of the number of rooms. This fee covers the cost of training and assistance provided to the franchisees, the cost of quality control inspections, and support of the main office staff. For example, a hotel may charge an initial franchise fee of $300 per room or a minimum fee of $40,000.

❖ **Royalty fee.** This fee is based on a percentage of gross room revenue, and it varies among hotel chains. Some hotel chains levy a fixed charge per room rather than a percentage of room revenues. The royalty fee is usually two to six percent of gross room revenues.

❖ **Adverting fee.** This fee is usually based on a percentage of room revenue, and it supports room revenues. The advertising fee is usually one to three percent of gross room revenues.

❖ **Reservation fee.** This fee is charged either as a percentage of room revenue (usually one to three percent) or as a fixed amount per room or reservation. This fee supports the hotel or motel chain's national reservation system. Many lodging chains require franchisees to purchase or lease reservation equipment.

Conclusion

Real estate is the basic foundation on which the hospitality industry is built. The fact that most students do not have the opportunity to study real estate applications in detail does not diminish the importance of the subject. Real estate is a complicated and detailed expertise that requires many years of training. This chapter has focused on the general nature of real estate and the important area of franchising.

Development of hospitality products in this country has depended upon not only the service aspects of the individual properties but also on their strategic location and cost of acquisitions. This requires the developer to consider not only marketing of a property, but also its financing, form of ownership, franchise selection, and most importantly, its location.

For the student who wants to specialize in the development of hospitality properties, a number of consulting firms exists that specialize in real estate aspects of hospitality development. By working for such a firm, the associate will see a wide variety of property owners and how each one approaches deciding where and when to build. It is a priceless education that will prepare the associate for a rewarding career in hospitality real estate.

Questions and Assignments

1. Discuss briefly the role of real estate in the hospitality industry.

2. What is one of the reasons that the hospitality industry saw an overbuilding of lodging properties in the late 1980s?

3. Please discuss with your team or classmates why you would never see a *McDonald's* at the end of a dead-end street. Include your own examples of hospitality companies that are not likely to consider a "dead-end" location. List the important issues. Can you think of a

hospitality company that would profit from a "dead-end" location? Please justify your response.

4. Pick a location of your choice such as your hometown. Contact the local chamber of commerce and ask for information relevant for a market analysis. Develop a list of data you will request prior to contacting the chamber. You can develop such list by considering the issues in your text and in discussion with your teammates or classmates. Bring the information to class and discuss it with your team or classmates. Which of the locations that you each gathered data on appears **most**

attractive to you for hospitality development? What type of hospitality establishments may be relevant? Discuss why this location is the most attractive of the "available" locations.

5. Using your preferred web browser visit the news desk at Lodging Research Network (http://www.lodgingresearch.com) or Hospitality Net's Real Estate and Finance page (http://www.hospitalitynet.nl/news/finance.htm), and search for articles that bear upon one of the issues or concepts discussed in this chapter. Review the article.

6. Establish the key elements of supply analysis.

7. Using your library resources or your preferred web browser and search engine, identify a hospitality location of your choice and list five demand generators for that location.

8. What is the key to obtaining a hospitality mortgage?

9. Seven types of business entities are discussed in the text. List and describe them.

10. Define franchising.

11. Review the advantages and disadvantages of franchising for potential franchisees. Do the same for franchisors. Following this discussion find an article that discusses a dispute within hospitality between a franchisor and a franchisee. Review the article, and establish whether the dispute can be tied to one of the disadvantages reviewed. Use your library resources or your favorite web browser and search engine. In addition to the web pages in item 5, the web pages listed in earlier chapters may be relevant.

12. List and discuss the costs associated with franchising mentioned in the chapter.

13. Using your library resources or your preferred web browser and search engine, identify a financial services company that works with hospitality financing. Perform a company/organization research on this firm. The approach is discussed in Chapter One.

Bibliography and Suggested Readings

Andrew, P. & Schmidgall, R. S. (1993). *Financial Management for the Hospitality Industry*. East Lansing, MI: The Educational Institute of the American Hotel & Motel Association.

Raleigh, L. E. & Roginsky, R. J. (1995). *Hotel Investments: Issues and Perspective*. East Lansing, MI: The Educational Institute of the American Hotel & Motel Association.

Rushmore, S., Ciraldo, D. M., & Tarras, J. (1997). *Hotel Investments Handbook*. New York, NY: Warren, Gorham & Lamont.

Law, Ethics, and the Hospitality Industry

Linda K. Enghagen, *Department of Hotel, Restaurant, and Travel Administration,*
UNIVERSITY OF MASSACHUSETTS AT AMHERST

ABSTRACT

This chapter will establish the basic structure of the American legal system and consider the general nature and origin of law in our society. Basic concepts, such as truth and fairness, will be defined from the legal perspective. Distinctions between civil and criminal law will be established and discussed. Essential legal issues that are current and uniquely relevant to hospitality will be introduced and considered. Finally, the constructs of law and ethics will be differentiated, and ethical behavior as it applies to hospitality will be reviewed.

OBJECTIVES

At the end of this chapter the student should be able to:

1. Distinguish between law and ethics.

2. Discuss the interrelationship of law and ethics.

3. Define the basic foundation and nature of U.S. law.

4. Establish the legal definition of truth and fairness.

5. Describe the structure of the U.S. legal system.

6. Discuss the various sources of law.

7. Establish the court structure in the U.S.

8. Distinguish between criminal and civil law and lawsuits.

9. Establish and discuss several key legal issues that hospitality is confronted with.

10. Discuss the role and importance of ethics in hospitality.

Introduction

The relationship between law and ethics in the hospitality industry is the same as the relationship between law and ethics in any other human endeavor. The law establishes what is minimally acceptable behavior. Ethics says, that may not be enough.

The legal system can sanction behavior only when the law is broken. For example, consider a common situation such as one where a hotel company enters into an agreement with a vendor. If that agreement complies with the legal requirements of a contract and the hotel company fails to honor it, the vendor can successfully sue the hotel company for breach of contract. However, if the agreement does not satisfy the legal requirements of a contract and the hotel company fails to honor it, the vendor cannot successfully sue the hotel company for breach of contract.

While the law establishes minimally acceptable behavior, complying with the law only is not a guarantee that the behavior is ethical. Consider a situation where two friends agree to meet for a movie. This constitutes an agreement, though not one the law recognizes as a contract. It is simply an agreement between friends. If one of the friends changes her mind and doesn't show up without even attempting to let the other know, she has not broken the law. Nevertheless, she has not done the right thing. While legally acceptable, being rude is not socially acceptable. Being rude to people is not the right thing to do; it is not ethical.

One doesn't need to look far into the law to find examples of laws that wouldn't be necessary if people behaved more ethically. Employment discrimination laws, child labor laws, consumer protection laws, and liquor liability laws are but a few of the areas of law which evolved as a response to the perception that too many people couldn't be trusted to do the right thing. A strong argument can be made that if more people behaved ethically there would be fewer laws.

In the hospitality industry, most encounters with the law involve alleged violations of civil law. Civil lawsuits are one of two basic types of lawsuits allowed under state and federal law. Generally speaking, a given lawsuit will be civil or criminal. While that may sound obvious, a full appreciation of the role of civil lawsuits requires an understanding of the nature of law generally and the U.S. legal system specifically. Consequently, before looking at examples of current legal issues confronting the hospitality industry, the nature of law will be examined and the basic structure of the U.S. legal system will be outlined.

Finally, ethical issues confronting the hospitality industry today will be examined. In addition to considering examples of ethical issues, a framework for identifying and analyzing such issues will be discussed.

The Nature of Law

The nature of U.S. law evolved from a blend of historical concepts. When monarchies dominated as the form of government, laws were believed to derive from the divine right of kings. That is, kings were held to be appointed to serve at and as the right hand of God. Consequently, any laws established by the king were deemed to be divine in origin; they were based on what was right and their rightness emanated from God. As the divine right of kings lost its influence in political theory, theories about the nature of law evolved. Law as custom formed the basis of a second theory of the nature of law. This concept of law focused on custom and tradition as the proper nature of law. A third concept of law emphasized law as command. That is, the basic nature of law was to serve as a series of rules (commands), which were issued pursuant to the authority of the government, and which could result in sanctions from the government when they were disobeyed. The most modern concept of the nature of law is that of law as the battleground of

social engineering. This concept of law focuses on the dynamic role of law as a vehicle for directing social, political, and economic change. It recognizes that law provides a means for balancing competing values and interests toward the end of the common good.

Modern U.S. law possesses elements of each of these concepts of the nature of law. At its most fundamental level, law establishes minimal requirements for what is acceptable conduct in our society. It recognizes the inevitability of individuals encountering one another in sometimes unpleasant exchanges, which they are unable to resolve on their own. By offering a set of rules which carry sanctions if violated, as well as a forum in which the disputes can be heard, it seeks to eliminate and minimize as much unnecessary harm as possible while offering relief when it can't be completely avoided. In other words, law is one of the means by which civilization is defined and maintained.

Certain assumptions underlie the nature of law. In the U.S., one of these assumptions is that the law and the legal system reflect basic principles of justice and truth. That is, the law and the legal system are designed to provide for just results based on the truth. However, to understand truth and justice in the U.S. legal system, it is necessary to understand what those terms mean. Truth as it is defined in the legal system (legal truth) is not the same as the truth (absolute truth) referred to in the everyday usage of that word. Absolute truth is what really happened. It is the most pure objective reality. Metaphorically, absolute truth is what God knows. In contrast, legal truth is what a judge or jury says it is. That is, a judge decides what the truth is when a trial takes place without a jury (called a bench trial). And, the jury decides what the truth is when a trial takes place with a jury (called a jury trial). When deliberating about the truth, judges and juries are limited by the information (evidence) presented at trial. That is, they can consider only the information in front of them. There may be information that is significant and telling but was never introduced during the trial. Perhaps a potential witness died between the time of the incident and the trial. Perhaps the rules of evidence did not permit a document to be admitted because only a photocopy was available (not an original). Perhaps evidence was seized in violation of the Constitutional prohibition against illegal searches and seizures. Justice (fairness) demands that judges and juries consider only the information properly in front of them. As a result, absolute truth and legal truth are sometimes at distinct odds with one another. The drug dealer whose paraphernalia was illegally seized is, in an absolute sense, absolutely guilty. Yet, in a legal sense, that same drug dealer is innocent and as pure as the driven snow. And despite the cries of some that this is nothing more than legal technicalities run amok, it is, given the broader structure of our legal system, justice.

The U.S. legal system operates within the greater structure of a democracy with deep traditions of revering and protecting freedom and individual liberties. In an effort to avoid the pitfalls of their forbears, the Founding Fathers established certain freedoms, which are spelled out in the Constitution. These freedoms and rights were deliberately designed to limit the power of the government toward the ends of preventing abuses of power and preserving democracy. Using illegal searches and seizures as an example, it is without a doubt unfortunate when true criminals avoid prosecution or conviction because illegally obtained evidence cannot be used at trial. However, allowing law enforcement officials unfettered authority poses a risk as well. Consequently, the system has evolved with built-in checks and balances. Law enforcement officials are supposed to do their jobs within certain rules. The courts serve as a check on that authority. In the long run, democracy is at greater risk from

law enforcement officials who have no real limits to their authority than from some criminals avoiding prosecution and conviction. The justness of suppressing illegally obtained evidence flows from this rationale. Now it is certainly true that not everyone agrees with this line of reasoning. However, if a democracy is the preferred form of government, then some method must be designed to preserve the many freedoms taken for granted as part of daily life.

The U.S. Legal System

The U.S. legal system is one component of the government which is a representative democracy grounded in a commitment to federalism (i.e., separation of powers). This commitment to federalism permeates not only the legislative bodies where power is divided between the state and federal governments, but is carried through to the legal system as well. In total, there are fifty-one (51) legal systems in the United States. On the national level, the federal court system serves as the primary forum for resolving cases involving questions of federal law. On the state level, each state developed its own court system which is the primary forum for resolving cases involving its state law.

Sources of Law

Before examining the structure of the court systems, it is important to understand where our laws come from. Or, to put it more simply, what is law? While this might sound like a decidedly elementary question, it is the source of immense confusion. The laws of the United States derive from five sources and each and every one of them is law. To think of it another way, if confronted with the question, where do I find the law; the answer is that one must look in each of these five places to determine if each holds any laws relevant to the issue in question. And, it is not uncommon to find laws from more than one source

which regulate the same issue. For example, laws prohibiting employment discrimination can be found in federal statutes (e.g. The Civil Rights Act of 1964 and the Americans With Disabilities Act), state statutes (e.g., individual state civil rights acts), the U.S. Constitution (e.g., equal protection clause), and state constitutions (e.g., state counterparts to the federal equal protection clause). The five sources of law are: constitutions, statutes, common law, administrative regulations, and treaties.

Constitutions

There are fifty-one (51) constitutions which serve as sources of law. In addition to the U.S. Constitution, each of the fifty (50) states has a constitution. The U.S. Constitution is sometimes referred to as a social compact or social contract. It is the basic agreement between the government and the people. It establishes the framework of the government and creates rights guaranteed to the people. The U.S. Constitution is the standard against which the legitimacy of all other law is tested. That is, any other law which violates the terms of the U.S. Constitution can be declared unconstitutional (i.e., void) by a court of law. This does not, however, mean that other laws must imitate the U.S. Constitution. Other types of law can afford more protection to the people than that given in the U.S. Constitution; they can't give less. For example, the Massachusetts Constitution has a specific clause guaranteeing a right of privacy to people within the Commonwealth. Even though there is no such specific provision in the U.S. Constitution, Massachusetts is allowed to do this because it gives people within the Commonwealth more protection from invasions of privacy than that afforded by the U.S. Constitution. In contrast, it would be unconstitutional for any state to attempt to put a provision in its constitution eliminating the warrant requirement for searches and seizures because the U.S. Constitution prohibits such searches and seizures.

Statutes

Statutes are the type of law which typically come to mind in reference to the word "law." Statutes are the laws enacted by legislatures. Congress enacts statutes on the federal level and state legislatures enact statutes for each of the states. Statutes are the type of laws most directly connected to the political process.

Common Law

Common law is the type of law most closely connected, historically, to the English system of law. Common law is sometimes referred to as case law or judge-made law. It is the body of rules (laws) which evolves from cases where there are no specific written laws (i.e., there is no constitutional provision, statute, administrative regulation, or treaty). Some fields of law are almost entirely regulated by common law. For example, most of the body of law in the field of torts is common law; the rules governing negligence cases or misrepresentation cases are found in the common law. Because the common law is comprised of judges' decisions in prior cases, the common law is physically located in the written decisions (or opinions) from actual cases.

The doctrine of *stare decisis* ("Let the matter stand"), which requires judges to follow prior precedents originated as a common law doctrine. Today, it applies to cases using common law rules as well as to cases interpreting the other four sources of law. That is, a judge interpreting a constitutional provision, statute, administrative regulation, or treaty is bound, by the application of the doctrine of stare decisis, to follow previous interpretations of that same law.

Administrative Regulations

Administrative regulations are laws created by administrative agencies. For example, the Environmental Protection Agency establishes regulations governing acceptable levels of pollutants. The Occupational Safety and Health Administration regulates safety standards for the workplace. While these examples are federal agencies, state agencies may promulgate regulations as well. However, not all agencies have the authority to create regulations. Only those agencies that have been given that authority by Congress or the state legislature have the power to engage in making laws. Typically, these powers are given when the subject matter is highly technical or complex. The reasoning goes that legislators have neither the time nor the expertise to properly regulate in such fields. Critics of administrative regulations counter that it is undemocratic to give agencies rule-making power because agencies are not accountable to voters in the same way as politicians.

Treaties

Treaties are the agreements entered into between the United States and native tribes or foreign governments. Only the federal government has the power to enter into treaties: individual states may not.

The Court Systems

There are fifty-one (51) court systems in the United States. In addition to the federal court system, each of the fifty (50) states has a court system which is modeled after the federal system. There is no requirement that states model their courts after the federal system, but historically this has been the case.

Federal Court System

The federal court system has three (3) levels of courts. The highest court is the U.S. Supreme Court. The intermediate level of courts is the U.S. Circuit Courts of Appeal, and the trial courts are known as the federal district courts. There are thirteen (13) U.S. Circuit Courts of Appeal. Eleven (11) of these courts are distributed throughout the country. The remaining two circuit courts are the District of Columbia Circuit Court of Appeals and the United States Court of Appeals for the Federal Circuit. There are approximately one hundred (100) federal district courts distributed throughout the states. The number of federal district courts in a particular state is based on the caseload of that state.

With limited exceptions, cases filed in the federal court system begin in a federal district court. That is why the district courts are referred to as the trial courts; they are where the actual trials occur. The significance of this is that trial courts serve as the "trier of fact." That is, trial courts are the place where the judge or jury determines what happened—the facts of the case. Once a trial court has established the facts of a case, the facts cannot be challenged (except in rare instances) or relitigated on appeal. As a general proposition, appeals can be made to a higher court, but appeals can be made only on issues of law. Were the right laws applied to the case? Did the judge err in allowing or disallowing certain items of evidence? Were the instructions to the jury proper? In addition to the requirement that a proper appeal must be based on an issue of law, appeals must be based on a "perfected record." That is, the trial transcript must show that the side filing the appeal made a proper objection at the proper time during the original trial. In other words, lawyers must object to certain things during a trial in order to create a record which allows the possibility of a later appeal. The failure to raise proper objections can result in no opportunity for an appeal, and, depending on the specific facts might constitute malpractice on the part of the attorney. Generally, an appeal from a federal district court goes to the U.S. Circuit Court of Appeals. Appeals from the circuit courts go to the U.S. Supreme Court.

State Court Systems

While the names of the courts are often different, most states model their state court systems after the federal court system in that they use trial courts as the triers of fact, and they have at least two levels of appeals courts.

A Court's Authority Over Cases

In order for a court to have the authority to hear a case it must have jurisdiction over the subject of the dispute and over the parties to the case. Having the authority to hear the type of dispute in question is known as subject matter jurisdiction. For example, in most states only probate courts have the authority to hear divorce cases or settle estates. A divorce action started in a district court would be thrown out for lack of jurisdiction. In addition, the court must have jurisdiction over the parties or persons involved in the case. With both subject matter jurisdiction and personal jurisdiction, the court has the authority to hear and decide the case. If a case is filed in a court which lacks either or both of these types of jurisdiction, the case will be dismissed for lack of jurisdiction. It can be re-filed in the proper court.

Civil and Criminal Lawsuits

The U.S. system of law operates as a single system that handles all types of cases. Nevertheless, there are two important divisions of law, which are critical to an accurate understanding of the manner in which cases are handled. First, under the umbrella of the U.S. Constitution, all law is divided between two categories: civil law and criminal law. In its simplest terms, civil law deals with private disputes between private parties (the government can be one of those private parties). In contrast, criminal law deals with offenses against society. That is, criminal law addresses conduct which is potentially threatening to all members of society in a manner which renders it more serious than civil violations of law. This distinction is not meant to diminish the significance of civil violations. A per-

son whose economic livelihood is threatened because someone else unlawfully breaks a contract has been seriously wronged. However, it is deemed to be less serious than the wrong suffered by the victim of a violent, physical assault. Civil law and criminal law are each further subdivided. Both civil law and criminal law possess separate and independent bodies of procedural and substantive law. Procedural law is the body of law which governs how a lawsuit is filed and processed by a court. It specifies such things as which pieces of paper must be filed, when and where they are to be filed, the amount of the filing fee, how the accused is to be notified, and how long the accused has to respond. Substantive law is the body of law which defines what is and is not lawful. Any lawsuit may be won or lost on either procedural grounds or substantive grounds.

Criminal Lawsuits

Consistent with the theory that crimes are offenses against society, not only offenses against individual victims, criminal lawsuits have multiple objectives: punishment, rehabilitation, and deterrence. Punishment as an objective is meant to serve as society's collective judgement that the criminal's conduct was so offensive that a penalty must be imposed. Typical punishments are probation, fines, and incarceration. Rehabilitation is meant to serve both society and the convicted criminal. At least in theory, society benefits from having one more productive member and the convicted criminal benefits from creating a better life. There are two types of deterrence—specific and general. Specific deterrence is best exemplified by the death penalty. When the death penalty is imposed and carried out, that specific individual is permanently deterred from ever again committing a crime. Unfortunately, the death penalty is the only technique which guarantees successful specific deterrence. General deterrence refers to the notion that most

people will be deterred from committing a crime simply because they know it is against the law and/or because they know that if caught they might be punished.

Because crimes are considered to be more serious than civil violations of law, they carry more serious consequences. In states which continue to impose a death penalty, the ultimate sanction of loss of life is possible. Even where the death penalty is not possible, incarceration can be imposed for anything from a few days to life without parole. Incarceration is a serious deprivation of liberty. Given the seriousness of these consequences, the criminal justice system was designed with certain safeguards. One of these safeguards is the presumption of innocence. In criminal lawsuits (but not civil lawsuits), the accused is presumed innocent until proven guilty. There are a multitude of human judgements which must be made before a conviction is won. The police must engage in an investigation. The prosecutor must decide if there is enough evidence to go forward with a case. Both the prosecutor and the defense attorney strategize over how to best present their side of the case. The judge and jury must sort through mountains of evidence. Even when everyone is acting in complete good faith and to the best of their abilities, mistakes are not only possible but sometimes occur. The presumption of innocence offers some measure of protection from honest human error. Based on the theory that it is less onerous to let a guilty person go free than to imprison or put to death someone who is innocent, it is a deliberate decision to tip the scales in favor of the accused.

The criminal justice system has other safeguards built into it. One of these is the burden of proof. The burden of proof refers to how strong and convincing the evidence must be before the defendant can be found guilty of violating the law. In criminal lawsuits, the burden of proof is that of proof beyond a reasonable doubt. Or, to put it more simply, the evidence must be strong enough to convince the judge (in a bench trial) or jury (in a jury trial) to a moral certainty that the defendant committed each and every element of the offense alleged. For example, the traditional definition of burglary has five elements: (1) breaking and entering, (2) into a dwelling house, (3) of another, (4) in the nighttime, and (5) with the intent to commit a felony. For someone to be found guilty of burglary, each element must be proven by proof beyond a reasonable doubt. If the prosecutor can prove all of the elements except the fourth because the crime occurred in broad daylight, the accused is innocent of burglary. Instead, the accused is guilty of a simple breaking and entering which does not require the incident to have occurred after dark. This example also highlights the importance of the decisions a prosecutor makes when deciding what crimes to charge someone with in a particular case.

Another safeguard for criminal defendants is found in the protection afforded under the U.S. Constitution. The Fourth Amendment protects criminal defendants from unreasonable searches and seizures. The Fifth Amendment protects them from double jeopardy and self-incrimination while guaranteeing the right to due process and, in federal cases only, the right to a grand jury before being charged with a capitol offense. The Sixth Amendment guarantees six rights to those accused of crimes. They are the right to: a speedy and public trial, be informed of accusations, confront witnesses, present witnesses, and competent representation by an attorney. Finally, the Eighth Amendment guarantees freedom from excessive bail and from cruel and unusual punishment.

Civil Lawsuits

Civil lawsuits are materially different from criminal law suits. Civil lawsuits are designed for one primary purpose—to compensate individuals for their losses. It is news to some that

lawyers did not invent the fact that civil lawsuits are about money. They were never designed or intended to be about anything else. And because they are primarily designed to be about only money, they do not have the built-in extra protections designed into the criminal justice system. There is no presumption of innocence in civil lawsuits. Which is not to say that there is a presumption of guilt, it is more accurate to say that both parties start from a position of neutrality. Further, because the stakes are less severe than in criminal lawsuits, the constitutional protections previously outlined do not apply. Finally, and again because the cases carry less serious consequences, the burden of proof in civil lawsuits is easier to meet than that of criminal lawsuits. The burden of proof in civil lawsuits is a preponderance of the evidence, which is roughly defined as more likely than not. That is, for a plaintiff (the person who brought the lawsuit) to win a civil lawsuit, the judge or jury must be persuaded that the plaintiff's version of the case (as supported by the evidence) is more likely than not accurate. This is far less stringent than a criminal lawsuit's standard of to a moral certainty.

Civil and Criminal Allegations of the Same Name

One source of confusion concerning the difference between civil and criminal lawsuits is the fact that the same incident can be a violation of each. For example, assault is both a crime and a violation of civil law. The victim of an assault, therefore, may be involved in two separate lawsuits even though both are based on the same incident. Typically, the prosecutor brings the criminal lawsuit and the victim is a witness. Only the victim can bring the civil lawsuit. The criminal lawsuit is intended to, among other things, punish the wrongdoer. The civil lawsuit is intended to compensate the victim for his or her injuries (e.g., medical bills, lost wages, pain and suffering).

Legal Issues Confronting the Hospitality Industry

With this understanding of the nature of law and structure of the U.S. legal system, it is easier to appreciate the legal challenges confronting the hospitality industry. Like their counterparts in other fields, businesses in the hospitality industry must operate within the limitations and requirements of the legal system and applicable law. In fact, given the possible financial cost associated with running afoul of the law, it is fair to say that complying with applicable law is simply another dimension of running a competitive business. Businesses operate in a capitalistic economic system to, among other things, generate a profit. Given that making money is a primary goal, it seems appropriate that money is one of the prices extracted when the law is violated.

Broadly speaking, the legal issues confronting the hospitality industry fall into two categories. One category includes the full range of issues which businesses in virtually any industry might encounter. For example, banking law, antitrust law, franchising law, employment law, and contract law are but a few of the areas of law which cut across industry boundaries. The other category includes those areas of law which have evolved exclusively or primarily in response to issues in the hospitality industry. For example, tip reporting law, liquor liability law, and food sanitation law are more industry specific. The following sections will take a closer look at selected issues confronting the hospitality industry today. The first issue, employment references, illustrates a case against a retired restaurateur. While liability for employment references can arise in any industry, this specific example arose in a hospitality business. The second issue, reservations systems, is more industry specific. While the case illustrated arose against U-Haul, its reservations practices and the problems they encountered are instructive for hotels as well.

Employment References

References are an important part of the job hunting and employee selection process. Nevertheless, it is not uncommon for businesses to decline to give references beyond basic information such as dates of employment, salary or wage level, and job titles held. This is because many businesses are afraid of getting sued for defamation as the result of offering a subjective assessment of someone's performance. Defamation occurs when someone makes false statements about another which injure that person. So, in the context of employment references, if a former employer falsely states that a former employee performed below average and as a result that employee does not get the new job, a defamation lawsuit could result.

While most employment reference cases involve allegations of defamation and negative information, in an unusual twist, a Massachusetts restaurateur is being sued because she gave her former bookkeeper a good reference.[1] The lawsuit is based on the theory of negligent misrepresentation and is being brought by the new employer who relied on the positive reference. The basic facts are as follows. The restaurateur decided to retire and close her restaurant. She notified her employees and gave them general letters of reference. Her bookkeeper applied for another job (as a bookkeeper) with a local contracting company. The bookkeeper used the reference letter and the contracting company confirmed its contents by a phone call to the restaurateur who confirmed the positive recommendation. Subsequently, the bookkeeper was hired by the contracting company where she embezzled in excess of $150,000. While a criminal investiga-

tion against the bookkeeper was underway, she died.

At this point, the contracting company is trying to recoup its losses from the restaurateur. As it turns out, the bookkeeper had embezzled money (approximately $50,000) from the restaurant as well. The basis of the negligent misrepresentation case is that the restaurateur negligently withheld material information. That is, she failed to disclose important information which would have affected the contracting company's hiring decision. While the restaurateur acknowledges she was aware of the embezzlement from her restaurant, she claims she did nothing illegal because she did not learn of the embezzlement until after the phone call confirming the positive recommendation. The contracting company counters with two claims. First, it asserts that she did know of the embezzlement before the phone conversation confirming the glowing recommendation. Second, it argues that even if she didn't, she had a legal responsibility to correct her mistake when she became aware of it (which according to court documents was no more than one month after the phone conversation).

Because this case is pending, its outcome is unknown. Nevertheless, it illustrates the importance of giving accurate information in employment references. Remember, regardless of whether an employment case is based on a theory of defamation or, as in this case, negligent misrepresentation, the heart of the case is that the recommendation contained information that was material and false. Employers should not be afraid to confirm negative information about a former employee as long as it is the truth. However, they must be careful in how they do so.

While focusing her discussion on Arizona law, the advice of employment attorney Jane Eikleberry is instructive for all employers. She offers a list of thirteen (13) guidelines for minimizing the risk of a lawsuit when giving employment references.

1. Limit the information provided to that which concerns job performance, education, training, and experience.

2. Establish a practice of regularly completing written employment evaluations and written reprimands when necessary, which are preserved in the employee's personnel file and can be used to create an employment reference or substantiate the contents of an employment reference, if necessary.

3. Do not repeat gossip about the employee.

4. Do not disclose the employee's living arrangements, marital status or sexual preference.

5. Do not report information concerning the employee's use of illegal drugs or alcohol unless the employee has failed a drug or alcohol test or the employee's use of illegal drugs or alcohol has interfered with the employee's job performance and the effect of the drug or alcohol usage on job performance is truthful and verifiable.

6. Ideally, provide a written reference and comply with the statute [this is a requirement of Arizona law] by mailing a copy to the employee at his or her last known mailing address.

7. Do not label the employee as a "troublemaker" or as a "claimsmaker" because he or she has filed a claim, such as a charge of discrimination, a worker's compensation claim, or has reported illegal activity on the part of the employer to an appropriate recipient of such information.

8. Do not provide information which cannot lawfully be used by the prospective employer in making a hiring decision, such as details regarding the employee's health, or identification of the employee's race, color, religion, or national origin.

---

[1] *Willard and Duffy v. August and Jack August's, Inc.*, Hampshire Superior Court Dept. Civil Action No. 96-168 (Massachusetts).

9. Crimes unrelated to the employee's job performance, education, training, experience, and qualifications should not be reported, but information relating to crimes or other matters which is clearly material to a hiring decision should be disclosed to a potential successor employer to avoid a suit being filed by the successor employer for misrepresentation.

10. Do not speculate about the causes for poor job performance or a high rate of absenteeism: for example, if it is suspected, but not verified, that drug or alcohol problems, emotional instability, or a disability may be the cause of the poor performance or absenteeism rate, only report the verifiable facts and avoid speculation as to the cause.

11. Do not give "off the record" references.

12. If possible, refer all reference requests to one person who examines the employee's personnel file and discusses the reference to be provided with those knowledgeable about the employee's job performance.

13. Finally, and obviously, never communicate information which is known to be false.[2]

Reservations Systems

Many types of businesses use reservations systems. Airlines, hotels, car rental companies, and rental centers utilize such systems not only to track reservations and the availability of services and products, but also to maximize revenue by overbooking. Unlike traditional retail establishments where inventory not sold today can be sold tomorrow, airline seats, hotel rooms, rental cars, and other rental products not rented today rep-

Photo courtesy Thomas A. Kelly/© Corbis.

The hotel room not sold today can't be sold twice tomorrow to recoup lost revenue.

resent revenue that is lost forever. The hotel room not sold today can't be sold twice tomorrow thereby recouping lost revenue. A car not rented today can't be rented twice tomorrow thereby recouping lost revenue. Consequently, businesses which sell such services often engage in a practice known as overbooking. That is, they accept more reservations than they have services available. For example, one-hundred (100) room hotel may make one hundred and five (105) reservations for the same night. This protects the hotel from lost revenue as a result of cancellations and no-shows (customers who don't show up and often do not bother to cancel). If the hotel's projections are correct, five (5) customers either cancel or are no-shows. The one hundred (100) guests who do arrive are accommodated, the hotel is at a 100% occupancy rate which maximizes revenue and everyone is happy.

Unfortunately, it doesn't always work that neatly. Sometimes the hotel overbooks by too high a margin and then cannot accommodate all the guests who have reservations. As a result, the hotel ends up "walking" some guests, usually by locating accommodations at another hotel. Despite the folklore of the hotel indus-

try which perpetuates the myth that because airlines can overbook and bump passengers, hotels can overbook and walk guests, the law has long held that "walked" guests have suffered a breach of contract.[3] Airline overbooking is regulated by federal regulations which permit the bumping of passengers on overbooked flights. However, the regulations further require the airlines to inform passengers of this through a disclosure on tickets and to offer specific types of compensation to bumped passengers.[4] Apparently, the myth assumes that the same laws apply to hotels. They do not. Hotels are regulated by the laws of the individual states in which they operate. Consequently, whether it is legal to walk hotel guests who have reservations is a function of state law.

A recent Consent Judgment entered into by the Massachusetts At-

[2]Eikleberry, Jane L., Job References: A Legal and Management Paradox, *Arizona Attorney*, October 1995, 41.

[3]*Dold v. Outrigger Hotel*, 501 P.2d 368 (Haw, 1972) and *Odysseys Unlimited, Inc. v. Astral Travel Service*, 354 N.Y.S.2d 88 (Sup. Ct. N.Y. 1974).

[4]Enghagen, Linda K. and Wilson, Robert, Challenging Conventional Wisdom: A Different Look at Selling Rooms, *Hospitality & Tourism Educator*, Vol. 7, No. 1, Winter 1995, 18–19.

torney General and U-Haul International, Inc. only reinforces the legal risk associated with certain reservations systems' practices.[5] The portion of the Consent Judgment relevant to hotel reservations systems relates to U-Haul's claims regarding what were allegedly "Guaranteed Reservations." U-Haul advertising offered "Guaranteed Reservations" for customers reserving trucks and vans. A reservation could be "guaranteed" by the customer paying a deposit when the reservation was made.

As substantiated by numerous customer affidavits filed with the complaint, many customers who paid the deposit to secure a "Guaranteed Reservation" did not receive a rental vehicle when they arrived at the agreed on date and time. One of these dissatisfied customers filed a complaint with the Consumer Protection Division of the Massachusetts Attorney General's Office. Following its investigation, the Attorney General's Office filed suit against U-Haul. Among other things, the complaint took issue with characterizing a reservation as "Guaranteed" and then not delivering the equipment as agreed. The complaint claimed that this constituted an Unfair or Deceptive Act or Practice under Massachusetts's consumer protection law.

In the end, U-Haul entered into a Consent Judgement with Massachusetts which permanently prohibits it from "Making any representation, directly or indirectly, that any reservation of trucks, trailers, vans or other equipment is guaranteed. . . ."[6]

There are distinct parallels between U-Haul's reservations practices and what is often done in hotel reservations systems. When making a hotel reservation, a guest is typically asked if he or she would like to "guarantee" the reservation with a credit card. Typically, the hotel's over-

booking practices are not disclosed and guests are sometimes walked even though they had a reservation that was allegedly "guaranteed." Given these parallels, it is clear that hotels who walk guests with "Guaranteed Reservations" need to be concerned with whether that practice violates applicable consumer protection laws.

Both the prior case law and the U-Haul Consent Judgment highlight the importance of making sure reservations practices comply with contract law and consumer protection law. There are a number of strategies a hotel might employ to minimize the possibility of liability in this area.

1. Advertisements and reservation confirmations should state that the hotel management sometimes overbooks with the result that a guest is walked. Further, the policy of hotel management relative to providing alternative accommodations and other benefits should be disclosed.

2. Hotels should develop and post a policy (similar to that of airlines) informing guests [of] what they will receive in the event of a denial of a reservation and what their obligations are in the event of late cancellations or no-shows.

3. Hotel guests should be educated concerning the cost and inconvenience to the hotel caused by guests who cancel late or simply don't show. Over time, this should be effective in motivating . . . some guests to change their behavior.

4. Hotel management should create and publicize policies which will reduce or eliminate most no-shows. In addition to education, contractual claims can be enforced against no-shows. Guests could be charged via credit card at the time the reservation is made. When guests know that a hotel enforces its policy of requiring guests to pay for reserved rooms, the number of no-shows will drop.

5. Hotels should try to eliminate the overbooking which results in the walking of guests. They should become more accurate and more conservative in predicting the number of no-shows.[7]

Ethical Issues Confronting the Hospitality Industry

Ethical issues confronting the hospitality industry are like legal issues confronting the industry in that some are industry specific and others cut across industry lines, that is, they can affect businesses of any type. At its core, ethics is about decision making that in some way goes to issues of right and wrong. Many decisions (perhaps most) have nothing to do with ethics—they are morally neutral. The routine tasks of daily life require constant decision making—what to eat for lunch, which route to take to school or work; nevertheless, these decisions typically are not of any moral significance. Similarly, many routine business decisions have no moral significance. Such decisions as which vendors to use and where to advertise typically do not involve questions of ethics. However, there are a multitude of personal and business decisions that do involve questions of ethics.

Students' Perceptions of Hospitality Industry Issues

In 1992, students from six different hospitality and tourism programs were surveyed and asked to identify the most important ethical issues confronting the hospitality and tourism industry.[8] Most of the issues identified

[5]*Commonwealth v. U-Haul International, Inc., et al*, Suffolk Superior Court Dept. Civil Action No. 97-2441-E (Massachusetts).

[6]Ibid.

[7]Wilson, Robert H., Enghagen, Linda K. and Sharma, Prashant, Overbooking: The Practice and the Law, *Hospitality Research Journal*, Vol. 17, No. 2, 1994, 103.

[8]Enghagen, Linda K. and Hott, David D., Students' Perceptions of Ethical Issues in the Hospitality and Tourism Industry, *Hospitality Research Journal*, Vol. 15, No. 2, 41–50.

by the students cut across industry lines while only two are specific to the hospitality industry. In the ranking of issues, eleven were identified with two tied at the eighth rank.

- ❖ Solid waste disposal
- ❖ Conditions of employment
- ❖ Nonspecific discrimination
- ❖ Race discrimination
- ❖ Employee theft
- ❖ Sex discrimination
- ❖ False advertising
- ❖ Sexual harassment
- ❖ Vendor honesty
- ❖ Sanitation violations
- ❖ AIDS discrimination
- ❖ AIDS in foodservice[9]

Three of these issues involve questions of honesty: employee theft, false advertising, and vendor honesty. Five involve questions of fundamental fairness: conditions of employment, nonspecific discrimination, race discrimination, sex discrimination, sexual harassment, and AIDS discrimination. The remaining issues are more safety oriented in focus: solid waste disposal, sanitation violations, and AIDS in foodservice.

Questions of honesty, fundamental fairness, and safety all raise ethical concerns. Being dishonest with others prevents them from making informed and accurate decisions. Treating others in an unfair manner denies them a fair opportunity. Unsafe practices put people at risk. Consequently, it is not surprising that the students surveyed raised these types of concerns.

A Formal Definition of Ethics

It is one thing to ask people to identify ethical issues; it is another matter to define ethics. As discussed earlier, it has something to do with decision

making that goes to issues of right and wrong. Beyond that, while there are common themes involving the distinction between right and wrong, its meaning is dependent on context. For example, to a philosopher, ethics is the study of moral reasoning. To an individual who is a member of a profession (such as a doctor, lawyer, or accountant), ethics is the rules of good conduct in that field.

Outside of such specialized contexts, ethics can be defined in a somewhat different manner. One such definition is advanced by ethicist Michael Josephson: "Ethics refers to standards of **conduct**, standards that indicate how one *should* behave based on moral duties and virtues, which themselves are derived from principles of right and wrong" (emphasis in original).[10]

Making Ethical Decisions

If ethics is about standards of conduct, the next logical question becomes whose standards? There are many models of ethical standards. Josephson's standards and decision making model will be illustrated here. Josephson begins by identifying what he calls "Six Pillars of Character" or core ethical values: trustworthiness, respect, responsibility, fairness, caring, and citizenship.[11] In Josephson's decision making model, these core values become the guiding principles for differentiating right conduct from wrong conduct. When differentiating right from wrong is not readily apparent, Josephson's decision making model, sometimes known as Golden Kantian Consequentialism, offers a systematic way to approach the problem.

Golden Kantian Consequentialism

1. *All decisions must take into account and reflect a concern for the interests and well being of all stakeholders.*

2. *Ethical values and principles always take precedence over non-ethical ones.*

3. *It is ethically proper to violate an ethical principle only when it is clearly necessary to advance another true ethical principle which, according to the decision maker's conscience, will produce the greatest balance of good in the long run (emphasis in the original).*[12]

Josephson's core values and decision making model offer one approach to ethical decision making which can be utilized in both personal and business endeavors. For example, in the previously cited survey, students identified vendor honesty as one of the most important ethical issues confronting the hospitality industry. Under normal circumstances, the selection of a vendor is a morally neutral event. However, when a vendor is known to conduct business in a dishonest manner, then vendor selection takes on an ethical dimension. If the vendor's dishonesty is unrelated to your business dealings with the vendor, it is tempting to take the "not my problem" approach to the decision. Consider, however, how this could be analyzed under Josephson's approach. Even if it does not adversely affect you, in a very direct way, knowingly doing business with a dishonest vendor does not support the core value of trustworthiness. And, while more remote, doing so may put other stakeholders at risk. Perhaps another company, unaware of the vendor's dishonesty, is aware of your doing business with the vendor and takes that as an endorsement of the vendor's business practices. This is not to suggest that you necessarily have an obligation to go public with your knowledge. It is simply to suggest that the decision to do business with such vendors can lead to, on some level, an endorsement of that company and its business

[9]Ibid., 46.

[10]Josephson, Michael, *Making Ethical Decisions*, Josephson Institute: Marina del Rey, 1995, 2.

[11]Ibid., 8–17.

[12]Ibid., 26–27.

practices. Under Josephson's model, the ethical decision is to decline to do business with dishonest vendors. Other stakeholders may be adversely affected. The core ethical value of trustworthiness takes precedence over other considerations that are not of ethical significance.

Conclusion

Like all businesses of any industry, the hospitality industry must be aware of and endeavor to comply with applicable law. For those who take seriously the notion that ethics is a concern in business, the practice of ethics must be undertaken as well. Compliance with the law only is not enough because law is the beginning, not the end, of moral discussion.

Questions and Assignments

1. Discuss the relationship between law-abiding behavior and ethical behavior. To what degree is a person complying with the law an ethical person? Use examples from hospitality to highlight your discussion.

2. Establish and discuss four concepts of the nature of law.

3. Discuss the legal definitions of truth and fairness.

4. Establish and define the five sources (origins) of U.S. laws.

5. Using your library resources or the web browser and search engine of your choice, identify an administrative regulation, statute, or common law that has a bearing upon hospitality. Summarize the key points.

6. Establish the hierarchy of the federal court system.

7. Distinguish between a criminal lawsuit and a civil lawsuit. What are the key presumptions and differences?

8. How is it that the same matter may be considered in a criminal suit as well as a civil suit?

9. What legal concerns/considerations are relevant for a hospitality manager in terms of employment references? Using your library resources or the web browser of your choice, identify an article that can be used to demonstrate a key issue you have reviewed.

10. Why should hospitality professionals be concerned about hospitality reservation systems from a legal perspective? Using your library resources or the web browser of your choice, identify an article that can be used to demonstrate a key issue you have reviewed.

11. Using your library resources or the web browser of your choice, identify a current legal issue or case that is currently relevant to hospitality. Summarize your finding.

12. Define ethical behavior.

13. Using your library resources or the web browser and search engine of your choice, search for an article or other information on "Golden Kantian Consequentialism." Summarize your findings and be prepared to discuss your findings with your team or classmates.

14. Consider the list of eleven ethical issues that are listed in the chapter. Can you think of additional concerns? Have you observed any unethical, or for that matter highly ethical, behaviors in your hospitality experience. Be prepared to discuss these with your team or classmates.

Bibliography and Suggested Readings

Gerlin, A. (1994). How a jury decided that a coffee spill is worth $2.9 million. *The Wall Street Journal*, September 1, A1.

Hansen, M. (1998). Suing bosses over beliefs: Bill proposed to accommodate workers' religious tenets. *America Bar Association Journal*, April 1998, 30.

Lindberg, K. & Hawkins, D. E. (1993). *Ecotourism: A Guide for Planners & Managers*. Bennington, VT: The Ecotourism Society.

Miller, L. (1997). When vacations go wrong, more travelers sue. *The Wall Street Journal*, May 2, B1.

Press, A. (1995). Justice: Are lawyers burning America? *Newsweek*, 125(12), 32–35.

Perspectives on Restaurants and Other Commercial Food and Beverage Establishments

Clayton W. Barrows, Ed.D., *Department of Hotel, Restaurant, &*
Tourism Administration, UNIVERSITY OF NEW ORLEANS

ABSTRACT

This chapter describes several segments within the commercial foodservice industry with an emphasis upon those segments that are currently experiencing higher than average growth. Opportunities for hospitality graduates are discussed and recommendations are made for students wishing to enter the various segments. The chapter also looks at some of the current trends that are occurring within the foodservice industry and affecting those same segments including brewpubs, coffeehouses, and catering.

OBJECTIVES

At the end of this chapter the student should be able to:

1. Describe and distinguish between the various commercial food and beverage segments of the hospitality industry.

2. Establish and discuss reasons for growth and decline in the various commercial food and beverage segments.

3. List and describe leading companies within each of the commercial food and beverage segments.

4. Discuss various trends that are impacting commercial food and beverage establishments.

Introduction

This is an exciting time in the commercial foodservice industry. The industry is currently undergoing some major changes and continues to experience significant growth as previously highlighted by numerous authors and industry analysts. According to the National Restaurant Association, the industry, as a whole, is expected to generate more than $336 billion in 1998—numbers befitting a sizable industry by any standard! The commercial foodservice segment has always maintained the lion's share of total industry performance. Of the projected total, the commercial foodservice segment represents approximately 90 percent. The remaining segments, institutional foodservice and military foodservice, generate the difference. The commercial sector is clearly driving the industry.

What are some of the factors that are causing the industry, and particularly certain segments of it, to grow at such a rate? The simple answer is that sales continue to grow as a result of not one but many factors. Lifestyle changes, the public's increasing reliance upon all services, and general increases in consumers' propensity to eat out are just a few of the factors driving growth. Others factors include what is generally perceived to be a healthy economy (which in turn drives consumer confidence), and that foodservice establishments are continuing to offer an array of new products and services to their customers.

Some segments, as mentioned earlier, are growing at a faster rate than the industry as a whole. This means, however, that similarly, a few segments are performing at levels below the average. A few of the more visible commercial segments are explored further in this the chapter.

Fine Dining Restaurants

Much of the glamour and prestige associated with the restaurant industry can be attributed to the successes of the fine dining segment over the decades. White tablecloths, elegant surroundings, refined service, and high check averages often characterize fine dining restaurants. Fine dining restaurants are also an important part of our culture. Many people remember, with some vividness, a meal in a fine dining restaurant that they might have had to commemorate a special occasion or celebration. Such memories can be long lasting.

U.S. cities such as New York (*Four Seasons* and *Lutece*), Chicago (*Charlie Trotter's*), and New Orleans (*Commander's Palace* and *Emeril's*) are well known for their high profile fine dining restaurants. Indeed, some cities, such as those mentioned above, are synonymous with their restaurants. Annually, there are awards for restaurants, that provide the best food, the most outstanding service, have the finest wine list, etc. These awards can be very effective in increasing the visibility of individual restaurants and the segment as a whole. To take this one step further and to further differentiate this segment from others, many fine dining restaurants almost become destinations in themselves. In fact, it is not uncommon for a traveler to a particular city to make advance reservations at one or more well known restaurants—sometimes before those same individuals even make hotel or plane reservations!

One of the important qualities of the restaurants within this segment is that there is usually a single dynamic individual behind the restaurant—individuals otherwise known as entrepreneurs. The fine dining segment, and independent restaurants in general, have always been receptive to these types of individuals. Wolfgang Puck, Paul Prudhomme, and Emeril Lagasse are just a few such individuals who have made their reputations in the fine dining arena. Fine dining restaurants can be characterized as being a very heterogeneous mix of restaurants, which is one of the reasons it is such an appealing segment—to employees, owners, and customers alike.

While fine dining restaurants have historically been owned and operated by individuals or families as independent units, this is changing somewhat in these times of chain domination. Chains have been built around successful independents. This is particularly true with steak restaurants such as *Ruth's Chris Steak House* and *Morton's of Chicago*. Other examples of a different variety would have to include the *Peasant Restaurants* in Atlanta and the *Brennan Family of Restaurants* in New Orleans and Houston.

What was once the darling of the foodservice industry, however, is now suffering through some difficult times. While fine dining restaurants will always have their place for special occasions, business entertainment, or a special night out, a number of factors have contributed to their difficulties. Changes in tax laws (which now allow a lower amount to be deducted for business entertainment purposes), a greater desire for value, competition from other segments, and a general shift toward more casual and relaxed eating environments have all had their affect. Fine dining seems to be losing its appeal to the average consumer as evidenced by the number of high profile closings in recent years. Restaurants that were booked for weeks in advance in the 1980s have since been shuttered. Others, having reacted more effectively to changes in the market, actually opened more casual versions of their restaurants downstairs, next door, or across the street in an effort to retain their valued customers. As we shall see in the sections to come, customers now have many other dining options (more than ever before) where they can spend less money in a more casual atmosphere.

Casual Dining Restaurants

Where it was once the dream of many students to work for one of the high profile fine dining restaurants discussed in the previous section, many students are now choosing to go to work for one of the many casual dining chains upon graduation. Hospitality graduates, as well as customers, now seem to be attracted to all things casual. While fine dining may offer more glamour, quick service may offer more profits and casual dining restaurants seem to have found a permanent niche in the industry. A segment that was once limited to the likes of *TGI Friday's* has come a long way in the last quarter century and especially during the last decade. Many casual dining restaurants are able to combine all of those facets that customers seem to be looking for in a dining experience into one concise package: food, service, ambience (and in many cases, entertainment). Certain chains, such as *Houston's*, are able to offer the right combination of quality product and efficient service in building a strong customer base. Others, such as *Planet Hollywood*, have concepts that were developed around unique themes including the movie industry, rock and roll, etc. Others may even cut across segments, so to speak, such as *Rock Bottom* with its on-premise breweries (brewery or restaurant?), *Hard Rock Cafe* with its merchandise (retail store or restaurant?), and *Dave & Buster's* with its recreation theme (adult game room or restaurant?). When a business is able to derive over 50 percent of its revenues from some area other than food and beverage (as some of the aforementioned do) the restaurant portion becomes ancillary.

Some of the major factors that characterize the casual dining segment include:

❖ chain affiliation (and resulting brand recognition)
❖ an attention to detail
❖ a systems orientation
❖ strong management teams
❖ expanding markets

Some of the more recognizable chains include *Chili's Grill and Bar*, *TGI Friday's*, *Applebee's Neighborhood Grill and Bar*, *Bennigan's*, and *Ruby Tuesday*. There are dozens of others,

The Hard Rock Café offers a lot of merchandise to go with its food.

and as a segment they are becoming even more visible as a result of their on-campus recruiting efforts. These companies have definitely identified the hospitality graduate as a viable management candidate.

From a customer's perspective, when one considers all of the different alternatives available in the casual segment, it is not surprising that the segment continues to grow at a double-digit rate. The segment is proving to consumers that they don't have to pay top dollar for a menu that has variety and for a full service restaurant experience. From an operational perspective, this segment is able to achieve high volume without missing a beat. Where an annual sales figure of $2 million per restaurants was once the benchmark, the ante has been raised with some chains grossing upwards of $10 million per unit!

Obviously with those kinds of numbers, also comes a lot of hard work and stamina. On the other hand, the successful chains within this segment provide superior training and compensate their managers accordingly. In short, there are ample opportunities right now for hospital-

ity graduates, and the situation is not likely to change anytime soon.

Coffeehouses

A very different type of operation than the full service types of restaurants discussed earlier is the newly rediscovered coffeehouse. There has literally been an explosion of new operations across the country, and the segment continues to grow. While coffeehouses (and coffee shops and coffee bars) have been around for a very long time, originating in Europe, they are now experiencing a renaissance of sorts in this country. Independent coffeehouses have always had a presence in this country, but they were not taken very seriously by the industry until chains embraced them. Now the name *Starbucks* is well known, as are some of the other more prominent chains including *Gloria Jean's*, *The Coffee Beanery*, and *Barnies*. There are also many regional chains around the country such as *P.J.'s* and *CC's* in the New Orleans area. Now when people think of coffee, they undoubtedly think of one of the larger chain operations, whereas this was not the case only a few years ago. Indeed, chains *and* independents alike seem to be everywhere, bringing a new meaning to the word "saturation." Coffee is so popular that one would be tempted to suggest that total market saturation will never occur. To an extent, though, saturation already has occurred with some chains already exploring non-traditional sites, such as institutional foodservice settings, hotel foodservice, and even airlines (*Starbucks* coffee being available on United Airlines). This simply mirrors the same trend that occurred several years ago in the quick service segment.

Again, the success of the coffee segment cannot be attributed to any single factor but rather to several. One factor does stand out, however—as our lives become more and more hectic, people tend to look for things that provide a respite. Coffeehouses provide this and more. For many, they

Chains have exploded across the country and their popularity continues to grow.

are a home away from home—a place where they can go and see some familiar faces. In this sense, coffeehouses help us to meet our basic social needs. The newly conceptualized coffeehouse no longer just appeals to bohemians and college students. A visit to a local coffeehouse will reveal an interesting cross section of Americana with patrons varying greatly in all respects. Coffeehouses serve a whole host of needs but much of it comes right back to those basic social needs—which is, and has always been, one of the primary reasons people choose to dine out.

Coffee has always been the beverage of choice for Americans, but coffeehouses have brought the beverage to the forefront. *Starbucks*, et al. are capitalizing on consumers' renewed interest in beverages (some might say fascination) and decreased interest in beverages of the alcoholic variety. It is the universal beverage that has simply been repackaged and, in doing so, has found a new niche. It also provides new opportunities for hospitality graduates. *Starbucks*, a company that has received a lot of attention recently for their employee programs, is recruiting aggressively and even has a web site for employment opportunities. Other companies are sure to follow suit as the segment continues to grow.

Cafeterias

Just a few years ago, students living outside of the Sunbelt may not have been familiar with commercial cafeterias. The down-home format, which was actually developed in the West (and popularized in the Northeast) in the latter part of the 19th century became a fixture in the southern region of the U.S. Companies such as *Luby's* and *Piccadilly* dominated (along with some smaller regional chains) and consumers who grew up going to cafeterias continued to do so as adults. Traditional cafeterias were long characterized by their extensive service lines from which customers could choose from as many as 100 items— many of which changed on a daily basis. Customers would select the food they desired, receive the food of their choice, and collect it on their trays as they proceeded down the line. Food was usually well prepared and fresh, having been prepared in relatively small batches, but it was seldom dazzling. The physicality of individual units rarely deviated from the standard corporate model—most units were based on a prototype. There was never any element of the dining experience that would detract from the food. The food was the center of attention and it was meant to be that way.

Until recently, this panorama could have fairly represented most cafeterias, national or regional in scope. Now, however, this segment is one of the fastest changing segments in the entire foodservice industry. This is a direct result of the segment, which is just now coming out of a financially difficult period, attempting to "get in line" with the times. Until recently, few of the major chains did any advertising to speak of and, as a result, continued to serve the same type of customers they had always served over the years.

Change is coming quickly to the segment, however. Some of the changes that have been made, in addition to media advertising, include:

- ❖ contemporizing their menus
- ❖ adding take-out service
- ❖ offering self serve buffets
- ❖ extending meal periods
- ❖ scaling down their units
- ❖ refurbishing their restaurants

In short, the entire segment (and concept) is being invigorated. One of the more successful changes has been in their attempt to capitalize upon the trend towards Home Meal Replacement (HMR) as chains such as *Boston Market* have done. Cafeterias have accomplished this through offering prepared meals for take-out in their traditional restaurants, offering "take and bake" items, and opening scaled down versions of their traditional restaurants in strategic locations such as what *Piccadilly* has done in partnering with several supermarkets. All of these strategies have allowed a well-established concept to become more in tune with the foodservice needs in the 1990s. In summary, these changes are proving to be beneficial to the industry, financially and otherwise. For example, four cafeteria chains recently appeared within the top 100 grossing chains in the Restaurants and Institutions 400: *Old Country Buffet, Luby's, Piccadilly* and *Morrison's Fresh Cooking* (*Restaurants and Institutions*, 1997). It should be noted that in 1998, *Piccadilly* purchased *Morrison's*.

Cafeterias are probably most similar to the family restaurant segment (e.g., *Cracker Barrel*, *Denny's*), with their relatively low check averages and variety offered. In a recent study published by *Consumer Reports* (1996), however, the segment fared quite well when compared to the family restaurant segment. The key for these chains in the future will be for them to maintain their identity (and reputation for value) without being cannibalized by other segments. The future looks bright for this segment though. As chains, several of the larger companies are able to offer extensive training programs to new managers and competitive salaries—two factors that should be of interest to students. A recent study indicated that, among other things, cafeteria companies try to identify potential managers who have strong food production skills (Barrows, 1994). For students who are interested in the "food" side of the business, the cafeteria segment offers some very good opportunities.

Quick Service

A segment that is quite different, and certainly more familiar than cafeterias, is the quick service restaurant segment (QSR). No longer known as fast food, the quick service segment of the industry has also gone through some changes of late. After many years of unprecedented growth owing to continued growth of the already large chains as well as new chains entering the market, saturated markets became the norm rather than the exception. Quick service companies developed their own strategies for managing market saturation and now the entry of quick service operations into nontraditional sites (such as universities and businesses) is old news. What is of some significance, however, is that the segment continues to grow, albeit more slowly (at about 2 percent per annum, real growth). Part of this growth is due to a reemphasis

upon the domestic market (in conjunction with international markets). Also, the big just keep getting bigger. There seems to be no slowing down of the biggest quick service chains. The top three companies (*McDonalds*, *Burger King* and *KFC*) all increased their sales a minimum of 5 percent between 1995 and 1996. In addition, some of the fastest growing foodservice companies are in the quick service segment. In fact, five out of the top ten fastest growing chains in the Restaurants and Institutions 400 are quick service chains.

With everything that is happening in this segment, it is somewhat ironic that it is often overlooked by students when it comes to making career decisions. For whatever reason, quick service seems to lack the glamour that many college students are looking for. On the other hand, the quick service industry is often on the cutting edge when it comes to several critical areas including:

❖ human resource management
❖ employee development
❖ research and development
❖ technology usage
❖ marketing

Photo courtesy Nik Wheeler/Corbis.

There seems to be no slowing down of the biggest quick service chains.

For these reasons alone, the quick service industry is deserving of consideration. In addition, several companies offer comprehensive management training programs that help to better prepare new entrants into the field. One example of a company with a strong training program is *Popeye's* (a division of America's Favorite Chicken in Atlanta). Their management-training program is a nine-week program, which combines on-the-job and classroom training. Further, once the initial training has been completed, *Popeye's* provides their managers with extensive professional development opportunities. Companies such as *Popeye's* recognize the importance of training and development and the positive influence that it has on the entire company. *Popeye's* is not alone in this regard, either, as the entire segment has a reputation for its strong training of managers.

"Fast food" restaurants have become entrenched in our society and are playing an ever-important role in the lives of Americans. Restaurants in this category, just like the others discussed, are in need of talented managers willing to commit themselves to the industry. At this point in time, this segment continues to drive the entire commercial foodservice industry, and that is not going to change anytime soon. As our lives become even busier, the need for quick service will only increase as will the need for both employees and managers.

Vending

Another one of the foodservice segments that is often overlooked by hospitality students is vending. It is an intriguing segment, however, because it combines operational characteristics of both foodservice and traditional retailing. The vending segment is larger than many people realize. According to the International Foodservice Manufacturers Association (1995) vending accounted for over 6 percent of all foodservice sales in 1994. Vending is, and has been for a long time, an integral part of the foodservice industry. Many foodservice management companies were started originally as vending companies (e.g., *ARAMARK*). Others started in foodservice management and branched out into vending. To this day, it can be hard to separate foodservice management from vending as many of the larger companies do both.

Vending is very much like other forms of foodservice in that many of the same activities must take place—production, distribution, sales, etc. As mentioned earlier, several of the national foodservice management companies have vending divisions, but there are also smaller, regional companies that specialize in vending. These companies, whether national or regional, typically enter into an agreement with a host institution (such as a business, hospital, or university) to provide vending services. These services can run the gamut from simple snacks and drinks to a variety of both hot and cold entrees. Sometimes the same company that provides foodservice for the host institution will provide vending services as well. Other times, different companies will handle the different responsibilities.

Both the variety and quality of products has improved dramatically in recent years. One reason for this is that the technology behind the machines has become more sophisticated. One example where major improvements is quite visible is with coffee. Machines are now available which can grind coffee beans to order, and then prepare them in any number of ways including espresso, cappuccino, and lattes. Improvements have not just been limited to beverages, either. Technology also has helped develop machines which can fry french fries upon order and also serve individual pizzas. Such innovations have changed the face of the industry as well as the public's perception.

While this segment of the market may not offer the same range of career choices and growth opportunities that other segments might be able to. However, it is an area that students should know about, particularly if they are thinking of working for an on-site foodservice management company.

Lodging Foodservice

Perhaps no other area of the foodservice industry is as multifarious or as fragmented as the lodging segment. In no other area is there as much variety and as many challenges as are faced by foodservice operations in lodging facilities. Foodservice and lodging have long gone hand in hand and for many years general managers of hotels were well-schooled in food and beverage. In most cases, general managers came up through their respective companies having had extensive food and beverage experience. As a result, hotels took their food and beverage programs very seriously even though they were generally not very profitable and even lost money in some cases. The prevailing belief in the full service lodging industry was that if you ran a hotel, you were also in the foodservice business. Further, the belief was such that a hotel should have as many restaurant outlets as it could support, which contributed to the tiered structure that became so common (e.g., a choice of upscale, midscale, and budget dining). Then there are always banquets and catering, room service, and lounges, which also fell under the purview of the food and beverage department. All in all, lodging foodservice operations tended to require a lot of time and energy on the part of hotel executives—without the financial benefits that most would have liked.

As with the foodservice industry in general, many changes have taken place in this segment, particularly over the last few years. The lodging foodservice market experienced one of the lowest growth rates of any commercial segment in 1997, at .6 percent (*Restaurants USA*, 1996). Many hotel food and beverage programs are now expected to stand on their own merits. As a result, many full service hotels no longer offer such an array of dining choices. Some do, and in fact some hotels, such as *Four Seasons* and the *Ritz-Carlton* hotel chains have very fine reputations for their foodservice. Others such as *Holiday Inn*, *Sheraton*, *Hilton* and *Marriott* have substantial investments in food and beverage and are among the leading foodservice providers in the foodservice industry. But changes are occurring at every level of the lodging industry. In many cases, companies are exploring alternative arrangements in running their food and beverage departments. These changes range from some hotel companies simply outsourcing certain food products (e.g., baked goods) to others which have completely turned their foodservice operations over to outside contractors. And some hotels have eliminated their foodservice entirely. Almost every major hotel company has scrutinized their food and beverage programs in recent years and made subsequent changes.

Changes have been particularly evident in the budget and economy segments where more and more hotels are not providing any foodservice at all, but rather locating their properties next to full service restaurants such as *Denny's*. This relieves the hotel company of the responsibility of providing foodservice while remaining confident that foodservice is readily accessible to guests. Other companies have outsourced their foodservice operations much in the way that institutions have been contracting their foodservice out for years. For instance, in New Orleans, which is well known for its restaurants, several boutique hotels have leased space to local restaurant operators, including the *Brennan's* whose family operates two hotel restaurants. Also, some of the local hotels in the mid-scale segment, such as *Holiday Inn*, have brought in restaurants that fit well with their concepts, such as *TGI Friday's*. Such arrangements seem to work well for both parties. Furthermore, because of the direction that lodging foodservice has taken in recent years, there are now companies, such as *HSC Hospitality*, which is based in Dallas, which specializes in managing lodging foodservice operations. Companies such as HSC will contract with a hotel to manage their entire foodservice operation, including room service and banquets.

Finally, there are unique arrangements that can be likened to the branding trend that is occurring in on-site foodservice where hotels have partnered with foodservice operators, both on a local and national basis, to varying degrees. These types of arrangements would include those established between *UNO Foods* (*Pizzeria UNO*) and *Doubletree Hotels*; *Starbucks* and *Sheraton*; and *Embassy Suites* and *Bennigan's*.

Needless to say, lodging foodservice in no way resembles what it did even ten years ago. Hotel executives have recognized that they can now turn their foodservice operations over to reputable operators, cut down on the high costs associated with running such departments, and make a profit to boot. Such arrangements have worked out well for hotels and foodservice operators alike. As a result of these changes, some of the opportunities for students in hotel food and beverage are not what they once were. On the other hand, new opportunities have arisen as more foodservice companies have begun to target hotels and are developing a niche for themselves.

Private Clubs

Private clubs are a fascinating segment of the hospitality industry. They are to be found in many communities around the country and the world. Clubs are able to offer their members a unique blend of products and services in whatever combination that they might desire. In a sense, many clubs are similar to resorts whose services are limited to members only. Often, the mix of services includes some combination of recreation (golf,

tennis, etc.) and foodservice. In fact, foodservice is an integral component of most private clubs. It can play an important role in attracting new members and in retaining current members.

Food and beverage operations in clubs are unique in the sense that no two are exactly alike. One club may have a simple snack bar while another may have an extensive foodservice operation with multiple outlets. It is going to vary depending upon the type of club (country, city, yacht, etc.), size, and makeup of its membership. Unlike traditional restaurants, they also tend to combine several different foodservice dimensions in one operation. This is especially true in country clubs, which may have as many as three or four different dining rooms, banquets and catering services, snack bars, lounges, and mobile cart service. Given the complexity of foodservice operations in clubs, there is a definite need for qualified individuals to manage these varied outlets. In fact, foodservice plays such an important role in clubs that a recent study indicated that over 80 percent of general managers had a background in food and beverage. The next closest area was a hotel background (17%) (*Operations and Financial Data Survey*, 1996).

Because of the importance of food and beverage operations in clubs, a good avenue for students wishing to enter the field is through food and beverage. Even students who have not worked in a club, but who have extensive food and beverage experience, could become management candidates at some clubs. Another way to learn more about the area is to consider joining a student chapter of the Club Managers Association of America. There are numerous chapters on college campuses around the country and most managers consider it an asset when evaluating a student who is involved with a CMAA chapter.

As with many segments of the foodservice industry, the basics of foodservice management are also

present in clubs. But the pleasure of dealing with a repeat clientele (the members) and the different type of working environment are two of the factors that make club food and beverage different. Graduates who appreciate those two factors about the club industry are likely to find the private club industry a fulfilling career.

Banquets and Catering

The banquet and catering business has always been unique unto itself. First, it has never been a clearly defined segment since many different types of operations provide catering services including many fine dining restaurants, casual dining restaurants, hotels, private clubs, foodservice management companies, and the list goes on. As one can readily determine, it can be a confusing segment to study. This section will describe some of the simpler characteristics of the segment.

The banquet and catering segment (or "social catering" as it is commonly referred to) as a whole is growing at a rate of just over 2 percent (real growth) (*Restaurants USA*, 1996). Catering generally can take place in one of three places: (1) on the premises of the caterer, such as a banquet hall or hotel (on-premise catering); (2) at the customer's home or business (off-premise catering); or (3) at the site of a third party such as a plantation home or municipal park. Off-premise catering accounts for the most business overall, but this sub-segment can be hard to track because of the number of small businesses involved in off-premise catering. Also, more and more restaurants, hotels, and even hospitals are providing off-premise catering. Further, the lines are blurring between what is a restaurant meal and what is a catered meal with the popularity of Home Meal Replacement. There are now numerous companies that provide pre-prepared meals which customers pick up and take home to reheat. This too, is a form of catering. When one thinks about the number of spe-

Somebody has to manage the food service at weddings, birthday parties, and other events!

cial events that take place that require some form of foodservice, one can quickly understand how large this segment is. Everyone has attended a wedding, anniversary party, birthday party, festival, dinner party, or any number of other events. Somebody has to manage the foodservice at these functions. Some very successful caterers have even gotten their start while they were college students catering parties on a part-time basis!

Catering has also been a popular entree into the restaurant business for a long time. The startup costs can be relatively low for an off-premise catering operation. They are obviously higher, on average, for an on-premise operation. Many restaurant operators have gotten their start in the business by developing a name for themselves through catering and then opening a restaurant. For students interested in learning more about this segment, the National Association of Catering Executives (NACE) is a good place to start. NACE is a national organization, which has a number of local chapters.

Brewpubs

The final segment of the industry that will be profiled in this chapter is the brewpub segment. And an interesting segment it is! Brewpubs are defined as operations that both brew and serve their beer at the same location. Most also serve food. The first brewpub in the U.S., in modern history, opened in 1982. Brewpubs, which were once identified as an innovative and somewhat unique combination of the craft brewing and restaurant industries, have been experiencing unprecedented growth since the late 1980s and particularly over the last five years.

How new is the brewpub concept? As with many segments of the hospitality industry, what appears to be new and innovative is really just an older concept that has returned to popularity in a slightly different form. Brewpubs are quite common, and have always been, in many parts of Europe. They were also quite common in the U.S. in the 1800s. At one time in this country's history, most of the beer sold to consumers was consumed in brewpubs (or taverns where the owner made his/her own beer). Modern brewpubs are simply an updated version of the original pub concept, a concept which is still common today in Belgium, Germany, and Great Britain (Jackson, 1988). The craft brewing industry is simply a continuation of a great brewing heritage in the U.S., which began when the early immigrants brought with them their favorite recipes from the "old country." At one time in the late 1800s, there were over 4,000 breweries spread across the U.S., many of which were brewpubs. When the Volstead Act took effect in 1920, some 2,000 breweries were forced to close (Erickson, 1987). The repeal of Prohibition in 1933 allowed breweries to flourish once again, but they were never able to reach the same level of saturation as they had in the 1800s. By the 1960s, due to a number of mergers and acquisitions the num-

ber had once again been greatly reduced—this time to fewer than 250.

The successful brewery of the 1960s was one that could produce in large quantities, maintain low unit costs, and distribute a product that would appeal to a wide variety of consumers. By the mid-1970s, consumers in search of a "European" style beer had few choices other than to drink imported European beer. The consumer was put in somewhat of a compromising position, however, since at this time, many of the imports were priced higher than domestic beers and did not always arrive in peak condition.

The total number of brewpubs operating in the U.S. now stands at about 600 and counting. The brewpub landscape continues to change and influence the greater restaurant and brewing industries. Prominent investors, celebrity chefs, and corporations have all been attracted to the popularity of the brewpub concept. In many cases, brewpubs are the joint effort of principals who have respective experience in the brewing and restaurant industries.

A sign that brewpubs have come of age was when the *Rock Bottom Brewery* of Denver appeared on Restaurants & Institution's annual list of top grossing independent restaurants (Weinstein, 1994). No longer are brewpub operations just limited to independent operators. The *Rock Bottom Brewery* is in the midst of an expansion project which includes additional units in several other states. As brewpubs continue to develop as chain operations, they will require more professional managers and will undoubtedly begin to look at hospitality programs more and more.

Industry Trends

Thus far, this chapter has discussed a variety of segments of the commercial foodservice industry. It would be difficult to have a complete understanding of the various segments, though, without also understanding what some of the trends are which are affecting the individual segments and the industry as a whole. A few of the more relevant trends will be discussed in this final section.

Some of the more obvious trends, which cut across multiple segments, have already been mentioned. These include:

❖ the increase in take-out and delivery (even in fine dining)
❖ continued penetration into nontraditional sites
❖ a growing preference for more casual dining experiences
❖ the elevated role that entertainment is playing in the dining experience resulting in a resurgence of theme restaurants
❖ a myriad of new products, services, and innovations
❖ branding and co-branding

In addition to these trends that have been extensively documented, several other significant trends are also impacting the industry. These would include:

❖ a return to meat and potatoes oriented menus (note the increased popularity in steak restaurants)
❖ more eclectic restaurant menus (borrowing from several different cultures)
❖ an increased focus on quality (of both food and service)
❖ more independent concepts being operated as chains (e.g., Lettuce Entertain You in Chicago)

❖ Scaling down of physical operations after years of getting bigger (this is happening in almost every segment)

These are just a few of the trends that will continue to influence the way foodservice operations are managed for years to come. There are many others including the popularity of special events (wine dinners), the continued backlash against smokers, and the proliferation of heart healthy menu items. It would be impossible to chronicle all of the trends currently impacting the industry. One of the signs of a good manager, however, is one that takes the time to observe the trends that are occurring instead of just getting wrapped up and consumed by day-to-day activities. Further, a manager should be able to evaluate how these individual trends influence his or her foodservice operation and how they should react or respond to them, making the appropriate changes as necessary.

◈Conclusion

The commercial foodservice industry continues to change and grow. New segments are emerging and new markets are being developed. This is one of the things that make the industry as exciting as it is. Students would be well advised to study the various opportunities that are available and identify one or two that seem to coincide with their professional interests. Each of the segments discussed has its own advantages. Fine dining will always have its place and can provide

an exciting and dynamic work environment, but it is declining in popularity. Casual dining offers good career opportunities, but there are some significant differences in chains' operating philosophies. Coffeehouses are probably seeing the greatest growth, but, at this time, most do not offer the range of food and beverage products that many students are looking for. Commercial cafeterias, a unique segment, have seen some difficult times but seem to be on the rebound. Quick service restaurants continue to grow and evolve. The greatest management opportunities may be in quick service. Vending is another unique segment worthy of consideration, particularly by students wishing to explore the area of on-site management. Perhaps the greatest changes are taking place in the area of lodging foodservice. While some opportunities have dissipated in this area, others have emerged with the evolvement of foodservice firms specializing in this area. Private clubs represent another career opportunity and may be one of the last bastions of fine dining. As with some hotels, students can experience a variety of foodservice operations under one roof. Banquets and catering represent a fragmented part of the industry with multiple opportunities for independence and growth. Finally, brewpubs are a fast growing segment, which should interest students who have an affinity for both food and beverage. Among these segments, and the others that exist, students are sure to find one that offers the right opportunities and matches well with their career aspirations.

Questions and Assignments

1. Discuss some of the factors that are influencing growth or decline in commercial food and beverage operations. Using your library resources or your web browser of choice, find two articles that discuss the growth or decline within two segments of commercial food and beverage operations. Summarize your findings, and be prepared to discuss your results.

2. Choose one of the segments discussed in the chapter. Using your library resources or your web browser and search engine of choice, identify a company within that segment and perform company/organization research on this firm. The approach is discussed in Chapter One.

3. Using your library resources or your web browser and search engine of choice, identify an article that discusses an entrepreneur within one of the segments discussed in the chapter. Summarize your findings, and be prepared to discuss your results.

4. List the major factors that characterize the casual dining segment. Using your library resources or your web browser and search engine of choice, find an article that describes a casual restaurant. Discuss the article in light of the major factors characterizing the segment.

5. What are the primary reasons that coffeehouses are successful?

6. Describe briefly the cafeteria segment. Using your library resources or your web browser and search engine of choice, identify an article that discusses an element of this segment. Summarize your findings, and be prepared to discuss your results.

7. Define home-meal replacement (HMR). Using your library resources or your web browser and search engine of choice, identify an article that discusses HMR. Summarize your findings, and be prepared to discuss your results.

8. Would you consider employment with a quick service restaurant (chain)? Please establish the potential advantages and disadvantages as you see them. Summarize your opinion and be prepared to discuss your results.

9. Why do some lodging companies opt not to provide foodservices themselves?

10. What options or approaches are available to a lodging company in terms of providing foodservice to their guests?

11. Using your library resources or your web browser and search engine of choice, identify an article that discusses the club segment. Summarize your findings and be prepared to discuss your results.

12. Define and discuss brewpubs. How are they different from other food and beverage companies? Why are they increasingly popular? Using your library resources or your web browser and search engine of choice, identify an article that supports your position. Be prepared to discuss your findings with your team or classmates.

13. List and discuss five key trends that are currently influencing the commercial food and beverage establishment. Using your library resources or your web browser and search engine of choice, identify an article that supports your position. Be prepared to discuss your findings with your team or classmates.

Bibliography and Suggested Readings

Barrows, C. W., (1994). Generating Interest in the Commercial Cafeteria Segment, *Hospitality & Tourism Educator*, 6, (3), 65–66.

Looking for a Good Meal?, *Consumer Reports*, September, 1996, 10–17.

Erickson, J., (1987). *Star Spangled Beer*. Red Brick Press: Reston, VA.

IFMA, (1995). Vending Foodservice. *Foodservice: A Segmented Industry*. International Foodservice Manufacturers Association, Chicago.

Jackson, M., (1988). *The New World Guide to Beer*. Running Press: Philadelphia.

Operations and Financial Data Survey, (1996). Club Managers Association of America. Alexandria, VA.

1997 Restaurant Industry Forecast, *Restaurants USA*, (1996). 16, (11), F1–F24.

Weinstein, J. (1994). Top 100 Independents, *Restaurants & Institutions*, 104, 34–56.

The Managed Services Perspective

Jerry L. Fournier, Jerry A. McVety, Robert A. Willis, *HDS Services*

ABSTRACT

This chapter will review and discuss the managed services segment of the hospitality industry. The history, current growth, and vitality within managed services at large, as well within various sub-segments will be discussed. Distinctions between self-operated companies and contract management companies will be made and companies from all sub-segments will be profiled.

OBJECTIVES

At the end of this chapter the student should be able to:

1. Define the managed services segment and discuss its relative size and importance.

2. Establish some of the historical foundations for the managed services segment.

3. Identify the leading managed services companies.

4. Define and describe the various segments within managed services.

5. Discuss the key services provided by managed services companies.

6. Identify and describe several managed services companies.

7. Discuss and consider career opportunities within managed services.

Introduction

In order to gain a complete understanding of the concept of managed services it is important to have a full understanding of the composition of the foodservice industry. The foodservice industry consists of two major market segments. The commercial segment represents approximately 68.6% of the industry and the non-commercial segment represents approximately 31.4%. The combined purchases of these segments during 1997 were approximately $128.6 billion.[1] (See Figure 1.)

Historical Overview—Managed-Services Companies

Since the 1950s many of these non-commercial segments began the trend toward utilizing managed-services companies (or "contract feeders"). This trend, also known as "outsourcing," became necessary because the internal administrations of these segments did not maintain the necessary expertise to keep these foodservice operations innovative and cost effective. In order to remain competitive, they reduced levels of management in

the non-core areas such as foodservice and directed further resources to their core business including manufacturing, education, healthcare, etc. Managed-services companies established sophisticated programs to increase revenues and control costs to more than offset their fees and charges, in-

cluding profit contributions, while at the same time reducing or eliminating the managed facilities subsidy to operate their foodservice programs. During the 1980s and 1990s significant growth for managed-services companies has occurred as demonstrated in the following segment comparison:

Figure 1. Major Segment Share of Market.

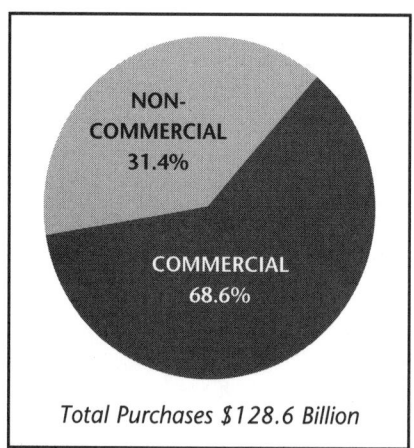

Total Purchases $128.6 Billion

[1]Technomic, Inc. (1997). "Forecast and Outlook." Annual Seminar, September 1997. Chicago, IL: Technomic, Inc.

T1 — Commercial Segment—Types of Operations

Segment	% Commercial	% Total Industry
Restaurants and Bars	80.1%	55.0%
Supermarket Delis	5.5%	3.8%
Lodging	4.6%	3.1%
Recreation	4.3%	2.9%
Other Retailers	2.9%	2.0%
Convenience Stores	2.6%	1.8%
TOTALS	100.0%	68.6%

T2 — Non-commercial Segment—Types of Operations

Segment	% Non-Commercial	% Total Industry
Business and Industry	26.6%	8.4%
Vending	22.9%	7.2%
Schools	14.1%	4.4%
Hospitals	9.3%	2.9%
Colleges/Universities	8.7%	2.7%
Nursing Homes	6.2%	1.9%
Military	4.1%	1.3%
Airline	2.1%	.7%
Other*	6.0%	1.9%
TOTALS	100.0%	31.4%

*Prisons, Elder Care (CCRC's), Child Care, Convents, Seminaries, and Railroads.

T3 — Estimated Share of Market Controlled by Foodservice Management Firms

Segment	1984	1997
Airlines	50–55%	85–95%
Business and Industry	75–80%	85–95%
Colleges/Universities	43–53%	65–70%
Hospitals	15–20%	25–35%
Nursing Homes/Elder Care	10–15%	15–20%
Penal Institutions	1–3%	10–20%
Primary/Secondary Schools	5–10%	15–20%
Recreation	30–35%	35–45%

Source: Technomic, Inc. (1997). "Forecast and Outlook." Annual Seminar, September 1997. Chicago, IL: Technomic, Inc.

As you will note airlines, business and industry, education, and health-care make up the bulk of the non-commercial segment of the foodservice industry. These are the same business lines for many of today's managed-services companies.

The Market and Its Leaders

Managed-services companies can be divided into two categories. The first group comprises numerous small and midsize companies, normally under $250 million in annual sales. They generally are privately held, target geographic regions, organizationally centralized, focus on a limited number of market segments, and concentrate on a single core service. The second group, with sales in excess of $250 million, often are publicly held or have a broader ownership base, are often global, and have diversified beyond foodservice into other support service areas such as housekeeping, facilities-maintenance, and laundry-linen distribution and management.

Market Segments— Description and Characteristics

Airlines

Some type of food and beverage service has been available to passengers since airlines began offering commercial/passenger services. United Airlines initially offered "boxed" lunches with limited beverage service. With the improvement of the services provided to passengers along with better galleys on board the planes, food and beverage service now runs the full gamut from basic juice, coffee, and bagel for breakfast, to a five course dinner with all the complements including real silverware and cloth napkins.

Over the years, airlines have been changing their views of foodservice offered passengers based primarily on cost. For a period of time in the 1980s, airlines basically offered mini-

Rank	Company/Location	1996 Worldwide F&B Sales ($MM)	1996 Total Accounts
	T4 Leading Contract Management Companies		
1	Compass Group—London (in U.S., Charlotte, NC)	$5,400.0	8,550
2	Sodexho—Paris (in U.S., Waltham, MA)*	5,300.0	14,000
3	Marriott Management Services— Bethesda, MD*	4,300.0	3,500
4	ARAMARK—Philadelphia, PA	4,100.0	2,280
5	Delaware North Cos.—Buffalo, NY	1,214.0	223
6	SHRM—Marseille, France (in U.S., Lafayette, LA)	818.3	1,321
7	The Wood Co.—Allentown, PA	400.0	352
8	Restaura—Phoenix, AZ	370.0	395
9	Daka Restaurants—Danvers, MA	328.0	328
10	Servicemaster—Downers Grove, IL	240.0	295
11	Morrison's Health Care—Atlanta, GA	220.0	300
12	Fine Host Corp.—Greenwich, CT	203.0	750
13	HDS Services—Farmington Hills, MI	153.2	186
14	Bon Appetite—Menlo Park, CA	122.0	88
15	Guckenheimer—Redwood City, CA	121.0	211

*Marriott/MMS and Sodexho consolidated in the 3rd quarter of 1997 and are now referred to as the Sodexho-Marriott/MMS Alliance.

Source: R&I August 15, 1997 individual companies

mum foodservices that were *easily prepared—served quickly* and yet provided the passengers something to eat.

For the most part, beverage service has been the same for decades, and there appears to be no change in the near future. The beverage format for almost all airlines on domestic flights is to offer non-alcoholic beverages at no charge, and beer, wine, and liquor can be purchased (in cash) and is free in business and first class. On international flights *all* beverages are typically free.

Some airlines have started to feature premium wines and beers. These airlines do this primarily to present themselves to the passengers as "full service" and upscale. Just like the hotel/motel industry, foodservice for airlines is directly related to the "type" of airline you choose. Southwest Airlines compares itself to economy motels with very limited service overall and very basic food served. On the other hand, JAL and Lufthansa, for example, tote themselves as an upscale airline and offer sushi and so on.

In the 1990s, passengers expect more from all airlines and have been vocal about their desire to have more and better foodservice available on all flights. Airlines are quickly recognizing this need and are addressing it immediately. In 1992, the per passenger food expenditure hit a high of $5.78 as compared to $4.33 per passenger in 1995. At least for the next five years, this per passenger expenditure will again be on the rise.

Airlines are also starting to feature brand name products such as *Starbucks* coffee, *Ben & Jerry's* ice cream, and *Snapple* beverages. In addition, local chefs from major restaurants across the country are developing the menus for business and first class passengers on intercontinental flights.

At least while the economy is good, airline food and beverage service will play a bigger part in satisfying the passengers. Airlines and their foodservice providers (see Table 5 for a list of leading providers) will have to remain alert to foodservice trends

Leading Airport/Airline Foodservice Providers

Company	1996 F&B Sales ($MM)	Contracts or Sites	Production Kitchens
LSG Lufthansa Service/Sky Chefs Arlington, TX	$1,530.0	250 airlines	128
Host Marriott Services Corp. Bethesda, MD	1,015.0	200 sites	N/A
Dobbs International Services Memphis, TN	750.0	80 airlines	64
Ogden Aviation Services Flushing, NY	192.0	100 airports	11
CA One Buffalo, NY	184.5	36 airports	30
United Airlines Elk Grove Village, IL	17.3	2 airports	2

Source: R&I August 15, 1997 individual companies

and passengers' needs. Concurrently, and because the airline business is cyclical, airline foodservice providers are also seeking non-traditional markets in malls, supermarkets, and airports that will provide them with additional business.

Business and Industry Foodservice

Foodservice in business and industry really evolved during World War II because of the competition for labor and their demand to have on-site foodservices in plants. Hence the "industry" demand for foodservices. This demand for in-plant foodservices continues today, and for the most part some type of foodservice is written into labor contracts.

Foodservice in plants usually involves one or more cafeterias offering a minimum of complete breakfast and lunch menus. If the plant operates more than one shift, the cafeterias could operate 24 hours per day. This would include breakfast, lunch, and dinner. The number of cafeterias in a plant depends on the population and the physical layout of each plant. In the older facilities, it is not uncommon to find at least two cafeterias located at each end of the plant.

In addition to the manual service (cafeterias), plants usually have a lot

of vending stations that are clustered throughout the plant for easy and quick access. Vending banks, as they are called, will consist of cold and hot beverage machines, candy, ice cream, soup, and juice machines. Very often there will also be a multi-purpose machine (sometimes referred to as a grand gourmet) which would offer fresh sandwiches, entrees, and other specialty food items. In addition to the vending machines, one would also find bill change makers (sometimes part of the actual vending machine) along with microwaves and condiment stations. Depending on the size of the plant, there may be a mobile cart that travels a set route each day throughout the plant to provide limited food and beverage service to workers.

In the 1970s the office based business foodservices began to grow. Once more, the main purpose for companies to offer foodservice to its employees had to do with retention of existing employees and attracting new ones. Foodservice was looked upon as an employee benefit even though today this is not necessarily the case.

Foodservices for the business segment again includes cafeterias, vending along with private executive dining areas, and on-premise catering. Initially prices were well below market and services were plentiful.

In the 1990s, with the downsizing of corporate America, foodservices in both business and industry has been challenged to reduce costs. Until recently, business and industry foodservices operated at a subsidy (at a loss). Now the pressure is on foodservices to reduce cost and to at least operate at a break-even level of performance. Needless to say, this challenge has a significant impact on pricing, menu variety, and the amount of service offered.

To enhance the foodservices, particularly in the business segment, the operators are now labeling the operations as dining services. Branding is being introduced in an effort to attract more customers and be more competitive to the commercial market. Foodservices in business and industry are managed by both foodservice management companies and are self-operated. Some of the leading self-operated facilities are in Table 6.

Schools

School foodservice began in the mid-19th century as an incentive to encourage classroom attendance. In the 20th century it grew rapidly in the United States primarily as a result of the National School Lunch Program introduced in 1946. Thereafter, the Child Nutrition Act of 1966 provided the sizable government funds required to feed schoolchildren.

The availability of government funding was what first attracted foodservice companies to schools. Now, state and federal cost-reduction programs and the cost savings possible through hiring efficient foodservice "experts" have increased the demand for managed-services companies in elementary and secondary schools throughout the country. This segment is a profitable environment for many companies.

Traditionally, it has been students who attack school lunches. Recently, many foodservice managers have been under siege by stronger forces, including government nutrition mandates, block-grant programs, and private contractors.

Company	1996 F&B Sales ($MM)	Units	Transactions per Day	Chain Brands
Motorola Schaumburg, IL	21.0	46	48,000	N
Ford Motor Company Dearborn, MI	7.6	30ᴬ	30,000	Y
J.P. Morgan & Company New York, NY	5.5	4	8,300ᴮ	N
Aetna Life & Casualty Hartford, CT	5.0	11	14,700	N
Abbott Laboratories North Chicago, IL	4.0	11	13,000	N
Minnesota Mining & Manufacturing Co. (3M) St. Paul, MN	3.1	17	5,600	N
Electronic Data Systems Corporation Plano, TX	2.6	12	9,500	N
Pharmacia & Upjohn Kalamazoo, MI	2.0	13	7,500	N
Steelcase Grand Rapids, MI	2.0	10	5,000	N
Hallmark Cards Kansas City, MO	1.7	4	4,550ᶜ	Y
Pitney Bowes Stamford, CT	1.7	4	3,800	N
Procter & Gamble Cincinnati, OH	1.4ᴰ	8	2,600	N

Source: R&I August 15, 1997 individual companies; (A) 20 main cafeterias with 10 mini food outlets; (B) includes 6,500 100%-subsidized lunches daily; (C) Kansas City and Liberty locations; (D) excludes sales from 40% of locations (operated by *ARAMARK*)

Perhaps most significantly, schools felt the full impact of the U.S. Department of Agriculture's Healthy Meals Initiative during the 1996–97 school year. On July 1, 1996, all school districts receiving federal subsidies for meal programs (approximately 89,000 schools) were to bring menus into compliance with the latest set of Dietary Guidelines for Americans. Under the guidelines, school lunches are to derive no more than 30% of calories from fat and no more than 10% from saturated fat over the course of a week. Meals must also limit sodium and contain more produce and grains.

Most schools have taken the new requirements in stride. Some districts have been working toward meeting the guidelines on their own. Most schools are modifying current menus with measures such as baking instead of frying and substituting low-fat cheeses and meats.

Compliance with nutrition regulations isn't the only issue school districts have with the federal authorities. The USDA commodities program is destined to play an even more complex role. Though all schools in the school lunch program rely on commodities, not all seem to have the same amount of control over what they receive. For most schools, participation is the name of the game. According to 1996 government data, expenditures for the

Child Nutrition Program and National School Lunch Program are holding steady, with increases of only 0.9% and 0.8%, respectively. While lunch programs grew slightly, the real growth segment was the School Breakfast Program, which saw 1996 participation rise 4.3% from the previous year. See Table 7 for a breakdown of leading school districts.

Foodservice departments also are coming up against the issue of privatization. The General Accounting Office published its most recent findings on school foodservice privatization in August 1996. According to the report, 8% of the school foodservice operations nationwide that participated in the lunch program during the 1994–95 school year used foodservice management companies, this was up from 4% in the 1987–88 school year. Other advantages include being able to bypass district purchasing rules and being able to take advantage of well-funded training and education programs.

Many schools offer commercially packaged snacks and chain-brand tacos and pizzas—though most remain reluctant to allow fast-food outlets into their buildings.

Universities and Colleges

At universities and colleges foodservice includes cafeterias, student-union foodservice, catering, and other on-campus outlets. Students expect quality, value, and a wide range of offerings, including ethnic foods and brand-name products. This segment is appealing to many managed-services companies and has become a cornerstone of business for most. Although, many universities are still self-operated (see Table 8 for examples).

At universities across the country, the food-court concept is more and more common, and even colleges that refuse to sign on with contractors are increasing brand-conscious. Many universities have found that combinations of nationally branded and self-operated spots work best. Increasingly diverse student bodies have prompted

District/Location	Total F&B Sales ($MM)	Value of Commod. ($MM)	Schools	Enroll- ment (000)	Meals Served (000)	% Breakfast/ Lunch	% Free or Reduced
New York City Board of Education	$91.0	$11.0	1,410	1,152	747	19/81	91
Los Angeles Unified School District	83.0	13.5	594	666	597	36/64	93
Chicago Public Schools	63.0	7.0	595	413	354	22/78	95
Dade County Schools Miami, FL	37.0	5.3	327	328	242	24/76	81
Philadelphia School District	23.8	2.5	259	212	159	25/75	92
Broward County Schools Fort Lauderdale, FL	19.1	3.1	190	235	177	26/74	64
Hawaii Statewide School System Honolulu	19.0	3.5	250	180	171	20/80	41
Hillsborough County Schools Tampa, FL	17.1	1.4	174	143	146	22/78	53
Dallas Independent School District	14.9	3.8	203	157	148	21/79	71

Source: R&I August 15, 1997 individual companies

menu changes. This is the result of having more students from all over the world.

University foodservice operations also continue to feel pressure to come up with alternate revenue streams. Catering is increasingly important, as

Photo © 1998 PhotoDisc, Inc.

At universities across the country, the food-court concept is more and more common.

are cash operations. Some colleges are trying self-branding.

Labor remains a challenge as well, and in some cases it affects food presentation as well as behind-the-lines employment practices. There is a use of self-service. More universities have made a conscious attempt to bring student foodservice workers into the industry once they graduate. In keeping up with trends, many college operations are offering wraps, custom stir-fry stations, chef demonstrations, cooked-to-order steaks, and other elements that serve up a custom dining touch. What campus these days is complete without an espresso bar staffed by conversationalists? The result: Students may be majoring in fast food, but there seems to be more room than ever in the curriculum for a personal approach.

Recreational

Fans watching a game at a major-league stadium were once content with hot dogs, peanuts, soda, and beer. Today a concession stand in a sports complex may carry sushi, tofu burgers, smoked-chicken pizza, and fruit smoothies. Convention

centers are also becoming more robust in their food offerings. A market only for the larger managed-services companies (because of the requirement of a considerable cash investment tied to a long-term contract), this is a segment that is both profitable and challenging.

Firms that manage small-scale recreational facilities such as country clubs, golf courses, indoor tennis facilities, comprehensive fitness centers, and the like fall into a different industry category known as concessionaires.

At sporting and entertainment arenas, the food has been elevated to match the rarefied atmosphere of private suites and box seats. On cruise ships, expanded room service and pizzerias offer alternatives to formal group dining. In casinos, variety is the name of the game as players try to distinguish themselves with menus to suit every taste. Table 9 contains large recreational foodservice providers.

Stadium

Before Boston Garden closed, hungry fans were provided with predictable fare, such as hot dogs and draft beer. At its replacement, the FleetCenter,

University	Total F&B Sales ($MM)	Board-plan Sales ($MM)	Board-plan Meals Served ($MM)	Cash-op Sales ($MM)	Enrollment
Pennsylvania State University, University Park	$20.8	$ 6.9	$5.7	$11.9	39,800
Michigan State University, East Lansing	15.1	10.3	4.5	8.9	41,545
Brigham Young University, Provo, UT	12.5	8.5	3.8	12.3	28,000
Harvard University, Cambridge, MA	9.1	7.0	3.1	5.0	18,500
University of Notre Dame, Notre Dame, IN	9.1	6.2	2.4	2.5	10,000
Purdue University, West Lafayette, IN	8.8	5.7	3.0	6.9	35,100
University of Maryland, College Park	7.9	5.5	NA	6.7	34,400
University of Illinois, Urbana-Champaign	7.5	6.5	2.4	2.3	36,100

Source: R&I August 15, 1997 individual companies

they now can dine on grilled turkey sausage while sipping a daiquiri served by waiters. Selection is important to the growing number of fans for whom a sporting event is no longer a lazy afternoon in the bleachers. It's a night out in a skybox, a place to see and be seen. When fans (or their corporate hosts) are paying dearly for the privilege, popcorn and greasy nachos don't quite cut it.

Cruise Ships

Evening dress used to be the rule during dinner onboard cruise ships. These days, it's T-shirts and shorts— even bathrobes—at least some of the time. Carnival, Princess, and Royal Caribbean are among industry leaders giving passengers a wider array of dining options, most of which focus on casual fare. After 24-hour pizzerias proved popular on its three newest ships, Carnival installed them fleetwide. Another new concept, the Seaview Bistro, serves a buffet dinner of salads, pasta, and desserts. It seems to have filled a niche: An estimated 70% of week long cruise passengers opt for the bistros at least once.

Royal Caribbean Cruise Lines has expanded the menu for its 24-hour room service to include more hot items. Passengers also can bypass the dining rooms and choose from steaks, salads, and pastas at the Windjammer Cafe. Alternative dining also is aimed at attracting new passengers who might be turned off by scheduled mealtimes.

Casino

Casino foodservice also is making news, not least of all for sheer volume. As legal gambling takes root and expands across the country, so too do restaurants that lure new customers and keep them coming back. "We offer variety and quality," says Bill Estes, director of investor and lender relations at Mirage Resorts in Las Vegas. The 30 restaurants on its four properties range from an upscale steakhouse to a 24-hour coffee shop. A similar lineup awaits at other casinos. Another impressive player, Mohegan Sun in Connecticut feeds 25,000 people a day everything from prime rib to Asian cuisine.

Organization	1996 F&B Sales ($MM)	Properties	Type of Business
The Walt Disney Co. Burbank, CA	$960.5*	4	Theme parks
Harrah's Memphis, TN	400.0	16	Gaming
Carnival Cruise Lines[A] Miami, FL	331.0*	22	Cruise ships
Volume Services Spartanburg, SC	228.0	90	Stadiums/arenas
Mirage Resorts Las Vegas, NV	224.4	4	Gaming
AMC Entertainment Kansas City, MO	222.9	228	Theaters
Sportservice[B] Buffalo, NY	221.1	66	Stadiums/arenas
Circus Circus Enterprises[C] Las Vegas, NV	210.4	15	Gaming
Club Corp. International Dallas, TX	209.0	240	Private Clubs
Royal Caribbean Cruises Miami, FL	120.0	11	Cruise ships

Source: R&I August 15, 1997 individual companies; *R&I estimate; (A) includes Carnival and Holland America lines; (B) a subsidiary of Delaware North Cos.; (C) includes 50% stake in three casino properties.

Correctional Facilities

After the 1970 Attica Prison riot in upstate New York in which poor food quality was cited as a source of the inmates' unrest, concerted efforts were directed toward implementing standards in foodservice. In 1977 the American Correctional Association developed the first such standards, which many other agencies have since adopted. The stringent specifications are most easily met by managed-services companies, and the nation's rising inmate population and increasing need for cost containment has led to increased privatization. Foodservice in correctional facilities is now a promising, if not booming, market.

Correctional foodservice is the hottest growing market segment of contract management services of the past five years (see Table 10 for the leading correctional operations). The reasoning for this is, quite simply, cost. Like most supporters of contract management, correctional clients are looking for the highest possible quality for the lowest reasonable cost. To meet these needs, a correctional foodservice manager has several unique challenges.

Staffing

Depending on the correctional facility—most accounts use inmate labor in the kitchens. This can be a positive resource in that you have a ready supply of labor, which can be used to maintain higher standards of sanitation. However, a correctional foodservice manager must be cognizant of management style. The inmate's motivation to work in the kitchen is for food access, not to be a valued employee. An inmate usually doesn't react positively to threats, pressure or coercion. Also, the experience and skill level of the inmate worker is usually not of the caliber needed for most skilled production tasks. Overall work ethics are not prevalent, requiring closer supervision and follow-through. Also, there is an extremely high turnover of the inmate labor. The illiteracy rate and language barriers are more challenging in the penal setting requiring more patience, detailed instruction, and training time. The correctional foodservice manager must be confident, but not overbearing, patient and possess good teaching skills.

Security

Correctional kitchens are usually one of the few places where utensils and knives are considered potential weapons. Therefore, these items must be accounted for daily. Greater care must be given to document access through signature forms and daily counts. Other items can also be used as weapons; the serrated edge of foil cartons, chemicals, padlocks placed in socks, and stirring paddles to name a few. The potential for violence is greater with inmate workers. Therefore, care must be given for warning signs of potential conflict, such as groups of inmates herding together, extreme quiet or extreme noise and arguments, missing utensils, and inmates not in their work areas.

Also, non-violent security issues center around food. Food is used as a "monetary" source and must be secured at all times. Theft is prevalent and can be extensive if not controlled. Theft occurs from the receiving dock, to the storerooms and coolers, to production, and through portion control on the serving line. Many incarcerated inmates have drug and alcohol addictions and crave sweets. Also, sugar and bread are used to make "hooch," a rather rank alcohol derivative. The most prevalent high theft items are: coffee, sugar, candy bars, cookies, fresh fruit (apples, oranges, bananas), boxed raisins, bakery items (jelly and syrup), and vanilla (which has alcohol). Supplements for weight gain such as instant breakfasts and high protein items are also sought after by inmates to "bulk-up." Regular "zone" sweeps through the kitchen are necessary to find "stashes" of contraband items. A successful corrections foodservice manager must be organized and manage by walking around.

Portion Control

Most correctional menus contain a high number of starches and casseroles, which are more difficult to regulate than piece menu items. The formula for forecasting production quantities must be consistent. Production quantities are essential to meeting aggressive food costs. Portion control is critical for maintaining costs and eliminating potential dining room disruptions. If an inmate server over portions by as much as an ounce in a facility feeding 500, this could lead to a shortage of 166 (3 oz) portions. Obviously, if you run out of food, the potential for disruption is intensified. Therefore, a correctional foodservice manager must have strong knowledge of forecasting, portion control, weights and measures, and a working knowledge of modified and caloric intake diets. Scales are critical pieces of equipment necessary in the kitchen and on the serving line. The proper serving utensils are equally necessary.

Another reason for proper portion control is caloric intake. Depending on the facility, caloric intake can range from 2,100 calories (for a non-working holding facility) to 4,400 calories (for a working penitentiary, generally in the South, also depending on the state). These intake amounts are critical to meeting state and federal guidelines as well as food costs. Not meeting these caloric intake levels can result in regulatory discrepancies as well as litigation initiated by inmates.

Sanitation/Regulatory Issues

Many correctional foodservice facilities are older structures which require more attention to pest control and sanitation procedures. These must be documented and consistently reviewed. Inmates are generally less educated regarding personal hygiene, therefore ridged health precautions must be monitored. Inmates must be physically screened prior to working, taught solid universal precautions and monitored for cuts, coughs, scratches, and infections. Proper serving gloves,

T10 Leading Corrections Operations

System	1996 F&B Sales ($MM)	Population	Facil-ities	Food Service Units
California Dept. of Corrections Sacramento	$136.0	152,138	79[A]	202
Federal Bureau of Prisons Washington	86.6	110,035	89	89
Texas Dept. of Criminal Justice Huntsville	60.0	134,000	105	120
Florida Dept. of Corrections Tallahassee	52.0	64,132	53	53
New York State Dept. of Corrections Rome	40.0	72,000	71	71
Pennsylvania Dept. of Corrections Camp Hill	38.0	36,600	26	30
Illinois Dept. of Corrections Springfield	36.8*	41,000	44	44
Ohio Dept. of Corrections Columbus	36.0	47,000	30	30
Michigan Dept. of Corrections East Lansing	34.4	42,107	40	56
Virginia Dept. of Corrections Richmond	29.9	25,500	52	45
New Jersey Dept. of Corrections Trenton	26.0	21,713	14	14
Georgia Dept. of Corrections Atlanta	22.0	35,000	70	70

Source: R&I August 15, 1997 individual correctional systems; *R&I estimate; (A) includes 38 camps.

hand soap, and showers are also essential.

Life safety and disaster policies must be created and prepared for. Correctional facilities have a higher degree of power and utilities stoppages than most foodservice accounts. Plans for feeding the population during these situations are critical. No electric, no water, use of field kitchens, lockdowns for riot situations—all call for pre-planning. A successful corrections manager should have a working knowledge of state and local penal regulations.

In summary, the habits and job routines of a successful correctional foodservice manager are not unlike those of other segments within this industry. However, the routines must be customized to include the above stated challenges and the specific requirements of the individual facility.

Health Care Facilities

Managed-services companies typically divide health care into hospitals, skilled nursing and extended care facilities, and retirement centers. While hospitals have existed for thousands of years, it was not until the 19th century that standards of treatment—including dietary needs—were created. A result was radical changes in foodservice, starting with specialized diets and kitchens designed specifically for preparing food for patients. Today there are a host of preparation and delivery systems and new technology—including computerized diet analyses and integrated robotics in

centralized kitchen facilities—being used. Those modifications have helped managed-services companies respond to an environment of increasingly complex guidelines and reduced government reimbursement rates.

Hospital foodservice directors are attracting new business by turning their facilities into retail- and service-oriented operations. Massachusetts General Hospital is a good example (see Table 11). The 886-bed hospital became one of the first hospitals to debut the marketplace concept in a health-care facility. This concept features exhibition-style cooking with a wok, charbroiler and flat-top grill, plus a fresh salad bar, *Papa Gino's* pizza station, and a *Friendly's Ice Cream* parlor.

Other hospitals use other methods such as display cooking, rotating hot bars, theme days—and good food—to attract customers. Additional features: Culinary Institute of America trained staff chefs, catering divisions, ethnic kitchens, breakfast carts, multiple choices for meals (up to 11 choices per meal), meat carving stations, yogurt, and specialty coffee machines.

Skilled-nursing and extended care facilities are a relatively new growth area. Several factors have created a high demand for managed-services companies in this sector. First, the facilities are highly regulated by the government and require much expertise in foodservice. Second, recent cuts in reimbursements from Medicare and Medicaid have required an ability to manage costs. Finally, because good food can translate into comfort, pleasure, and security it has not only a nutritive role but also a therapeutic one. This segment also offers many more such facilities today than, say, 25 years ago, and this expansion—and its attractiveness to managed-services companies—is likely to continue as healthy (and demanding) baby-boomers reach their 70s and 80s.

Retirement centers, or senior residential communities, provide a variety of services. They cater to

Facility	1996 F&B Sales ($MM)	Beds	% Occupancy	Avg. Stay (Days)	Non-patient Transactions Per Year (000)
Greater Metropolitan Health System[A] New York	$6.7	2,137	84.0	7.2	700
Massachusetts General Hospital Boston	4.5	886	89.0	6.2	2,986
The New York Hospital New York	4.1	770	80.0	6.0	1,243
New York University Medical Center New York	3.5	814	90.0	8.0	2,250
Cedars-Sinai Medical Center Los Angeles	3.1	793	76.9	5.5	807
The Medical Center at University of California San Francisco	3.0	960	65.8	6.4	1,334
Cook County Hospital Chicago	3.0	698	60.0	6.0	364
St. Vincent Medical Center Little Rock	2.9	699	54.0	6.4	1,800
Baptist Memorial Hospital Memphis	2.8	2,000	72.7	5.0	1,387
Carolinas Medical Center Charlotte, NC	2.7	878	80.0	4.6	1,259

Source: R&I August 15, 1997 individual facilities; (A) a June 1997 partnership of Beth Israel Health Care System and St. Luke's-Roosevelt Health Care System.

relatively healthy people and feature upscale dining facilities, housekeeping services, social activities, transportation, and on-site medical personnel. Foodservice at these facilities illustrates the transition from institutional feeding to gourmet dining.

Continuum of Care Retirement Community (CCRC) is a residential facility which encompasses multiple levels of care including one or more of the following: nursing care beds, sub-acute beds, assisted-living units (provision of room, board, and personal services such as bathing, help with walking, eating, etc.), and independent living units (activities, meals, housekeeping services, etc. may be provided, but no personal services as in assisted living.) The campus may include freestanding villas or cottages for seniors with no services provided. Typically, this type of format offers seniors the opportunity to receive any services that are necessary without moving from the community.

Programs Offered by Managed Services Companies

Managed-services companies have established their advantages over the traditional self operative modes by developing sophisticated programs supported by highly experienced people to improve quality, increase revenues, control costs, and allow the upper management of these organizations (client's facility) to spend more time managing their core business. The two main ingredients of this *support through expertise are **people and programs***.

The People

In addition to assigning qualified on-site managers to their businesses, managed-services companies provide a team of corporate specialists to support these managers. The first level of support above the unit manager is often referred to as the Regional Director of Operations (a.k.a. District Manager). A Regional Director of Operations is normally someone who has been promoted from the level of unit manager, has a degree in foodservice management, and possesses the necessary skills to implement the various programs offered by a company, motivate the staff, and successfully communicate with the facility client to demonstrate the value and effectiveness of the company. A Regional Director of Operations will typically supervise 12–15 managers (facilities).

The next position in the hierarchy would be a Regional Vice President, or Area Manager, who often would supervise four or more Regional Directors of Operations. This person is responsible for an entire geographic region and or segment line for the company. Typically the various Regional Vice Presidents would report to a Vice President of Operations.

In addition to the direct line support positions, the operations department of the managed-services company will consist of various staff support positions such as:

❖ Purchasing
❖ Recruitment and Personnel
❖ Training and Development
❖ Computer Support
❖ Program Development
❖ Nutrition and Clinical Dietetics
❖ Accounting and Data Processing
❖ Sales and Marketing

These staff support people provide the additional expertise and value that would be associated with reasons why a business would decide to outsource their foodservice operation(s). Similar to a multiple restaurant chain/operation, a management company's greatest asset and value stems from the system, contracts, program, people, and standardization they can provide to a client versus the very limited resources available in a self-operative situation.

The Programs

Product/Commodity Management

Managed-services companies develop sophisticated programs, often times computerized, that encompass all the processes that contribute to the provision of the end product—a meal. These programs provide the keys to assuring high quality, increased sales, and cost control. These processes include the following components:

❖ Product Specifications
❖ Product Purchasing
❖ Product Receiving
❖ Product Storage
❖ Menumatics
❖ Recipe Resource

❖ Product Utilization
❖ Portion Control

Product Specifications

Selection, control, and usage of clearly defined purchasing specifications impact food cost. Development of concise product specifications give managers and vendors sufficient flexibility yet provide quality controls along with price optimization. Specifications not only control the grade of raw product, but also eliminate the chance of major improper product selection.

Product Purchasing

The purchasing segment involves three basic steps that seriously effect food cost:

1. Obtaining the highest quality products at the lowest prices as a direct result of consolidating buying power. Most managed-services companies utilize *Prime Distributor Programs*.
2. The *Prime Distributor* purchasing program normally includes direct order/entry and computer linkage/communication.
3. Utilization of *Commodity* purchasing guides to control the amount of product purchased.

Product Receiving

The receiving aspect requires an accurate auditing procedure to compare

deliveries with what is ordered and at the quoted price. This provides management with the ability to avoid receipt of items that are not needed, as well as isolated instances when crucial products needed to fulfill menu requirements are left off deliveries. It also provides a check to prevent vendor over charging.

Product Storage

The storage aspect requires experience in food handling procedure and knowledge of food chemistry and quality preservation. Managed-services companies strive to reduce inventory as much as possible to a point where turnover is maintained four times per month. The logic behind this goal is to free up cash, rather than having it tied up in inventory, and eliminating the opportunity for waste by maintaining a minimum amount of food on hand.

Menumatics

Providing menus that exceed customer satisfaction targets is paramount. Additionally, positive financial results can be achieved through the development of cost effective menus and offerings which can be adjusted frequently and effectively. When market conditions change, the menus should be altered to maintain focus on financial targets. The objective is to maintain a balance between menu items/selectivity, scratch production, and food/labor costs.

Figure 2. Components of Product/Commodity Management.

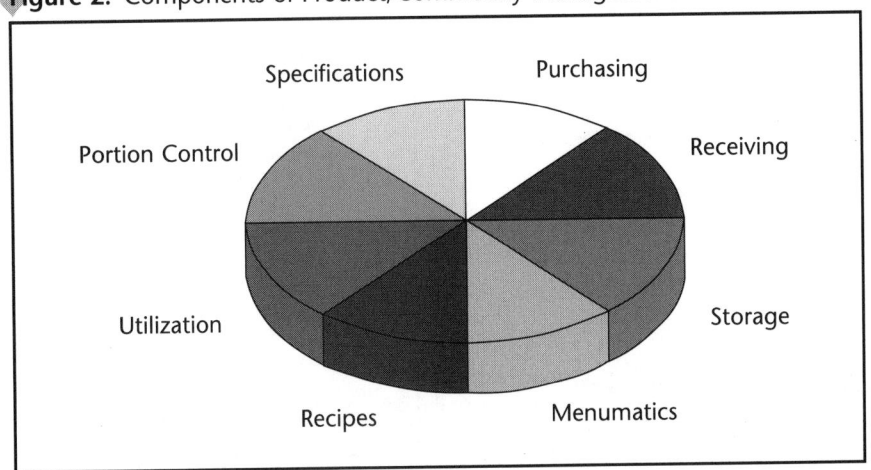

Product Utilization/Recipes

The effective use of production records is a vital management tool that affects food cost. Standardized recipes are used in the production process to control food usage and product quality. Practically all leftover food products can be carried over for future use, but this requires detailed supervision, planning, and imagination.

Portion Control

Proper portioning is extremely important and requires the use of scales, proper portioning tools, and continuous supervision. The distribution and holding process is important from the standpoint of maintaining product quality to assure that all portions will be served and not wasted due to deterioration. Some products may be held at serving temperature for several hours, while other more delicate products require batch cooking.

Staff Training and Development

Labor cost is typically the largest component of cost in a foodservice operation. The professional capabilities of the salaried and hourly staff are a key to a well-run cost-effective operation. Exciting . . . motivating . . . service-oriented . . . films, videotapes, audiocassettes, and printed materials are made available to stimulate employee learning. Resource libraries include materials focused on management, quality assessment and improvement, menu development, environmental impacts, service standards, safety, sanitation, proper food handling, and an ever-expanding array of contemporary foodservice topics. Managed-services companies' goals are typically to provide improved direction through training, reorientation, reorganizing, and rescheduling. Positive employee relations are an important priority. Through one-on-one and group meetings, employees are given the opportunity to discuss their positions and contribute to improvements. Regularly scheduled evalua-

tions give them a clear idea of their strengths and weaknesses, and help them develop a professional approach in their foodservices responsibilities.

Total Quality Management/ Continuous Quality Improvement

Managed-services companies realize the importance of exceeding the customers' expectations and that it is the most important key to survival. A quality management approach involves the entire work force in quality improvement where employees have fun at doing the job right the

first time and are a cooperative team. Increasing quality also results in higher productivity and lower costs. In today's climate of rising costs, and satisfying both external and internal customers, change is crucial. Continuous Quality Improvement (CQI) is the long-term answer.

Managed-services companies have taken the initiative to develop quality management within their organizations. Companies realize that quality improvement is not a program. A program has a beginning and an end. Total Quality Management (TQM) is a process. *There is no end to quality improvement.*

Figure 3. Together for Quality: Executive Model.

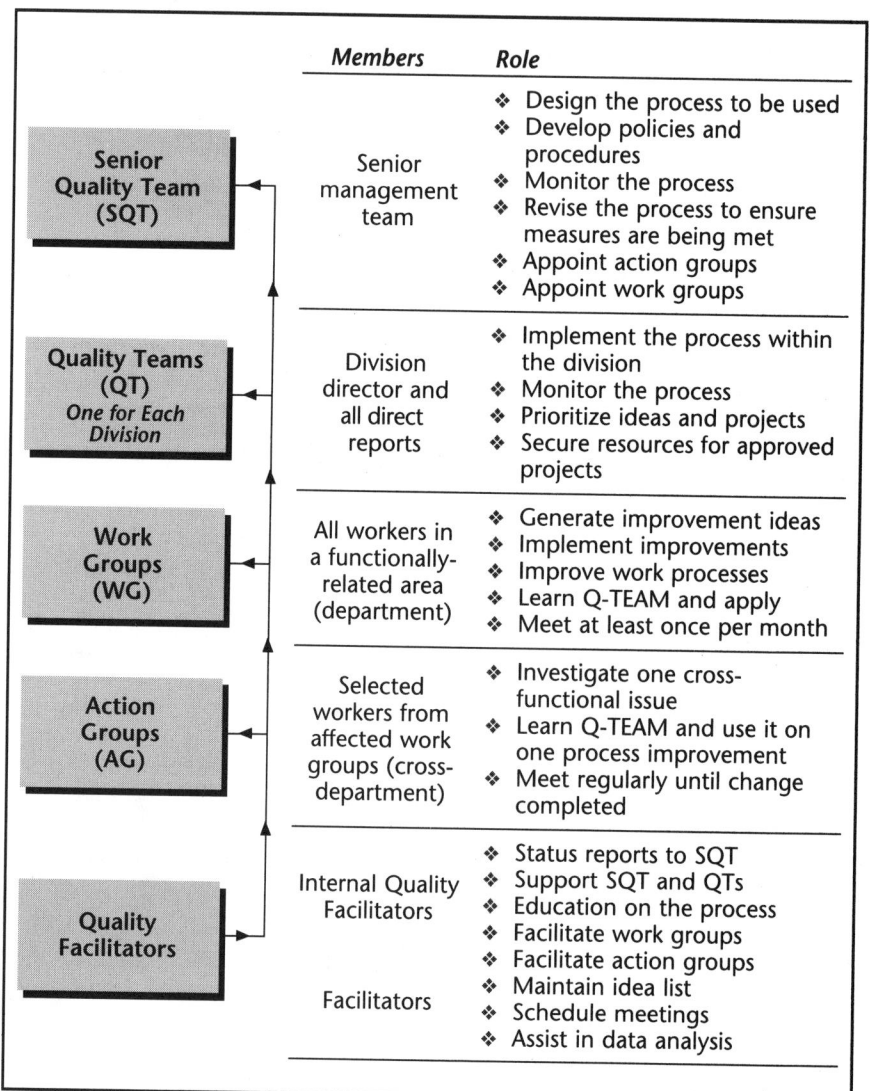

	Members	Role
Senior Quality Team (SQT)	Senior management team	❖ Design the process to be used ❖ Develop policies and procedures ❖ Monitor the process ❖ Revise the process to ensure measures are being met ❖ Appoint action groups ❖ Appoint work groups
Quality Teams (QT) *One for Each Division*	Division director and all direct reports	❖ Implement the process within the division ❖ Monitor the process ❖ Prioritize ideas and projects ❖ Secure resources for approved projects
Work Groups (WG)	All workers in a functionally-related area (department)	❖ Generate improvement ideas ❖ Implement improvements ❖ Improve work processes ❖ Learn Q-TEAM and apply ❖ Meet at least once per month
Action Groups (AG)	Selected workers from affected work groups (cross-department)	❖ Investigate one cross-functional issue ❖ Learn Q-TEAM and use it on one process improvement ❖ Meet regularly until change completed
Quality Facilitators	Internal Quality Facilitators Facilitators	❖ Status reports to SQT ❖ Support SQT and QTs ❖ Education on the process ❖ Facilitate work groups ❖ Facilitate action groups ❖ Maintain idea list ❖ Schedule meetings ❖ Assist in data analysis

Ongoing Retail Enhancements

One other very important reason that businesses utilize managed-services companies has to do with the approach these companies take in promoting the day-to-day food-service business. In many ways, it is perceived that employees working in a building are somewhat "captive" for the foodservice operation. This is truly a myth. Employees in any building have *many* options regarding food and beverage services and if the foodservice operation becomes complacent by offering the same mundane menu everyday, business can really drop off. The managed-services companies recognize this danger and have developed a variety of promotions to keep the building employees interested in the "in-house" food and beverage operation(s). Several key factors that managed-services companies offer include:

❖ Cycle and seasonal menus
❖ Fresh product
❖ Variety/selection
❖ Weekly calendars showing menus for the entire week
❖ Menus announced via internal e-mail
❖ Branding (both proprietary and/or regional/national brands)
❖ Theme meals
❖ Salad Bars

❖ Deli Bars
❖ Breakfast Bars
❖ Dessert Bars
❖ Professional Signage
❖ Professional Decor Package

and the list goes on.

Conclusion: Career Opportunities (Not Just a Job!)

By now you have certainly recognized that managed services is a major part of the foodservice industry. Within this one area there are many different segments of business (Airlines, Business and Industry, College/University, Hospitals, Nursing Home/Elder Care, Penal Institutions, Primary/Secondary Schools, Recreation, etc.).

For many years, managed services were referred to as institutional management—not a very appealing name. Therefore, the whole concept of working the field of institutional management prevented many good and qualified individuals from entering into employment in this area of foodservice. Needless to say, this image/perception has greatly changed. The growth in all segments of managed services has been phenomenal and will continue to expand rapidly concurrent with the desire for outstanding services. Now managed-services companies are viewed as more professional rather than institutional.

With the growth of business for managed-services companies comes the demand for more people—people at all levels (cooks, chefs, supervisors, managers, and executives) and in all areas of business (foodservices, human resources, accounting, etc.). The career opportunities within managed services are bountiful. Managed-services companies offer much more than just a job—you have a career. There are many opportunities to excel within managed-services companies.

The companies offer solid, independent training programs, very competitive salaries and benefits, reasonable work schedules, and a team approach to doing business. Since these companies are all regional, national, and/or international there is an additional opportunity to relocate to new geographic areas along with new and different assignments. For many, working for a managed-services company fulfills a person's aspirations both professionally and personally.

Figure 4. Advantages of Employment with a Managed-Services Company.

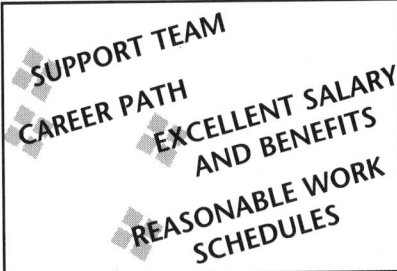

Questions and Assignments

1. List and briefly describe each of the non-commercial foodservice segments.

2. Discuss the historical trends in managed-services companies. Using your library resources or the web browser and search engine of your choice, identify an article that discusses managed services. Summarize the article, and be prepared to discuss your findings with your team or classmates.

3. What are the two broad categories that managed services companies can be divided into?

4. Consider one of the *Leading Contract Management Companies* discussed. Using your library resources or the web browser and search engine of your choice, perform a company/organization research on one of the companies mentioned. Do not repeat a company you have already investigated. See Chapter One for details of research.

5. Using your library resources or the web browser and search engine of your choice, find an article that discusses airline food and beverage service or one of the *Leading Airport/Airline Foodservice Providers*. Summarize the article, and be prepared to share and discuss the content with your team or classmates.

6. Briefly summarize the change and growth over the years in *Business and Industry Foodservice*.

7. Consider one of the *Leading Self-Operated B & I Dining Services* discussed. Using your library resources or the web browser and search engine of your choice, identify an article that discusses the foodservice at one of the companies mentioned. Alternatively, find an article that discusses self-operated B & I as a concept. Summarize the article, and bring your findings to class prepared for discussion.

8. Using your web browser of choice go to http://www.nacufs.org and perform a *virtual tour*. Summarize your findings and bring to class.

9. Using your library resources or the web browser and search engine of your choice, find an article that discusses a *Recreational Foodservice Provider*. Summarize the article, and bring your findings to class prepared for discussion with your team or classmates.

10. Summarize and discuss the key concerns relative to foodservice at correctional facilities.

11. Would you consider employment in a correctional facility foodservice? Justify your response, and support it with a relevant article.

12. Using your library resources or the web browser and search engine of your choice, find an article that discusses health care foodservice. Summarize the article, and bring your findings to class, prepared for discussion.

13. Consider the discussion on TQM/CQI. Using your library resources or the web browser and search engine of your choice, find an article that discusses TQM/CQI further. Summarize your findings and bring to class prepared for discussion.

Bibliography and Suggested Readings

Cornyn, J., Coons-Fasano, J. & Schechter, M. (1995). *Non-commercial Foodservice: An Administrator's Handbook*. New York, NY: John Wiley.

Matsumoto, J. & Dulen, J. (eds.). (1997). *Restaurants & Institutions*, August 15, 1997.

McCool, A. C., Smith, F. A. & Tucker, D. L. (1994). *Dimensions of Non-commercial Foodservice Management*. New York, NY: Van Nostrand Reinhold.

Warner, M. (1989). *Recreational Foodservice Management*. New York, NY: Van Nostrand Reinhold.

Warner, M. (1994). *Non-commercial, Institutional and Contract Foodservice Management*. New York, NY: John Wiley.

The Casino Gaming Perspective

John M. Tarras, *The School of Hospitality Business*, MICHIGAN STATE UNIVERSITY

ABSTRACT

This chapter will introduce the reader to the history and current status of casino gaming. The most important growth areas will be discussed. Gaming terminology and gaming specific positions will be introduced and defined. The key role that marketing plays in casino gaming will be emphasized. The chapter ends with a discussion of social considerations.

OBJECTIVES

At the end of this chapter the student should be able to:

1. Briefly describe the history of gaming in the United States.

2. Describe the growth of gaming.

3. Identify and describe several important gaming locations/destinations.

4. List and define important gaming terminology.

5. Describe several gaming companies.

6. Understand and discuss career opportunities within gaming.

7. Introduce and discuss the social and economic impacts of gaming.

Introduction

Gambling can be found in almost every area of the world. No one knows for sure when gambling first started, but it is safe to say that gaming has been around almost as long as mankind. As far as the United States is concerned, gambling has been part of our culture since the founding of the nation. Lotteries were a popular way to raise funds for public projects in early America until scandals caused many states to outlaw their use.

Gaming establishments expanded westward in the early to mid-19th century. During the California gold rush, San Francisco became one of the largest gambling centers in the United States. Slowly, states found gambling to be socially offensive and eventually all states outlawed legal gambling. However, illegal gambling still flourished with private clubs and with the playing of numbers (a form of street lottery) filling the void for people who wished to continue to gamble.

The modern era of legalized gambling in this country started when Nevada, in an attempt to improve its financial well being, legalized gambling in 1931. Nevada, was the only state with legalized gambling until New Jersey allowed casinos to operate in Atlantic City in 1976.

At the start of gaming in Nevada, Reno was the major city and had the toughest enforcement of gaming laws. Famous casino firms such as Harrah's got their start in Reno soon after it became legal. However, it was the building of Hoover Dam in the 1930s that soon allowed the small town of Las Vegas to become a major player in the casino business. Being a frontier town with little infrastructure, Las Vegas was ripe for organized crime to move in and profit from the lax atmosphere. Although many erroneously believe Benjamin "Bugsy" Siegel to be the founder of modern Las Vegas, the truth is that Las Vegas was already being established as a gaming center for the Los Angeles,

CA market well before he arrived on the scene.

Soon organized crime saw the benefit of operating casinos in Las Vegas; the house always had the odds in its favor, therefore, there was no need to cheat the customer. Because of its near monopoly on gambling, organized crime did little to draw attention to itself, henceforth, Las Vegas became one of the safest gaming markets in the world. With money illegally borrowed from the Teamsters Union, organized crime managed to build Las Vegas into the premier gaming center of the world.

Soon pressure from state regulators and Federal Bureau of Investigation began to take a toll on organized crimes hold on Las Vegas. When a wiretap in Kansas City, MO on the local crime family revealed the extent of the mob's activity in Las Vegas, it was the beginning of the end for organized crime in Las Vegas. Legitimate business people then began buying up the casinos. Most notable of these individuals was Howard Hughes.

The experience of organized crime in Las Vegas had one positive effect on the gaming industry in that regulation of the casinos became very strict. When New Jersey legalized casinos at Atlantic City in 1976, the state put in place elaborate control devices intended to keep organized crime out of the city. In fact, Hilton Corporation was once denied a casino license because one of their attorneys was accused of being associated with organized crime.

Today there is some form of gaming in all the states except Hawaii and Utah. As gaming has expanded throughout the country, new career opportunities have been created for hospitality majors. Competition has increased as casinos have expanded, and it is no longer a monopoly type operation with the attitude of "build and they shall come." Today's casino manager has to be service driven with a keen eye on the bottom line just like any other business. The casino industry today focuses not only on casinos, but the

total entertainment experience. In fact, Harrah's changed their name to Harrah's Entertainment to reflect the total experience it hopes to create for its customers. In today's modern casinos you will find first rate production shows, fine dining restaurants, first class rooms, attached shopping centers, and more, as casinos attempt to satisfy the needs of an ever demanding public. However, gaming is still the engine that drives the casino industry.

Gaming Industry Today

Las Vegas

Las Vegas is still the king of worldwide gaming with over 30 million visitors expected to visit the city each year. Las Vegas now has over 100,000 hotel rooms with more being constructed. Las Vegas is a major convention center hosting the Comdex computer show each year, which is the largest convention in the United States. Tourists from the entire world come to Las Vegas to enjoy the wide range of gaming and entertainment offered from the city in the desert.

As new and bigger casinos open, there becomes a point when the market will become saturated just like any business, and growth will slow down. In fact, recent mergers of gaming companies may suggest that the Las Vegas market may begin to reach that saturation point. This will mean that growth will only occur by taking business away from other casinos. Customer service and marketing will take on a new importance as casinos fight to keep their customers.

Atlantic City

The second largest gaming complex in the United States is Atlantic City, New Jersey. Here the casinos have clustered around the boardwalk that made the city famous. Atlantic City has the competitive advantage of being within a day's drive of the millions of inhabitants who live on the East Coast. Therefore, Atlantic City has relied more on the transient traveler who comes either by car or bus coach. During the early 1990s most Atlantic City casinos were losing money, and many thought that gaming was slowly coming to an end in the city. But new casinos and a revived economy provided the needed impetus to turn the gaming market around. Atlantic City has diversified itself by adding theme properties similar to Las Vegas and expanding the convention center in order to attract greater variety of customers. As competition increases, Atlantic City is adding more entertainment value for its gaming customers.

Riverboats

When the recession in the late 1980s began, states began looking for ways to raise revenue without increasing the taxes. Iowa was the first state to come up with the idea of issuing gaming licenses to riverboats. Iowa placed numerous restrictions on the boats' operations, including rather modest limits on gambling per person. Even still, the riverboat became a huge success and attracted attention from Iowa's neighbors.

Soon, Illinois passed its own riverboat legislation but without the loss restrictions that Iowa had. The boats in Iowa quickly lost market share and went out of business. Shortly thereafter, Louisiana, Missouri, Mississippi, and most recently Indiana added riverboat gambling.

Mississippi then went beyond riverboat gambling by only requiring that the casino float on water. Therefore the casinos could be put on barges, and land based hotels could be built next to them. Soon cities such as Biloxi, Tunica, and Gulfport became major gaming centers in the South. In fact, Mississippi is the third largest gaming market after Nevada and New Jersey.

Indian Gaming

One of the fastest areas of casino development has been on Indian reservations. Since Congress passed the Indian Gaming Regulatory Act in 1988, native Americans have been able to offer casino style gaming if the state offered similar games. Since most states did not offer slot machines, Indian tribes had to agree to sign compacts with the states, and, usually, pay a percentage of slot revenue to the state for the right to have slot machines. Since reserva-

tions are considered "sovereign nations" they are exempt from state betting limits or taxation.

The largest casino in the United States is the Pequot Indian tribe's Foxwoods casino located in Ledyard, Connecticut. In fact, tribal casinos have grown rapidly throughout the United States and have played a major role in the local economies where they are located. There has been controversy, though, that a few tribes are reaping the lion's share of profits, while tribes located in more remote areas have received little benefit from Indian gaming.

Other Markets

In 1996 Michigan voters approved a referendum allowing three casinos to operate within the city of Detroit. When these casinos are built, Detroit will be the largest city in the United States to have legalized casinos. The outlook for the expansion of casinos into other markets, however, is not as optimistic. There seems to be a trend among the states to limit the further expansion of casinos in this country.

❖ Voters in Colorado and South Dakota, where low stakes gaming is approved for a few old mining towns, failed in state referendums to raise the betting limits.

❖ A land based casino planned for downtown New Orleans, LA has been put on hold due to political infighting after the project went bankrupt during the construction of the permanent casino.

❖ The first Indian tribe casino went out of business in northern Washington, when Vancouver, Canada liberalized their casino rules and Canadian citizens stayed at home to gamble.

Casino gaming has spread to markets all over the country with mixed results. Some areas are opposed to the introduction of casinos on moral grounds, and others see casinos as just a convenient way to tax their con-

Photo courtesy Atlantic City Convention & Visitors Authority.

Atlantic City's casinos are clustered around the boardwalk that made the city famous.

stituents. Whatever the reasons, it appears that casino gaming is here to stay, and there will be a greater need for well-educated managers if the casino industry is to remain profitable.

Terms Used in the Industry

Like any business, casinos have their own particular language to describe transactions or customers. For instance, a "whale" is a very high roller that will get the royal treatment from any property where they chose to stay. The suites reserved for whales are small palaces and the whale has his own personal host to make sure that his every whim is taken care of. And why not—a typical whale can be betting millions of dollars during a single visit. It is estimated that there are only about 300 such customers who qualify as whales in the world, and the competition for this market is fierce.

Looking at the casino operation from the manager's point of view, there are some key concepts that must be understood. Since casinos deal a lot with cash, control and daily reporting of cash is an extremely important part of casino management. It is not surprising that the following terms deal with cash type transactions. The drop, handle, win, and hold percentage are the key reports a casino manager will monitor.

Table Drop

The table drop is basically the amount of money and markers that is placed into the drop box at a gaming table. This represents the amount of money the customer is willing to bet by exchanging his cash for chips. It does not mean that the customer will bet all the chips in his possession, but it does represent a cash transaction at the table. Therefore, the table drop is not a very accurate measurement of profit, since it does not measure the money actually wagered. However, it is an important control

device and for the table games a necessary part of the calculation in determining table wins.

Table Win

The table win is the amount that each table earns from its game. It is the gross winning before any operating expenses such as salaries and fixed cost are subtracted.

The calculation of the table win can be shown by the following example:

Cash drop	$	1,500
Markers (credit drop)	+	500
Redeemed markers	−	1,000
Total Drop	=	1,000
Opening chip totals		25,000
Fills	+	1,000
Credits	−	500
Chips available	=	25,500
Closing chip totals	−	24,700
Cost of Games	= $	800
Total Drop	$	1,000
Cost of Games	−	800
Win	= $	200

"Opening chip total" is the amount of chips the table is stocked with at the beginning of the shift. The dealer will verify the total before opening the table by comparing the chips in the till to the final inventory slip from the previous shift. The "fill" is the amount of chips that are added to the table after play has started. The fill usually occurs because the table is losing, markers are issued, or players purchase a large number of chips and leave the table. Fills are ordered by management and brought over to the table by security from the cashiers' cage. "Credits" occur when the chips are sent back to the cashiers' cage. This occurs only when the table has more chips than space to accommodate them. This is a very rare occasion for casinos.

In the example above, the casino has won $200 from table play. The table win will vary greatly in a casino over a period of time based on the fluctuations of wins and losses. But over the longer period of time the casino's win should be very close to the house advantage on the table game.

Hold Percentage

The hold percentage is the percentage of gaming revenue retained by the casino divided by the casino activity. It is the percentage of the drop the casino wins. The casino's hold percentage should be close to equal the percentage of expected casino advantage percentage over a period of time. In our example above the table hold percentage would equal 20% ($200 win/ $1,000 drop).

The drop, win, and hold percentages are used by management to monitor the gaming activity on the individual table games. It is similar to management in a hotel reviewing the occupancy and average daily room rates.

Slot Machine Drop

The term drop for slot machines has a different meaning. First the gross amount of coins and currency put into a slot machine is called the slot handle. This is the gross amount of betting by the customer on a given machine. The slot drop is the final amount of coins in the bucket and currency in the bill acceptor when the machine is cleared out. The slot drop is the coins or tokens that fall into a hopper that has reached its predetermined level. These coins and tokens are then automatically diverted into the drop bucket located in the slot cabinet below the slot device.

Slot Win

The slot win is the slot drop minus any jackpots that were hand paid and minus any hopper fills. The following example demonstrates how slot winnings are accounted for:

Coins in (handle)	Can go in hopper or drop bucket	$5,000
Currency in	Goes into bill acceptor box	700
Total handle		$5,700
Slot Drop	Coin comes out of the hopper	
	Coins in bucket and currency in bill acceptor	$1,145
Jackpots paid by hand		− 45
Hopper fills		− 700
Slot wins		$ 400

The slot win percentage then would be 8% ($400 win/$5,000 coin handle). The management would again monitor these figures and compare them to the theoretical win percentage. Over time the win percentage and theoretical win should be close to equal.

Casino Management

The casino industry is one of the most structured organizations in any business setting. This is due in part to the heavy emphasis on controls needed to ensure honesty and compliance with governmental regulations. At the top of the casino hierarchy is the director of casino operations. This person is responsible for all that goes on in the casino. He usually has vast discretionary powers to ensure that the casino is operating in an efficient and effective manner. However, his power is limited by strong internal controls and government regulations that prevent him from entering sensitive areas such as surveillance and counting rooms. These rules are designed, as are most of the rules in a casino, to prevent criminal collusion or evidence tampering. Also, in most jurisdictions the casino management must go through a rigorous process of being approved to work in the casino by the state's government regulatory agency.

The next level of management is the assistant casino director who works with the casino director. His job usually consists of ensuring that

the detail requirements of the casino are being taken care of, and he will be the acting casino director when the casino director is absent.

Shift Managers

Casinos operate twenty-four hours a day and divide the workday into three shifts for the casino (day, swing, and graveyard). Casinos use three shift managers to manage the personnel for each shift. The shift managers become the authoritative source in the absence of the casino director or assistant casino director. The shift managers are responsible for directing the activities of the casino personnel. They need to understand the games and spend a great deal of their time in the operations area to make sure the casino is operating properly. All the pit bosses report to the shift managers.

Pit Bosses

For all the table games (blackjack, dice, baccarat, roulette, Caribbean stud poker, etc.) in the casino, an individual is placed in charge of a group of tables known as the pit. It is the pit boss's job to complete the work schedules and supervise the floorpersons. However, the pit boss's primary job is to monitor all gaming activities within his area. He may also be required to approve credit for a customer, settle player disputes, and make sure that all the rules of the casino are being followed correctly.

Floorperson

The floorperson is under the pit boss and is the first management line in the casino. He is usually assigned four tables or less to monitor and makes sure the games are operating according to prescribed internal control rules.

The primary duty of the floorperson is to track the table game players for betting habits and rating the higher betting players. Floorpersons usually rate players based upon the average bet and duration of play. The floorperson will fill out a rating sheet and that sheet will be entered into the computer to determine the level of *comps* a player can receive. The "*comps*" are the free perks that a player may receive (see page 162).

The floorperson is responsible for replenishment of tables short of chips and handling any minor player disputes. He will also verify chip amounts brought to the hotel by security, and he maintains a running count of money paid in and paid out during the shift.

Slot Department

The slot machines are becoming an increasingly important part of casinos. In some casinos they can represent over 75% of the gaming dollars taken by the casino. Because of the computerization of today's slot machines it is very easy to rate players and reward them based on their level of play.

A slot manager heads the slot department. This person is responsible for maximizing revenues from slot machines by determining the type and denominations of machines on the floor. He also coordinates slot tournaments and other promotions with the marketing department to enhance slot play.

As with table games, the slot manager is responsible for determining the number and location of personnel in the slot department. He also has the responsibility of ensuring that the slot machines meet the standards of regulatory agencies and the internal control department. Also, the slot manager is responsible for the overall running of the slot club. This is an important marketing tool which awards points for money spent by the casino slot guest. These points can be redeemed for prizes or cash depending on the particulars of the casino's slot program.

Each shift is headed by a shift manager who is in charge of the day to day details of the slot operation. He can usually be found on the slot floor moving from area to area ensuring that the slot operation is running smoothly and handling any major disputes that may arise.

The slot floorperson is assigned a specific area and is responsible for the payment of any "handpay" jackpots (when the machine runs out of coins or the payoff is larger than the machine can handle, the floorperson will "handpay" the jackpot). Also, any jackpots paid in excess of $1,200 require a tax declaration form, which is usually handled by the slot floorperson. Finally, when a machine is out of coins, the slot floorperson ensures that the machine is filled from the cashiers' cage in accordance with casino policy.

Slot departments make it easy for slot players to cash out by establishing one or more slot booths. The slot booth cashiers sell rolls or racks of coins and also redeem coins or tokens from slot players. The coins are usually dumped into an automatic counter, which sorts the coins and registers on a meter how much the player has coming.

Often casinos have special progressive or special-attraction slot machines in a round or rectangular configuration known as a carousel. A carousel attendant will stand on a platform behind the machines and dispense coins to patrons who wish to play.

Finally, the casino will have a "change person." This person walks with a cart around the slot area selling coins to slot patrons. However, with bill validators becoming more

Slot machines are becoming an increasingly important part of casinos.

and more popular, the changeperson is slowly going the way of the mechanical slot machine. Future generations of players will more than likely prefer the easier and faster method of sliding paper money into the bill validator.

Casino Marketing

As the casino industry matures, casino marketing is becoming an increasingly important department in casinos. The salaries of casino marketing managers tend to be much higher than marketing executives of hotel companies. The reason is simple; the dollar amounts involved are much higher for a casino. The marketing manager uses many techniques to attract customers for a particular casino. For instance, the casino director working with the casino marketing manager may target certain gamblers who bet large sums of money. It is important for this type of customer to be extremely pleased with his experience so that he will return over and over again. Therefore, some upscale gaming properties may offer free corporate jet and limousine service, large suites, gourmet meals, and private gaming areas, all at no cost to the customer. Obviously the casino hopes to make the money back through the customer's play.

Not all casinos target high rollers; many casinos offer low room rates and loose slots to attract the small time gambler to a property. They are more concerned with winning a little money on each customer but having a large volume of business. Other

casinos appeal to upper income individuals who may not gamble much, but who expect luxury rooms, good service and friendly dealers, upscale eating establishments, and are willing to pay for those amenities.

Each property is different. What they all have in common, though, is service to the guest. The casino industry is really the entertainment industry. Gone are the days when a casino would open and people would flock into the casino just to gamble. Today, the typical gambler, and for that matter the non-gambler, is looking at gaming as just one aspect of his or her entertainment experience. That is why today's casinos are full-service entertainment complexes offering shows, fine dining, arcades, special attractions, amusement rides, and themes. Such casinos are looking at the property to make a profit on many different levels, not just from the casino.

Comps

The most important marketing tool for casinos is the "comping" of guests for their play. The idea of comps is to return to the player a certain percentage of the money lost through gambling. The one comp that everybody qualifies for is free drinks if you are actively gambling; any comps after that depend on the level of the guest play. Usually, comps are divided between table players and slot players with each having their own set of criteria for comping by the hotel. For a table player, the average bet, amount of playing time, and the theoretical win percentage for the house are taken into account in measuring the amount of comps to be rewarded. In blackjack, because it is a skill game, the casino will also rate the player based on his playing skill. The casino has a theoretical win percentage on each game and returns a portion of that theoretical win to the player. For instance, if the theoretical win percentage from blackjack is 2% and the average bet for a trip is $4,000 per hour ($100 a hand for 40 plays an hour), the casino would expect to win $80 and may return up to 40% of that win to the player, or in this case $32. This $32 multiplied by hours played would determine the level of comps the player would qualify for. The more the player is willing to risk the higher the return to the guest by the casino. So a player who averages a bet of $25 per hand of blackjack for four hours of play a day may qualify for a reduced room rate. A player who averages $50 dollars per hand of blackjack for four hours of play may qualify for a free room, and a player who averages $75 per hand of blackjack for four hours a day may qualify for free room and meals. Players who are willing to risk thousands of dollars per hand may qualify for free airfare, free suites, free food and beverage, show tickets, etc.

Not all casinos have the same comp schedule and it is important for a player to ask the casino what qualifies for complimentary treatment. Obviously, a high roller establishment will have greater qualifying limits than a small family-style casino.

In order to cater to the frequent gambler, most casinos have hosts whose job is to see to it that the play of the gambler is recorded accurately, and that his or her needs are taken care of within the parameters for that type of bettor. For instance, a host can analyze a player's record on the computer and make an immediate determination as to what comps the player is entitled to. Also, each player is different and the host will often smooth the way for a guest to get special consideration, especially if the guest has been a long-term customer of the casino.

Casinos today are much more sensitive to the type of guest who is staying at a property. For instance, a convention guest usually will not gamble as much as a typical visitor and so the casino will often charge a higher room rate for this type of guest. So, casinos have gone to yield management techniques when filling rooms. During the off-season a person may be able to stay at first class hotel for $70 a night while during the convention season that same room will cost the guest $250 a night. Casinos are making an effort to turn all departments into profit centers and identifying those gamblers who rate the special room comps.

Slot hosts, on the other hand, are more noticeable within the casino. The slot machines are computerized and players are given cards, which when inserted into a slot machine accurately record their play. Since slots theoretical win is already built into each machine, the cards can accurately record the play of the guest and award comps based on a point system developed by the casino. Therefore, a slot host booth is usually set up with various merchandise and awards so that the slot player, by inserting his or her card in a validator, can see how many points he or she has accumulated. The accumulated points will determine which type of merchandise or comps the player is entitled.

Promotions

One of more common methods of drawing guests back to the casino is to offer special promotions. The most common promotion used by casinos is the slot tournament. Slot tournament invitations are usually mailed out to the best slot customers with a special bank of slot machines reserved for tournament play. The players are usually given generous room and food discounts and at the end the player with the highest point total wins a large cash prize. Some casinos hold tournaments for the general public on a daily or weekly basis. These tournaments involve a fee and a percentage of the fees collected are returned to the winning players as prize money.

Another type of promotion is the direct mailing offers. Casinos, during traditional slow periods, will offer promotions to their customers in the hope of generating additional business that they otherwise would not get. Depending on the value of the customer, the promotion could be a reduced room rate or a full room, food, and beverage comp for a limited number of days. Other promotions include parties for selected guests, golf tournaments, boxing matches, tennis matches, and any special event that will attract large numbers of people and gamblers.

Casino Host

The casino host is to ensure that premium players are treated properly. They coordinate the room reservations, maintain computer reports on players assigned to them, meet the premium player at the airport or hotel entrance, and arrange for show tickets. Many casinos have special check-in areas for the invited player so that they do not have to wait in line, and even at times, a hostess will greet the player at check-in to make sure his or her needs are taken care of personally. The primary functions of a casino host are soliciting and booking major players for the casino, and making sure the guest experience is truly exceptional for the high roller.

◆ Social Considerations

Although gaming has spread throughout the country, there are many questions about the social cost of gaming and its effect on society. Many would argue that gambling is a vice that takes advantage of people who are least able to afford the losses. On the other hand, there are those who view gambling simply as one of many choices a person has on which to spend his entertainment dollar. Both sides believe strongly in their own arguments. The fact remains, however, that people more and more see gaming as an acceptable form of entertainment. Gaming has grown so fast in this country that it is very difficult to measure the impact gaming has had on society as a whole. Some concerns of the public towards gambling are briefly discussed below.

Compulsive Gambling

There is no doubt that certain individuals have trouble with gambling. They spend more than they have and they get into economic trouble due their gambling compulsion. What is not clear however, is how big a problem it really is. Recent studies have cast some light on the subject, but there remains much to be researched before the extent of the problem is known.

What is known is that the compulsive gambler needs to stop gambling, just as the alcoholic needs to stop drinking. To that end the gaming industry has been funding programs for compulsive gamblers, including the national organization called Gamblers Anonymous that publishes literature on the subject of problem gambling. Help for compulsive gamblers is available through local chapters of Gamblers Anonymous. An addicted gambler has a serious problem and there are no easy solutions.

Increase in Crime

Opponents state that gambling increases the crime rate in the area of the casino. Again, studies differ on this point. Some studies show that crime rate does go up. However, other studies show that the actual per capita rate of crime decreases when a casino opens. The reason often put forth is that the security present in casinos is actually a deterrent to criminal activity. Crimes such as check forgery, child abandonment, prostitution, and drunk driving, which occur due to casino activity, have not been studied enough to render a firm opinion on the extent of the problem.

Hurts the Poor

Casino opponents argue that people who can least afford to gamble are the ones who lose the most. Instead of spending money on the necessities of life, the gambler spends his or her money in the casino. The truth is that there is no evidence that gaming contributes to a lower standard of living for most individuals. Some would argue that, outside the small percentage of compulsive gamblers, gaming has a positive impact on the local economy, and thus on many poorer individuals.

Diverts Money Away from Other Businesses

The argument here is that gambling is a service industry and does not produce any goods and products, and that bowling establishments, theaters, restaurants, etc. are all hurt by the casino. Although a person's discretionary income is limited, proponents would argue that people are free to spend their money as they see fit, and one should let the market decide.

Conclusion

Gaming in the United States and around the world is growing at a rapid rate. Casinos can be found in the majority of states and countries around the world. Its acceptance has created a service industry that has grown into the largest entertainment industry in the world. The need for professional managers is growing faster than the supply that is currently available. Like any service industry, those companies that provide the best total amenities in the customer's mind are going to dominate. Therefore, savvy casino companies are recognizing, for the first time, the need for well-trained professional staff and managers to keep their guests in an ever-increasingly competitive environment.

The future of the casino industry from a career perspective has never been more attractive. As the baby boom generation nears retirement, more and more of them will be available to the gaming industry. However, people are looking for value for their dollars and if a casino does not measure up, the consumer will take his or her business elsewhere.

Gaming in the U.S. and around the world is growing at a rapid rate.

Questions and Assignments

1. Summarize the history of gaming in the United States.

2. Using your library resources or the web browser and search engine of your choice, develop a summary statement of gaming and hospitality in Las Vegas. Bring your findings to class prepared for a discussion.

3. Choose a gaming location that is not in Nevada. Using your library resources or the web browser and search engine of your choice, develop a summary statement of gaming and hospitality at that location. Bring your findings to class prepared for a discussion with your team or classmates.

4. Using your library resources or the web browser and search engine of your choice, identify a gaming company. Perform organization/company research as discussed in the first chapter of this text.

5. Define and differentiate the following gaming terms: table drop, table win, hold percentage, slot machine drop, slot machine handle, and slot win.

6. Define and discuss the role of the gaming-specific employees discussed in the chapter. Do not include a discussion of positions found in other segments of the hospitality industry.

7. Using your library resources, or the web browser and search engine of your choice, identify a current (no older than one year) article that discusses gaming and hospitality. Summarize your findings, and be prepared to discuss your results with your team or classmates.

8. Discuss gaming from the marketing perspective. How does casino marketing differ from traditional hospitality marketing?

9. Summarize the social considerations mentioned in the chapter. Using your library resources or the web browser and search engine of your choice, identify an article that discusses one or more social concerns raised by gaming. The following web site may be a good starting point: http://www.americangaming.org

10. Identify two positive aspects of gaming development. Using your library resources or the web browser and search engine of your choice, identify an article that supports your position. Be prepared to discuss your findings with your team or classmates.

11. Using your library resources or the web browser and search engine of your choice, identify a non-U.S. gaming location and describe in summary fashion the available gaming and hospitality services and products. The following web sites may be helpful starting points: http://www.euroslot.com, http://www.wheretobet.com

Bibliography and Suggested Readings

Hashimoto, K., Kline, F. S. & Fenich, G. G. (1998). *Casino Management*. Dubuque, IA: Kendall-Hunt Publishing Company.

Marshall, L. H. & Rudd, D. P. (1996). *Introduction to Casino and Gaming Operations*. Englewood Cliffs, NJ: Prentice Hall.

UNLV International Gaming Institute (1996). *The Gaming Industry: Introduction and Perspectives*. New York, NY: John Wiley & Sons.

10

The Lodging Perspective

A.J. Singh, *The School of Hospitality Business*, MICHIGAN STATE UNIVERSITY

ABSTRACT

This chapter will cover the lodging industry from the middle of this century through 1997. The major economic fluctuations and trends will be highlighted and discussed. The proliferation of brands and industry consolidation will be introduced and explained in terms of industry impacts and structural changes.

OBJECTIVES

At the end of this chapter the student should be able to:

1. Describe the developments in the U.S. lodging industry since the 1950s.

2. Discuss the central factors that are seen as contributing to the lodging industry recession and recovery.

3. List and explain the primary characteristics of several lodging brands.

4. Describe in detail one of the top twenty-five management companies with an eye on career opportunities.

5. Establish the growth rates of chains versus independent lodging companies.

6. Explain the characteristics of various lodging company structures.

7. List and describe the various lodging market segments.

8. List and describe the anticipated impacts of industry consolidation.

9. Define various lodging terminology.

Introduction

The modern hotel industry had its genesis in the period following World War II. However, the structure of the industry during that period bears little resemblance to the hotel industry of today. In 1948, hotels with fewer than 50 rooms dominated the industry. They represented about 85 percent of all hotel establishments and 40 percent of the number of rooms. Almost all hotels were independently owned and operated. Less than 5 percent belonged to a hotel chain (Winfree, 1996). The number of rooms in the industry has grown from 1,854,044 in 1948 to 3,525,000 in 1997.

The post World War II period (1945–1950) represented a time when travel in the United States became increasingly popular. An improving economy, shorter workweeks, increased disposable income, construction of highways, and improvements in automobile and air travel stimulated this trend. However, the shortage of material and capital during the war years resulted in a hotel room product that was aging. Thus this period saw a significant amount of updating, replacing, and building of hotels after years of neglect through the depression and war.

A new type of highway-oriented hotel called the motel began appearing in the 1950s. This was in response to the burgeoning number of automobile travelers. Table 1 indicates the percentage shift in the number of establishments from hotels to motels in this period. These early motels were small "no-frill" facilities with basic (very limited) amenities. As the industry saw the coexistence of hotels and motels, competition between the two segments became heated. Motels started to offer more amenities and started to resemble hotels, while hotels started to lower room rates to compete with motels. As a result the distinction between the two segments started to erode.

T1	**Distribution of Hotels by Type Establishment**	
Year	Hotel Percentage	Motel Percentage
1939	67.4	32.6
1948	53.4	46.6
1954	45.7	54.3
1958	41.4	58.6
1963	35.3	64.7
1967	36.0	64.0
1972	23.8	76.2
1977	24.2	75.8

Source: *Hospitality in Transition.* Albert J. Gomes. 1985

Lodging Industry in the 1950s and 1960s

The Birth of Franchising

One of the major drawbacks of motels and hotels during this period (1950s) was that their services were not standardized, as a result, hotel guests did not know what type of product to expect when they checked in. This deficiency in the hotel product was first detected and rectified by Kemmons Wilson, who founded Holiday Inn in 1952, and who is credited for introducing the concept of a standardized hotel product. The Holiday Inn concept revolutionized the hotel industry by introducing a motel with standardized service, a recognizable name, and moderate prices (Rushmore, 1992).

Expansion

In the 1960s U.S. hotel chains such as InterContinental Hotels and Hilton Hotels began to expand their operations into South America and Europe. Further, lodging chains expanded through vertical integration. Trans World Airlines (TWA) purchased Hilton International (1967), United Airlines purchased Westin Hotels and American Airlines started to acquire hotels under Americana Hotels. This strategy was conducted in the belief that accommodations and transportation companies are synergistic and therefore more viable as

one company. Later divestitures indicated that this strategy did not have the intended outcome.

Other factors during this period that influenced the rapid increase in the supply of hotel rooms include the passage of the Interstate Highway Act of 1956, which laid out a blueprint for the establishment of a network of national highways. On the demand side, population growth and migration, increase in household formation, rising incomes, increase in leisure time, and business development in the suburbs resulted in more travel. A by-product of increased business activity was the introduction of the meeting and conventions market, which resulted in the creation of convention hotel products, such as the New York Hilton in 1963 (Winfree, 1996).

A final factor that influenced hotel supply during this period was a change in income tax laws in 1954, which allowed accelerated depreciation. This change in the accounting rule resulted in the development of hotels to take advantage of tax benefits provided by the new depreciation method, which allowed them to take larger depreciation in the early years of the investment. A major drawback of this type of investing was that in order to keep up the high depreciation and interest deductions, new properties had to be added continuously to an investor's portfolio, resulting in occasional poor investment choices, (Rushmore, 1992). This factor, unlike the others, was not demand related, and resulted in hotel development decisions dictated not by the economics of the operation but by the tax savings offered by the hotel real estate venture. Similar, "tax driven" supply increases were to plague the hotel industry later in the century.

Lodging Industry in the 1970s

The increase in the hotel room growth trend of the 1960s continued into the early 1970s. Many of the chains established in the 1950s and 1960s started to carve a niche in the budget segment of the industry. These companies were now established as franchisors, and they used the franchising vehicle to aggressively establish critical mass.

Combined with aggressive corporate growth strategies, financing was readily available, especially through mortgage and equity REIT's (Real Estate Investment Trusts). Rushmore (1992) states that the high leverage finance companies created allowed small investors to participate in real estate mortgages and equities, making billions of dollars available to finance real estate projects. As a result, many lenders became so overwhelmed with new money that their underwriting procedures broke down. The net result of aggressive franchising policies and readily available capital was overbuilding and the development of hotels in poorly located sites. National occupancies dropped to 59 percent in 1972.

The supply/demand imbalance put pressure on lodging companies to find new ways to grow. As they were not able to grow by increasing demand for their product, chains started to pursue multiple segments, whereby, one chain may have more than one brand, targeting a different type of customer. Thus the lodging industry chains were introduced to the concept of market segmentation, which has continued to the present period. The advent of market segmentation was a sign of the maturation of the lodging industry (Ader & Lefleur, 1997).

The bubble burst in 1973 with the Arab oil embargo and the subsequent energy crisis. Annual hotel occupancies plummeted due to decreased travel and many marginal properties were foreclosed. This was followed by a recession in 1975.

The late 1970s was a period of rough equilibrium between supply and demand. New construction was constrained because of the recent losses incurred by lenders on hotel properties. A combination of higher demand during the 1977–1979 period coupled with high inflation resulted in Average Daily Rates (ADR) escalating. Between 1977–1980 ADRs increased at a compounded annual rate of 16.8 percent (Ader & Lefleur, 1997). As a result of high inflation, interest rates were raised resulting in an increase in the cost of borrowing, and developing new hotels became expensive. With a reduction in new room growth, and a continued increase in demand, this period saw an increase in occupancy from 63.9 percent in 1975 to 72.6 percent in 1979 (PKF, Trends in the Hotel Industry, 1988–1997).

Lodging Industry in the 1980s

The 1980s was a turbulent period for the hotel industry. The decade started with a building boom as a result of tax incentives for real estate investment, availability of capital, and product segmentation.

Tax Incentives

Beginning in 1981, the passage of the Economic Recovery Tax Act (ERTA) made investment in commercial real estate very attractive. ERTA cut corporate, individual, and capital gains taxes. Further, by changing the depreciation rules, it made investment in commercial real estate (including hotels) profitable on an after tax basis. In addition, the rules of taxation allowed passive investors (such as those in a limited partnership) to offset income generated in other activities to be offset by losses incurred by their participation in these limited partnerships. This resulted in the formation of syndicated limited partnerships to take advantage of these tax benefits. Thus capital flowed to finance the industry for "non-economic" deals (non-cashflow generating).

Availability of Capital

On the debt side, the Depository Institutions Deregulation and Monetary Control Act of 1980 (DIDMCA) and the Garn-St. Germain Depository Institutions Act of 1982 deregulated the Savings & Loan (S&L) industry. This allowed them to make commercial loans for the first time. As a result massive infusion of debt capital flowed to the lodging industry by inexperienced lenders. Many of these loans were made with minimal underwriting standards and insufficient regard for the substantial risks involved in hotel development (for further discussion, see Flannery & Flannery, 1990).

In 1986 the Tax Reform Act (TRA) was passed and it took away the previous tax benefits of commercial real estate investment. Depreciation schedules were increased to 31.5 years, the investment tax credit was repealed, and earned income could no longer be sheltered by passive investment losses. Many of the hotels that had been built to take advantage of the tax laws were now exposed because of their uneconomical capital structure (very high leverage) and inadequate debt coverage. This resulted in many of the hotel owners defaulting on their loans and many Savings & Loan Institutions that had over extended themselves into commercial real estate became insolvent. This was known as the "S&L Crisis."

From 1983 to 1987 annual growth of room supply was more than 4 percent each year, and in 1987 it was over 7 percent. Demand could not keep up with the frenzied pace with which new hotels were being added. Hotel operators competed by slashing room rates.

Product Segmentation

The third factor that "assisted" the over development scenario was that the market segmentation strategy adopted by chains evolved into "product segmentation." With the increase in competition, chains saw that the only way to grow was by creating new products. In the words of one management consultant, "Proliferation of new products has been overdone by lodging companies, which dreamed up more concepts than there are real and discernable market segments" (Trice, 1992). These products were being created by franchisors who realized that the creation of certain critical mass is important for franchise brand awareness. Transactions, a research report by Hotel Motel Brokers of America (HMBA, 1991), summarized the situation correctly. It states, "In retrospect, the rationale for the 80s hotel construction boom is easy to see; franchisors created new products for developers to build; lenders had capital to lend; and developers could acquire capital on "soft" terms with construction profits financed as part of the package."

During this period, the only truly new products created were the extended stay and all-suite products. The all-suite product was based upon the theory that many of the business travelers do not use facilities such as meeting, banquet, and restaurant space. By eliminating this space and providing additional space in the guestroom by converting them into suites, a hotel would provide more value to the guests. Since their introduction the all suite segment has been the fastest growing segment in the U.S. lodging industry.

The extended stay product was designed to target a traveler who stays in an area for longer periods, either due to relocation or extended projects. The facilities in these hotels resemble a residential atmosphere. So much so that checking into one of these accommodations does not involve going to the front desk. Further, the layout of the guestrooms is more like a mini-apartment or studio.

Although not a completely new product, the "Microtel" may be considered the 1980s version of the original budget motels of the late 1950s. Now, as then, the motels that started as budget started to add amenities (due to competitive pressure) and eventually, moved up into the mid-price category. The Microtel filled the vacuum thus created, and are smaller, less expensive to construct, yet provide all the basic amenities.

Five Category Classification

Pannell Kerr Forster (PKF) has developed a five-category classification scheme for hotels. This is presented in Table 2. It is clear that by the 1980s the industry evolved from the simple dichotomy of hotels vs. motels (of the 1960s) into its present structure consisting of multiple products. The impact of the profusion of products is seen later in the chapter, which outlines the various current brands in the industry.

Management Contracts

Although the history of management contracts in the hotel industry can be traced back to the 1960s and 1970s, they were not as prevalent. Owners generally operated their own hotel. As Charles A. Bell (1993) points out, there were less than 22 management contracts in 1970, this increased to 182 in 1975, and by 1980, there were too many to count. The primary reason for this growth was the increase in passive investors that owned hotels during this period to take advantage of the hotel real estate tax benefits discussed earlier in this section.

The introduction of the management contract presented a fundamental change in the structure of the lodging industry—this was the separation of lodging ownership from its management. The former represents the real estate component while the latter its business component. Hotel companies realized that the hotel business was really a hybrid of two businesses, real estate and lodging. "Hotel companies began selling ownership of the existing hotels to, and developing new projects with, investment groups who sought the benefits of real estate ownership, but who had no interest or expertise in hotel operations. In return, hotel companies kept long-term management contracts, giving them operational control over the properties for a stipulated management fee. The arrangement could either include the right to use a brand name along with the management services (e.g., Mar-

riott), or include just management services (eg. Interstate), with the brand provided by a third party franchiser (e.g., Choice or HFS)" (Ader & Lefleur, 1997).

Lodging Industry Structure from 1990 to the Current Period

Recession

As the lodging industry entered 1990's it was severely impacted by the national recession which now occurred. The excesses of the 1980's resulted in a dramatic increase of hotel rooms. Now this overbuilt scenario faced the brunt of declining demand for rooms due to reduction of overall travel as a result of the Persian Gulf War (1990–91) and the recession. As noted in Table 3 national occupancies bottomed out at 61.8 percent. Due to the oversupply of rooms, hotels had to reduce room rates, which further impact profitability. Table 3 shows the negative profitability of the hotel industry during this period.

Economic Impacts

Hotels have different economic occupancy levels based upon a variety of factors, such as changes in tax laws, cost of capital (interest rate), and changes in Average Daily Rate. The economic occupancy is the level at which new construction can be justified. Prior to 1986, a new hotel could be justified at occupancy levels as low as 59.5 percent. However, once those tax benefits were taken away, economic occupancy levels rose up to 70 percent. The predicament that the hotel industry found itself in was that hotels, which were constructed on the basis of pre-1986 economics, now had to perform at much higher levels of occupancy to survive. As Ader and Lefleur (1997) state in their analysis of the lodging industry, by 1991 every $0.15 out of every dollar in revenue was going to pay debt. This compares to $0.06 of every dollar in 1977.

Five-Category Classification Scheme for the Hotel Industry

Price	Function	Location	Market Served	Distinctiveness of Style or Offerings
BUDGET/ECONOMY 1. Rooms-only 2. Little public space 3. No food and beverage	**CONVENTION** 1. Large hotels 2. 500+ guest rooms 3. Extensive public space 4. Extensive meeting space	**DOWNTOWN** 1. High rise structures 2. Attached parking 3. Wide mix of facilities and amenities	**EXECUTIVE CONFERENCE CENTER** 1. Secluded settings 2. Smaller properties 3. Less than 300 rooms 4. Small meeting rooms 5. Audio visual facilities 6. Variety of recreation facilities	**ALL-SUITE** 1. Larger than normal guestrooms 2. Separate living and sitting areas 3. Minimum public space 4. Facilities equipped for extended stay
MIDDLE-MARKET 1. Wider range of facilities and amenities	**COMMERCIAL** 1. Functional guest rooms 2. Ample work area 3. Small meeting and conference rooms 4. Limited recreation	**SUBURBAN** 1. Low to mid-rise structures 2. Surface parking 3. Meeting and banquet facilities	**HEALTH SPA** 1. Catering to market with specific need (weight loss or hedonistic experience) 2. Variety of trained professionals on staff (dieticians, therapists, and counselors)	**HISTORIC CONVERSION** 1. Well known historic buildings and landmarks renovated or converted to hotels
LUXURY 1. Upscale décor and furnishings 2. Concierge service 3. High quality public space 4. Higher than average employee to guestroom ratio		**HIGHWAY** 1. Low rise structures 2. Surface parking 3. Exterior corridors 4. Some have outdoor pools **AIRPORT** 1. Adjacent or attached to airports 2. Efficient and functional	**RESORT** 1. Emphasis on recreation 2. Extensive food and beverage 3. Banquet facilities 4. Picturesque setting	**HOTELS IN MXD'S** 1. Mixed use developments consisting of hotels, retail, and other attractions

Source: PKF Consulting

Note: Many types of hotels can be defined by more than one classification scheme. For example, a resort hotel can be defined by market, location, and style of offerings.

Analysis of Lodging Industry Performance (1990–1992)

Year	Supply % Change	Demand % Change	Occu-pancy	Occupancy % Change	ADR*	ADR % Change	REVPAR**	REVPAR % Change	GOP***	Fixed Charges	Profits $Billions
1990	3.2%	1.9%	63.5%	(1.1%)	$57.96	2.9%	$36.82	2.9%	25.5%	32.1%	–5.7
1991	1.4	(1.3)	61.8	(2.6)	58.08	0.2	35.91	(2.5)	27.4	29.7	–2.8
1992	0.7	1.9	62.6	1.3	58.91	1.4	36.87	2.7	29.5	26.5	0.0

Source: Smith Travel Research

*Average daily rate

**Revenue per available room

***Gross operating profit

To further compound the problem, many of the loans made in the 1980s were now coming due. The structure of these loans required a large lump sum payment at the end of the loan term. This type of financing structure is known as a "bullet loan." The consequence of this negative economic situation was an increase in the number of non-performing loans, leading to increased case foreclosures. The number of delinquent loans increased dramatically during the period from 1990 to 1992. After 1992, as loans were restructured, new loans were cut back, and the overall performance of the lodging industry started to gradually improve, the amount of foreclosures also began to reduce.

The direct result of these non-performing hotel loans was the virtual elimination of new hotel loans to the industry from traditional financing sources such as commercial banks, life insurance companies, and savings and loan institutions. Furthermore, the 1989 Financial Institutions Recovery and Enforcement Act of 1989 (FIRREA) required more stringent capital standards for thrift institutions.

Reduction of Hotel Values

The oversupply of hotel rooms during this period also impacted the value of hotel real estate, which started to plummet and finally reached rock bottom in 1991. Hotel properties that were taken back by the lender in a foreclosure, or were part of the REO portfolio (Real Estate Owned) of savings and loans and were acquired by the Resolution Trust Corporation (RTC), sold at especially discounted prices (see Table 4 for average selling price per room). The majority of the sellers during this time were financial institutions.

During this period, to take advantage of the exceptionally low hotel values, the lodging industry saw an infusion of foreign capital, especially European and Japanese investors that found U.S. real estate inexpensive. Domestic investors with capital access were also buyers of hotel real estate.

T4	Average Selling Price of Hotels 1987–1991	
Year		Average Selling Price Per Room
1987		$20,713
1988		23,630
1989		20,688
1990		21,539
1991		18,400
1992		18,741
1993		17,411
1994		19,068

Source: Hotel Motel Brokers Association (HMBA)

Lodging Industry Recovery

The lodging industry gradually began to recover in 1992. Hotel occupancies increased to 62.6 percent. This was the result of a 1.9 percent increase in demand and only a 0.7 percent increase in room supply. Financing was still difficult to find during this period, as lenders were still trying to dispose of their hotel real estate. Hotel values started to increase over 1991, which was a reversal from the declining trend of the past three years.

This period also saw a proliferation of management companies. Many of these companies managed as few as two or three hotels, and signed short term management agreements with an owner, especially a financial institution that needed to reposition and sell a distressed property. Due to

the flood of management companies during this period, management fees dropped to an all time low. Some companies would sign on for as low as a half percent of revenue. Many of these companies came to be known as "Work out" specialists, which meant that they improved the profitability of a hotel primarily to increase its market value and make a quick sale.

The year 1993 was critical for the lodging industry on its road to recovery. Occupancies and room rates showed an up tick and the industry was once again profitable. This was a combined result of a reduction in debt service due to the sale or restructuring of most distressed hotels and tighter controls instituted by the management companies discussed above. Table 5 and Table 6 show the increasing operational efficiency of the lodging industry, as measured by key expense ratios and the ratio of employees per room revenue. Table 7 shows the "de-leveraging" in the capital structure of the lodging industry, as it reduced its interest expense from a high of 14 percent in 1990 to 8 percent in 1993.

Consolidation of the Lodging Industry

The U.S. lodging industry in the 1990s is characterized as a mature industry. A mature industry is one in which growth has slowed down. As Maurice Robinson of KPMG Peat

T5	Key Expense Ratios 1990–1996					
	Full Service			Limited Service		
Year	Debt Expense	Fixed Charge	Interest Expense	Debt Expense	Fixed Charge	Interest Expense
1990	48.7%	30.3%	12.5%	27.1%	41.3%	19.8%
1991	45.4	28.9	11.1	27.9	34.9	15.6
1992	44.9	25.6	9.2	27.6	28.8	12.3
1993	44.5	22.8	7.8	29.5	25.4	9.7
1994	42.9	21.1	7.0	27.3	23.6	7.9
1995	41.4	19.5	6.2	27.1	20.6	6.5
1996	40.6	16.3	4.9	25.9	17.6	4.3

Source: Coopers & Lybrand, Smith Travel Research

T6	Employees Per 100 Rooms	
Year	Employees	
1986	81.0	
1987	78.0	
1988	79.5	
1989	78.5	
1990	78.5	
1991	77.5	
1992	75.5	
1993	75.0	
1994	74.5	
1995	75.0	
1996	75.2	

Source: Coopers & Lybrand

T7 — Interest Expense as a Percentage of Revenues

Year	Interest Expense	Year	Interest Expense
1977	6.0%	1987	11.2%
1978	6.8	1988	12.0
1979	6.8	1989	13.5
1980	6.8	1990	14.0
1981	7.2	1991	12.0
1982	8.5	1992	10.0
1983	8.0	1993	8.0
1984	9.0	1994	7.5
1985	11.2	1995	7.0
1986	10.0	1996	7.0

Source: Coopers & Lybrand

Marwick states (1997), "the lodging industry is a mature industry where top brands have been fighting for market share for years. Segmentation or 'nichemanship' is mostly the result of the battle for "shelf space." Consolidation or cannibalization, is the growth strategy most often utilized in these mature industries, once growth in demand for the product levels off."

The growth in the 1990s for hotel companies is different from the 1960s where growth came through franchising and vertical integration (United Airlines and Westin). Now, as Robinson (1997) states, the growth strategy is consolidation. Increasing access to capital through public equity and debt markets fuels this growth. Other factors such as the improved performance of the lodging industry (and consequent inflation of stock prices), providing economies of scale, strategic fit, and globalization are also contributing to the increased merger and acquisition (M&A) activity.

Steve Bollenbach of Hilton Hotel states (1997), that M&A activity is inevitable and will continue to grow. "In a unit-expansion business, the only way you can expand your company is by acquiring properties. Today it is cheaper to acquire than build them . . . there is plenty of product to buy because the bulk of the construction done in the 1980s and the product controlled by Japanese investors has come into the market."

As noted in Table 8, merger and acquisition (M&A) activity increased from one in 1992 to 15 in 1996 and 1997. In 1997 the total M&A activity announced was valued at $23.5 billion (Shroeder & Co. Inc., *Lodging Industry Review*, Feb. 28, 1998). Some of the most notable hotel deals of 1997 are listed in Table 9. It is very clear from the industry consolidation that the major acquirers of hotel companies were REITs. REITs accounted for ten out of the fifteen deals in 1997. This trend continues into 1998.

T8 — Mergers and Acquisitions 1991–1997

Year	1991	1992	1993	1994	1995	1996	1997
M&A	—	1	7	9	10	15	15
Spinoffs	—	—	—	1	3	2	—

Source: National Hotel Realty, Smith Travel Research and the Conference

T9 — Largest Lodging Deals in 1997

Acquirer	Target	Deal Size (Millions)
Starwood (REIT)	ITT	$13,748
Promus	DoubleTree	1,704
Patriot American (REIT)	Interstate	2,142
Starwood (REIT)	Westin	1,570
Patriot American (REIT)	Wyndham	773
Marriott International	Renaissance	908
Patriot American (REIT)	Carnival	485
Starwood (REIT)	HEI	327
Sunstone (REIT)	Kahler	322
Patriot American (REIT)	WHG	266
Extended Stay America	Studio Plus	296
Boykin Lodging (REIT)	Red Lion Inns	271
Patriot American (REIT)	Cal Jockey/Bay Meadows	239
Prime Hospitality	Homegate	132
Wyndham	Clubhouse	130

Source: Securities Data Corp.

The consolidation of the lodging industry is changing the industry in many ways. Listed below are some of the major impacts of the consolidation trend.

1. The first major impact is that consolidation is resulting in a larger number of hotel rooms being controlled by fewer companies.

2. Although it is not evident as yet, consolidation also has the effect of reducing competition, as the number of lodging companies are reduced.

3. The surviving companies are growing larger in size. The industry as a whole should become more efficient, and have more access to capital. At the same time, many industry observers are presently asking the question, how big is too big?

4. As each company grows, they acquire multiple brands and types of products, and thus become more diversified. Many of the larger hotel companies are either acquiring or merging with firms that operate casinos. Companies such as Cendant, which started as a lodging company (Hospitality Franchise Systems), no longer operate only hotels. They have diversified into car rental, real estate, marketing, and insurance businesses. (*Hotel Business*, Jan. 21–Feb. 6, 1998). Some consolidations, such as the DoubleTree/Promus merger are examples of brand consolidation. Promus did not have an upscale, full service brand, and DoubleTree did not have midscale brands. Together, they cover a wider range. Furthermore, Double-Tree was strong as a management company while Promus's strength was the brand. Other portfolio diversification includes major hotel companies such as Hyatt, Marriott, Westin, and Four Seasons.

5. Lodging companies are becoming part of conglomerates. Bass Plc., a U.K. based conglomerate, added InterContinental Hotels to its growing umbrella of firms, which include Holiday Inn (*Hotel Motel Management*, March 16, 1998). Another example is La Quinta, which was acquired in 1998, by Meditrust, a non-hotel REIT (*Hotel Business*, February 7–20, 1998).

6. Newer, consolidated companies are likely to put money into renovating many of their hotels that are approaching the end of their economic lives.

7. The collective purchasing power of consolidated firms will lead to greater discounts, technology investments, shared central costs, and marketing synergy that should have a positive impact on the profitability, effectiveness, and competitiveness of these consolidated companies.

8. The consolidation trend is also resulting in acquisition of U.S. based hotel firms by foreign companies. As a result of consolidation, U.S. companies are gaining access into foreign markets. For example, the acquisition of Renaissance Hotels by Marriott International will give them access to markets such as Vietnam, China, and Indonesia.

Many experts predict that after the equals have finished merging, the next wave of mergers will be of large companies acquiring smaller companies. According to Bjorn Hanson, an industry consultant, these will be "survival mergers" in which the operating environment will make it very difficult for these smaller companies to have the marketing or financial clout of the large mega-hotel organizations. Paul Nussbaum, Chairman of Patriot American (a REIT) states "we'll see smaller capitalized companies, especially those that have a higher cost of capital, become targets of larger firms. As securitization increases (as source of capital) growth companies will continue to acquire non-growth companies."

Table 10 contains a summary of recent lodging brand introductions. This increase of new brands in the past few years has further added confusion to the structure of the lodging industry, which in the minds of many has created more brands than clearly discernable products. In 1995 and 1996 a total of 25 new brands were added to the lodging industry.

In Table 11, the growth rate of the brands by market segment is displayed, while Table 12 is a matrix of brands by market segment. The budget segment has recently had a negative growth rate, while the limited service and full service brands enjoyed the highest rates of growth from 1992–1995. Limited service hotels accounted for two-thirds of the overall brand growth during this period.

Ownership Structure and Business Activities

The increasing complexity of the lodging industry is further illustrated by the various company structures

T10 New Hotel Brands 1991–1997							
Product	1991	1992	1993	1994	1995	1996	YTD 3rd Qtr 1997
Limited Service	—	—	—	1	—	4	—
Full Service	2	1	3	1	5	—	1
Extended Stay	—	2	—	—	2	6	2
All Suite	1	1	—	1	3	5	—
Luxury	1	—	—	—	—	—	—
Total	4	4	3	3	10	15	3

Source: National Hotel Realty, Smith Travel Research and the Conference Board

that exist today and the multiple business activities that each could be involved in. A Hilton or a Marriott could be corporate owned, or individually owned, franchised and managed by an independent management company. Tables 13 and 14 categorize the various company structures in existence today and the business activities in which the large public companies are involved.

T11 — Brand Growth By Market Segment

Market Segment	Hotels in 1995	Variance 1992–1995	Percentage of Total Change
Budget	812	–78	–3.0%
Limited Service	5,976	1,729	66.5
Full Service	9,096	800	30.8
First Class	2,027	146	5.6
Luxury	57	7	0.1
Total	17,968	2,604	100.0%

Source: National Hotel Realty

T12 — A Market Segmentation Map (A Selection of Hotel Chains and Market Segments)

Chain	Lower-range Economy	Upper-range Economy	Middle-range Full Service	Upper-range Full Service	Luxury	All Suite	Other
Choice	Sleep Inn Econolodge Friendship	Comfort Inn Rodeway Inns	Quality Inns	Clarion Hotels		Comfort Suites Quality Suites Clarion Suites	
Doubletree			DoubleTree Club	DoubleTree Hotels		Guest Quarters	
Forte	Thriftlodge	TravelLodge	TravelLodge Hotels	Exclusive Hotels		TravelLodge Suites	
Hilton			Hilton Garden Inns	Hilton Hotels		Hilton Suites	
Holiday Inn		Holiday Inn Express	Holiday Inns	Crowne Plaza Holiday Inn Select			Sunspree Resorts Crowne Plaza Resorts
HFS	Super 8	Park Inns Days Inn Wingate Hojo Inn Ramada Limited	Howard Johnson Ramada Inns		Ameri Suites		
Hyatt			Hyatt Regency	Grand Hyatt Park Hyatt		Hyatt Suites	Hyatt Resorts Hyatt Vacation Clubs
ITT Sheraton			Four Points	Sheraton Hotels	Luxury Collection	Sheraton Suites	
Marriott		Fairfield Inns	Courtyard by Marriott	Marriott Hotels	Marriott Marquis	Residence Inn Marriott Suites	Marriott Marriott Timeshares
Promus		Hampton Inns				Embassy Suites Homewood Suites	
Wyndham			Wyndham Garden				Wyndham Resorts

Source: PKF Consulting

Type Lodging	Characteristics	Advantages	Examples
Franchisor	❖ Owns hotel brand and sells right to use name, logo, reservation system and other services to franchisee. ❖ Franchisee to operate hotel according to standards established by franchiser. ❖ Franchisee owns hotel and may self-manage or hire third party management company.	**Franchisee** ❖ Greater customer recognition of a hotel. ❖ Access to a reservation system and a variety of support services. **Franchisor** ❖ Ability to increase the number of hotels that bear its brand without expending capital to build or buy hotels, creating enhanced brand value. ❖ Incremental costs associated with enhanced revenues are minimal, yielding strong profit margins.	❖ HFS ❖ Marriott International ❖ Hilton Hotels ❖ U.S. Franchise Systems ❖ Holiday Inns
Chain Management	❖ Owns and/or manages hotel that are affiliated with chain management. ❖ May participate in hotel ownership.	**Owner** ❖ Greater customer recognition of a hotel. ❖ Access to reservation system and variety of support services. **Chain Management** ❖ Ability to increase the number of hotels that bear its brand without expending capital to build or buy hotels, creating enhanced brand value. ❖ Steady revenue stream through management fees with limited financial risk.	❖ Marriott International ❖ Hilton Hotels ❖ Holiday Inns
Independent Management Company	❖ Retained to manage a hotel on behalf of owner. ❖ Often independently managed property retains a franchise to enhance customer recognition and benefit from chain services. ❖ May participate in hotels ownership.	**Owner** ❖ Close alignment of owner and operator goals rather than the management of a "brand." ❖ Independent management often has regional expertise. **Independent Management Company** ❖ Steady revenue stream through management fees with limited financial risk of upfront capital costs.	❖ Interstate ❖ Prime Hospitality ❖ Richfield
Owner/Operator	❖ Owns and operates hotel(s). ❖ May have its own brand, be a franchise, or operate a combination of own brands and franchised hotels. ❖ Ownership position may be large or small.	❖ Owner/operator participates in hotel profits and capital appreciation.	❖ John Q Hammons ❖ Bristol Hotel Company ❖ Extended Stay America
Non-REIT Owner	❖ Owns the hotel but retains a chain or independent management company to operate the hotel. ❖ Owners are entrepreneurs, limited partnerships, financial institutions, pension funds, governments or corporations specifically formed to own hotel real estate.	❖ Assumes all ownership risk and rewards including greater profits and asset appreciation.	❖ Host Marriott

Source: Bear Stearns & Co., Ltd.

T14 — Business Activities of Publicly Traded Lodging Corporations (1997)

Lodging Corporation	Franchisor	Chain Management	Independent Management	Owner/ Operator	Owner/ Non REIT
Amerihost			X	X	
Bristol Hotels				X	
Candlewood	X	X		X	
CapStar			X	X	
Chartwell Leisure				X	
Choice Hotels	X	X		X	
DoubleTree	X	X		X	
Extend Stay America				X	
Four Seasons		X			
HFS Inc.	X				
Hilton Hotels	X	X		X	
Homegate Hospitality				X	
Homestead Village				X	
Host Marriott					X
Hudson Hotels	X	X			
Interstate Hotels		X	X	X	
ITT Corp.	X	X		X	
John Q Hammons				X	
La Quinta Inns				X	
Marriott International	X	X			
Prime Hospitality			X	X	
Promus Hotel	X	X		X	
Red Roof Inns	X			X	
Servico			X	X	
Sholodge	X			X	
Studio Plus				X	
Suburban Lodges of America	X			X	
U.S. Franchise System	X				
Wyndham Hotel	X	X		X	

Sources: Bear Stearns & Co., Coopers & Lybrand

T15 — Chain vs. Independent Hotels (U.S. Lodging Industry) 1980–1997

Year	Room Demand Chains	Room Demand Independent
1980	55%	45%
1985	59	41
1990	61	39
1995	66	34
1997	70	30

Source: Smith Travel Research, 1997

Chain versus Independents

The lodging industry has become more organized and dominated by large chains, which is reflected in change in the chain vs. independent share of room demand. Table 15 shows this change. In 1980 the independents commanded 45 percent of the room demand, which reduced to 30 percent in 1997. Based on room conversion tracking by Smith Travel Research (1997), in the past four years 64,000 rooms converted from independent to chain status.

The conversion to chains is also demonstrated by Table 16, which shows the growth rate of hotel brands. The growth in brands is impacted by a number of factors, such as the changing demographics of travelers who prefer recognizable products, conversion of independents to brands, availability of capital to construct new hotels, the physical aging of hotel products from the 1970s and 1980s, and international expansion of U.S. lodging companies (Transactions HMBA, 1995). A development survey conducted by National Hotel Realty (Ford, 1996) concluded the following after studying the growth patterns of 40 major U.S. brands over four years:

1. Brand consolidation is nearly over. Few national brands remain that can be bought outright.
2. Brand growth among the top 40 brands was generally slow, averaging 5.3 percent per year.

Photo courtesy Kevin Fleming/© Corbis.

There are currently over 3.5 million hotel rooms in the U.S. lodging industry.

Growth Rate of 40 Major United States Hotel Brands

Brand	1992	1993	1994	1995
BUDGET				
Friendship	170	146	130	53
Motel 6	754	769	769	759
LIMITED SERVICE				
Budgetel	83	97	102	117
Econolodge	789	753	737	640
Fairfield Inn	125	140	172	234
Knights Inn	179	183	187	163
Red Roof Inn	210	210	220	231
Sleep Inn	65	76	118	74
Super 8	946	1,061	1,220	1,353
Travelodge	422	418	425	450
Comfort Inn	1,060	1,291	1,491	1,373
Hampton Inn	327	372	437	525
Homewood Suites	24	24	26	30
Holiday Inn Express	79	150	240	385
La Quinta Motor Inn	212	221	227	235
Shoneys	56	58	74	102
FULL SERVICE				
Days Inn	1,330	1,441	1,586	1,652
Howard Johnson	543	566	582	523
Park Inn	39	39	45	
Rodeway Inn	108	11	141	151
Best Western	3,388	3,385	3,423	3,462
Clarion	95	97	96	84
Courtyard	210	216	231	254
Holiday Inn	1,545	1,560	1,591	1,602
Quality Inn	598	601	645	564
Ramada	593	676	775	804
FIRST CLASS				
Crowne Plaza	66	86	97	107
Doubletree	81	82	91	105
Embassy Suites	103	107	107	114
Hilton	200	213	225	222
Marriott	246	255	257	273
Radisson	235	235	271	319
Residence Inn	178	183	189	196
Sheraton	426	407	388	349
LUXURY				
Four Seasons	23	26	27	26
Hyatt Hotels	163	167	169	176
Omni Hotels	44	45	42	41
Ritz Carlton	27	30	31	31
Renaissance/Stouffer	85	85	75	72
Westin Hotels	85	54	57	53
Grand Total	15,881	16,636	17,716	17,968

Source: Adapted from Transactions by HMBA. Various Issues

3. Many full service, mid market brands with aging inventory have failed to keep up with the changing tastes and preferences of consumers.

4. A slow down in the international economies has reduced the rate of franchise expansion overseas.

Table 17 shows the top 25 management companies as of year-end 1997. These companies represent 316,360 rooms and 1,878 properties managed. Evaluating the individual companies, they represent average hotel size as low as 63 rooms and as high as 615 rooms, with the total average of the top 25 at 168 rooms. This diversity in size is the result of the wide range of hotel products.

Shifts in the 1990s

There are currently over 3.5 million hotel rooms in the U.S. lodging industry. From an investment perspective, it is important to understand that supply of hotel rooms is not homogeneous. The lodging room supply may be differentiated either by the price segment, product type location, or region. An analysis of the changes in the lodging room supply is important in any study of capital flow, as it is indicative of the type of products, locations, and regions to which capital is being attracted. The series of tables that follow describes the characteristics of the U.S. lodging industry room supply.

The total net change in room supply from 1990 to 1996 for each of the price segments is described in Table 18. The economy and mid-price segments without food and beverage (F&B) have both added the most rooms to the inventory. This has been done through construction and conversion activity. Much of the new construction in the 1990s was a result of an aging of the room supply. Limited service hotels constructed in the 1970s would be at the end of their economic lives in the 1990s. Economic lives for a limited service hotel ranges from 15 to 20 years (Winfree, 1996). Independents and the mid-priced segment with F&B have actually reduced their inventory, primarily by converting out of these concepts.

The changes in share of room supply by each of the price segments are shown in Table 19. Although independents represent the largest percentage of hotel rooms, they have been losing their market share. This is primarily through conversions to branded properties. The upper scale and upscale have remained steady in their share of supply. The mid-scale product with F&B is losing popularity and has shown a reduction in supply, while midscale without F&B is the fastest growing segment. The economy segment has shown a slight increase while the budget segment has a minor reduction in share.

The changes in room supply from 1990 to 1996 for each of the price segments is shown in Tables 20–26. Although the independents have the largest number of rooms, they are steadily decreasing in size primarily through conversions.

The number of hotel properties and rooms opened from the early part

T17 — Top 25 Management Companies 1997

Company	Rooms Managed	Properties Managed	Average Size of Hotel Managed
Interstate Hotels	45,329	223	203
Bristol Hotels	28,799	101	285
Capstar Hotel Co.	24,287	121	200
Prime Hospitality	19,513	140	139
Tharaldson Property Management	15,829	250	63
Unihost	14,400	132	109
American General Hospitality	13,398	65	206
Ocean Hospitality	13,026	77	169
Richfield Hospitality Services	12,989	55	236
Westmont Hospitality Group	12,912	63	205
Remington Hotel Corp.	11,500	70	164
Winegardner & Hammons	10,228	49	209
Beck Summit Hotel	10,000	60	204
Lane Hospitality	9,708	53	183
Sage Hospitality	8,103	56	144
Barrington International	7,800	34	229
Hostmark Management Group	7,385	33	224
Amerihost Properties	7,112	89	80
Davidson Hotel Co.	7,000	28	250
Westcoast Hotels	6,906	32	216
Tishman Hotel Corp.	6,768	11	615
Horizon Hotels Ltd.	6,634	33	201
Boyd Gaming Corp.	6,177	12	515
Ramkota Cos./Regency Inns	5,542	43	129
White Lodging Services	5,485	48	114
Total	316,360	1,878	168

Source: Adapted from Hotel Motel Management, March 2, 1998

T18 — Net Room Change by Chain Segment 1990–March 1997 (Thousands)

Segment	Net Room Change (B+C)	Net Rooms Constructed (B)	Net Room Conversions (C)
Upper Scale	43,838	42,924	914
Upscale	63,909	37,891	26,018
Midscale, with F&B	–6,705	21,605	–28,310
Midscale, no F&B	156,794	118,667	38,127
Economy	132,121	97,514	34,607
Budget	19,335	17,410	1,925
Independent	–66,393	6,089	–72,482

Source: Smith Travel Research, 1997

T19 — Share of Room Supply by Segment

Segment	1990	1994	1997 Ytd March
Upper Scale	12.6%	12.3%	12.5%
Upscale	6.5	7.0	7.4
Midscale, with F&B	21.5	20.8	19.6
Midscale, no F&B	4.8	6.6	8.5
Economy	9.9	10.8	12.2
Budget	7.0	7.2	6.8
Independent	37.7	35.3	33.0
Total	100.0%	100.0%	100.0%

Source: Smith Travel Research, 1997

T20 — Growth in Room Supply 1990–1996, Upper Upscale Chains

Year	Net Rooms Constructed	Net Room Conversions	Net Room Change	Ending Room Inventory
1990	19,122	(2,891)	16,231	401,625
1991	8,729	(8,053)	676	402,301
1992	6,704	(2,082)	4,622	406,923
1993	1,266	(4,730)	(3,464)	403,459
1994	312	(491)	(179)	403,280
1995	3,807	6,901	10,708	413,988
1996	2,016	9,166	11,182	425,170

Source: Smith Travel Research, 1997

T21 — Growth in Room Supply 1990–1996, Upscale Chains

Year	Net Rooms Constructed	Net Room Conversions	Net Room Change	Ending Room Inventory
1990	12,313	3,698	16,011	207,407
1991	5,037	(134)	4,903	212,310
1992	3,107	1,777	4,884	217,194
1993	622	3,353	3,975	221,169
1994	1,830	5,654	7,484	228,653
1995	3,502	8,611	12,113	240,766
1996	7,843	3,381	11,224	251,990

Source: Smith Travel Research, 1997

T22 — Growth in Room Supply 1990–1996, Midscale Chains with F&B

Year	Net Rooms Constructed	Net Room Conversions	Net Room Change	Ending Room Inventory
1990	4,511	(2,408)	2,103	683,613
1991	2,783	(2,875)	(92)	683,521
1992	1,215	(1,913)	(698)	682,823
1993	864	(158)	706	683,529
1994	119	(291)	(172)	683,357
1995	3,434	(12,242)	(8,808)	674,549
1996	7,487	(7,614)	(127)	674,422

Source: Smith Travel Research, 1997

T23 — Growth in Room Supply 1990–1996, Midscale Chains without F&B

Year	Net Rooms Constructed	Net Room Conversions	Net Room Change	Ending Room Inventory
1990	13,130	2,919	16,049	151,007
1991	9,333	6,272	15,605	166,612
1992	7,863	4,388	12,251	178,863
1993	8,167	8,232	16,399	195,262
1994	14,099	5,726	19,825	215,087
1995	23,803	5,600	29,403	244,490
1996	34,126	3,689	37,815	282,305

Source: Smith Travel Research, 1997

T24 — Growth in Room Supply 1990–1996, Economy Chains

Year	Net Rooms Constructed	Net Room Conversions	Net Room Change	Ending Room Inventory
1990	20,908	5,296	26,204	313,644
1991	7,964	(6,769)	1,195	314,839
1992	7,327	401	7,728	322,567
1993	6,274	3,377	9,651	332,218
1994	11,317	8,382	19,699	351,917
1995	15,968	13,330	29,298	381,215
1996	22,538	8,616	31,154	412,369

Source: Smith Travel Research, 1997

T25 — Growth in Room Supply 1990–1996, Budget Chains

Year	Net Rooms Constructed	Net Room Conversions	Net Room Change	Ending Room Inventory
1990	4,338	2,451	3,789	220,859
1991	2,176	20,336	22,512	243,371
1992	899	(68)	831	244,202
1993	718	(3,424)	(2,706)	241,496
1994	572	(4,326)	(3,754)	237,742
1995	1,465	(13,102)	(11,637)	226,105
1996	5,956	(101)	5,855	231,960

Source: Smith Travel Research, 1997

T26 — Growth in Room Supply 1990–1996, Independent Chains

Year	Net Rooms Constructed	Net Room Conversions	Net Room Change	Ending Room Inventory
1990	8,446	(9,065)	(619)	1,197,070
1991	(7,796)	(8,777)	(16,573)	1,180,497
1992	(14,477)	(2,503)	(16,980)	1,163,517
1993	4,273	(6,650)	(2,377)	1,161,140
1994	5,723	(14,654)	(8,931)	1,152,209
1995	(2,333)	(9,098)	(11,431)	1,140,778
1996	10,985	(17,137)	(6,152)	1,134,626

Source: Smith Travel Research, 1997

of the decade to the present period is displayed in Table 27. The rate of development has doubled in the past two years as compared to the early 1990's. This is the result of the increasing availability of capital. The average size of a new hotel opened in 1997 was 93 rooms. There has been an increase in smaller projects since 1994 when capital again became available. As the industry showed further signs of recovery, larger hotel projects were financed.

An interesting analysis is to compare changes in room supply by price segment to the changes in the revenue per available room (REVPAR). It would be expected that the segment adding the most rooms would also create a more competitive environment, thus having a negative impact on room rates and, therefore, room revenues. Consequently, there should be a negative correlation between growth in room supply for a segment and the growth in REVPAR for that segment. The data in Table 28 supports this, where, generally, segments with higher supply growth have lower growth in REVPAR.

The lodging industry supply may also be analyzed by price segment and product type. Table 29 identifies the percentage of different type of hotel products in each of the price segments. Most of the hotels, convention, casino, and all suite products are concentrated in the luxury and upscale segments. While the motels make up most of the mid-price, economy and budget segments of the industry.

Table 30 shows the distribution of lodging room supply by location. As noted, suburban and highway location currently has the highest share of hotel rooms in the U.S. This is indicative of the move of businesses from the central business district locations (CBDs) to the suburbs, and by the use of the auto as the primary travel method by most travelers.

The growth in the room supply by location from 1994 to 1997 is in Table 31. Suburban and highway lo-

T27 — Development of New Hotels 1991–1997

Year	1991	1992	1993	1994	1995	1996	Ytd 3rd Qtr 1997
Properties opened	475	394	410	540	799	1,054	945
Number of Rooms opened	51,197	36,547	39,750	44,838	64,092	91,150	84,754
Avg. size of new hotels	108	93	97	83	80	87	93

Source: National Hotel Realty, Smith Travel Research and the Conference Board

T28 — Room Supply Growth as Compared to REVPAR Growth

Segment	1994–1997 CAGR* Room Supply	1997 Growth in REVPAR and Rank
Midscale, no F&B	14.3%	4.1% (4)
Economy	7.6	1.0 (7)
Upscale	4.9	5.6 (3)
Budget	2.2	2.9 (6)
Upper Upscale	2.0	7.7 (1)
Midscale, with F&B	–0.3	3.8 (5)
Independent	–0.4	6.7 (2)

Source: Schroder & Co. and Smith Travel Research
*CAGR = Compound Annual Growth Rate

T29 — Distribution of Lodging Rooms by Price Segment and Product Type

Segment	Hotel	Motel	Convention	Casino	All Suite
Luxury	29.4%	1.6%	60.9%	20.9%	37.7%
Upscale	39.5	17.7	25.8	33.9	40.2
Mid-Price	19.9	29.9	11.5	15.2	15.2
Economy	5.5	21.5	1.9	13.7	4.2
Budget	5.4	28.9	0	17.3	1.6
Total	100.0%	100.0%	100.0%	100.0%	100.0%

Source: Smith Travel Research, 1997

T30 — Percentage of Room Supply by Location 1990 and 1998

Location	Total Rooms (1990)	Share of Rooms	Total Rooms (1998)	Share of Rooms
Urban	485,658	15.9%	518,634	14.4%
Suburban	995,675	32.7	1,243,815	34.6
Airport	219,310	7.1	244,865	6.8
Highway	982,946	32.2	1,158,669	32.2
Resort	364,679	12.0	427,527	12.0
Total	3,048,268	100.0%	3,593,510	100.0%

Source: Smith Travel Research, 1997

cations continue to lead other locations in supply growth rate.

Most urban hotels are either in the luxury, upscale, or mid-priced segment. Suburban hotels tend to be upscale, mid-priced, or budget properties. Airport hotels are clustered mainly upscale or mid-priced, while highway properties are mostly low priced. Not surprisingly, resort hotels are mostly luxury or upscale. Please see Table 32.

The distribution of rooms by regions is described in Table 33. The largest share of hotel rooms in the U.S. is located in the South Atlantic region (24%). The New England area, with 4 percent, has the least number of hotel rooms.

Conclusion

As the demand caught up with the supply and finally exceeded it in

---

T31 — Percentage Change in Rooms Available 1994–1997

Location	CAGR* Percent
Suburban	3.3%
Highway	2.7
Resort	1.1
Airport	0.9
Urban	0.8

Source: Smith Travel Research, 1997
*CAGR = Compound Annual Growth Rate

T32 — Distribution of Lodging Rooms by Price Segment and Location 1997

Segment	Urban	Suburban	Airport	Highway	Resort
Luxury	35.1%	9.5%	12.0%	1.7%	23.8%
Upscale	28.5	23.2	25.2	16.6	42.8
Mid-Price	20.1	28.4	34.5	27.3	17.4
Economy	6.9	17.2	15.2	22.5	7.0
Budget	9.4	21.7	13.2	31.8	9.4
Total	100.0%	100.0%	100.0%	100.0%	100.0%

Source: Smith Travel Research, 1997

T33 — Distribution of Room Supply by Region

Region	Rooms January 1998	Share of Rooms	Rooms January 1997	Share of Rooms	States
New England	142,989	4.0%	140,151	4.0%	ME,NH,VT,MA,RI,CT
Middle Atlantic	307,701	8.6	301,147	8.7	NY,NJ,PA
South Atlantic	860,843	24.0	827,646	24.0	DE,MD,DC,VA,WV,NC,SC,GA,FL
East North Central	425,966	11.9	407,044	11.8	OH,IN,IL,MI,WI
East South Central	228,921	6.4	216,356	6.2	KY,TN,AL,MS
West North Central	247,298	6.9	236,148	6.8	MN,IA,MO,ND,SD,NE,KS
West South Central	367,149	10.2	350,364	10.1	AR,LA,OK,TX
Mountain	436,006	12.0	417,889	12.1	MT,ID,WY,CO,NM,AZ,UT,NV
Pacific	576,637	16.0	566,044	16.3	WA,OR,CA,AK,HI
Total	3,593,510	100.0%	3,462,789	100.0%	

Source: Smith Travel Research, 1997

T34 — Analysis of Lodging Industry Performance

Year	Supply Change	Demand Change	Occupancy	Occupancy Change	ADR	ADR Change	REVPAR	REVPAR Change	GOP	Fixed Charges	Profits $ Billions
1990	3.2%	1.9%	63.5%	(1.1)%	$57.96	2.9%	$36.82	2.9%	25.5%	32.1%	−5.7
1991	1.4	(1.3)	61.8	(2.6)	58.08	0.2	35.91	(2.5)	27.4	29.7	−2.8
1992	0.7	1.9	62.6	1.3	58.91	1.4	36.87	2.7	29.5	26.5	0.0
1993	0.3	1.7	63.5	1.4	60.53	2.8	38.42	4.2	30.5	23.3	2.4
1994	1.0	3.0	64.7	1.9	62.86	3.8	40.70	5.9	36.2	22.8	5.5
1995	1.2	1.7	65.1	0.6	65.81	4.7	42.83	5.2	37.0	19.8	8.5
1996	2.1	2.3	65.2	0.2	69.66	5.9	45.47	6.2	38.2	18.3	12.5

Source: Smith Travel Research, 1997

1992, room rates, occupancies, and profits have been improving. The mid-priced and particularly the upscale and luxury segments have been performing better in recent years than the economy and budget segments. Demand growth for these segments has been weak in the last two years. Equity analysts at BT Alex Brown feel that this weakness may be partly attributed to the aging of the budget and economy product. Many of these hotels were built in the 1960s and 1970s and may be reaching the end of their economic life. Further, they feel that the introduction of the mid-price segment, which is much newer, offers a higher price value relationship to the customer. The strength of the overall economy has also allowed many companies to afford higher priced rooms for their executives, which benefits occupancies at upscale and luxury hotels.

As the lodging industry recovered in the middle to late 1990s, it was reflected in its profitability. Table 35 shows the growth in the lodging industry's profitability, which increased from net losses in the early 1990s to double-digit profits in recent times.

T35 Analysis of Lodging Industry Profitability, Pre-Tax Income (Loss)

Year	Full Service	Limited Service
1990	(10.2)%	(1.5)%
1991	(6.0)	1.9
1992	(1.4)	10.5
1993	2.6	13.8
1994	6.8	14.6
1995	9.6	23.0
1996	15.7	27.0

Source: Smith Travel Research, 1997

Questions and Assignments

1. What can be seen as the impetus for the modern hotel industry?

2. List and briefly discuss the key occurrences that took place in the lodging industry in the 1950s through the 1970s. Be prepared to discuss your findings with your team and classmates.

3. What three factors are seen as providing an impetus to the early 1980s lodging building boom? What was the outcome of the building boom? Summarize your findings and be prepared to discuss them.

4. Using your library resources or your web browser and search engine of choice, identify two lodging properties. Where do they fit in the Five Category Classification Scheme (Table 2)? Justify your choices.

5. Describe briefly the characteristics of the lodging industry in the early 1990s. Summarize your findings and be prepared to discuss them.

6. Consider the proposed impacts of the lodging industry consolidation. Using your library resources or your web browser and search engine of choice, identify an article that discusses the lodging industry consolidation. Which of the proposed impacts does the article refer to? Summarize your findings and be prepared to discuss them.

7. Consider Table 12. Choose one of the brands listed and describe the brand. Use an article to demonstrate your description.

8. Consider Table 13. Which of the company structures do you personally favor? Justify your response. Use an article to demonstrate. Summarize your findings and be prepared to discuss them.

9. Choose one of the top 25 management companies listed in Table 17. Perform organizational/company research on this company. The procedure to use is described in Chapter One.

10. Describe the changes that have taken place in the lodging industry in the late 1990s. Summarize your findings and be prepared to discuss them.

Bibliography and Suggested Readings

Ader, J. N. & LaFleur, R. A. (1997). *U.S. Lodging Almanac*. New York, NY: Bear Stearns Equity Research.

Arnold, D. E. & O'Mara, W. P. (1984). *Hotel/Motel Development*. Washington, DC: The Urban Land Institute.

Bell, C. A. (1993, February). Agreements with chain hotel companies. *Cornell Hotel Restaurant Administration Quarterly*, 34(1), 27–33.

Boorstin, D. J., (1958). *The Americans: The Colonial Experience*. New York: Random House.

Cendant emerges from $14 B merger between HFS and CUC. *Hotel Business*, Jan 21–Feb 6, 1998.

Choi, J. G., Olson, M. D. & Kwansa, F. A. (1997). Hotel industry cycle. In Bosselman, R. H., Bowen, J. & Roehl, W. S. (eds.). *Advances in Hospitality and Tourism Research. Proceedings of the Second Conference on Graduate Education and Graduate Students Research*. University of Las Vegas, Nevada.

Cline, R. (1997). The urge to merge. *Lodging Hospitality*, 53(2), 24–28.

Days of M&A's are not done yet. Discussion of Lodging Industry professional reported in the *Real Estate Forum*, October, 1997.

Ford, P. (1998). The state of real estate financing. *Lodging*, 23, February, 70–73.

Flannery, M. J., Flannery, J. J. (1990). Causes of hotel industry distress. *Real Estate Review*, 19, 35–39.

Giovanetti, T. (1998). Meditrust to use La Quinta management. *Hotel Business*, February, 1.

Gomes, A. J. (1985). *Hospitality in Transition. A Retrospective and Prospective Look at the U.S. Lodging Industry*. Washington, DC: American Hotel and Motel Association.

Hanson, B. & Vo, S. (1998). Lodging market overview. *Urban Land*, 57, January.

HMBA transactions. (Various issues 1991–1996). *Hotel Development Highlights*.

HMBA transactions (1992). HMBA analysis of the hotel real estate market (1987–1991).

Kundu, S. K. (1993). Explaining globalization of service industries. (Doctoral Dissertation, Rutgers State University). *Dissertation Abstracts International*, 55/04, 1030. Oct 1994.

Laventhol & Horwath. (1986–1988). *U.S. Lodging Industry*.

Locker, K. (Speaker) (1997, November). *Real Estate Investment Trusts in the Year 2000 (panel discussion)* (cassette recording 047-10). Washington, DC: Urban Land Institute.

Mandelbaum, R. (1994). It feels so good when I stop. *KPMG Peat Marwick Trends Report*. Chicago, IL: KPMG Peat Marwick.

Mutkowski, M. & Maher, B. A. (1997). *Lodging Industry Overview*. New York, NY: BT Alex. Brown Research.

Nardozza, F. (1996). Future opportunities in lodging. *KPMG Peat Marwick. Real Estate Report*. Chicago, IL: KPMG Peat Marwick.

Nozar, R. A. (1998). Acquisition adds to Bass global umbrella. *Hotel & Motel Management*, 151, 1, 9.

PKF Consulting and Urban Land Institute (1996). *Hotel Development*. Washington, DC: Urban Land Institute.

Pannell Kerr Forster. (1988–1997). *Trends in the Hotel Industry, USA Edition*.

Promus and DoubleTree gain merger approval. *Hotel Business*, Jan 21–Feb 6, 1998.

Robinson, M. (1997). And then there was one . . . consolidation in the hospitality industry. *KPMG Peat Marwick Trends*. Chicago, IL: KPMG Peat Marwick.

Rohs, J. J. & Gump, W. (1998). *Lodging Industry Annual Review*. New York, NY: Shroder & Co. Inc.

Rushmore, S., Ciraldo, D. M. & Tarras, J. (eds.) (1997). *Hotel Investments Handbook*. Boston: Warren, Gorham & Lamont.

Rushmore, S. (1992). *Hotels and Motels: A Guide to Market Analysis, Investment Analysis, and Valuations*. Chicago: Appraisal Institute.

Raleigh, L. E. & Roginsky, R. J. (eds.) (1995). *Hotel Investments Issues & Perspectives*. East Lansing, MI: Educational Institute of the AH&MA.

Smith Travel Research. (1997). *The Host Study*.

Tarras, J. M. (1991). *A Practical Guide To Hospitality Finance*. New York, NY: Van Nostrand Reinhold.

Trice, D. R. (1992, June). Finance: A new partnership for the hotel industry. *Cornell Hotel Restaurant Administration Quarterly*, 33(3), 15–19.

Winfree, M. W. (1996). Historical perspective. In PKF Consulting and Urban Land Institute (Ed.), *Hotel Development*, 1–9. Washington, DC: Urban Land Institute.

Year of the deal. (1997). *Lodging*, 22, October, 11.

The Service Management Perspective

Alex M. Susskind, *School of Hotel Administration*, CORNELL UNIVERSITY

ABSTRACT

This chapter will establish that hospitality companies are service organizations, yet different from many other service organizations. Key issues in delivering and managing quality service will be discussed. The role that service intangibility, guest needs, and expectations and habituation of expectations will be explained. The dual importance of content and process will be introduced and discussed. The customer service equation will be defined.

OBJECTIVES

At the end of this chapter the student should be able to:

1. Define and discuss customer service as it relates to hospitality enterprises.

2. Introduce and describe the service equation.

3. Understand the importance of intangibility of services.

4. Differentiate service content and service process, and establish their role in service management.

5. Differentiate needs and expectation.

6. Understand and describe the role that habituation plays in guest satisfaction.

7. Understand the role of standards and training in service management.

8. Define service guarantee.

9. Describe the steps that must be considered in order to establish an effective service guarantee.

10. Understand the role of explicit and implicit feedback in service satisfaction.

11. Define and describe the service exchange process.

12. Discuss the role of the guest in hospitality success.

Introduction

Today's market economy has clearly and consistently transformed from a manufacturing-based economy to a service-based economy. This is evidenced through the increasing number of service-based industries (e.g., food and lodging, communications, financial, and medical services to name a few), and the fact that over 70% of the national income is accounted for through these industries (Heskett, 1987). This gradual transformation to a service-based economy has been occurring for over thirty years and continues to be the source of much of the new growth and expansion realized in our economy. The service industries have generated over 44 million new jobs during this steady expansion, and they are expected to be a continuous source of employment opportunities in the years to come (Heskett, 1987). In terms of employment opportunities, the service industries—specifically the hospitality industry—appear to have an insatiable need for both managers and employees to perform and execute service-related jobs.

When looking at how service-based organizations function, it may be difficult to clearly identify each part of the service process, and how the service process progresses from a consumer's needs and wants through the ultimate delivery of service. Typically, the service process (*service equation*) involves three inter-related participants, each who have an important role in the delivery of service. The three main participants are:

1. Guests—who have a need for a particular service, request or seek the service, and ultimately receive and evaluate the output of the service
2. Service employees—who are mainly responsible for the provision of service to guests and support the majority of direct contact with guests seeking service
3. Management—whose main responsibility is to coordinate the

efforts and experiences of both employees and guests to ensure satisfaction (Schneider & Bowen, 1995). Each of the three participants plays a varied but crucial role in the service process. Therefore, it is neither possible nor desirable to determine which of the three participants in the service equation are the most important. Excellent and satisfying service does not occur unless all three groups of participants work toward a common goal.

Photo © 1998 PhotoDisc, Inc.

Service employees are mainly responsible for the provision of service to guests.

Definition of Service

The term service as we know it today is derived from the Latin word *servitium* which refers to the duty or condition of a slave (Webster, 1988). A servant's duty was to the master, and each servant was expected to please the master unconditionally. Fortunately, slavery is no longer practiced in free society, but the need for service still remains. Rather than associating the concept of service negatively with servitude, it is best to positively associate service with hospitality. Hospitality, on the other

hand, is defined as providing for a cordial welcome, or offering a pleasant or sustaining environment (Webster, 1984). In modern times, service providers are commissioned to provide hospitality to their guests in exchange for fair compensation and the satisfaction of providing assistance to those seeking services.

In a service-based economy, services are provided to those who are interested in paying for them. In this exchange, a guest (or consumer) identifies a need or desire for a particular service, and solicits that desired service. Services can be sought out in lodging facilities, restaurants, clubs, gaming establishments, resorts, and retail outlets (to name a few). As illustrated in Figure 1, an individual wishing to purchase a meal, such as a cheeseburger, french fries, and a soda will have to go through a variety of steps to complete the purchase and consumption of the meal. The mere desire to obtain a particular service may not lead to the purchase of that service due to other considerations that influence the service exchange process. For example: (a) the service provider must agree and be able to provide the said service, (b) the services offered must be agreeable to the consumer, and (c) the consumer must be able to pay for the services rendered. This relationship may appear to be simple, but it is truly complex and requires attention to detail in order to consistently execute service to the guests' satisfaction.

Service is an intangible product of the hospitality business. In Figure 1, a guest sought out and purchased a meal at a foodservice establishment. While it is true that guests receive a few tangible products during service episodes, most of the service process is not tangible. This means a guest cannot touch or hold on to friendly, efficient service, but can expect it to consistently occur. What makes a service operation unique is that very few products are separated from the service establishment where they are offered. It is true that you can touch and taste your cheeseburger and

Figure 1. An Example of Guest Service in Terms of the Service Exchange Process.

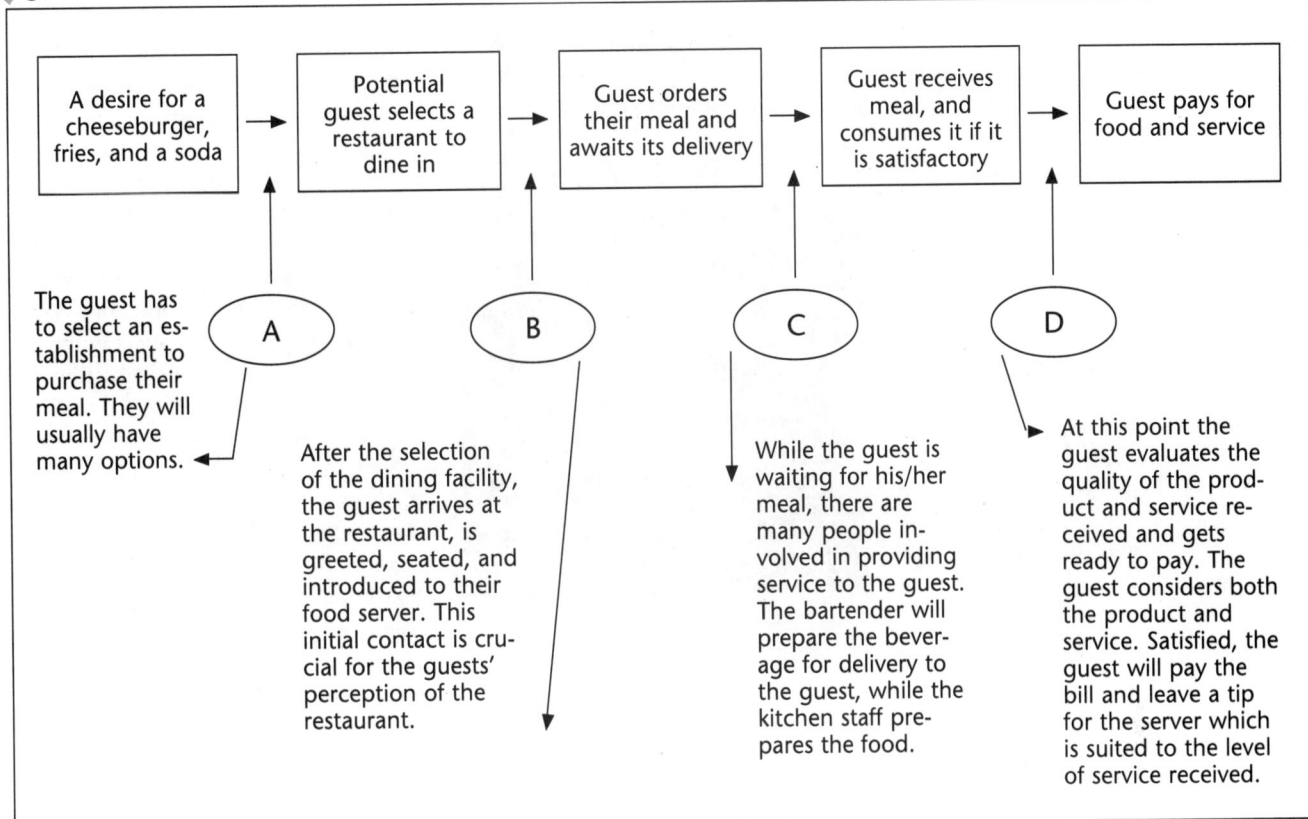

| A desire for a cheeseburger, fries, and a soda | → | Potential guest selects a restaurant to dine in | → | Guest orders their meal and awaits its delivery | → | Guest receives meal, and consumes it if it is satisfactory | → | Guest pays for food and service |

(A) The guest has to select an establishment to purchase their meal. They will usually have many options.

(B) After the selection of the dining facility, the guest arrives at the restaurant, is greeted, seated, and introduced to their food server. This initial contact is crucial for the guests' perception of the restaurant.

(C) While the guest is waiting for his/her meal, there are many people involved in providing service to the guest. The bartender will prepare the beverage for delivery to the guest, while the kitchen staff prepares the food.

(D) At this point the guest evaluates the quality of the product and service received and gets ready to pay. The guest considers both the product and service. Satisfied, the guest will pay the bill and leave a tip for the server which is suited to the level of service received.

french fries, but normally you consume your products and service while still in the service establishment. When done, you are left only with a memory of your dining experience.

Your service experience is likely to be influenced by: (a) the ambiance of the service establishment, (b) the features of the people who greet you and serve you, (c) the products you select and consume, (d) other patrons in the service establishment, and (e) the management responsible for the operation (Lockwood & Jones, 1989). The influences listed above may have a direct or indirect role in shaping a guest's service experience. For example, a guest who is sitting adjacent to a loud and boisterous party in a dining room may perceive a different experience than a guest seated quietly in front of a fireplace regardless of the quality of the food and service offered. In sum, service is a multidimensional process involving many elements with each element of

the process influencing a guest's service experience in either a positive or negative manner.

You can't hold or touch friendly, efficient service, but you can expect it to be there.

Guest's Needs Versus Expectations

Needs

Guests begin their *quest for service* when they realize that they have a need which is not being met. This unmet need, in terms of the hospitality industry's domain, could come about in many forms. The need could arise out of: (a) hunger or the desire for food and beverage, (b) an overnight stay in a city, or (c) a need for social interaction or relaxation at a club or resort. Once the need has been identified, the guests will subsequently search to have the need filled. The guests will consider the available alternatives and choose a means to attempt to have the need met or serviced from those viable alternatives. For example, guests visiting a city will most likely have a need for some type of lodging. For argument sake, let us assume that they have a need for commercial lodging accommodations. Prior to arriving in the city the guests will have some general idea of the price that they are willing to pay for accommodations (e.g., per night), the general location of the facility (e.g., downtown, at the airport, or off the interstate), and the type of lodging establishment available (e.g., budget, mid-range, or luxury). Based on the evaluation of alternatives or options, the guests will choose the alternative which appears to match their needs most completely. Once selected, the guests will form expectations of how that service will be provided, and they will eventually evaluate how the service was delivered. Keep in mind that guests can only evaluate a service during and after its delivery (LeBlanc, 1992). This phenomenon (unique to the provision of service) emphasizes the intangible, perishable, and non-transferable nature of service (Schneider & Bowen, 1995).

Expectations

As a guest, expectations are based upon norms or standards set by the service providers. For example, within the hospitality industry there are numerous types of organizations with varying levels of service offerings. These levels are evident in foodservice (i.e., quick service, full service, or delivery service), lodging (i.e., budget, mid-range, or luxury), and even retail (i.e., discount outlets, specialty stores, or department stores). For each service, and each type of service, consumers anticipate certain features of that service to be consistent with their expectations. Specifically, the statement, *"I recommend the 'Big Mac™', Sir. The fry-chef has prepared it eloquently this afternoon"* would not be anticipated by a drive-through patron at a quick-serve restaurant. However, in a full service restaurant, consumers often rely upon the "expert" advice of their service providers to help make their food and beverage selections (Borchgrevink & Susskind, 1996). Based on the "lodging selection" example above, if the

Consumers anticipate certain features of a service to be consistent with their expectations.

travelers had opted for a budget hotel room, their expectation would most likely be to find a clean room including a bed, television, closet, and a functioning full bathroom. If the room provided less than those basic amenities without notice, the guests' satisfaction with that service is likely to be low (Evans, Clark & Knutson, 1996). On the other hand, if the same guests were to walk into a "budget" room ensconced in gold and marble with a complementary fruit basket sitting on the desk, they would surely be pleasantly surprised and most likely happy with the unexpected "extras." It is very important to meet and exceed guests' expectations consistently, but one must be cautious of "habituated" expectations (Schneider & Bowen, 1995).

In the process of service delivery, guests become accustomed to the services offered, and therefore, if the level of services provided is consistent, it will become normalized (habituated) to the guests. Any deviation from guests' normalized expectations (which are created by the service operation) will be perceived as a failure on the part of the service provider and is likely to create guest dissatis-

faction (Evans, Clark & Knutson, 1996). When your expectations are being met or exceeded, you pay less attention to the service process because you are being serviced as expected; it is only when your expectations are not met that you notice the failure in service. Schneider & Bowen (1995) use the following example of telephone service to illustrate habituated expectations and how they operate. When a need to make a phone call arises (assuming one subscribes to telephone service and has an account in good standing), the individual simply picks up a telephone, listens for a dial tone, and proceeds to make a call as anticipated. Under normal circumstances this is a simple process with few complications, as a telephone customer expects to hear a dial tone when the telephone receiver is lifted. Conversely, if the telephone customer did not hear a dial tone when lifting the receiver, he/she would then attempt to determine why. The reason for the service failure could be the fault of the phone company, the telephone unit itself, or some other factor. Regardless of the cause, the customer must now seek to have the desired telephone service restored as the habituated expectations have been violated (Schneider & Bowen, 1995). In reality, customers are not interested in listening to excuses as to why the service process has failed, they are only interested in having the service restored or remedied quickly and properly (Marvin, 1992, Schneider & Bowen, 1995).

The alignment of customers' expectations of service and an organization's *actual* delivery of service is crucial to developing and maintaining customer *and* employee satisfaction (Schneider & Bowen, 1995), and this has great implications for the training and socializing of a service-based workforce (Bowen, Siehl & Schneider, 1989; Kelly, 1992; Schneider & Bowen, 1992, 1993). It is crucial that service is delivered consistently to guests. Consequently, it is important to train your guest contact staff to provide excellent customer service. However, it is equally important to train and inform your guests concerning your product and services to eliminate any misalignment in their needs and expectations for customer service.

Content Versus Process

As described above, service is a series of actions that are designed to meet certain needs and expectations of guests. While equally important, both the content and process of a service episode determine how a service will be received and evaluated by your guests.

Content

Content of the service process is defined as the actual product(s) which are exchanged and the surrounding environment in which the service episode occurs. For example, in any given city it is possible to purchase a cheeseburger through many different sources. One can select quick-service establishments (such as Wendy's or Burger King), full-service chain restaurants (such as Chili's, TGI Friday's or Bennigan's) or a local independent operation (unique to that city). Each establishment will have its own decor and theme and will generally follow similar guidelines for service. For example a quick-service restaurant usually offers limited service in exchange for speed (i.e., counter service or drive-through service), while full-service restaurants typically offer an extended stay and a larger variety of options (i.e., table service or expansive take-out service). Assuming that each of the service establishments mentioned above offers cheeseburgers on their menus, you are able to select the *content* of a cheeseburger with ease. It is safe to say, however, that even though each establishment may sell cheeseburgers, there is considerable variation in the content between establishments. Cheeseburgers can be served with lettuce, tomato, and onion, on a variety of breads, and with numerous condiments. Additionally, the meat and cheese used

can vary in how it is offered and served in the establishment (i.e., fresh ground or frozen, made from ground sirloin or ground chuck). In short, the apparently simple selection of a cheeseburger has many variable components which a guest needs to choose from. The content of a cheeseburger is tangible and will certainly influence a guest's preference for the selection of that product and hence service.

Process

On the other hand, *process* can be defined as the means by which products and services are delivered to guests for their consumption. While content of a service episode is mostly tangible, process is mostly intangible. The specific content of a cheeseburger mentioned above can be ordered, prepared, and served in a variety of manners. Process is where each individual organization is given the opportunity to become and remain unique. The process of service involves the human element along with other procedures and policies. A quick-serve restaurant may have a policy of serving food that is prepared

Photo © 1998 PhotoDisc, Inc.

Quick-service restaurants usually provide limited service in exchange for speed.

to order and served within 7 minutes to each guest from a well-trained, friendly employee. While one may believe that this "procedure" can be easily copied (much like content), the consistent implementation of policies and procedures remains a challenge for the operators of service establishments. The decision to implement the policy of *food prepared to order, served within 7 minutes of a guest's arrival to the establishment, and served from a friendly employee* requires that the establishment maintains at a minimum: (a) a staff which is fully aware of the procedure and why it is being used, (b) a staff which is willing to implement the procedure, (c) a staff which is trained to effectively implement the procedure, (d) sufficient staff and equipment to accommodate peak service times (i.e., lunch and dinner "rush"), and (e) a means of evaluating the output of the process. Not unlike content, the process must be carefully monitored and implemented to ensure that it is being used as planned. Process and content are inseparably related in service-based organizations. Orders can be taken and delivered quickly by a friendly, informed staff, but if the content of the product is not consistently offered, the service episode is likely to be seen as not satisfying for the consumer. Conversely, excellent content and poor process will inevitably lead to a similar level of dissatisfaction.

In sum, the goal of a service operator should be to keep both the content and the process within the organizational context consistent to ensure that guests' expectations are not violated. This should be maintained through proper training, socialization, and evaluation of both service content and process (Lewis & Nightingale, 1991).

The Customer Service Equation

As mentioned earlier, the customer service process is dynamic and multidimensional in nature. It requires a series of interactive components that are arranged by all of the participants in the service process (i.e., guests, employees, and managers). The quest for service begins with a guest identifying a need and seeking a particular match for that need. The process ends with an evaluation of the service process that is used as feedback for subsequent service episodes. In between needs and evaluation, there are issues of: (a) service content, process, and delivery, (b) guests, employees, and managers, and (c) service quality, expectations, and guest satisfaction. The employees and managers of service-based organizations and their guests coequally influence the customer service equation. Please see Figure 2.

Guests in the Service Equation

Guests are the driving forces behind any service business. Guests select products and services that they believe are best suited to match their needs, and they hope to have their expectations met or exceeded during each step of the service process. For the guest, selection decisions can be either routine or unusual depending upon the circumstances and their particular needs. When faced with uncertainty (i.e., attempting to find a restaurant for dinner in a city never visited), guests will either seek a familiar solution (i.e., a national quick-service restaurant), seek additional information to make a decision (i.e., advice of a concierge, Zagat or Frommer's guides), or conquer the unknown. Either way, the guest will: (a) consider the potential quality of the offerings (based on needs and expectations), (b) seek to experience output from the service process, and (c) eventually evaluate it. In the process of receiving the output, the guest will have contact with service-based employees and management. Each party will influence the service episode in different ways.

Whether solicited or not, a guest will evaluate the service process in terms of quality and satisfaction. This evaluation, in terms of feedback, will be used by the guest to influence future service choices. A guest offers feedback to the employees and operators of service-based operations in terms of appearance (e.g., looking satisfied), compensation (e.g., paying the bill or tipping appropriately), or written and/or verbal comments (e.g., comment cards or a discussion with service or management personnel). Feedback can be positive or negative and should be used judiciously by each participant in the service process.

Guest feedback can help service operators identify strengths and weaknesses in their service processes. While some guests may freely offer feedback and suggestions to service providers, more often than not, guests do not offer any "formal" feedback following service. It is beneficial to regularly solicit feedback from your customers to continuously improve and maintain your service processes.

Employees in the Service Equation

The customer service employee has become an important factor in the customer service process because employees act as a bridge between the guests and management (Schneider & Bowen, 1995). In short, service employees are responsible to maintain service quality and guest satisfaction, while operating within the organizational guidelines set by management.

The job of service provider is particularly difficult because there is little or no separation in regard to the task of producing service, consumption of the service by the guest, and evaluation of the service by the guest *and* management. This differs greatly from manufacturing settings where production and consumption activities are typically separated. A service provider is charged with the responsibility of adapting to each guest's specific requirements (within reason of course).

With instantaneous feedback from guests and management there are many behavioral implications which should be addressed with employees of service-based organizations. Often, service employees have to deal with

Figure 2. The Customer Service Equation.

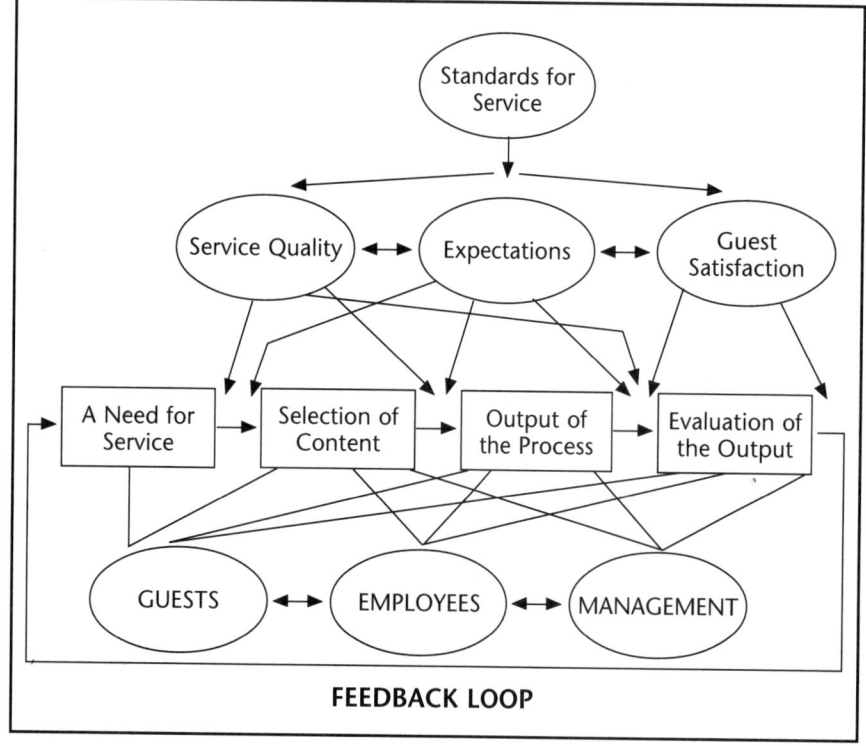

upset guests, disgruntled employees, understaffing, and high turnover among employees. To say that the service industry is over-stimulating at times would be a grand understatement. As such, the climate of a service organization greatly influences how workers perceive their service-related duties in terms of job satisfaction and organizational commitment. If workers are happy in their jobs, they will show greater commitment to the organization and its operational objectives. Likewise, employees' perceived support from coworkers and supervisors influences how they relate to their duties in terms of possessing a guest orientation (Kelly, 1992; Susskind, Kacmar, Borchgrevink, & Brymer, 1998), and they have a sense of being an internal customer (Lewis, 1989; Susskind, et al., 1998). In this case, *guest orientation* is defined as workers having a primary focus on providing exceptional service to their guests, while being an *internal customer* suggests that the workers believe they are viewed as valuable to the service process. These factors all highlight the interactive nature of service-based duties, and this suggests that the key to effective service comes not only from good policies, procedures, and processes, but the people who effectuate them.

Managers in the Service Equation

Managers of service-based business serve the function of coordinating the entire service process (Schneider & Bowen, 1995). This is a complex task that involves coordinating the activities and experiences of both guests and employees. If guests are to be truly satisfied, they must consistently receive excellent service. Likewise for employees to be satisfied, they need to feel that their contributions to the service process are valuable and they can make a difference through the provision of the service to their guests. It is difficult to sum up a manager's duties in a page or two. Managers, at all times, must balance

Photo © 1998 PhotoDisc, Inc.

If workers are happy in their jobs, they will show greater commitment to the organization and its operational objectives.

the often-conflicting needs of their guests and employees. As with any equation, it will not balance unless all components are properly in place. They must carefully interpret the feedback they receive from their guests and employees to regulate the service process.

For example, a hotel guest may be unhappy with a room service order placed and received. Based on the complaint of the guest, the manager must first identify the cause of the guest's dissatisfaction and attempt to determine where the breakdown occurred. With room service it could have been an issue of an incorrect order, improper service, product quality, or a variety of reasons. The manager must promptly and correctly identify the problem, address the guest to recover from the service failure, and point out to the employees involved in the service episode where the breakdown occurred and what should be done in the future. Managers must institute corrective feedback to address the problem for both the guest and the employee. This is one example of many daily occurrences which must be addressed and coor-

dinated by management. As with the employees and guests, the goal of the service process is to provide satisfying service episodes in terms of service quality, guest satisfaction, and employee satisfaction.

Service Quality and Guest Satisfaction

When looking at the service process in organizations, service quality and customer satisfaction are consistently identified as two points of evaluation used to assess the service process (Oh & Parks, 1997, Susskind, Kacmar, Borchgrevink, & Brymer, 1998). Service quality is framed as a long-range issue, which places the appraisal of service episodes on a continuum typically ranging from "excellent down to awful." Over time, service is evaluated and "labels" are attached to describe the services offered. For example, the statement, "Restaurant X serves excellent food, but there is always a two hour wait to get a table," implies that the food quality and service is perceived as excellent, and for the most part guests are willing to wait for it. However, the "two hour wait" portion of the evaluation of the service establishment evidently presents a concern. Conversely, customer satisfaction is episodic in nature and symbolizes an individual's perception of a particular service experience (Bitner, 1990; Cronin & Taylor, 1992, 1994). For example, a budget hotel may be well known for providing exceptional value in their products and services, but may dissatisfy customers periodically for a number of reasons. The distinction between service quality and customer satisfaction implies that guests' perceptions of service episodes are influenced by multiple factors (Susskind et al., 1998). Whether referring to service quality or customer satisfaction, consumers want to be treated hospitably and receive products and services consistent with their expectations and perceptions of the organization (Ford, 1995; Ford & Etienne, 1994). Recently, much attention has been paid to both of these issues, and organizations remain interested in developing processes to ensure consistency in product and service offerings to achieve the ultimate goal of repeated guest satisfaction (Oh & Parks, 1997).

Managers and employees of service-based organizations should understand that customer satisfaction and service quality are crucial elements that lead to success in the service business. However, this alone does not translate into conduct which produces satisfying customer service interactions on the front lines among customer service employees and their guests (Susskind, et al., 1998).

Standards

Standards for service outline the elements of the service process and act as a gauge by which comparisons are made. Standards from an organizational standpoint can be defined as perceptions of: (a) organizational goals and objectives, (b) managerial expectations for job performance, and (c) the implicit importance placed upon those goals, objectives, and performance demands (Litwin & Stringer, 1968). In large bureaucratic settings, such as a hospital or public utility company, there are typically distant and fuzzy relationships among the employees, the services or products offered, and organizational objectives in terms of organizational members' task identity and task significance (Hackman & Oldham, 1976). In customer service organizations, however, standards are generally more pronounced due to the fact that the service provider is more involved with the production *and* delivery of the product or service and frequently receives feedback concerning the service process during or immediately following its consumption whether solicited or not (Schneider & Bowen, 1995). Standards for service are typically an important part of a service-based organization's strategic mission and act as a gauge by which products and services are produced in a service organization. For employees to consistently uphold standards for service set by the organization, they must feel that they are supported by the organization to maintain those standards.

A Service Guarantee

A service guarantee is a strategic and operational commitment on behalf of an organization to ensure that each guest is *unconditionally* satisfied with the output of the service process. In effect, with a service guarantee, the service provider is willing to ensure that guests do not pay for services or products with which they are not satisfied. The service guarantee fills the gap between service quality and guest satisfaction. A service guarantee can be implicit or explicit, publicized or not; either way, a service guarantee is put in place to make guests happy (Evans, et al., 1996; Marvin, 1992). The concept of a 100% service guarantee was coined and introduced to the service industry by L.L. Bean, and continues to be the standard by which companies institute service guarantees within their organizations (Evans, Clark & Knutson, 1996). Likewise, many food companies, such as Nabisco and General Mills, have had product guarantees in place for many years. You need just read the label of any box of General Mill's breakfast cereal to find the statement:

> "**We're committed to quality.** In fact we unconditionally guarantee it. If you are not satisfied with the quality of this product, a prompt refund or adjustment of equal value will be made. Your comments and questions are welcome. **Save and send your box and** . . . call: [toll free phone number], write: [address], e-mail: [address]."

In the preceding service guarantee, the company is willing to stand behind their product unconditionally if the consumer is not happy with it. This is the same type of policy that has also been adopted by retailers such as Kmart, Land's End, Sears, and Nordstrom. Furthermore, it has also worked its way into many lodging companies (i.e., Hampton Inn, Comfort Inn, and Howard Johnson) and foodservice companies (i.e., Pizza Hut, Papa Johns, and Burger King). The only difference in a service guarantee between retail outlets and hospitality businesses is that, with retail businesses, consumers must: (a) purchase the product, (b) take the product home (or at least away from the store), and only then are they able to (c) evaluate the product's quality and their satisfaction with that level of quality. Hospitality operations (with the exception of take-out services) provide products and services to their guests while they are present in the establishment. This requires that the guests concurrently consume and evaluate the services received. Furthermore, in most cases, the guest has yet to pay for the services received prior to consuming them. This unique feature of the hospitality industry would lead one to believe that some form of a service guarantee is needed.

In order for a service guarantee to be effective, management must be committed to consistently reimbursing dissatisfied guests for the products and services, which did not meet their expectations. Each employee, whether they have direct contact with guests or not, should be trained to utilize the policy and understand why it is in place. In regard to the guests, employees, and management there are eight interrelated steps to an effective service guarantee policy:

1. Guests need to be aware of *your desire* to have them be unconditionally satisfied with the services offered.

2. The guests *and* employees need to know that dissatisfied guests will not have to pay for services which do not meet their expectations, regardless of the reason.

3. Clearly identify the source of the guests' dissatisfaction.

4. Never assign blame to anyone—management must personally take full responsibility for the lapse in service and quickly correct the problem for the guests involved.

5. Ensure the guest that the problem will not reoccur in the future and inform employees of any deficiencies.

6. Thank the guests for their patience and understanding.

7. Reassure your guests that they are the reason why you are in business (make sure your employees know that too).

8. Make a clear record of each reported incident and follow-up in a week or two with a written confirmation of the problems the guests had and what was done to permanently address the problem (if applicable).

If consistently applied, a service guarantee can help a business gain the trust and loyalty of their guests. For a service guarantee to be effective there must be clear policies and procedures in place, effective training for employees, and a commitment to achieve ultimate guest satisfaction (Evans, Clark & Knutson, 1996).

Problems with a Service Guarantee

When an operation has a service guarantee in place there is the potential for abuse by customers and employees. Any good policy, plan, or procedure needs to be monitored and controlled for effectiveness. For example, if a hotel company offers guests their money back if they are not 100 percent satisfied with their stay, as stated above they should make note of the incident and keep a record of it. Should a guest frequently be dissatisfied, the company should inquire as to why they continue to return if they can never be made happy. If a guest is abusing a courtesy, they can then be disqualified from receiving the benefit. It is extremely important to never accuse a guest of abuse without being sure of wrongdoing on their part. Remember the guest is dissatisfied until proven satisfied. Handle the situation tactfully, and gather sufficient information and evidence of abuse prior to refusing a guest remuneration for a reported incident of dissatisfaction. Regardless of what policies are in place to ensure guest satisfaction, it should be the goal of every hospitality business to make all of their guests happy. That is the fundamental premise behind the service equation, which drives the concept of the hospitality industry.

◆ Conclusion

It is essential to remember that the delivery of service is dependent on the three inter-related participants of the service equation, namely the guests, the service employees and management. All three are equally important as either one can derail the delivery of high quality services making the experience unsatisfactory.

Given the relative intangibility and perishability of the hospitality experience it is important to align the actual delivery of hospitality services with the guests' needs and expectations. It is particularly important to be aware of potential habituated experiences that guests may have, as failing to meet such expectations are particularly annoying and dissatisfying to guests.

In providing quality services both the service content and the service process needs to be considered. A useful tool in delivering high quality service is the service guarantee. To be effective, however, management and service employees must be fully committed to the promise of the guarantee and must consistently enforce the guarantee. This will help build guest satisfaction, trust and loyalty.

◆ Questions and Assignments

1. List and describe the three major components of the service equation.

2. Define service from the hospitality perspective. Use an example from your hospitality experience to demonstrate. Establish what the key issues were that led to satisfaction or dissatisfaction. Be prepared to discuss your definition and example with your teammates or classmates.

3. Using your library resources or the web browser and search engine of your choice, identify an article that discusses service in hospitality. Summarize the key points, and bring your findings to class, prepared to share and discuss your findings with your team and classmates.

4. Define and differentiate need and expectation.

5. What does it mean that an expectation becomes habituated? Use an example to demonstrate. Be prepared to discuss your definition and example.

6. Discuss briefly the role of process and content in service management. Is either more important? Use an example to illustrate. Summarize the key points, and bring your summary to class, prepared to share and discuss them with your team or classmates.

7. Summarize the chapter discussion of the relationship between service quality and guest satisfaction. Using your library resources or the web browser and search engine of your choice, identify an article that discusses this further. Summarize the key points, and bring your findings to class, prepared to share and discuss your findings with your team and classmates.

8. Using your library resources or the web browser and search engine of your choice, find a hospitality company service guarantee. Discuss the guarantee in light of the eight steps to effective service guarantees. Summarize the key points, and bring your findings to class prepared to share and discuss your findings with your team and classmates.

◀Bibliography and Suggested Readings

Bitner, M. J. (1990). Evaluating service encounters: The effects of physical surroundings and employee responses. *Journal of Marketing, 54*, 69–82.

Borchgrevink, C. P. & Susskind, A. M. (1996). Beverage Communication: A pilot study of the experiences and preferences of restaurant customers. *Hospitality and Tourism Educator, 8*(1), 19–23.

Bowen, D. E., Siehl, C. & Schneider, B. (1989). A framework for analyzing customer service orientations in manufacturing. *Academy of Management Review, 14*, 75–95.

Cronin, J. J. & Taylor, S. A. (1992). Measuring service quality: A reexamination and extension. *Journal of Marketing, 56*, 55–68.

Cronin, J. J. & Taylor, S. A. (1994). SERVPERF versus SERVQUAL: Reconciling performance-based and perceptions-minus-expectations measurement of service quality. *Journal of Marketing, 58*, 125–131.

Evans, M. R., Clark, J. D. & Knutson, B. J. (1996). The 100–percent, unconditional, money-back guarantee. *Cornell Hotel and Restaurant Administration Quarterly, December*, 56–61.

Ford, W. S. Z. (1995). Evaluation of the indirect influence of courteous service on customer discretionary behavior. *Human Communication Research, 22*, 65–89.

Ford, W. S. Z. & Etienne, C. N. (1994). Can I help you? A framework for interdisciplinary research on customer service encounters. *Management Communication Quarterly, 7*, 413–441.

Hackman, J. R. & Oldham, G. R. (1976). Motivation through the design of work: Test of a theory. *Organizational Behavior and Human Decision Processes, 16*, 250–279.

Heskett, J. L. (1987). Lessons in the service sector. *Harvard Business Review, (March–April)*, 118–126.

Kelly, S. W. (1992). Developing customer orientation among service employees. *Journal of the Academy of Marketing Science, 20*, 27–36.

Lewis, R. C. (1989). Hospitality marketing: The internal approach. *Cornell Hotel and Restaurant Administration Quarterly, November*, 41–45.

Lewis, R. C. & Nightingale, M. (1991). Targeting service to your customer. *Cornell Hotel and Restaurant Administration Quarterly, August*, 18–27.

Litwin, G. H. & Stringer, R. A., Jr. (1968). *Motivation and organizational climate*. Boston, MA: Harvard University Graduate School of Business.

Lockwood, A. & Jones, P. (1989). Creating positive service encounters. *Cornell Hotel and Restaurant Administration Quarterly, November, February*, 44–50.

Marvin, B. (1992, September 9). Exemplary service guaranteed. *Restaurants and Institutions*, 108–112, 117–121.

Oh, H. & Parks, S. C. (1997). Customer satisfaction and service quality: A critical review of the literature and research implications for the hospitality industry. *Hospitality Research Journal, (20)*, 35–64.

Schneider, B. & Bowen, D. E. (1992). Personnel/human resources management in the service sector. *Research in Personnel and Human Resources Management, 10*, 1–30.

Schneider, B. & Bowen, D. E. (1993). The service organization: Human resources management is crucial. *Organizational Dynamics, 21*(4), 39–52.

Schneider, B. & Bowen, D. E. (1995). *Winning the Service Game*. Boston: Harvard Business School Press.

Susskind, A. M., Kacmar, K. M., Borchgrevink, C. P. & Brymer, R. A. (1998). The use of referent climate to examine customer service behavior and attitudes: Further evidence for a climate for customer service." Working Paper, Department of Hospitality Administration, Florida State University, Tallahassee, FL.

Webster's Ninth New Collegiate Dictionary (1988). Springfield, MA: Merriam-Webster, Inc., Publishers.

The Hospitality Marketing Perspective

Bonnie J. Knutson, *The School of Hospitality Business*, MICHIGAN STATE UNIVERSITY

ABSTRACT

The Hospitality Marketing Perspective focuses on the making and keeping of customers at a profit. With this as a foundation, hospitality marketing is seen as having three functions: Identifying demand, influencing demand, and servicing demand. Therefore, the hospitality perspective is built on the belief that marketing and operations cannot be separated; they are two sides of the same coin. Whereas marketing makes a promise, operations must keep that promise.

OBJECTIVES

At the end of this chapter the student should be able to:

1. Define hospitality marketing.
2. List and discuss *Eight Ps of marketing*.
3. Describe marketing related activities.
4. Discuss the role of the guests in hospitality success.
5. Describe the importance of marketing information.
6. List and discuss the various components of situation analysis.
7. Explain the importance of perception.

Introduction

It could be suggested that Levitt's admonition (Levitt, 1960) is just plain common sense not some cutting edge revelation. On the other hand, the growing competitiveness of the hospitality industry has forced many firms to believe that the purpose of business is making money. The focus on profits, ROIs (Return on Investment), growth in sales and number of units, mergers, buyouts, and a series of sophisticated business school jargon has drawn attention away from the real purpose of business: to *make and keep customers*. If you doubt the validity of this conclusion, just look at how management is evaluated. Emphasis in any business plan is placed on costs, controllable expenses, and profit margins. Rarely is the manager's performance judged in terms of guest counts, guest frequencies, guest satisfaction, and market share. And as famed business consultant Michael LeBoeuf reminds us, *you get more of the behavior you reward* (LeBoeuf, 1987).

No one is suggesting that profit is not important. It is critical. Without profit (and cash flow) a business "'ain't no more"! Think of the following analogy: If you claim that the purpose of business is making money, you might just as well say that the purpose of life it to eat. Eating is a requisite, not a purpose in life. The same is true

of profits. Making profits is a requisite, not a purpose in the life of a business. Mike Hurst, owner of the famed 15th Street Fisheries and former president of the NRA correctly says: Profits *follow people* (Hurst, n.d.). So to give Levitt's definition a hospitality marketing perspective, we modify it to: The purpose of hospitality marketing is to make and keep guests at a profit (Smith, n.d.; Stevens, 1988). This hospitality marketing perspective confirms the marketing philosophy begun by The General Electric Company that became known as The Marketing Concept. The Marketing Concept views the consumer (i.e. people) as the focal point of all marketing activities (Harvey, Lusch, and Cavarkapa, 1996). In his classic article, "Marketing Myopia" (1960), Levitt reinforced this belief. Before this re-orientation was introduced, marketing focused on what the company could produce, promote, and sell. It was called The Selling Concept. Folklore of the day maintained, in fact, that Henry Ford reflected this philosophy with his claim that, *You could have any color of Ford, as long as*

Henry Ford was a proponent of the "selling concept."

it was black. This basic switch in how marketing was viewed reshaped the field of marketing to focus on the "customer is king" philosophy. From this reorientation came the practice of segmentation, target or niche marketing, competitive advantage, product differentiation, positioning or image building, and consumer research.

As a hospitality manager, you will need to understand computers, managerial accounting, how to compute ROIs (Return on Investment), establish cost control procedures, and manage your staff. Each of these functions are essential *supports* to the purpose of your business—*your guests*. It is marketing that focuses a business on the value of making and keeping its customers—i.e. its guests.

While many people may be influenced to try a hotel, restaurant, or attraction through the mass media, loyal guests are made one at a time. This appears to be a mind-boggling task. Think about a hotel that checks in 800 guests a day, or a restaurant that serves 500–2000 people daily, or the hundreds of thousands who walk through the gates at Disney World every day. The hospitality managers that manage these operations, and thousands more like them, must have knowledge, understanding, and managerial skills to establish a standard operating *performance* (notice I didn't say procedure) for hospitality or caring. The customer who first walks through their door can be turned into a loyal guest only through the well-selected, trained, and motivated employee. Thus, in reality, it is impossible to separate marketing from operations/line management. They are two sides of the same coin. Every employee is both a salesperson and a goodwill ambassador for your business. In fact, to your guest, he or she *is* your business.

Therefore, you have to view hospitality marketing as a process with three major functions:

❖ *Identifying* opportunities to increase sales and/or guest counts.

- *Influencing* guest choices through image building and promotion.
- *Servicing* guests to develop loyalty, gain repeat business, and generate word-of-mouth (or radial) advertising.

Sometimes, these functions are known as identifying, influencing and servicing demand, where demand is defined as consumers who are ready, willing, and able to buy. Whatever the label, each of these three marketing responsibilities involves a variety of marketing functions: research, positioning, packaging, differentiating, pricing, promotion, calendars, budgeting, and analysis—all of which serve the purpose of increasing guest count—in other words *making and keeping of customers.*

Marketing and operations can't be separated. They are two sides of the same coin.

Identifying Marketing Opportunities to Increase Sales and Guest Counts

Professionals in the business of hospitality know that marketing information systems (MIS) is the basis for effective management decisions. If you talk with successful managers in successful hospitality chains—McDonald's, Taco Bell, Hyatt International, Hilton, or any other first tier enterprise—you will get the same response: *Marketing Information Works.* They all believed in it, do it, and use it. It stands to reason that if we develop new products, services, or concepts, the market had better want them and be willing to pay what we need to charge to cover our costs. We are in the business of solving our guests' problems better than our competition does, so we had better carefully observe and listen to our guests and prospective guests.

Every once in a while, you'll find an entrepreneur who manages a small hotel or restaurant. He may huff a little and cry, "That stuff! Who needs it?" Don't listen to him because that response can't really be taken at face value. Chances are, he *is* gathering market information, he just doesn't know it. Is he:

- recording and monitoring customer counts, sales information, and costs?
- personally on the floor at meal times or at peak check-in times observing guests' behavior?
- using comment cards?
- talking with his bussers and dishwashers to find out what is being left on plates or watching how a guest moves furniture in the hotel room to make it more convenient?
- visiting competitors, attending seminars, and reading trade magazines?

If he is doing any of these things (and chances are he is), then he is using marketing information systems. Why? To get feedback from his customers and competition and make better management decisions. More often than not, when restaurateurs and hoteliers say, "I cannot afford to conduct market research; I'm a small business operation," they deal with guests on a daily basis. They don't need sampling when they have the whole universe in front of them. They understand guests' wants and needs by being close to those being served. They really do believe in marketing information. It's just not a formalized process.

The growth of multi-unit operations brought with it a need to formalize the guest information system. This is because the final decision-makers (corporate management) have become removed from the end-user (guest); and because the impact of a management decision on hundreds or thousands of units is far greater than on one. Therefore, the lack of a formalized system can cause financial disaster.

The owner/operator of a 200-seat restaurant finds it relatively easy to obtain feedback from guests and employees. She can be on the dining room floor almost every meal period, observing guests, and probing for perceptions, preferences, and habits. Her method of adapting to changing guest needs can be trial and error. Before listing an item on a menu as a regular offering, it can be carefully tested for taste (by sampling), appearance (again, by sampling), portion size, and price (usually first as a special). Single unit owner/operators continually obtain feedback from guests and employees to aid in predicting what the customers will like/buy and what they won't.

On the other hand, the president of a 2,000 unit hamburger chain finds it impossible to have the same personalized and direct marketing formation umbilical cord to guests. As the distance between decision makers and customers gets bigger, the greater the need for accurate, thorough, and continual market information. Thus, there is the need for a formalized system. Of course, it is still critical for the head(s) of the company to "get down in the trenches" and deal with guests one-on-one.

The bottom line is this: Marketing information is necessary whether you

Art Gunther, a former president of Pizza Hut, was another marketing guru who understood the purpose of his business was to make and keep pizza-eaters. Supposedly, when he was flying from one place to another in the corporate jet, he would often tell the pilot on route to "set down here" or "set down there." Once on the ground, he used to go into the nearest store, unannounced and unrecognized. He pretended he was a customer, experiencing his restaurant as a customer—all the while watching the operations—with special attention to observing the guests and what they were doing.

are the manager of a 10-room bed and breakfast or a 1,000 unit chain. It works. The question is:

1. How to do it?
2. How to use it? and
3. What can realistically be expected from it?

That is what developing a marketing plan is all about.

Relationship Between Identifying Opportunities and Marketing Information

Before you go on a vacation to a new place, you might get a brochure about the resort, search the Internet for attractions in the area, and get a road map to decide the best way of getting there. In other words, you need information before you decide to go. In much the same way, before you decide on a marketing strategy, you need information. You need to *look before you leap*, so to speak. This process is often called a *Situation Analysis* or a *Business Review*. Its purpose is just what it says: to analyze the current and future business situation for the company.

Most *Situation Analyses* have six major components.

Performance

Sometimes called Historical Analysis or Sales Analysis, a manager needs to know what has been and is going on within the hotel or restaurant itself. How are sales? Costs? Profit margins? How many guests are being served? In which market segments? Are the numbers going up or down? What are your guests buying? How effective have your promotions been? Successful marketers are continually collecting and analyzing this internal quantitative data so that they have an accurate picture of how their unit(s) is performing and what opportunities might be there. As a snapshot, this information by itself isn't really helpful; but when compared to sales levels

over past years, and when compared to industry averages, or to other units in your company, or even the competition, you have useful data. So, when possible, gather data that will allow you to compare your performance to:

❖ Similar properties in your company and to corporate averages.
❖ Industry averages for your segment.
❖ Major competitors in your segment.

Finally, try to collect three to five years of data for each of these categories. This will allow you to determine performance trends for your business.

Successful marketers are also talking with their servers, bussers, bartenders, cooks, and dishwashers. They are talking with their bellman, housekeepers, front desk, and room service personnel. Successful marketers know that employees are an essential source of performance information because they are the closest to the *boss*—i.e. the customer. Front line employees hear the compliments and complaints; they respond to requests and special needs; they see what food guests leave on their plates or how

a business traveler rearranges the furniture in his hotel room to make it more efficient. Sometimes, employee input can be the most valuable information of all when looking for new marketing opportunities. For example, one hotel added pizza to its room service menu after housekeepers started reporting that they were finding a lot of Domino's boxes being left in rooms or in the hallway outside the door. After conducting some additional research, the hotel launched an aggressive promotional campaign designed to position its pizza as hotter, fresher, and quicker than the "30-minutes-or-free" competition. It worked. Room service sales were up and housekeeping didn't find any more competitors' boxes.

Product

The hospitality product is unique in two distinct ways. First, when guests walk in your door, they have already made the decision to buy something from you. It's a rare occurrence when someone makes a hotel reservation, enters the lobby, then decides to leave without spending the night. It's similar for restaurants. People usually decide where to eat before they walk

Photo © 1998 PhotoDisc, Inc.

Successful marketers know that employees are an essential source of performance information.

in. *Gee, I feel like ribs tonight. Let's go to Damon's.* This isn't the case with most retail operations. When you go to the mall to buy a new sweater, you may walk into Eddie Bauer's, J.C. Penny's, and Macy's before you actually spend your money. Second, by definition, a critical element of the hospitality product is *hospitality*. It is that intangible aspect that makes a guest feel valued, special, and welcome. You can't touch, feel, taste, see, or hear it, but it is real. We sometimes call it Service Quality.

A Product Analysis must evaluate both the tangible and intangible components. There are a variety of ways to get this information. There are shoppers' studies, guest surveys, and walk-arounds. Most involve comparing what the hotel or restaurant has or does with an established benchmark or to the competition—cleanliness, convenience, room amenities, atmosphere, prompt service, knowledgeable employees, decor, menu— ad infinitum. The key to any product analysis is objectivity. While you may note that the carpet is worn in the hallway or that one of your servers didn't know the menu items too well, more accurate information is always gathered through fresh eyes. Large organizations often have a separate department, or it hires outside firms, to conduct this analysis for you. If this isn't available, you can turn to a local university's marketing class, work with your advertising agency, or even arrange with another manager in the area to "shop" and evaluate each other's property.

Competition

The overall goal of this analysis is to find out how your property compares to its' competition. Therefore, the same categories that you use in your product analysis apply here. The difficulty, of course, comes in getting some of the competitive data. While you may not be able to directly obtain sales figures or occupancy rates for the guy across the street or down the road, you can use their corporate publications, industry publications, and media spending to get a sense of their situation.

You also need to shop your competition in much the same way you would shop your property. Have your chef and servers make brunch reservations at the restaurant down the street. Send your sales staff to the competitors' lobbies to find out which meetings or conventions are being held there. Have someone call for information about holding her wedding reception in their ballroom? And, of course, you can conduct market research studies to find out what consumers think about you and your competition. Your overall goal is to find out how the market compares you to your competition. Where are you doing better? Where do you need to improve? What is the competition doing that you're not? Is there something that consumers want or need that the competition isn't providing?

Market

By far, understanding your current guests and potential guests is the most important thing you can do in marketing. This is a *sine qua non*. (That's Latin for "without this you're nothing.") The better you understand your target market(s), the better you, as a marketer, will be able to fulfill guests' needs and effectively market to them.

A market analysis will give you a format for sorting guests/potential guests into segments. Such segmentation allows guests to be grouped according to similar characteristics. These characteristics could be demographics, such as age, gender, income, education, occupation, or location. You can also segment by psychographics; that is, their attitudes, beliefs, interests, and personality traits. It's an attempt to really get inside the consumers' minds. In marketing, psychographics are really more important to know than demographics. How many people do you know that are the same age and gender, have comparable education and income levels, live in the same neighborhood and have similar families? Yet, one may drive an expensive conservative car, belong to a country club, and eat out several times a week. The other drives a Sports Utility Vehicle, has a summer home in the woods, and would rather barbecue in the back yard. Clearly, they have different attitudes, values, and interests. They probably read different magazines, watch different television programs, and contribute to different charities too. In other words, you need to market to each differently. This requires knowing psychographics.

Guests can also be segmented by use. For a hotel, there are leisure guests, business travelers, and group business. In a restaurant, there are guests who come there for breakfast, for happy hour, to celebrate a birthday, or just because they don't feel like cooking at home. Each of these groups is fulfilling different needs and derives different benefits from coming to your property. You can also segment guests by frequency. The market research industry often uses such labels as heavy users, light users, or non-users. Understanding why they come and what they get out of the experience helps you design effective marketing strategies.

Trade Area and Industry Trends

The final two sections of a Situation Analysis are the Trade Area and Industry Trends. A trading area is the geographical territory from where your customers come. It's how far your customers travel to eat at your restaurant or stay at your hotel. In general, the more convenience driven your product, the smaller the trade area. For a restaurant at lunchtime, that is usually three to five miles; at dinner, that same restaurant can expand its trade area to 10 or more miles. A hotel, on the other hand, can draw its guests regionally, nationally, or internationally. You can iden-

Guests can be segmented by use, such as business guests or leisure guests in a hotel.

Influencing Customer Choices Through Image Building and Promotion

In your basic marketing course, you probably learned about the "4 Ps of Marketing"—Product, Price, Place, and Promotion (McCarthy, 1960). This model of The Marketing Mix served us well in the past; now there is a more complex and competitive business environment. Couple this with the uniqueness of the hospitality industry, it makes a lot more sense to expand the paradigm of the 4 Ps and think of marketing in terms of 8 Ps (Smith, n.d.; Stevens, 1988). The 8 Ps are more than just 8 words that happen to begin with the letter "P." In reality, they are *tools* to be understood, used, manipulated, developed, and perfected in order to reach the ultimate marketing goal of *making and keeping customers at a profit*. Just as you would use a hammer, saw, and nails to fashion wood into a piece of fine furniture, you use these ten elements to fashion raw marketing information into a successful marketing plan. You use them to influence consumers to come into your place, and once there, to influence what they buy.

People

The first "P" requires you to ask the question, *Who are your guests and prospective guests?* This means that you need a real good understanding of:

❖ *Who* is your current and prospective user (guest)?
  ◆ Demographics
  ◆ Psychographics
  ◆ Behaviors
❖ *Why* do they come to your business instead of going someplace else?
❖ *How* do they compare you to your competition?
❖ *What* do they see as your strengths and weaknesses?
❖ *When* do they come to your place? To your competition?

tify your trade area in a variety of ways. Hotels can use its reservation or registration systems, mailing lists, credit card information, business-cards-in-a-fishbowl, sophisticated market surveys, or a simple in-house questionnaire to find out where its guests live and work. Restaurants can use the same techniques, or others. I know one restaurateur who also walks around his parking lot looking at the license plates to find out where his customers are from.

Knowing your trade area is important from a media-purchasing standpoint, for determining future site locations, and for determining possible opportunities and threats for your business. Assume, for example, that you are a hotel with a strong business clientele. Most of your guests are in town for meetings with XYZ Corporation, which is located less than a mile away. As the marketing director, what do you do if you discover that the XYZ Company is "downsizing" that location in favor of expanding another office across town? Conversely, let's say you are the marketing manager for a 300 seat casual restaurant

and learn that the Planning Commission has just rezoned 100 acres across the street from agricultural to office and multi-unit development. Or what if you run a popular pub in a state that is considering reducing it's definition of intoxicated from .1 to .08? Offices, housing, attractions such as theme parks, stadiums, or shopping centers are all *demand generators* for your business. Roads, extension of utility lines, designation of public lands, and legislation can affect your target markets. Changes in anything that affects demand affects your marketing strategy.

Finally, keeping up with lifestyle and industry trends is a must for any marketer. Most managers spend too much time reading invoices and inventories, but not enough reading *Nation's Restaurant News, Restaurants & Institutions, Lodging, Lodging Management, CREST Reports, American Demographics, Advertising Age, Clicking, U.S. News & World Report, Time, Newsweek,* and even *USA Today.* Some of the greatest marketing opportunities are found by looking at the broad picture.

- How *often* do they come (frequency)?
- How do they get to your place? In terms of time? Transportation? From where?
- How can they be influenced?

Underlying the needs, wants, and expectations of your guests/prospective guests are changing lifestyle trends. These shifts in overall demographics, psychographics, and behaviors alter how consumers think of or position your products and company. Just think of the healthy eating and fitness trend. Before we all started counting calories and fat grams, fried foods were goooooooooooood! Now, we may still eat them (look at the millions McDonald's sells every year), but we *think* of them differently.

In addition to trends, an important part of the People "P" is *elbows*. Who guests "rub elbows with" has a lot to do with your marketing strategy and how good your guests think you are. Certainly the price/value relationship is affected. Being around other people—the *right* other people—is part of why you go to a certain bar, join a certain club, or book a cruise on a certain ship. Market segmentation is heavily related to homogeneity.

Product

Product is what your guests "order," not necessarily what they "buy." The second "P" asks what business you are in and what products (both tangible and intangible) you really sell. While you might think that McDonald's is in the hamburger business, they are really in the safety and security business. Whether you eat at the golden arches in Minneapolis or Moscow, you know what you're going to get. There are no surprises; you feel safe in your food choices. Similarly, Disney World is really in the entertainment business not the theme park business. And what about Michelin Tires? While they may *sell* tires, they are actually in the insurance business. Who can watch those cute babies

riding around in a tire on television and not feel that, with Michelin, they are *insuring* the safety of their loved ones?

Your product is the *sum* total of all the tangibles and intangibles of need/want satisfying benefits. As mentioned earlier, it includes the physical as well as the psychological product. The *physical product* involves the tangible aspects of your business that the guest can experience with his or her senses. This includes such things as the taste of a menu item, the decor in your lobby, the aroma of baking bread, the choice of "elevator music," the shape of the swimming pool, the comfort of seats or beds, and even the distance a guest has to park from the front door. Anything that the guest can see, hear, smell, touch, or taste at your property becomes part of the physical product. So, as you can see, the *product* is more than what a guest has to eat in your restaurant, or whether you have one or two chairs in your hotel room. It is quite a total. And you can design each aspect of the product to influence your market.

On the other hand, the *psychological* product relates to perceived benefits. It involves all the need/want satisfying intangibles that exist and can't be touched by the five senses. Such things as personalization, the feeling of security, recognition, exclusivity, reputation, status, and experience are all *mind-related* values that become part of what your guest is buying. And it comes back to the basic question of knowing just what business you are in.

Position

Positioning requires that you look at how guests and prospective guests: 1. classify and 2. rank your product in relation to your competition (Ries and Trout, 1986). It asks the question, *"What image do you want to win in your guests' minds?"* Positioning is the strategic marketing term that provides a hospitality business a reason for being. It results in management's determination to deploy resources to

develop a competitive advantage in the minds of the prospective audience (guests and potential guests). And it focuses three to five years into the future, because positioning is a battle fought in the prospect's mind. It takes time to alter how people look at you, so positioning strategies have to be long term.

Your positioning strategies also have to be related to your mission statement. It would, for example, be unrealistic for Taco Bell to want to "win" a fine dining position in consumers' minds when its mission centers around southwestern fast food at a low price point.

Hospitality firms can be positioned (classified and ranked) on a motivation spectrum. At one end of the spectrum are higher-order needs such as Maslow's Self-Actualization. At the other end are the lower-order needs such as food, water, shelter, safety and security. If you think about the restaurant industry and the lodging industry you could easily place four classifications along the lines illustrated in Table 1.

Since *positioning* is a mental game and since *perception is reality*, there may be a lot of variations on these classifications. For example, to some, staying in a Holiday Inn may be akin to status, while for others, it might strictly be a convenience choice. That is why you really have to understand what your market thinks—how they classify and rank your business. This begs the following questions for you to think about:

- What kinds of guests will you be serving?
- What is your competitive advantage? On what marketing element will you position your hotel or restaurant?

According to Porter (1985), a business can only be positioned on one of three things:

- **Price**—If your mission statement allows you to position on price, then the key is to be seen as either

Positioning of Some Hospitality Businesses by Motivation

Lower Order Needs		Higher Order Needs	
← Convenience	Home Replacement	Experience	Entertainment/Status →
❖ McDonald's ❖ Arby's ❖ Taco Bell	❖ Old County Buffet ❖ Pizza Hut	❖ Planet Hollywood ❖ Houlihan's	❖ Private Clubs ❖ Polo Lounge
❖ Motel 6 ❖ Red Roof Inn	❖ Holiday Inn ❖ Embassy Suites	❖ Disney ❖ Greenbrier	❖ Waldorf Astoria ❖ Beverly Hills Hotel

the *least expensive* or the *most expensive*. You can't get caught in the middle. Don't misunderstand me, your pricing strategy may be middle-of-the-road, but if you *position* (i.e. want to be known as) your company on price, then you have to be at one extreme or the other. New York Carpet World positions itself on the pricing element. It wants to be known as the cheapest place in town to buy carpet. Taco Bell took a major step in positioning itself on price when it launched its 49-69-89 cent campaign. On the other end, you will find that companies such as Cartier's, The Regent Hotel, and Mercedes Benz are all top of the line when it comes to cost, but that is their niche.

❖ **Segment**—You can also position yourself by the market niche you go after. The clearest example of this is a private club. Clubs are not out to be all things to all people. They go after a very narrow band of the market. Maybe it's golfers or people who like to work out, or drink imported beer. Whatever the product, a hospitality organization that narrows its focus to a special target market is really selling homogeneity, friendship, and exclusivity. Its physical product is only a vehicle for their real product.

❖ **Differentiation**—If you don't position yourself on price or market segment (people), then you have

to position yourself on some other element on the marketing mix—i.e. one of the other "Ps." You have to be known for *something*—have *some* uniqueness. You might determine that you could put out the best pizza in the world, in which case your choice would be *Product*. Look at Gino's Pizza in Chicago. Or how about being known as the hotel for business travelers. In fact, a few years ago, Hilton capitalized on "product" with its slogan: *America's Business Address*. Think about the elements of *Packaging*. Maybe you serve a London Broil with British flair, or your salad bar is extensive and spectacular to look at. The meat may be the same cut as served in other restaurants, and a salad bar is commonly found. It's just that you do them differently . . . and better than the competition. So either can become what you're known for in the minds of the consumer. You would be positioned then, as the place with the best salad bar in town, or where the London Broil is presented with great showmanship by a server dressed in an English bowler, with a British-flag printed tea towel over his arm, and carrying a sizzling platter, complete with a small flag inserted in the meat. In my hometown, there was an ice-cream store that sold "rainbow" cones in "junior" and "senior" sizes. Their ice cream was like most other stores in the

area—no better or no worse. But it was what they *did* with their ice cream that made the positioning difference. To make the rainbow cone, they would layer 5 (junior size) or 7 (senior size) flavors of ice cream on a regular cone using a type of spatula scoop. This special scoop would produce a layer of ice cream about four inches long, about three-quarters of an inch thick, and the width of the cone. When one flavor was put in, the next was laid along side of it, extending a little further out of the cone. This would continue until all the flavors were layered, resulting in a "rainbow" of color and flavor bands. People could drive for an hour just to get one of Walt's Rainbow Cones. Now that's what I call positioning on packaging . . . not on the ice cream, but what they *did* to the ice cream. You can position on *Place* when you are the "most conveniently located," or when you're "only five minutes away." That is strictly a location factor. In *Promotion*, you're strictly known as "the business with . . ." One of the most successful hospitality campaigns in this area is Absolut Vodka. They are known far and wide for their unique print ads. And then there is the Energizer Bunny, Garfield with Embassy Suites, and of course, "I love ya' man!" and the "Da Da Da." Each has a quality product, but to stand out from the others, they use a unique message on which they position themselves.

When thinking about positioning, you have to consider the trends that can impact your position in the next three to five years. What changes are taking place that might alter how people classify and rank your business? A classic case is that of Kentucky Fried Chicken. Having been born and bred as a southern cooking, heavy food alternative, it saw the writing on the wall relative to the health and fitness trend. So the company added lighter fare to its menu and changed its name to KFC in a direct attempt to get people *not* to position it in the "greasy, fatty fast food" category. *Clicking* (Popcorn & Marigold, 1996) and *Rocking the Ages* (Smith & Clurman, 1997) are two books that can be a big help to you in thinking about positioning for future consumer trends.

Package

When we talk about a box of cereal or a bottle of perfume, the idea of packaging is obvious. The same is true when we think about take-out or delivery. What does the "box" look like? While that's one way to look at packaging, in hospitality marketing, this "P" is actually more complex than that. There are really three levels of packaging that we can use to help market our products.

The first one is the actual container itself. For "BK" it might be the Styrofoam™ container the Whopper comes in. In a traditional restaurant, it is the actual china, flatware, and presentation of the food and garnishes.

The second level is what we think of as the decor and ambiance of the place. It includes color, texture, lighting, and sound, also, furniture design and any theme used. This type of packaging produces a warm or cool feeling, one that is open or cozy, even formal or hospitable.

The third level includes all the symbols you use to reinforce your positioning. The company logo and signage, how the building looks, its landscaping, and surrounding neighborhood. Add to these the feel and look of your advertising, where you place your ads, get publicity, and how you generate public relations.

Many times, packaging is left to chance—particularly when it comes to levels two and three. But we live in a very visual culture; your customers have grown up with TV, glossy magazines, and alluring brochures. So when something in your total package is *out of sync* in your customer's mind's eye, the "P" becomes a weak

link in your marketing mix. A few years ago, we were working with a restaurant named *The America's Cup*. It had an eclectic menu of soups, salads, and sandwiches. As you might expect, when you walked in, you saw an array of nautical items to carry out the theme—pictures on the wall, roping and buoys, a sail hanging from the ceiling, and models of various racing hulls throughout. Even the dishes, napkins, and carry out containers carried out the theme. But the total package was out of sync. For in the midst of all the red, white, and blue sailing motifs, was a wait staff dressed in brown pants and orange shirts! Ouch! Why brown and orange you might ask? When we asked the same question, the owner simply said that he was saving money by using left over uniforms from another of his restaurants.

Too many times, the packaging "P" receives too little attention (beyond a Styrofoam™ box that is) in the marketing mix. As Julia Robert's character says in the movie, *Pretty Woman*, "Mistake. Big Mistake!" Always remember another golden rule of marketing:

What the eye sees, the eye buys!

Notice I didn't say "orders"; I said "buys." Packaging is an important part of the total product. A guest may "order" a steak, but he is buying the total ambiance, total experience, and total first impression. He is certainly not buying brown and orange uniforms in a nautical setting. A hotel guest may "book" (order) a room, but is buying safety, comfort, and a feeling that this is a home-away-from-home. She certainly is not buying a burned out bulb in the hall light outside her room, a lumpy bed, or a shower that doesn't have enough hot water and good pressure. (Incidentally, the part about the

shower is one of the biggest pet peeves for business travelers.)

This brings us to another rule of hospitality marketing:

Perception is Reality

And, the only perception that counts is the customer's! Think about the following examples that a colleague of mine often uses.

There is a little seafood restaurant on the channel side of Estero Island, Florida. It's flanked by Gulf-going fishing boats at harbor and has rustic wood, lots of windows, casually-dressed patrons (wearing socks is over-dressed), and even pelicans perched on dock posts in front. Everybody who goes there seems to order shrimp. There are no tablecloths, but plenty of paper napkins. Servers wear shorts, T-shirts, and deck shoes. There are even a couple of seashells on the table.

Contrast this with the Red Barn Steak and Seafood Restaurant located in a small rural Midwest town. The insides of the 200 seat red barn looks like a cross between a Big Boy and an International House of Pancakes. There are paper plates, paper napkins, and overturned coffee mugs on the table when you sit down. The plastic coated multi-page menu offers more than 100 items. There's a service bar in the back, but the bar business is less than 5%. The owner can't understand this, or why sandwiches and family-type entrees outsell steaks and seafood items nearly 6-to-1.

Hello! Every packaging symbol about the restaurant in Florida says, *We're serious about fresh fish.* What about the Red Barn? Because it has *Steak and Seafood* in its name and on the menu, and because it has a service bar, it indicates it really wants to be a dinner house . . . not a family type replacement house. But everything else—i.e., *Red Barn* in the name, decor, menu, staff uniforms, and tabletop design—says that it is a family coffee shop. While the owner may *think* it is a steak and seafood restaurant, the townsfolk *think* it's a coffee shop. You know what? It's a coffee shop. *Perception is reality* (Stevens, 1988).

Place

Place refers to the geographic location with respect to your target market[s], competition, employees, and distribution channels. It also includes relevant site characters such as convenient access to highways, airports, and exit ramps, proximity to other demand generators/attractions, restrictions on site development, and natural scenic features.

How important is location? That depends on a lot of factors. But most of all it depends on what kind of a need your customer is trying to satisfy—i.e. where on Maslow's hierarchy that need falls. The *lower* the need ("Gosh, I'm exhausted; we've been driving for 15 hours. What's at the next exit?"), the more important location is. The *higher* the need (Let's celebrate our wedding anniversary with a long weekend by ourselves.), the less important location is. In other words, the more **physi**ological the need, the more important is location; the more **psycho**logical the need, the less critical location becomes as a decision factor to your guests. Just remember that in today's fast paced culture, distance is measured in terms of time not in terms of miles. Think about place, then, relative to how long it takes people to get there . . . and . . . is it worth their time and effort to do so?

Price

The pricing "P" is what a guest pays to get your product. What you ultimately decide to charge (pricing strategy) is really a marketing decision that is too often driven by accounting factors. Price is:

- the single most tangible way for consumers to compare you to your competition,
- establishes the all-important perceived "price-value" relationship for guests, and
- must deliver the financial return on capital for your business.

To accomplish all this, you'll have to look at:

- What you need/want for your return on investment
- What your fixed, variable, and semi-variable costs/expenses are
- What is the actual/potential customer count (by segment)
- What are the actual/estimated revenues (average check or room rates)
- What are the competitive influences on consumer value perception
- What is the guest/potential guest ready, willing, and able to pay?

Pricing strategies that you'll work with are:

- Psychological Pricing
- Menu Engineering (which can be applied to rooms, too)
- Package or Value Added Pricing
- Providing the guest an opportunity to spend more, and
- Discounting/Couponing.

Whew! That's a lot of decision points for one little price. But remember that pricing is a marketing strategy in addition to a financial strategy. So you have the psychological aspect that takes the decision out of just a balance sheet and puts it into the consumers' minds. The bottom line in pricing is this question: With whatever price you ask your guests to pay, when they leave, will they feel that *you owe them* or that *they owe you*?

Promotion

Promotion addresses the question of how to best influence your guest to buy (within the parameters of your promotional budget). Generally, promotion is thought of as advertising, special promotions, and direct sales. But in its broadest definition, it includes everything you do to influence people to come, and then influencing their purchase choices once they are there. In other words, promotion is all activities that are designed to influence consumers to choose your restaurant or hotel over your competition. Promotion can be subtle, building an image over time, or it can be hard-hitting and call for immediate action.

The overall goal of any promotion is to make a promise to the prospective guest . . . a promise that establishes an expectation higher than the competition's: *Jimmy's Pub: Center City's answer to Cheers.* Or . . . *Your most romantic weekend awaits you at the Moonlight Inn.* In designing your promotional strategy, remember that you must deliver on the promise and hopefully exceed guest expectations. This job falls to operations, reinforcing the belief that there is no way marketing can be separated from operations in the hospitality industry.

Marketing departments and advertising agencies are very creative and, by design, are aggressive promoters. Sometimes, in their exuberance, they can make a promise and set an expectation level that can't be delivered. A case in point: A new restaurant, built in a rather well to do suburb, did an excellent job promoting itself as

Common External Promotion Tools Designed to Influence Consumers to Come In.

- Advertising
- Special Events
- Public Relations
- Publicity ("free" media exposure)
- Word-of Mouth (the best form of advertising there is)
- Direct Sales Calls
- Merchandising (Tee-shirts, hats, etc.)

- ❖ Packaging
- ❖ Point of Purchase Materials (table tents, reader boards, etc.)
- ❖ Sampling (give one away to result in sales to other guests)
- ❖ Suggestive Selling (using your employees as sales people)
- ❖ Priming the Pump (table side cooking, theatrical presentations)
- ❖ Menu design and wording

the area's grandest "supper club." The advertising painted an inviting picture of a beautiful setting, outstanding dining and dancing, and top-notch service. To complete the promise, the restaurant heavily advertised an introductory two-for-one grand opening. The promotion was a huge success. Opening night attracted the press, business leaders, and other influential people from the community. But it was a disaster! The kitchen was overwhelmed with orders resulting in slow delivery; servers were not adequately prepared to handle the number of guests who came. And to top the evening off, the band's microphone system wouldn't work and the air conditioner failed. The restaurant couldn't live up to the great promotional promise made. It closed within the first year.

While the ultimate goal of your promotion is to make a promise to the guests, more specifically, your promotion must be designed to accomplish several goals. The first is to build consumer awareness, preference, and frequency. This is often called the AIDA Principle which stands for:

1. Grabbing consumers' **A**ttention,
2. Keeping their **I**nterest,
3. Building their **D**esire to buy your product, and
4. Convincing them to take **A**ction.

The second goal of your promotion is to break through the clutter of other promotional "noise." Every day, you are bombarded with messages to "buy me." Your message must be able to break through all that clutter in order to grab attention. This means that you have to be creative, keep the message simple and memorable, and repeat, repeat, repeat your message using a variety of media. There is an old formula, which says:

$$PE = F (D \times E \times B)$$

Translated, this says that the effectiveness of your promotions is a function of the interaction of

1. Desirability (Does this consumer want what you are promoting—i.e. the most romantic weekend),
2. Exclusivity (Can the consumer get the same benefits somewhere else or only at your place—i.e. your local answer to *Cheers*.), and
3. Believability (Does your promotion make sense to the consumer —i.e. is it believable that the new suburban restaurant is the grandest supper club in the area?) (adapted from Twedt, 1969).

Servicing Guests to Develop Loyalty, Gain Repeat Sales, and Make Your Customers Also Your Advertisers (Word-of-Mouth)

Performance

The final "P" represents the third function of marketing . . . that of servicing demand. Too many marketers see their job as simply getting guests to the door and operations as the folks who deal with the product, service, maintenance, accounting, staffing, scheduling, etc. But it costs six to ten times as much to get a new customer to the door as it does to get a present customer to return. If you fail to integrate operations into your marketing strategy, you'll end up with a big hole in your bucket.

Consistent top service quality is the name of the game here. You can "sell the sizzle," but you also must be able to deliver a great meal every day. You can promote your hotel as a haven for business travelers, but you must provide data ports, on-time wake up calls, prompt room service, and plenty of hot water and strong water pressure in the shower. Once you're well positioned, nobody can get your guests to switch to another hotel or restaurant as easily and quickly as you can. No one can knock you out of your market share unless you give a bad performance.

Performance is the consistent delivery of the *Promise of the Promotion*. It's management getting the needed/desired results through others. It's called operations. And it's the other side of the marketing coin.

A Closing Story

To help bring the marketing perspective into focus, let me tell you a story about my hospitality mentor and his marketing teacher and mentor. My mentor was (and is) Don Smith, former director of the hospitality program at Michigan State University and marketing genius *extraordinaire*. Those of us lucky enough to be taken under his wing call him *Coach*. His mentor and marketing teacher was the unparalleled visionary, Winston Schuler of Marshall, Michigan. Win Schuler knew the restaurant business technically, managerially, and conceptually. He was without equal. In the opinion of many, he was the most intuitive restaurateur of the 20th century. He also had the gift of communication and was always willing to share his wisdom with others.

In 1960, Coach was getting ready to open his first restaurant in Dundee, Illinois. He called Mr. Schuler, who graciously offered to spend a few hours giving him an overview of the business of hospitality. They met and talked in the lobby of Schuler's first restaurant in Marshall. What this genius talked about was not food costs, not profits, and not sales growth. Instead, he talked about *football!* For Don Smith, who happened to be leaving the coaching field after ten years, this was exciting.

The following is in Don Smith's own words:

"The three things that I will never forget about that meeting is how he viewed football coaching and restauranteuring as one in the same business. First, winning (within the rules of the game) is everything. He viewed the restaurant business as competing for customers, with that competition being won (or lost) one customer at a time inside the restaurant (our playing field).

"The reason we were sitting in the lobby was that Schuler could accomplish the most fundamental and important task of hospitality at his restaurant—greeting every customer personally and orchestrating their evening of good food, service, and atmosphere in a memorable experience. I have never seen another host so skilled at making a guest welcome as 'Win.' His ability to sincerely concentrate on guests and, in less than two to three minutes, build a bridge of friendship is still unmatched.

"Nothing was more important than the guest when he or she entered those front doors. He didn't have to speak to that importance, write in a policy manual or drum it into his employees' heads with platitudes. He lived and modeled caring for people every moment he was at work. Time after time,

he would interrupt our conversation or whatever he was doing the instant a guest walked into Schuler's. He literally jumped up to greet the guest and, through actions, demonstrated how important that person[s] was to him. The guests never doubted their importance to Win Schuler. He had a marketing person's single greatest attribute—he could listen. It was only minutes and he knew something special about that visit and was calling guests by name (the restaurant's greatest asset) as he seated them to explain that this dining room was especially suited to their needs that day.

"Second, Schuler was a fundamentalist and a master of the details of hospitality. The wizard of hospitality would shift from the role of a host to the role of an organizational man by turning the guests over to a team so well trained in the details of hospitable service, he was certain to win the competition for the guest. No one was going to provide a product (broad sense) as Win Schuler. He had established a system of guest satisfying standard procedures that exceeded the guests' expectations.

"Third, he orchestrated the Schuler hospitality through the most productive team of caring people I have ever seen in the industry. He constantly found ways of reinforcing the behavior of hospitality. The only individuals who received more attention than a Win Schuler employee was a Win Schuler guest.

"He was a great coach. He led by example, stayed close to the customer and found beauty in a relish tray. His enthusiasm galvanized his people into a caring team. And most of all, they gave the guest what they could never get anywhere else—Win Schuler hospitality." (Smith, n.d.)

But how many Win Schulers or Don Smiths are there, you might ask? How can you reproduce such personification and hospitality in another restaurant or hotel, let alone a chain of 50 or 1,000? You can't. Hospitality is in people, not restaurants, hotels, attractions, destinations, or any other place. **There are no great hospitality businesses, only great hospitality people!**

Can you be that great hospitality person? Of course you can! Just as Coach learned from Win Schuler, always remember the **Platinum rule of Hospitality**:

The Answer is always "Yes"!

Now, what was the question?

Don Smith was able to reproduce the Win Schuler standard procedures of hospitality at his restaurant in Dundee, *Chateau Louise*, which became one of the busiest and most profitable restaurants in the country. How was it done? Simple. Hard work, concentration on the guest, and pride. And that's what the hospitality marketing perspective is all about.

Questions and Assignments

1. Define hospitality marketing.

2. How does hospitality marketing differ from marketing of manufactured products?

3. Consider the statement that marketing and operations cannot be separated in that they are two sides of the same coin. Support or refute the statement. Using your library resources or the web browser and search engine of your choice, find an article in support of your position. Summarize your findings, and be prepared for discussion with your team or classmates.

4. List and explain the six components of situational analysis. Which of the components is most important in your mind? Justify your response.

5. List and review briefly the eight Ps of hospitality marketing.

6. Consider the eight Ps of hospitality marketing. Using your library resources or the web browser and search engine of your choice, find some marketing materials that have been developed by a hospitality company.

Review the materials in light of the eight Ps. Which Ps does the material address? Summarize your opinion and bring the material and the opinion to class. Be prepared for discussion.

7. Define and discuss the difference between what a guest "orders" and what a guest "buys." Summarize the key issues and be prepared for class discussion.

8. Consider the discussion of the "Red Barn" and perception. Why is this such an important issue? Do you have any similar examples to share?

9. Using your library resources or the web browser and search engine of your choice, find an article that discusses promotion in hospitality. Summarize the content and be prepared to share your findings in class.

10. Perform an informational interview with a hospitality marketing manager or a hospitality sales manager. The procedures are outlined in Chapter One. Check with your instructor on how to avoid contacting someone already interviewed.

Bibliography and Suggested Readings

Harvey, M. G., Lusch, R. F. & Cavarkapa, B. (1996). A Marketing Mix for the 21st Century. *Journal of Marketing Theory and Practice*. 4(4), 1–15.

Hurst, M. (no date). Personal Conversations.

LeBoeuf, M. (1987). *How to Win Customers and Keep Them For Life*. New York, NY: G.P. Putnam's Sons.

Levitt, T. (1960). Marketing Myopia. *Harvard Business Review*, 38 (July–August), 45–56.

McCarthy, E. J. (1960). *Basic Marketing*. Homewood, IL: Richard D. Irvin.

Popcorn, F. & Marigold, L. (1996). *Clicking*. New York, NY: Harper Collins.

Porter, M. E. (1985). *Competitive Advantage: Creating and Sustaining Superior Performance*. New York, NY: Free Press.

Ries, A. & Trout, J. (1986). *Positioning: The Battle for Your Mind*. New York, NY: McGraw-Hill.

Smith, D. (no date). Unpublished manuscript drafts.

Smith, J. W. & Clurman, A. (1997). *Rocking the Ages*. New York, NY: Harper Business.

Stevens, P. J. (1988). *Winning!!: Getting customers, keeping customers, and making money*. Okemos, MI: Hospitality Publications.

Twedt, D. W. (1969). How to Plan New Products, Improve Old Ones, and Create Better Advertising. *Journal of Marketing*, 33, 53–57.

13

The Financial Perspective: Understanding the Financial Scoreboards

Raymond S. Schmidgall, *The School of Hospitality Business*, MICHIGAN STATE UNIVERSITY

ABSTRACT

The purpose of this chapter is to introduce the most important financial scoreboards: the balance sheet, the income statement, and the statement of cash flow. They will each be defined and described and their interrelationship will be established. Important financial terminology will be discussed, and the uniform systems of accounts for restaurants will be introduced.

OBJECTIVES

At the end of this chapter the student should be able to:

1. Provide a definition of accounting.

2. Describe the various users of financial information.

3. Discuss the balance sheet.

4. Present and describe an income statement.

5. Provide a brief description of cash flow.

6. Establish familiarity with the Uniform System of Accounts for Restaurants.[1]

---

[1]Deloitte Touche LLP, *Uniform System of Accounts for Restaurants*, Washington: National Restaurant Association, 1996.

Introduction

The financial scoreboards tell the score of how a foodservice business is performing. These scoreboards further reflect what is owned, what is owed, and what residual belongs to the owners of the business. The financial scoreboards are commonly called the financial statements. The major financial statements, namely the balance sheet and the income statement, are prepared monthly by the accounting personnel of a business. They are considered to be the end products of the accounting process. Yet, once produced they then are to be used by department heads, general managers, lenders, suppliers, and owners in making decisions. These scoreboards reflect history, generally very recent history, for decisions to be made in the near future.

Accounting

Accounting is analyzing, classifying, and recording of economic information and the summarization on a periodic basis, generally monthly, of the financial activity in financial statements. Historically, bookkeepers have performed the detailed tasks of analyzing, classifying, and recording economic activity. The accountant prepares the financial statements and interprets the results.

Business transactions are classified by types of activity such as sales on account, purchases on account, cash receipts, cash disbursements other than payroll, and payroll disbursements. Separate accounting is conducted for each type of activity as the transactions are recorded in individual journals. For example, checks written to employees are recorded in the payroll journal while sales on accounts are recorded in a sales journal.

Each transaction is recorded with at least two entries. In the case of payroll, an expense account, such as wages expense, is charged and the cash account is reduced. When sales are made on account, the amount receivable must be recorded as well as the sales.

After the transactions are recorded in journals the totals are recorded in the individual accounts at the end of the period. The accounts are maintained in a ledger, which is simply defined as a book of accounts. A firm will maintain a separate account for each employee where the gross wages and related tax withholdings are recorded. This account reflects the total payroll payments to the employee as well as the dates of pay and the payroll check numbers. The book of accounts related to payroll is called the employee payroll ledger. Other ledgers maintained by a business include accounts receivable ledger, accounts payable ledger, and the general ledger.

At the end of the accounting period, usually monthly, financial statements are prepared. The income statement provides a summary of the operating activities of the firm as it reflects revenue and expenses for the month. The balance sheet reveals the assets and claims to assets as of the last day of the accounting period. The third statement is the statement of cash flows, which reveals the cash receipts and cash disbursements by type of activity of the firm for the accounting period.

Users of the Financial Scoreboards

Managers of a business are major users of accounting information. On a daily basis they make decisions based on the accounting information they receive. Other users of information emanating from the accounting system are as follows:

1. **Owners.** Those who have invested in the business—whether ownership is represented by one person in a sole proprietorship, two or more people in a partnership or limited liability company, thousands of people in a corporation—want to know how their investment is doing.

2. **Boards of directors.** Corporate stockholders elect persons to represent them overseeing the management of the corporation. They need accounting information in order to evaluate the effectiveness of the managers hired to run the operation. Likewise, boards of directors establish policies and guidelines that are used by management as business decisions are made. Of course, governing boards of institutions operating food services have these same concerns.

3. **Creditors.** Those lending money or providing terms for the purchase of products and/or services desire to know the likelihood that payment obligations will be met.

4. **Employee unions.** Accounting information is used by union officials and the membership to assess the abilities of an organization to meet wage and benefit demands.

5. **Governmental agencies.** Since income is taxable by our federal and most foreign governments—along with most states and many local communities—accounting information becomes the base upon which tax assessments are made. The Internal Revenue Service (at the national level), various state revenue departments, and local taxing authorities have a continuing interest in accounting records. Likewise, the Securities and Exchange Commission (SEC) has the authority and obligation to review audited financial statements as it approves prospective information developed by companies wishing to issue securities to the public.

6. **Financial analysts.** People outside of the organization who desire information about a firm—for their own or clients' purposes—require accounting information. Primary examples are investment analysts working for insurance companies and investment banks.

The Balance Sheet

The balance sheet, also known as the statement of financial position, reports the assets, liabilities, and net worth of a firm at a point in time (generally the end of the accounting period, usually a month). Thus, this statement provides a static view, that is, a still picture of the firm's financial position. If a second balance sheet were prepared for a foodservice operation even one day after the end of the accounting period, it no doubt would reflect a slightly different amount of assets, liabilities, and net worth than did the balance sheet prepared one day earlier.

Different users of financial information are interested in the balance sheet for different reasons. Therefore, it has several important purposes; the following are among the most important:

1. The balance sheet reflects the *cash on hand* at the end of an accounting period. All assets are ultimately converted, either directly or indirectly, to cash. This conversion process may result in a partial loss (such as uncollected accounts receivable). Alternatively, several months (or even years) may elapse before an asset is fully used (converted as an expense). Cash on hand is cash available for many future uses such as paying bills and disbursing to owners in the form of dividends.

2. By comparing cash and assets that can be fairly quickly converted to cash to meet current obligations, one is able to determine a firm's *liquidity* (the ability to pay current bills when due). A firm will not need to be concerned about debt payments five years in the future if it is unable to pay its bills at the present time. In this sense, the "future is now."

3. The balance sheet explains *details about assets*. A fairly high percentage of the assets of many firms in the hospitality industry are fixed assets. Several years are required to fully use these assets in the business. Everything else being the same, the longer the period to fully use fixed assets the greater the risk.

4. The *composition of debt* and *owners' equity* is shown by the balance sheet. This reflects how the foodservice enterprise has been financed. The greater the amount of debt financing with a given amount of equity, the greater the financial risk. A foodservice firm that has used debt to finance a large percentage of its fixed assets may have a difficult time securing more debt financing.

5. The balance sheet shows how much of the firm's *past earnings* have been retained in the business. Generally, the greater the retention of internally generated funds, the less borrowing will be required during an expansion period.

Contents of the Balance Sheet

The balance sheet is divided into two major categories, assets and equities. Assets equal equities, thus the name *balance* sheet has been tagged to this statement. Equities are further divided between claims of creditors to assets (liabilities) and residual claims of owners (owners' equity). Owners' equity can be referred to by several different titles depending, in part, on the nature of business (profit or not for profit) and how the business is organized (incorporated or unincorporated). Several common titles for "owners' equity" include the following:

Profit-Oriented Organization/ *Common Titles*

Sole proprietorship/*Proprietorship, Net worth, Owners' equity*

Partnership/*Net worth, Owners' equity*

Limited liability company/*Members' equity*

Corporation/*Stockholders' equity, Owners' equity*

Not-for-Profit Organization/ *Common Titles*

Corporation/*Fund equity, Members' equity*

Assets

Assets are normally subdivided into the four general categories: current assets, fixed assets, investments, and other assets. Each firm develops its own list of accounts depending on its specific needs.

Current Assets

Most balance sheets show current assets as the first category of assets. Current assets are cash, assets to be readily converted to cash, and other assets that are expected to be used in the foodservice operation within one year. Thus, a note receivable due in 18 months would be classified in a noncurrent category of assets, even though most notes receivable may be due within one year from the balance sheet date and would be recorded as a current asset. An exception to this definition is cash that is restricted as to use. Cash set aside for retirement of bonds classified as a noncurrent liability would be classified as a noncurrent asset.

Current assets are normally listed in the order of their liquidity; i.e., cash is listed first followed by the next current asset that is most quickly converted to cash. The major accounts included in current assets are as follows:

Cash. The cash account normally includes cash on hand in house funds, change banks, undeposited cash receipts, and cash on deposit with banks. It is common practice for different bank accounts to be shown separately on the balance sheet. For example, in addition to a general account, many firms maintain a payroll account.

Accounts Receivable. The accounts receivable account includes receivables from customers, credit card companies, employees and officers, and from others such as concessionaires. Accounts receivable should be shown on the balance sheet at their estimated realizable value, i.e., the total amount due is reduced by an "allowance for doubtful accounts" —the estimated amount of accounts receivable that is not expected to be collected. Promissory notes due to the foodservice firm should be recorded in a separate account titled notes receivable. Notes that are due beyond 12 months from the balance sheet date should be classified as a noncurrent investment. Notes receivable, just as accounts receivable, should be reported on the balance sheet at their net realizable value. Therefore, an allowance for doubtful notes should be established for any notes or portion of notes that may become uncollectible.

Inventory. Inventory consists of the amount of food, beverages, and other goods on hand at the end of the accounting period that is available for sale. This includes food in the storeroom, freezers, pantries, kitchens, and in storage warehouses along with beverages in stock at the beverage outlets and at warehouses.

Inventories ideally should be reported at the lower of cost or market value. However, because of the rapid turnover of inventory, many foodservice firms value their inventories at the specific cost of the item. This is accomplished by writing the cost of the item on the box, can, or bottle in which it is packaged. Alternatively, it is common for firms to value the inventories at the latest cost of each item. Regardless of the method used, the same procedure should be consistently followed each accounting period.

Prepaid Expenses. Prepaid expenses include unexpired insurance premiums, prepaid interest, prepaid taxes and licenses, and prepaid rent. Proper accounting dictates that disbursements for these items be shown as assets until the period the firm receives benefit (at which time the expense is recognized). Generally, these prepaid items are amortized on a straight-line basis, e.g., a 12-month insurance premium for $3,600 would be expensed at $300 per month.

Fixed Assets

These are also referred to as property and equipment, and includes those items that are tangible, material in amount, and benefit the foodservice firm for more than one year into the future. A writing utensil, such as an ink pen, may be used by a clerical employee over a period of two years, but would not be recognized as a fixed asset since its cost would be insignificant. The property and equipment group includes items used in the business such as land, building, furniture and fixtures, equipment, and leasehold improvements.

Land. This account is used for recording the purchase of land used by the business. Land purchased for future use or as an investment should not be shown as a fixed asset on the balance sheet but should be shown as an investment. The cost of land includes the purchase price and all costs related to the purchase such as brokers' commissions, legal fees, and title fees. The costs of clearing or otherwise *permanently* improving the land after it is purchased should be recorded as part of the cost of land. The cash receipts from materials salvaged in clearing the land, if any, should be subtracted from the cost of the land.

When expenditures are made for land improvements that have a limited life, such as paving the parking lot, these costs should be recorded in a separate account entitled "land improvements." Land improvements should be depreciated over their useful life.

Buildings. Purchases of buildings should be recorded in these accounts (with a separate account for each building). When a recently purchased building is renovated, this cost should be added to the cost of the building.

When buildings are constructed, costs capitalized include materials, labor, and overhead related to the construction. Also included are architect fees, building permits, and taxes during the construction period, and construction financing costs.

When land and buildings are acquired together for a single amount, the purchase price must be divided between the land and the buildings. Preferably, the purchase contract will provide a breakdown; however, if not, then an appraisal may be required. The appraisal values then serve as the basis for the allocation of the purchase price.

Buildings wear out over time and also become obsolete. Therefore, these fixed assets must be depreciated. Several methods of depreciation for depreciating fixed assets will be presented later in this chapter. Depreciation is recorded by charging depreciation expense and also recording the same amount in an accumulated depreciation account. Accumulated depreciation accounts are maintained for each fixed asset account for which a fixed asset is depreciated. For balance sheet presentation, the amount recorded in the accumulated depreciation account is subtracted from the fixed asset amount to yield a net book value (see the sample balance sheet format in Figure 1).

Cost of Improvements in Progress. These costs should be included as a component of fixed assets. When the improvements have been completed, the costs should be reclassified to buildings or leasehold improvements as appropriate. After the transfer, depreciation or amortization would commence.

Equipment. The equipment accounts cover a wide range of items that vary with the foodservice operation. It is desirable to maintain separate records for each piece of equipment; however, for balance sheet purposes, these generally are combined. Equipment includes kitchen equipment, cleaning equipment, point-of-sale equipment, delivery trucks, etc. The cost of equipment includes the purchase price, tax and duties on purchase, freight charge, insurance charges during shipping, and installation charges.

As with the building, equipment is depreciated over its useful life. The balance sheet presentation of equipment shows the net book value, that is, the cost less the accumulated depreciation related to the equipment.

Furniture and Fixtures. Furniture and fixtures include such items as desks, booths, tables, chairs, carpets, drapes, and showcases. These items are recorded at cost, which includes the purchase price plus taxes, freight, insurance in transit, and installation costs. As with equipment and buildings, furniture and fixtures are depreciated over their useful lives. Some foodservice firms combine furniture and fixtures with equipment as furniture, fixtures, and equipment—the abbreviated account title is FF&E.

Uniforms, Linen, China, Glassware, Silver, and Utensils. All of these items are normally combined for balance sheet presentation. These items should be reported at cost less the depreciation allowance. If a reserve stock of these items is maintained, the foodservice firm generally will report this portion at cost.

Alternatively, some foodservice firms choose to capitalize and depreciate their original china, etc., and expense all future purchases of these items. Although this latter approach lacks theoretical support, it is viewed by many as a more practical approach to accounting for these items.

Leasehold Improvements. Leasehold improvements are expenditures of a capital nature to property leased by a foodservice firm. For example, a building may be leased for 10 years and several partitions might be added to the building. The cost of the partitions is recorded as leasehold improvements. Leasehold improvements should be amortized over either the life of the leasehold improvement or the life of the lease—whichever is shorter. Certain leases of buildings and equipment meeting the requirements of the Financial Accounting Standards Board are capitalized. This results in these items being recorded as fixed assets and a liability is recognized.

Deferred Expenses

Organization Costs. The costs to organize a foodservice business should be initially recorded as an asset and amortized against revenue over a 3–5 year period. Expenditures recognized as organization costs include legal fees, promotional costs, stock certificate costs, accounting fees, and state incorporating fees.

Pre-opening Costs. The costs to open a new foodservice operation, such as payroll prior to opening, training costs, and promotional costs should be recorded in this account. Pre-opening costs are generally amortized over a 1–3 year period.

Bond Discount and Issue Costs. The cost to issue bonds includes legal fees, accountants' fees, and other costs, such as those of certificates and state registration. These costs should be amortized over the life of the bond issue. When bonds are issued at less than their face amount, they are issued at a discount. The amount of the discount is recorded in this account and is amortized over the life of the bond issue.

Other Assets

Other assets are all the assets not included within the previous three asset categories (current, fixed, and deferred expenses). Examples of "other assets" are now briefly described.

Rental Deposit. Some restaurant leases require a cash deposit for one-month's rent which is to be applied to the last month's rent per the lease contract. This amount is not readily available and should be shown as part of "other assets."

Franchisee Fees. Franchise costs normally include an initial franchise fee and continuing royalties based on sales. The initial fee should be recorded as an asset. In addition to the fee paid to the franchisor, the franchisee should also record in this amount the legal fees and other costs incurred in obtaining the franchise. The costs recorded in this account should be amortized over the life of the franchise agreement.

Goodwill. Goodwill is the summation of all special advantages, not otherwise identified, relating to a foodser-

vice operation. It includes the excellent reputation, well-trained staff, highly motivated management, and favorable location. However, goodwill is not recognized on the books of a foodservice firm unless it has been purchased. Purchased goodwill results when the cost of an acquired business exceeds the amount assigned to individual assets. Goodwill should be reported in the balance sheet at cost less the amount amortized. It should be amortized over the shorter of its life or 40 years.

Cash Surrender Value of Life Insurance. The amount of cash a foodservice organization would receive when a life insurance policy is cashed in should be reflected on the balance sheet as another asset. The portion of the premium that covers the insurance is recorded as insurance expense when the premium is paid.

Cost of Bar (or Other) License. The cost to acquire a bar and other licenses should be recorded in this account. The cost should be amortized over a reasonable number of years.

Liabilities

Liabilities are normally classified as to whether they are current or long term. The distinction is important since current liabilities are considered in the calculation of working capital and in the measurement of liquidity of the foodservice firm. As with assets, the list of accounts is not exhaustive as each firm has somewhat different accounts depending on its circumstances.

Current Liabilities

The first category of liabilities shown on the balance sheet is current liabilities. An existing liability is classified as current if it must be satisfied with current assets within one year. Therefore, debt that is to be paid within a year from the balance sheet date with sinking fund assets (a noncurrent asset) would not be classified as current.

Accounts Payable—Trade. This account is used to record goods and services purchased on account by the foodservice firm. Technically, accounts payable should be recorded when "legal title" to the goods purchased passes to the buyer. From a practical viewpoint, this title passage is generally assumed to be when the goods or services are received. If cash discounts are available and it is expected that the discounts will be used, the purchase should be recorded net of the cash discount.

Accounts Payable—Others.
Accounts payable due to concessionaires for collections from customers or large open accounts, from purchases of equipment, etc. should be shown separately on the balance sheet.

Notes Payable.
Notes payable includes notes to be paid within one year issued to suppliers, to banks for loans, to officer, and to stockholders. Notes should be recorded at their present value, that is, the amount it would take to retire the note at the balance sheet date. The net present value is the amount of the note when the interest rate on the note approximates a reasonable rate. However, if the note has no stated interest rate or an unreasonable rate, then the note should be discounted using the prevailing interest rate. For example, a noninterest-bearing note for $5,000 is issued for one year for equipment. Assuming a market interest rate of 12%, the note is recorded as follows:

Equipment	$4,464.29
Discount on notes payable	535.71
Notes payable	$5,000.00

The equipment amount was determined by dividing the amount of the note by 1.12 (1.00 plus the interest rate). The discount on notes payable, a contra-liability account, is amortized to interest expense over the life of the note. The note payable and the discount on notes payable accounts are netted for balance sheet reporting.

It is desirable to show separately notes due to different sources of funds such as bankers, trade creditors, and owners. This may be accomplished via a footnote to the financial statement.

Salaries and Wages Payable.
Unpaid salaries and wages earned by employees of a foodservice operation are recorded by an adjusting entry at the end of the accounting period. There is no need to identify the portions relating to tax withholdings and deductions. The amounts related to bonuses and commissions should also be recognized in this account.

Payroll and Withholding Taxes.
Separate accounts should be established for each different payroll and withholding tax. These normally include FICA, federal and state unemployment taxes, and federal income tax withheld. In a number of areas, foodservice firms must also withhold state and city income taxes. In addition to withholding FICA from employees' pay, the foodservice firm itself must pay a comparable amount for most employees.

Sales Tax Payable.
Most foodservice firms must charge sales tax on food and beverage sales. This tax, established by the states, should be recorded in the sales tax payable account when the sale is recorded. Periodically, monthly in most states, this amount is remitted to the proper sales tax authority.

Deposits on Banquets.
This account is used for recording cash received from customers for future goods and services to be rendered by the foodservice firm. When this occurs, this account is debited and a revenue account is credited. If the deposit is refunded without the provision of goods and services, the liability and cash are both reduced.

Income Taxes Payable.
This account is for income taxes relating to the foodservice firm's taxable income. On a monthly basis, the income taxes should be estimated and accrued via an adjusting entry. The estimated amount is adjusted based on the actual taxes due per the tax returns.

Accrued Expenses.
Accrued expenses include expenses incurred for the period but not payable until after the balance sheet date. Proper accounting dictates that these be recognized as liabilities along with the expense portions during the month incurred. The accrued expenses include rent, franchise royalties, interest, and utilities. For balance sheet purposes these may be combined; however, it is desirable to show separately any significant amounts.

Dividends Payable.
Cash dividends —declared by the board of directors of a foodservice firm—that are unpaid at the balance sheet date should be shown separately as current liability. Declared dividends become a liability at the "date of declaration" and stockholders become unsecured creditors for the dividends. Stock dividends are satisfied by distributing shares of stock and are not considered liabilities at any time. Dividends are a reduction of a firm's retained earnings and are never considered an expense.

Employees' Deposits.
Some foodservice organizations control uniforms, badges, and other similar items placed in custody of employees by requiring a deposit. The deposit should be shown as a current liability until it is returned to the employee.

Gift Certificates Outstanding.
Foodservice operations may sell gift certificates entitling their owner to food and beverages. When the certificates are sold, the amount received should be credited to this account. As the gift certificates are redeemed, this account is debited and the appropriate sales account is credited. Some certificates may be rendered void by lapse of time, and experience may indicate that a certain percentage of the certificates are not used. These factors should be considered at the balance sheet date to reduce this account balance to reflect the value of gift certificates expected to be redeemed in the future.

Current Portion of Long-Term Debt.
The amount of long-term debt

due within one year of the balance sheet date should be reclassified from long term to current. An exception to this reclassification arises when noncurrent assets, such as a sinking fund, will be used to retire this debt.

Long-Term Debt

The second major category of liabilities is long-term debt (also referred to as noncurrent liabilities). Several long-term debt accounts are now briefly described.

Mortgage Payable. This account is used to record long-term debt when a creditor has a secured prior claim against fixed assets of the foodservice firm. The portion due within one year of the balance sheet date should be reclassified as current.

Bonds Payable. Bonds are issued by foodservice firms to raise the capital needed for expansion, renovation of facilities, and other purposes. Generally, bonds have maturity dates of five years or more, and some bonds of corporations have had maturity dates of over 50 years. When bonds are sold, certificates are issued, and the debt should be recorded in the bonds payable account. Bonds sold for more than their face value are sold at a premium while bonds sold for less than their face are sold at a discount. The premiums and/or discounts should be recorded in separate accounts but, for balance sheet purposes, the unamortized portions are combined with the bonds payable account. This is accomplished by adding the premium to the bonds payable or, if the bonds were sold at a discount, subtracting the discount on bonds payable from the bonds payable account.

Due to Affiliated or Associated Companies. Amounts due to affiliated or associated companies that are not part of stockholders' equity and are not due within one year are shown in this account.

Due to Officers, Stockholders, Partners. Loans and other amounts due to officers and stockholders that are not part of stockholders' equity and are not due within one year are shown in this account.

Deferred Income Taxes. When foodservice firms account for certain items differently for tax purposes than for reporting purposes differences in income result. For example, a firm may use the straight-line method for depreciating its fixed assets for reporting purposes, but an accelerated method of depreciation for depreciating its fixed assets for tax purposes. In this case, in the first half of the life of the fixed asset, depreciation for tax purposes is greater than it is for reporting purposes, whereas in the second half of the life of the fixed asset the reverse is true. This difference is called a timing difference. The tax effect, basically the tax rate times the difference between the two methods on a yearly basis, is reported in the balance sheet as deferred income taxes.

Other Noncurrent Liabilities. Other amounts owed by the foodservice firm that are not due within one year of the balance sheet and are not material should be shown under this caption. Separate captions should be used for significant liabilities. Significant other liabilities may include employee benefit plans or long term leases.

Owners' Equity (Proprietorship)

Depending upon the type of organization, the final section of the balance sheet is owners' equity or proprietorship. First, the various accounts for corporations will be discussed, then the accounts for unincorporated businesses will be presented.

Corporations

Corporations are separate legal entities created by law that have an existence separate from their owners. Corporations are authorized by the state in which they are incorporated to issue stock to raise capital. Generally, stock may be freely traded by its owners without permission of the corporation. For many large foodservice and lodging firms such as McDonald's, Marriott International, and Hilton a price for its stock is established by the market system. For accounting purposes, the foodservice firm is not involved in the selling and buying of stock between stockholders even though it is very interested in keeping its stock prices as high as possible. Different classes of stock, described below, may be issued by a corporation and should be accounted for separately.

Common Stock Account. When a corporation issues only one class of capital stock, it is normally called common stock. This account is used to record par or stated value from the sale of common stock. The par value is the value assigned to each share of stock and is shown on the stock certificate. For example, a share may have a par value of $1. In some states where stock is issued with no par value, the board of directors is permitted to assign a value to each share called the stated value.

Preferred Stock Account. Capital stock that corporations issue that has preference over common stock is called preferred stock. Generally, the preference is to dividends and assets, if the firm is liquidated. The par or stated value of preferred stock is reported in this account.

Paid-In Capital in Excess of Par Account. Amounts paid by stockholders in excess of the par value are recorded in this account. For example, assume 100 common shares with a par of $1 are sold for $50 per share. The $5,000 received (100 shares at $50 each) would be recorded as $100 to the common stock account (100 shares at $1 each) and $4,900 to the paid-in capital in excess of par account (100 shares at $50 – $1 each).

Retained Earnings Account. Earnings retained by the foodservice firm are reported as retained earnings. The major changes to retained earnings are from dividends and results of operations. Dividends paid by a corporation are paid out of this account, thus reducing retained earnings. Profitable operations increase this account, while unprofitable operations result in a decrease in retained earnings.

Some foodservice firms choose to report the change in retained earnings on the face of the balance sheet. This is accomplished as follows:

Retained earnings at the beginning of the period	$ XXX
Plus:	
Net income	XXX
or	
Less:	
Net loss	(XXX)
Dividends declared	(XXX)
Retained earnings at the end of the period	$ XXX

Treasury Stock. Capital stock, either common or preferred, that is repurchased by the issuing foodservice firm for possible future reissue is called treasury stock. Stock is repurchased for several reasons including (1) to obtain shares for issuance to executives, (2) to invest excess cash temporarily, (3) to support the market price of stock, and (4) to improve earnings per share by reducing the number of shares outstanding. Treasury stock is normally recorded at cost and is reported in the balance sheet as a deduction in the stockholders' equity section.

Unincorporated Businesses

Unincorporated foodservice operations are generally organized as sole proprietorships (one owner), partnerships (two or more owners), or limited liability companies (two or more members). If the firm is a sole proprietorship, the equity section of the balance sheet consists of a single line such as "Proprietor's account" or "(Owner) Capital." This account includes the initial and subsequent capital contribution by the owner, less owner withdrawals, plus the results of operations. If the firm is a partnership or a limited liability company (LLC), common practice is to show the net

worth of each partner (partnership) or member (LLC) as follows:

Net worth	
Partner (member) A	$XXX
Partner (member) B	XXX
Partner (member) C, etc.	XXX
Total net worth	$XXX

Not-for-profit businesses, such as educational organizations, do not issue stock. They generally account for any foodservice activity separately from other activities. A separate balance sheet may be maintained showing the foodservice firm's assets, liabilities, and fund equity. Fund equity in this case is equivalent to the stockholders' equity section of an incorporated profit-oriented foodservice business. Fund equity is increased by profitable operations and reduced by unprofitable operations. There are no distributions of "profits" by nonprofit foodservice operations as there are for profit-oriented foodservice businesses.

Format of the Balance Sheet

The details of the balance sheet used by foodservice industry firms varies based on the size of business, the complexity of the business, the related businesses of the foodservice firm owners, and on how the firm is organized (i.e., sole proprietorship, partnership, LLC, or corporation).

Related balance sheet items are normally combined to provide a more concise presentation. For example, all cash accounts may be combined and reported as "cash." All inventory accounts may be combined and reported as "inventory." The account of consolidation first depends on the similarity of items, i.e., only similar items should be combined, and second on the complexity of items, i.e., consolidation should serve to make the balance sheet more understandable. Thus, the users' needs should be a major consideration in the preparation of not only the balance sheet but of all the financial statements.

When important details of various balance sheet items are not desirable in the balance sheet, they may be included in supporting schedules. For example, long-term notes may be shown as one item on the balance sheet provided there is a supplementary schedule listing of long-term notes and their interest rates and maturity dates.

Another way to enhance the balance sheet presentation is to use notations on the balance sheet. For example, the inventory may be shown as follows:

Inventory for resale (FIFO)	$22,300

This disclosure tells the reader the basis of inventory valuation. This technique is useful for several other items, such as marketable securities, accounts receivable, fixed assets, long-term debt, and capital stock.

Generally, foodservice firms provide balance sheets for the end of two periods. This comparative form enables the reader to compare two sets of financial information and determine some of the trends.

Balance Sheet—Uniform System of Accounts

The Uniform System of Accounts for Restaurants (USAR) contains a recommended balance sheet format and describes the various balance sheet accounts. A considerable portion of the previous discussion regarding the balance sheet was based, in part, on the discussion in the USAR. Figure 1 is the USAR's recommended balance sheet.

Statement of Retained Earnings

Some foodservice firms provide a *separate* statement depicting changes in retained earnings rather than include this detail on the balance sheet as just discussed. This approach results in a more concise balance sheet presentation but does require still an-

Figure 1. USAR's Recommended Balance Sheet, page 1.

Balance Sheet

NAME OF RESTAURANT COMPANY AS OF (DECEMBER 31, 19XX)

ASSETS

Current Assets		
Cash on Hand	$ 15,000	
Cash in Banks	80,000	$ 95,000
Accounts Receivable:		
Trade	90,000	
Employees	9,000	
Other	2,000	
Total Receivables	101,000	
Deduct Allowance for Doubtful Accounts	(11,000)	90,000
Inventories:		
Food	75,000	
Beverages	55,000	
Gift and Sundry Shop	8,000	
Supplies	2,000	140,000
Prepaid Expenses		25,000
Total Current Assets		**350,000**
Due from officers, stockholders, partners, and employees		5,000
Due from affiliated or associated companies		1,000
Cash held by trustee—restricted		4,000
FIXED ASSETS:		
Land	50,000	
Buildings	1,250,000	
Cost of Improvements in Progress	15,000	
Leasehold and Leasehold Improvements	40,000	
Furniture, Fixtures, and Equipment	112,000	
Uniforms, Linens, China, Glass, Silver, Utensils	29,000	
Deduct Accumulated Depreciation and Amortization	(125,000)	
Net Book Value of Fixed Assets		1,371,000
DEFERRED EXPENSES:		
Organization and Preopening Expenses	4,000	
Bond Discount and Loan Initiation Fees	6,000	10,000
OTHER ASSETS:		
Amount Paid for Goodwill	7,000	
Cost of Bar License	10,000	
Rental Deposits	3,000	
Cash Surrender Value of Life Insurance	5,000	
Deposit on Franchise or Royalty Contract	15,000	40,000
TOTAL ASSETS		**$1,781,000**

Figure 1 *(continued).* USAR's Recommended Balance Sheet, page 2.

LIABILITIES AND SHAREHOLDERS' EQUITY

Current Liabilities

Accounts Payable:

Trade	$ 115,000	
Others	4,000	$ 119,000

Notes Payable—Banks		15,000
Taxes Collected		4,000

Accrued Expenses:

Salaries and Wages	9,000	
Payroll Taxes	2,000	
Real Estate and Personal Property Taxes	6,000	
Rent	8,000	
Interest	3,000	
Utilities	1,000	
Other	1,000	30,000

Employees' Deposits	1,000
Deposits on Banquets	1,000
Income Taxes—State and Federal	7,000
Current Portion of Long-Term Debt	15,000
Dividends Declared and Payable	10,000
Total Current Liabilities	**1,466,000**

Due to officers, stockholders, partners	1,000
Due to affiliated or associated companies	2,000
Long-term debt, net of current portion	1,294,000
Deferred income taxes	9,000
Other noncurrent liabilities	7,000
TOTAL LIABILITIES	**1,515,000**

SHAREHOLDERS' EQUITY (if a Corporation):

Capital Stock	5,000
Description of Each Type of Stock,	
Shares Authorized and Issued,	
Stated Value per Share	
Paid-in Capital	120,000
Retained Earnings	141,000
Total Shareholders' Equity	266,000

NET WORTH (if an Individual Proprietor or Partnership):

Proprietor's Account	266,000
Partner A	133,000
Partner B	133,000
Total Net Worth	266,000

TOTAL LIABILITIES AND CAPITAL	**$1,781,000**

Note: Numbers used are for illustrative purposes only.

other statement. When this approach is used, the recommended form is as shown in Figure 2.

Footnotes to the Financial Statements

An integral part of the financial statements are the footnotes to the financial statements. They help to explain the content of the financial statements. They are meant to clarify, not to replace, the content of the financial statements. Footnotes deal with methods of valuation, the existence of contingencies, details of long-term debt, significant accounting policies, and any other matters that require explanation so as to render the financial statements understandable.

To illustrate what is covered by foodservice firms in footnotes, a major food-service corporation's footnotes in a publication of a recent annual report included the following:

1. summary of significant account policies;
2. restaurant acquisitions, dispositions, and number of restaurants in operation;
3. segment and geographic information;
4. income taxes;
5. property and equipment;
6. intangible assets, net;
7. debt financing and dividend restrictions;
8. lease of properties owned by others;
9. franchise arrangements;
10. other commitments and security deposits;
11. stock options and incentive plan;
12. preferred stock;
13. net income per share; and
14. quarterly results (unaudited).

Income Statement

The income statement reports the results of operations for a period of time. Alternative titles for this statement include "statement of operations," "income and expense statement," "profit and loss statement," and "earnings statement." The income statement is a flow statement in contrast to the balance sheet—which pertains to the last day of the accounting period. As a flow statement, the income statement reflects the revenues and expenses for the entire accounting period.

Users of the Income Statement

The income statement is considered to be one of the most useful of all financial statements by most users. However, no one statement by itself yields adequate information for making complex decisions. All the financial statements, including the footnotes, must be carefully studied and analyzed prior to making meaningful decisions. For example, a foodservice firm could have experienced an excellent year according to the income statement, yet have insufficient cash to make interest and principal payments during the next week. The result may lead to bankruptcy.

First, how does the information in the income statement meet the external users' (suppliers, bankers, investors, etc.) needs? These users are primarily interested in cash flows. Although the income statement does not reveal cash flows, it does show the firm's profitability. Profitability does not necessarily yield positive cash flows, but continuing profitable operations over a few years generally suggest positive cash flows. Thus, to some degree, the income statement may be used as an indicator of future cash flows. Everything else being equal, the greater the profitability of a foodservice firm, the more financial institutions will lend, the larger the amount of credit that will be provided by suppliers, and the higher the market value of the stock will rise.

Taxing authorities are interested in operations of the foodservice enterprise. Even though there are some differences between taxable income and "book income," the tax returns of foodservice firms contain much of the information from the income statement. Large foodservice firms whose stock is traded publicly provide detailed financial information, including their income statements, to the Securities and Exchange Commission annually in a required report.

The primary users of information contained in the income statement and supplementary statements are the foodservice firm's management. Years ago, most foodservice proprietors had an intuitive feel for the financial health of the firm, but today management relies heavily on the reports on operations in making decisions. This increased interest by management is due, in part, to the increasing complexity of foodservice operations. Today there are numerous chains of restaurants in which the top management are geographically removed from the many properties.

The income statement indicates revenues and expenses, for the ac-

◆ Figure 2.

STATEMENT OF RETAINED EARNINGS		
Foodservice Firm	Date _____	
Retained earnings at (date—beginning of period)		$XXX
Additions: Net Income	$XXX	
Other	XXX	XXX
Deductions: Dividends declared	XXX	
Other	XXX	XXX
Retained earnings at (date—end of period)		$XXX

counting period, which are compared to the financial goals expressed as budget figures. The income statement and supplementary statements provide answers to numerous questions such as the following:

- ❖ What were sales for the period?
- ❖ What was the food and beverage cost percentage?
- ❖ Which of several restaurants had the largest bottom line?
- ❖ How much was spent on advertising?
- ❖ What was the tax expense for the period?
- ❖ Was payroll kept within the budget for the year?

Large foodservice firms operate their businesses using the concept of responsibility accounting. Under this concept, revenues and expenses are reported by separate areas of responsibility. For example, a restaurant chain with five units and a separate manager for each would provide separate income statements for each. These reports most likely would contain revenues and expenses for the current and previous period in addition to the budget figures for the period.

Nature of Income

The primary purpose of commercial foodservice firms is to increase the wealth of the owners. The favorable results of operations of a foodservice firm over a period of time result in net income. Is the net income necessarily equal to the increase in wealth of the owners? This depends on how wealth and net income are measured. Net income, as reflected in the income statement of the firm, occurs when revenues exceed expenses. Both revenues and expenses are based on recorded transactions. The wealth of the owners may be increased due to increases in the value of the firm's building and land. Yet this increase is not reflected on the income statement until the building and land are sold. Thus, in this example, wealth is

based upon market values. The market value of the net assets at the end of the period, less the market value of the net assets at the beginning of the period, after allowing for owner contributions and withdrawals, equals the increase in wealth. On the other hand, net income in the income statement is the result of the "transaction approach" to measuring revenues and expenses occurring during operations.

The concept of income to be discussed in this chapter is net income based on the transaction approach. Next, revenues and expenses which appear on the income statement will be defined and discussed.

Revenue

Inflows or other enhancements of assets of the firm or settlement of its liabilities (or a combination of both) during a period from delivering or producing goods, rendering services, or other activities that constitute the entity's ongoing major or central operations.

Thus, increases in cash (assets) from business loans or sale of capital stock do not qualify as revenues. Further, increases in cash or other assets from a promise to perform, such as a cash receipt for a future banquet recorded as "deposit on banquets," do not qualify as revenues. Revenues may be called various names by foodservice firms, such as sales, interest, dividends, and rent.

Revenue has been defined but the question of revenue recognition remains; that is, when is the revenue recorded? For example, $100 may be received for a banquet to be held two months in the future. Assets have increased but so have liabilities since the restaurant has the responsibility for future performance. In this case, no revenue is recognized when the cash is received. Revenue should be recognized when two conditions are satisfied:

- ❖ The earnings process is completed.
- ❖ An exchange has taken place.

For the foodservice firm, the earnings process is completed when the food and beverage have been produced to meet the customers' expectation. The exchange takes place as the food and beverage is provided to the guest, and either cash or a promise to pay in the future (receivable) is received. Thus, the revenue is generally recognized by foodservice firms at the point of sale.

Expenses

The outflows or other using up of assets or incurrences of liabilities (or a combination of both) during a period from delivering or producing goods, rendering services, or carrying out other activities that constitute the entity's ongoing major or central operations.

The purchase of a fixed asset involves the using up of cash (and asset) but such "using up of cash" is not from delivering or producing goods, etc., and thus it is not recognized as an expense. For a foodservice firm, paying labor for producing and serving food is clearly an expense. Using a machine to slice meat to be served to customers is another example of an expense; however, no cash is directly involved. As the machine is used, its value normally decreases. Thus, the using up of the machine when rendering goods and services results in an expense.

Expenses are often categorized as direct and indirect. Direct expenses are closely related to the goods or services rendered. For example, the cost of the food sold relates directly to food sales. Further, the cost of labor to prepare and serve the food relates directly to the food sold. However, what about depreciation or the repairs and maintenance of the freezer in which the food was stored? These are commonly called indirect costs. Recognizing direct expenses generally causes no problem; assessing indirect expenses is more difficult.

Indirect costs are divided into two categories; those recognized as expense based on systematic and rational allocation and those expensed immediately. An example of a systematic and rational allocation is depreciation expense. The cost of most fixed assets is spread against revenue systematically using an acceptable (rational) method of depreciation. Costs with which no future revenues can be associated are expensed immediately. An example of this is the cost of settling a lawsuit.

Content of the Income Statement

The income statement reflects revenues and expenses, yet how and in what detail these are shown may differ substantially. The determination of the amount of detail shown on the income statement and supporting schedules should be based on the user's needs.

Generally, the income statement provided to outsiders (suppliers, bankers, investors, etc.) is much less detailed than the income statement and supporting schedules provided to management. Figure 3 is McDonald's income statement issued to stockholders for 1997. Notice the following: (1) The income statements are provided for three years. (2) The amounts are in millions of dollars. (3) All revenues and expenses are combined in only 17 lines of information. (4) Per share information is provided for income and dividends.

The income statement generally provided to management contains much more detail including numerous supplementary schedules not generally required by outsiders. The remainder of this chapter will cover the income statement recommended for management in accordance with the USAR.

The USAR presently in use is the revised edition published in 1996 by the National Restaurant Association. The USAR is highly recommended for internal use for the following reasons:

Figure 3. Income Statement from McDonald's Corporation.*

Consolidated Statement of Income

(In millions, except per common share data)	Years ended December 31, 1997	1996	1995
Revenues			
Sales by Company-operated restaurants	$ 8,136.5	$ 7,570.7	$6,863.5
Revenues from franchised and affiliated restaurants	3,272.3	3,115.8	2,931.0
Total revenues	11,408.8	10,686.5	9,794.5
Operating costs and expenses			
Company-operated restaurants			
Food and packaging	2,772.6	2,546.6	2,319.4
Payroll and other employee benefits	2,025.1	1,909.8	1,730.9
Occupancy and other operating expenses	1,851.9	1,706.8	1,497.4
	6,649.6	6,163.2	5,547.7
Franchised restaurants–occupancy expenses	613.9	570.1	514.9
Selling, general and administrative expenses	1,450.5	1,366.4	1,236.3
Other operating (income) expense–net	(113.5)	(45.8)	(105.7)
Total operating costs and expenses	8,600.5	8,053.9	7,193.2
Operating income	2,808.3	2,632.6	2,601.3
Interest expense–net of capitalized interest of $22.7, $22.2 and $22.5	364.4	342.5	340.2
Nonoperating (income) expense–net	36.6	39.1	92.0
Income before provision for income taxes	2,407.3	2,251.0	2,169.1
Provision for income taxes	764.8	678.4	741.8
Net income	$ 1,642.5	$ 1,572.6	$1,427.3
Net income per common share	$ 2.35	$ 2.21	$ 1.97
Net income per common share–diluted	2.29	2.16	1.93
Dividends per common share	$ .32	$ .29	$ .26
Weighted average shares	689.3	698.2	701.5
Weighted average shares–diluted	705.1	716.6	717.7

The accompanying Financial Comments are an integral part of the consolidated financial statements.

1. It is a time-tested system developed by the best accounting minds in the industry.
2. The USAR has been revised several times to keep it up to date with changes in the industry.
3. In order to make a reasonable comparison of a restaurant's operating results with published industry averages, one needs to have his/her financial statements prepared on the same basis as the industry statistics that are based on the USAR. Industry statistics are issued annually by the National Restaurant Association in conjunction with Deloitte Touche.[2] Industry averages are simply that—averages. The restaurants included in the survey to yield annual statistics consist of restaurants from Washington to Florida, from small to large, both independent and chain affiliated, and from fine dining to fast food. There is probably no single restaurant just like the industry average; thus, each user of industry averages must use them very carefully.

Finally, a compelling reason for new restaurateurs to adopt the USAR is that it nearly provides a "turn-key" accounting system. New restaurateurs thus have a time-tested system to rely upon. The author has observed investors in restaurants who used accounting systems based on other industries with which the investors were more familiar. Unfortunately, the income statements lacked meaning when compared to USAR statistics. The foodservice industry differs substantially from other industries, and this is reflected in the USAR.

The USAR presented below should not be viewed as a system to be strictly followed but rather as a guideline. It must be adapted as required by each user. It is *not* a

straightjacket but a flexible accounting system.

Figure 4 is the USAR's Summary Statement of Income (NRA, 1996) with hypothetical figures inserted. In Figure 4, operations are summarized with details being shown in 13 supplemental schedules. Sales in the summary statement are divided between food and beverages. Gift and sundry shop sales, commissions from vending machines, telephone, etc., rentals of banquet rooms, and other miscellaneous sales are recorded as "other income." Other income is shown just below repairs and main-

tenance with the operating expenses. Food and beverage cost of sales are subtracted from food and beverage sales to determine gross profit from food sales and beverage sales. This approach of reporting food sales and the related cost of food sales separately from beverage sales is useful in analyzing the operation. If this separation were not required, a poor food operation could be covered up by a highly profitable beverage operation or the reverse could also occur.

The next major category is "operating expenses." All ten expense line items under operating expenses have

Figure 4.

Summary Statement of Income			
NAME OF RESTAURANT COMPANY			
For the year of 19XX			
	Exhibit	*Amounts*	*Percentages*
SALES:			
Food	D	$1,000,000	66.7%
Beverage	E	500,000	33.3
Total Sales		1,500,000	100.0
COST OF SALES:			
Food		350,000	23.3
Beverage		100,000	6.7
Total Cost of Sales		450,000	30.0
Gross Profit		1,050,000	70.0
OPERATING EXPENSES:			
Salaries and Wages	F	450,000	30.0
Employee Benefits	G	100,000	6.7
Direct Operating Expenses	H	80,000	5.3
Music and Entertainment	I	10,000	0.7
Marketing	J	75,000	5.0
Utility Services	K	50,000	3.3
General and Administrative Expenses	L	20,000	1.3
Repairs and Maintenance	M	30,000	2.0
Occupancy Costs	N	20,000	1.3
Depreciation	N	75,000	5.0
Other Income	O	(5,000)	(0.3)
Total Operating Expenses		905,000	60.3
Operating Income		145,000	9.7
Interest	P	50,000	3.3
Income Before Income Taxes		95,000	6.4
Income Taxes		30,000	2.0
NET INCOME		$ 65,000	4.4%

[2] The foodservice industry statistics are published annually in Restaurant Industry Operations Reports by the National Restaurant Association, 311 First Street, N.W., Washington, D.C. 20001.

a supplementary schedule under the USAR. Therefore, considerable detail is provided for this major division of expenses.

All salaries and wages should be combined into one figure and shown as "salaries and wages." In a supplementary schedule, these can be separated by department, by position, etc. Employee benefits include payroll taxes, fringe benefits, and the cost of employee meals.

Expenses such as uniforms, laundry, cleaning supplies, menus, kitchen fuel, etc., are reported as "direct operating expenses." These expenses are incidental to service in the dining areas, kitchen, and storage areas.

Music and entertainment, when significant, should be shown separately. Many restaurants will have little or no music and entertainment expense. When this is the case, this expense, if any, may be recorded as part of direct operating expense.

The "marketing expense" category includes newspaper, magazine, radio, and television advertising. Similar expenses are for outdoor signs, direct mailings, donations, and entertainment that promote the business.

"Utility services" include the cost of all utilities (except for kitchen fuel which is treated as a direct operating expense). When facilities are rented and the foodservice operator pays the utilities, these should be recorded as "utilities" rather than rent.

The "general and administrative expenses" category includes expenses generally classified as operating overhead. These expenses are considered to be necessary to operate the business versus being directly connected with serving customers. This category includes office stationary, postage, telephone, data processing costs, general insurance, professional fees, protective service, etc.

"Repairs and maintenance expenses" include painting and decorating, maintenance contracts for elevators and machines, and repairs to the various equipment and mechanical systems of the foodservice operation.

"Occupancy costs" include rent of facilities and land, property taxes, and insurance on the fixed assets. These expenses will vary considerably from foodservice firm to firm.

"Depreciation expense" is the result of depreciating buildings, furniture, fixtures, and equipment. In addition, this figure should include the amortization of leaseholds and leasehold improvements.

"Other income" was discussed above. The total operating expenses is the sum of the ten expenses (salaries and wages through repairs and maintenance) less other income. Gross profit less total operating expenses equals operating income.

"Interest expense" is the cost of borrowing funds. Whether or not interest has been paid, it should be recorded in this account.

Finally, "income taxes" are shown prior to the bottom line for profit-oriented foodservice firms organized as corporations. This includes income taxes relating to all levels of government—federal, state, and city. Generally, foodservice firms organized as sole proprietorships, partnerships, LCC, and even certain corporations will not show income taxes, as these are the responsibility of the owners, as individuals, not the foodservice firms.

Supplementary Schedules

On the face of the Summary Statement of Income of the USAR (Figure 4), supplementary schedules D through P are referenced. In the remainder of this chapter, Schedule D is presented and discussed as a representation of these supplementary schedules. The other schedules are not included in this text; however, the reader interested in the details of these schedules is encouraged to obtain the Uniform System of Accounts for Restaurants from the National Restaurant Association.

Food Sales. Schedule D (see Figure 5) for food sales is designed initially to show the number of meals served and amounts by meal period and secondly by dining area. Food sales should include sales of coffee, tea, milk, fruit juices, and soft drinks, if there is no service of liquor, wine, and beer. If the latter beverages are sold, soft drinks should be reported on the beverage sales schedule.

Still another approach to reporting food sales is by menu item or food groups on the menu. This approach, though less common, is useful in determining the best selling menu items. Further, it lends itself to analysis called "menu engineering," recommended by Kasavana and Smith (1990).[3]

Bakery counter, takeout, and outside catering sales are also included in this schedule as recommended by the USAR. However, the USAR states that if the food sales in these areas are significant, then the sales and related costs of food sold may be shown separately. In this case, the departmental profit would be included with "other income."

Other Expenses

Five expenses will be explained in some detail as the accounting for these expenses is complicated and in total these expenses are substantial in amount.

Cost of Goods Sold

The cost of goods sold includes cost of food and the cost of beverages sold. The cost of food sold should be the actual cost of food sold after consideration for inventory on hand at the end of the accounting period, employee meals, meals provided to entertainers, etc. For many retail firms, the cost of goods sold is determined as follows: beginning inventory + purchases − ending inventory = cost of goods sold. This formulation is not acceptable to many foodservice operations, as employee meals and/or complimentary meals would be part of the cost of food. The formulation of cost of food sold for foodservice firms is as follows:

---

[3]Kasavana, M. L. and Smith, D. *Menu Engineering*, Okemos, Michigan: Hospitality Publications, Inc., 1990.

Figure 5.

FOOD SALES

	Meals Served	Amounts	Percentages
By Meal Period		$	%
Breakfast			
Lunch			
Dinner	_____	_____	____
Total Dining Room			
Banquets	_____		
Total Meals Served	_____		
Bakery			
Take-out			
Outside Catering	_____	_____	
Total Food Sales		$_____	____%

	Meals Served	Amounts	Percentages
BY LOCATIONS:			
Dining Room		$	%
Coffee Shop			
Luncheon Terrace			
Grill			
Cafeteria			
Patio			
Drive-Thru			
Take-out			
Banquets	_____	_____	_____
Totals Meals Served	_____		
Bakery			
Take-out			
Outside Catering	_____	_____	
Total Food Sales		$_____	____%

Beginning inventory of food	$_____
Add:	
Food purchases including freight and delivery charges	_____
Food available for sale	_____
Less:	
Ending inventory of food	_____
Cost of food consumed	_____
Less:	
Employee meals and other transfers	_____
Cost of food sold	$_____

An example is used to illustrate the calculation of cost of food sold. A restaurant had $15,000 inventory of food at the beginning of the account-ing period, while it had $18,000 of food at the end of the period. During the period, $40,000 of food was purchased including delivery charges on food received. Complimentary meals to entertainers and employee meals totaled $500 for the period. The cost of food sold is determined as follows:

Beginning inventory	$15,000
Add:	
Purchases of food	40,000
Food available for sale	55,000
Less:	
Ending inventory	18,000
Cost of food consumed	37,000
Less:	
Complimentary meals, etc.	500
Cost of food sold	$36,500

The calculation of cost of beverages sold is similar to the calculation of the cost of food sold. The formulation is as follows:

Beginning inventory	$_____
Add:	
Purchases (including delivery charges)	_____
Transfers to beverage department	_____
Total available	_____
Less:	
Ending inventory	_____
Transfers from beverage department	_____
Cost of beverages sold	$_____

Service Charges

Some foodservice firms, especially clubs, automatically add a service charge of a specified percentage to the customers' checks in lieu of voluntary tipping. This amount received for service charges then is distributed all or in part to employees.

The USAR recommends that the service charges billed to customers be credited to a revenue account titled "service charges" which is part of the "other income" category on the Summary Statement of Income. This approach, rather than recording the service charges as sales, will allow for better comparisons to other foodservice firms which do not charge a service charge.

When the service charges are distributed to employees, the USAR recommends that they be charged to the account, "service charges" resulting in a net amount of service charges retained. Again, this approach according to the USAR, rather than recording the distribution as payroll, will allow for better comparisons to other foodservice firms.

Employee Meals

Many foodservice firms provide their employees with complimentary meals after a specified number of hours worked. Failure to properly account for the cost of employee meals results in an overstatement of cost of food sold and an understatement of the cost of labor to the foodservice firm. The cost of employee meals should be subtracted from the cost of food consumed in determining cost of food sold and then charged to a separate account titled "employee meals."

The calculation of the cost of employee meals differs among foodservice firms. A theoretical approach to determining the cost of employee meals involves determining the actual food cost, labor cost, and overhead to prepare each employee meal. Probably no foodservice operators are willing to make this calculation, as the time and cost involved exceeds the value of information received. In practice, the cost of food only is considered in determining the cost of employee meals; that is, no labor or overhead is considered. Three approaches are suggested below for determining the cost of employee meals.

1. **Actual cost**. This approach involves a determination of the cost of each item served and tracking the various food items provided to employees. For example, if the *cost* of a cheeseburger is $.50, then 12 hamburgers provided to employees would result in a $6.00 charge to the employee meals account. In addition, other food items provided to employees would be costed-out and charged to the employee meals account.

The next two approaches are both estimates of the food cost provided to employees.

2. **Use of actual food cost percentage**. This approach uses the firm's food cost percentage and sales value of employee meals. The food cost percentage is multiplied by the sales value of the total employee meals to determine the cost of employee meals. For example, assume the food cost percentage is 35% for a foodservice firm and that during a 7-day period the sales value of employee meals based on menu prices to-taled $500. Then $175, determined by multiplying $500 by 35%, would be charged to the employee meals account.

3. **Government allowable amount**. This approach uses the amount allowed by the federal or state government. The federal government allows a specified amount per hour to be used in meeting the minimum wage requirement. Some foodservice firms use this amount in estimating the cost of employee meals. For example, assume $.15 per hour is allowed. If the employees of a foodservice firm worked 800 hours in a week, the amount recorded as cost of employee meals would be $120, determined by multiplying the total hours worked of 800 by $.15 per hour.

Depreciation

Depreciation is the reduction in value of a fixed asset. As fixed assets are used by foodservice firms, their future usefulness declines. This decline in value is recognized by recording depreciation expense. Several methods of depreciation are available. Three will be discussed in this chapter. Annual depreciation using the *straight-line* method is determined as follows:

Depreciation expense = $(C - SV)/n$,

where C = cost of fixed asset, SV = salvage value, and n = estimated life in years.

Of the above factors, two are estimates while the third, cost, is obtained from the accounting records. The salvage value is an estimate of the market value of the fixed asset at the end of its useful life. The useful life is an estimate of the length of time the fixed asset will benefit the foodservice firm. Therefore, since the calculation of depreciation expense is based on estimates, it is also an estimate of the decline in value of the fixed asset to which it relates.

The straight-line method of depreciation results in the same depreciation expense for a given fixed asset for each accounting period. Some other methods result in greater amounts of depreciation in the earlier years of the life of the fixed asset than in later years. These methods are called accelerated methods of depreciation. The double-declining balance and sum-of-the-years-digits methods are two methods that result in accelerated depreciation.

First, the *double-declining balance method* (DDB) will be presented. As mentioned previously, this method results in greater amounts of depreciation in the early years of the fixed asset's life and lesser amounts in the latter years. The formula for DDB is as follows:

1. First, determine the straight-line (SL) rate

Straight-line rate = $1/n$

2. Second, multiply the straight-line rate by 2 to determine the DDB%.

DDB% = $2(1/n)$, DDB% = $2/n$

3. Third, multiply the undepreciated amount of the fixed asset by the DDB% to determine the annual depreciation expense.

Depreciation expense = DDB% × (undepreciated amount).

The DDB ignores salvage value. In addition, when using DDB do not depreciate the fixed asset below its salvage value.

The second accelerated method to be discussed is the *sum-of-the-years-digit method* (SYD). Like the DDB, the SYD results in greater amounts of depreciation in the early years of the life of the fixed asset and lesser amounts in the latter years. The SYD formula is as follows:

Depreciation expense = $(C - SV)(RL/\frac{1}{2}n(n + 1)$

where C = cost of the fixed asset, SV = salvage value, RL = remaining life in years at the beginning of the year, and n = estimated life in years.

An example is used to illustrate

the calculation of depreciation using these three methods. A restaurant purchased a new point-of-sale device at a cost of $4,000. The estimated useful life is 8 years, and the machine is estimated to have a salvage value of $800.

Annual depreciation for years 1–8 for the three methods is shown in Figure 6.

Notice that the DDB yields the greatest amount of annual depreciation for years 1–3, while the SYD yields the greatest amount for year 4, and the straight-line method results in the greatest amount of depreciation fore each of the last 4 years.

All three of these methods of depreciation are acceptable for depreciating fixed assets for accounting purposes. The method selected by a foodservice operator should best reflect the decline in value of the fixed asset being depreciated. Once a method is selected for depreciating a specific fixed asset, it should continue to be used over the life of that asset. It is acceptable to use different methods of depreciation for different fixed assets. For example, a building may be depreciated using the straight-line method, while the DDB is used for kitchen equipment and the SYD for furniture.

For foodservice firms subject to income taxes, "depreciation" is useful for shielding income from taxes. In general, a foodservice firm should "depreciate" its fixed assets as quickly as possible to save on taxes and to expedite its cash flow.

Congress, in the last two decades, has passed tax laws which have replaced the concept of depreciation with the concept of cost recovery. In general, these tax laws have created classes of equipment with lives such as 3, 5, 7 and 10 years. The effect of this system from the "life" viewpoint is that, in general, the lives are considerably shorter than previously allowed by the IRS.

In addition, the cost recovery is based on statutory percentages that are similar to accelerated rates under accelerated methods of depreciation. These rates approximate the DDB rates discussed above.

A firm is not required to utilize the accelerated write-offs for tax purposes, but it may elect to use the straight-line method either over the shortened recovery period or extended periods as desired.

The cost recovery method used will determine the tax rates used when the fixed assets are sold at a later date, that is, either ordinary or capital gains rates. The foodservice operator should consult with the IRS or a tax consultant to determine the appropriate "depreciation" approach to minimize taxes over the long run, as further discussion of these concepts is beyond the scope of this text.

Figure 6.

ANNUAL DEPRECIATION

Year	SL[a]	DDB[b]	SYD[c]
1	$(4,000 - 800)/8$ $= \$400$	$1/8 = 12\frac{1}{2}\%$ $12\frac{1}{2}(2) = 25\%$ $4,000(0.25) = \$1,000$	$(4,000 - 800)(8)/\frac{1}{2}(8(9))$ $= (3,200)(8/36)$ $= \$711.11$
2	$400	$(4,000 - 1,000)(0.25)$ $= \$750$	$3,200(7/36)$ $= \$622.22$
3	$400	$(3,000 - 750)(0.25)$ $= \$562.50$	$3,200(6/36)$ $= \$533.33$
4	$400	$(2,250 - 562.50)(0.25)$ $= \$421.88$	$3,200(5/36)$ $= \$444.44$
5	$400	$(1,687.50 - 421.88)(0.25)$ $= \$316.40$	$3,200(4/36)$ $= \$355.56$
6	$400	149.22^1	$3,200(3/36)$ $\$266.67$
7	$400	-0-	$3,200(2/36)$ $= \$177.78$
8	$400	-0-	$3,200(1/36)$ $= \$88.89$
Total depr.	$3,200,000	$3,200.00	$3,200.00

[a]SL = straight-line rate. [b]DDB = double-declining balance method. [c]SYD = sum-of-the-years-digit method.

[1]The depreciation for year 6 is only $149.22 since the sum of the depreciation amounts through year five was $3,050.78. The calculated amount for year 6 was $237.30, but only $149.22 is used since when added to the accumulated depreciation through year five of $3,050.78 the total accumulated depreciation equals $3,200.00.

Income Taxes

Income taxes must be paid by profitable profit-oriented foodservice corporations to the Federal Government, to several state governments, and to some municipalities. Income taxes are shown on the summary income statement just above net income.

Income taxes are a function of taxable income as defined by the appropriate tax code. Taxable income on the firm's tax return and "income before taxes" on the firm's summary profit and loss statement generally are not the same. The differences between these two figures are called timing and permanent differences. A permanent tax difference results when either a revenue or expense item recognized for "book" purposes is not recognized for "tax" purposes or vice versa. For example, the cost of a traffic citation in the delivery of food is an expense of a foodservice firm and is shown on their income statement. However, the internal revenue code does not allow for the payment of fines in determining taxable income.

Timing differences result from an expense or revenue item being included in one year for "book" purposes and in a different year for "tax" purposes. For example, an expense that may cause a timing difference is depreciation. Assume a foodservice firm uses the straight-line method for "book" purposes and an accelerated method for "tax" purposes. Further, assume the amount of depreciation is $5,000 and $8,000 for "book" and "tax" purposes, respectively. The difference in taxable income and income before income taxes caused by the different methods is $3,000. Everything else being the same, if the income before income taxes is $10,000 according to the books, then the taxable income is $7,000 ($10,000 – $3,000 = $7,000). Assuming a tax rate of 20% for "book" purposes, the income tax expense is $2,000, while only $1,400 is shown on the tax return. The journal entry to record the income taxes is as follows:

Income tax expense	$2,000
Income tax payable	$1,400
Deferred income taxes	600

In the above example, the foodservice firm temporarily saved $600 in cash by using an accelerated method of depreciation for income tax purposes rather than the straight-line method used for calculating depreciation for "book" purposes. These cash savings may be invested, and it will generate increased earnings for the firm.

Statement of Cash Flows

The two financial scoreboards covered thus far were the balance sheet and the income statement. The third major statement is the statement of cash flows (SCF). The SCF reflects the changes in cash over an accounting period. This statement will be most useful in answering questions such as:

Figure 7. Classification of Cash Flows.

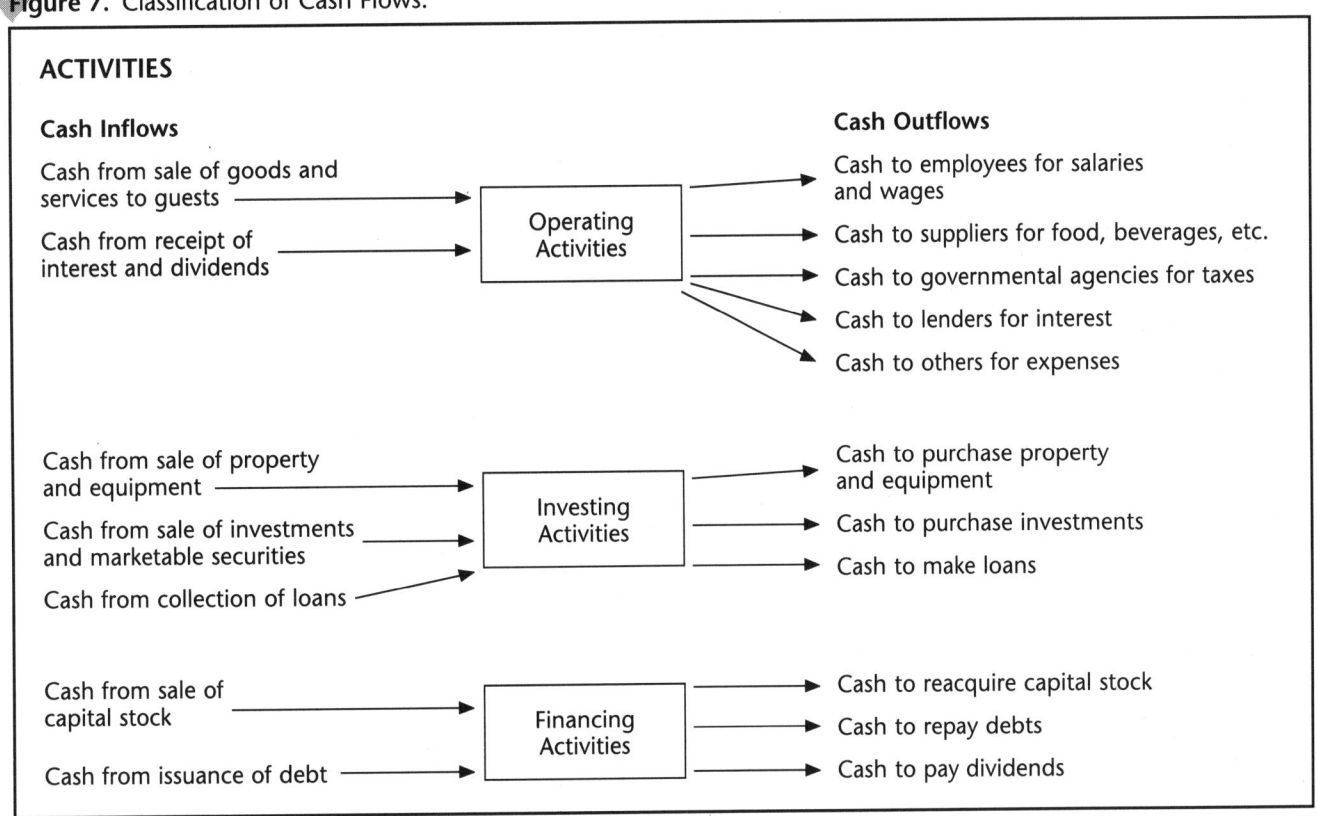

1. How much cash was provided by operations?
2. What dollar amount of fixed assets was purchased during the year?
3. How much long-term debt was borrowed during the year?
4. What amount of funds was raised through the sale of capital stock during the year?
5. What amount of dividends was paid during the year?

The SCF reports cash receipts and cash payments in three activity areas—operating, investing, and financing.

Cash flows from operating activities are the cash inflows and cash outflows that relate to operations. For example, cash sales is a cash inflow while the payment of employees for their services is an operating cash outflow. Figure 7 depicts cash inflows and cash outflows for each of the three activities.

Investing activities principally include the acquisition and deposition of fixed assets at most foodservice firms. Cash used to purchase a piece of equipment is a cash disbursement, while cash received from the sales of a delivery truck is an investing cash receipt.

Financing activities include the receipt of cash from owners and lenders to finance the firm. Further, financing activities include the disbursement of cash in retiring ownership interests, in paying dividends, and in retiring long-term debt. Cash received by a foodservice corporation from selling its own capital stock is a financing cash inflow, while the payment of dividends to the owners is a financing cash disbursement.

Figure 8 contains the SCF for a hypothetical company. Note the three sections and cash flows from each as follows:

Operating activities	$ 69,000
Investing activities	(28,000)
Financing activities	20,000
Net increase in cash	$ 61,000

The sum of the cash flows from the three types of activities equals $61,000. The cash at the beginning of the period is $60,000, plus the net increase in cash for the period equals the cash of $121,000 at the end of the period.

A brief examination of each section of the SCF is warranted. The activities section of the SCF starts with net income, which is also shown as the bottom line on the income statement. Several adjustments follow net income to essentially convert the net income to cash flows provided by operations. The income statement is prepared based on accrual accounting concepts which the SCF is a cash statement; therefore, all of these adjustments are required. The depreciation and provision for doubtful account numbers did not result in a use or source of cash, but since they are subtracted on the income statement to determine net income they must be added back to net income on the SCF. The loss on the sale of equipment reflects the difference between

Figure 8.

Statement of Cash Flows

NAME OF COMPANY
For the year of 19XX

CASH FLOWS FROM OPERATING ACTIVITIES:	
Net Income	$50,000
Adjustments to Reconcile Net Income to Net Cash Provided by Operating Activities:	
Depreciation	$18,000
Provision for doubtful accounts	1,000
Loss of sale of equipment	1,000
Change in current assets and liabilities:	
Decrease in accounts receivable	5,000
Increase in inventory	(10,000)
Increase in prepaid expenses	(1,000)
Increase in accounts payable and accrued expenses	5,000
Increase in interest and income taxes payable	2,000
Decrease in other current liabilities	(2,000)
Total Adjustments	19,000
Net Cash Provided by Operating Activities	**69,000**
CASH FLOWS FROM INVESTING ACTIVITIES:	
Proceeds from sale of equipment	2,000
Cash payments for leasehold improvements	(10,000)
Purchase of equipment	(20,000)
Net Cash Used in Investing Activities	**(28,000)**
CASH FLOWS FROM FINANCING ACTIVITIES:	
Long-term debt borrowed	15,000
Proceeds from sale of capital stock	10,000
Dividends paid	(5,000)
Net Cash Provided by Financing Activities	**20,000**
Net Increase in Cash	**61,000**
CASH, BEGINNING OF PERIOD	**60,000**
CASH, END OF PERIOD	**$121,000**

the net book value of the equipment sold and the proceeds from the sale. The proceeds of $2,000 are shown as an investing activity; however, the loss of $1,000 was subtracted in determining net income, so it must be added to net income on the SCF since the cash is shown in a different section of the SCF.

Changes in current assets and liabilities that are directly related to operations are also shown in the operating activities section. These accounts directly impact cash. For example, if a sale of $100 is made and the amount is charged to a customer's account then both accounts receivable and sales are increased. Sales is shown on the income statement and

directly impacts the net income. Yet, until the accounts receivable of $100 is collected, cash has not been increased. Therefore, changes in accounts receivable and similar accounts must be shown on the SCF.

The investing activities section in Figure 8 shows proceeds from sale of equipment which was briefly discussed above. In addition, cash was paid out to improve the leased space and cash was paid to purchase equipment.

The financing activities reflected in Figure 8 reveals the sale of capital stock, borrowing long-term debt, and paying dividends.

Clearly, the SCF reflects the different types of cash activity for a busi-

ness. These distinctions are most useful for understanding sources and users of cash.

Conclusion

All individuals that are involved in business considerations of one form or another need to understand financial scoreboards. To be involved in a business decisions or in business investments without such understanding and insight can be likened to attempting to drive a motor vehicle across town without knowing how a car operates, nor being familiar with the prevailing traffic laws and regulations. The likelihood of success is limited.

Questions and Assignments

1. Provide a definition for accounting.

2. List and briefly describe the various users of financial information.

3. What is the role of the balance sheet?

4. Define and differentiate assets and liabilities. Use examples to demonstrate.

5. Using your library resources or the web browser and search engine of your choice, obtain a balance sheet from a hospitality food service company. What is the ratio of liquid assets to current liabilities? Bring the balance statement and your ratio to class.

6. Discuss the extent to which an income statement provides a complete description of a foodservice operation's financial success? Be prepared to discuss and justify your conclusion.

7. Define revenue. Include examples of increases in cash that do not qualify as revenue. Summarize your finding and bring to class.

8. Define expense, differentiating direct and indirect expenses.

9. List and describe four benefits of using the USAR? Can you think of any disadvantages? Summarize your finding and bring to class.

10. Using your library resources or the web browser and search engine of your choice, obtain an income statement from a food service company. Establish the food and beverage sales percentages and the food and beverage cost percentages. If these percentages are reported, establish how they were developed. Bring the income statement and your findings to class.

11. List and describe the three approaches to determining the cost of employee meals.

12. Define depreciation. Illustrate with an example.

13. What is the role of the Statement of Cash Flow (SCF)?

14. How is the SCF different from the Income Statement?

Bibliography and Suggested Readings

Coltman, M. (1998). *Hospitality Management Accounting*, 6th ed. New York, NY: John Wiley & Sons.

Schmidgall, R. S. & Damitio, J. W. (1994). *Hospitality Industry Financial Accounting*. East Lansing, MI: The Educational Institute of the American Hotel & Motel Association.

Schmidgall, R. S. (1997). *Hospitality Industry Managerial Accounting*, 4th ed. East Lansing, MI: The Educational Institute of the American Hotel & Motel Association.

The Control Perspective in Food and Beverage Operations

Jack D. Ninemeier and Carl P. Borchgrevink, *The School of Hospitality Business,*
MICHIGAN STATE UNIVERSITY

ABSTRACT

This chapter will discuss various control routines and procedures that are essential tools in ensuring that a food and beverage operation is profitable and maintaining desired margins. Controlling will be explained as an element of the management process, and various standards will be discussed. Control procedures relevant to purchasing, receiving, storage, issuing, production and service will be introduced.

OBJECTIVES

At the end of this chapter the student should be able to:

1. Discuss the role that controlling plays in the management of food and beverage operations.

2. Define and describe a control system and the control process.

3. Discuss food cost and food cost percentages and menu prices.

4. Define and discuss various food and beverage standards.

5. Differentiate between various yield ratios, their interrelationship, and respective costs.

6. List and discuss key issues relative to each of the six components of the product control cycle.

7. Define and discuss the most commonly used service procedures.

Introduction

Foodservice managers must **control** all resources available to them. These resources include products (food and alcoholic beverages) labor, machines, time, methodology, energy, and money. Unfortunately, all these resources are in relatively scarce supply. The manager's task, then, is to make decisions about how to best use limited resources to maximize attainment of objectives.

Food and beverage products are typically the most expensive resources to be purchased. (In some operations labor costs are higher than product costs, but in all situations food and beverage costs are significant and demand careful control.) While the need to control product costs appears obvious, basic principles of control are frequently ignored. Perhaps, for example, managers do not recognize the importance of control believing that the operation will "manage" itself. Other managers desire to implement control practices but do not know how. Still others "invent" detailed control procedures which, while yielding accurate information, are not worth the time or effort required to generate the "numbers" helpful in the control process.

Hopefully, foodservice managers will develop practical systems to effectively manage product costs which lie between the extremes of no control and excessive control. The purpose of this chapter is to explain basic procedures which those managing commercial and non-commercial operations can use to control food and beverage costs.

Process of Control

In its most basic terms, a control system helps the foodservice manager to do four things:

1. To define what should be happening if there are no operating problems. In other words, a control system should tell the manager what food and beverage costs are ex-pected to be both as a percentage of revenue (in commercial operations) or as a percentage of total operating costs (in non-commercial operations) and in terms of dollars if there are no problems.

2. To understand what food and beverage costs actually are. This information, an output of the accounting system (see the previous chapter) indicates the actual costs as a percentage of revenue (in commercial operations) or as a percentage of operating costs (in non-commercial operations) and in total dollars for both types of operations.

3. To compare expected costs with actual costs. The manager can determine whether a problem exists (actual percentages and/or costs exceed expected percentages and/or costs) and begin to understand where priorities should be placed in "controlling" the operation. (Those costs representing the most "wasted" dollars should receive the highest priority for corrective action; each dollar of reduced costs brings one dollar to the bottom line!)

4. To evaluate the results of the corrective action(s) that was (were) taken. This is done to help assure that actual operating results more closely approximate the expected operating results.

Use of an effective control system is important. The manager who *plans* what costs ought to be (an operating budget is used for this purpose and is discussed below), and who accurately determines what actual costs are, will have available the basic information required to become an effective manager and to make "good" operating decisions.

Figure 1 reviews each of the five basic steps in the management process. The activity of control relates to each step. Let's see how:

❖ **Step One**—A manager must *plan*. As noted above the first step in control is to plan what expected product percentages and/or costs should be.

❖ **Step Two**—The second step in the management process involves *organizing*. Control requires that basic tools (some including standard recipes, standard meat yields, and standard purchase specifications, for example—are discussed below) must be in place to assure that quality goals are met while costs are not exceeded.

❖ **Step Three**—A manager must *coordinate* resources. Products must be controlled during purchasing, receiving, storing, issuing, producing, and serving as part of the coordinating task. These activities are discussed later in the chapter.

❖ **Step Four**—*Supervision* is critical. Managers must develop standard operating procedures to help assure that quality and cost goals are consistently attained. The super-

Figure 1. Basic Steps in the Management Process.

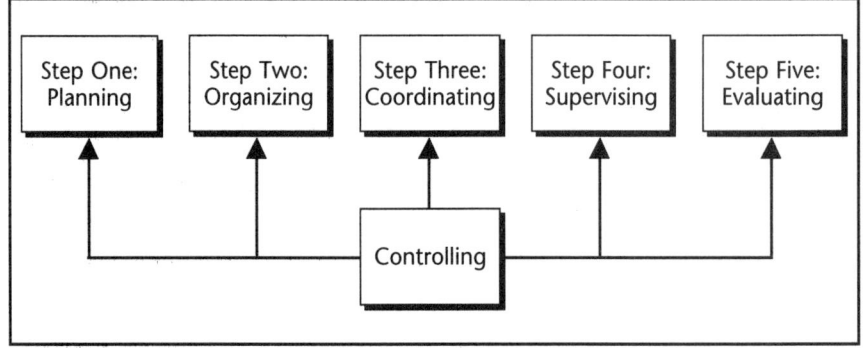

vision task helps the manager confirm that employees follow required procedures.

- **Step Five**—The manager *evaluates* actual costs by comparing them with expected costs. The manager also evaluates the results of corrective actions, which have been taken to assure that new operating results are more in line with expected results.

Designing Control Systems

A foodservice manager must use a separate control system to manage each asset (products, labor, etc.). This chapter focuses on only one resource: products (food and alcoholic beverages). A product control system involves much more than just physically doing something to reduce costs. Unfortunately, many managers believe that control only involves activities such as weighing incoming products, locking food storage areas, and assuring that portion control tools are consistently used. These and related activities are very important. However, other control tactics such as planning operating budgets and determining actual costs through accounting procedures have less to do with physical activities and more to do with creatively-developed "mental" plans, which provide the foundation for an effective control system.

Systems required to control product costs include:

- **A revenue and profit plan**—An effectively developed operating budget indicates what revenues should be, what costs should be incurred, and the level of profit, if any, which should result from managing financial resources to the level specified in the operating budget.
- **An information collection plan**—Accounting procedures to assess revenue and cost information in a practical, accurate and efficient manner are necessary. The procedures needed to compare expected and actual revenue, product cost levels, and to decide when a problem exists are integral parts of this plan.
- **An operational improvement plan**—The manager must know how to increase revenues and/or to reduce costs when the comparison of actual operating results with planned budget information indicates unacceptable variances.

Planning the Control System

The control system used to manage product costs must be practical and must yield reasonably accurate information. The foodservice manager will need to address certain limitations as the control system is designed. These include:

- Some resources (time and money) must be allocated to system design. While "better" systems do not necessarily result as more time or money is expended on the system design, it is also true that some priority must be assigned to the control task.
- The manager will need to assure that planned control procedures are, in fact, consistently used. For example, if budgeted food costs assume that meat items will be purchased according to strict specifications and prepared according to standardized recipes, these practices must be consistently implemented.
- Information must be provided on a timely basis. The manager who discovers a problem long after it has begun occurring has lost opportunities to decrease costs and increase profits.
- Information must be reasonably accurate. There is always a cost-benefit to be considered as control systems are planned. As the amount of desired accuracy increases, typically the amount of time required to generate the information also increases. (For example, the manager may wish to calculate actual food costs every day. However, to do this calculation accurately the changing values of inventory must be assessed. The time required to take a daily physical count of items in inventory may be better spent in other areas. If this is the case, food costs may need to be estimated based upon the values of issues to production rather than on net changes in inventory levels.)[1]

- Information must be cost effective—As suggested above, the system must be "worth more than it costs." (For example, to design a system costing $25 a day to save $10 a day is clearly unwise.) This unbalance can easily occur when significant amounts of high-paid management time are committed to developing and implementing control systems which save pennies.
- Data must be consistent—Information must be collected, analyzed, and utilized in the same way each fiscal period to be helpful. For example, if food costs include changes in work station inventory areas during one period and exclude this information in the next fiscal period, the "worth" of the food cost information becomes questionable: concerns about "comparing apples with oranges" become understandable.
- Control information must be practical—The manager's time is limited. The definition of *practical* often relates to the amount of time necessary to generate information. This time must be minimized without sacrificing the accuracy of the information that is generated.
- Information must be meaningful —Information from the property's unique control system is much

---

[1] In the future the calculation of inventory costs will be less of a problem: systems using optical scanning equipment and appropriate packing labels will automate this task and facilitate the taking of inventory.

better than "average" information generated from numerous properties that may (or may not) have something in common. For example, a manager may know the average food cost of large and small volume properties in all parts of the country with varying menus and guest markets; professional associations and trade magazines, for example, publish this data. However, knowledge of average food cost information is of little help to a manager in a specific property with a specific menu catering to the specific needs of a specific clientele.

What Should My Food (or Beverage) Cost Be?

Foodservice managers have several alternatives available to answer this question:

❖ They can assume that product costs should be those specified in the budget; when the operating budget is developed correctly this is probably the best source of what costs ought to be. (Details about developing an operating budget are presented later in this chapter.)

❖ Historical costs represent a much less useful source of control information. For example, a property manager with a 35% food cost last year (food cost ÷ food revenues = 35%) may use this as a goal for the current fiscal period. What if, however, product control procedures were lax last year and excessive product costs resulted? Utilizing the same goal would perpetuate these problems.

❖ Industry averages are a third source of control information. However, as suggested above, the manager desiring food costs to be equal to or less than an external average is doing a disservice to the operation. Food costs vary by geographic area, by menu design, by volume of business, etc., and

the development of benchmarks based upon an external average is easy but inaccurate!

◢ Product Control Tools

Foodservice managers must consistently use several standard food cost tools. These include standard recipes, standard yields for meats, and standard purchase specifications, among others. Each of these standard control tools is discussed in this section.

Standard Recipes

A standard recipe is an absolute must for any foodservice manager desiring to control product costs. It helps assure that the same ingredients in the same quantities are used for the production of a menu item each time it is produced. A standard recipe also helps assure that the same preparation procedures are used, that the product looks and tastes the same, and, as important, that it costs the same. Consistency is important from the perspectives of both the property and the guests. Each time the guest orders a product it should look and taste the same, and the portion size should be

Photo © 1998 PhotoDisc, Inc.

Consistency is important for both the property and the guests.

the same. As this is done the guest receives a constant value (price relative to quality) without any "surprises" about ingredients, portion size, flavor, and other characteristics that, from the guest's perspective, make an item "good" or "bad."

It should be the goal of every foodservice operation to standardize all recipes for all products so that the advantages of consistency can be realized by both the operation and the guests.[2] Figure 2 illustrates a sample format for a standard recipe. Note that it indicates the number of portions of a specific portion size which will be produced when the standard recipe is followed. Standard recipes should be pre-costed; the cost of all ingredients used in the recipe should be assessed. It then becomes possible to determine standard portion costs, which can be combined to determine the total expected food cost to produce a menu item. All objective menu-pricing plans use total food costs as a base to establish the item's selling price.[3]

Standard Yields for Meats

It does little good to cost ingredients such as fresh meats required for standard recipes when standard yields have not been considered. (The term "yield" refers to the difference between the purchased weight of a product (AP, such as when it is received), the edible portion weight (EP, after

---

[2]Details to develop standardized recipes are beyond the scope of this chapter. See, for example, Ninemeier, J. D. (1990). *Management of Food and Beverage Operations.* East Lansing, MI: Educational Institute of the American Hotel and Motel Association. (Chapter 7).

[3]Readers are referred to the discussion about operating budgets below: Data from the operating budget can be used to establish base selling prices. See also Ninemeier, J. D. (1998). *Planning and Control for Food and Beverage Operations,* 4th ed., Orlando, FL: Educational Institute of the American Hotel and Motel Association. (Chapter 5 reviews several objective menu pricing methods).

Figure 2. Example Standard Recipe Template.

STANDARD RECIPE FORM			
Date:		Page ____ of ____ pages	
Recipe Source:	Total Yield:	Servings:	
Category:	Portion Size:	Portion Utensil:	
Estimated Total Prep Time:			
Holding Procedure:		Cooking Temp:	
Storage Procedure:		Holding Temp:	
	Storage Temp:	Max. Storage Time:	
Mise en Place:			
Ingredients	Quantity		Procedure
Special Instructions:			

trimming and production loss) and the as-served weight (AS, which represents the final quantity of products placed on the plate.)

Yields are determined as a result of a series of tests which consider the original purchase specification for the product (purchase specifications are discussed below), the methods of trim during preparation, and the amount of further processing as products are plated.

Examples showing how knowledge of yields affects purchase and pricing decisions are presented in Box 1.

Purchase Specifications

A third tool helpful in managing product cost is the food purchase specification. This document provides information to suppliers, which details quality requirements which must be met for products being purchased by the foodservice operation. All suppliers should quote prices for the same quality of products. When the purchaser determines that quality requirements are met by all suppliers there is better assurance that the quality of products *ordered* and *paid for* is the quality of product which is *received*.

Figure 3 shows a sample format for a food purchase specification.

Suppliers can provide information about the desired quality of products to be incorporated into purchase specifications. For example, the foodservice manager can remove a meat product (such as New York Strip steak) from refrigerated storage if the item is currently on the menu. By asking the supplier to provide basic information about the product, it is possible to develop generic information useful in developing the purchase specification for the product.

There are a wide variety of sources which provide information about quality for products to be purchased. These include:

❖ Product suppliers. One of the roles of a supplier is to be knowledgeable about the specter of products carried and be able to suggest which products best meet the operator's needs.

❖ Industry-developed specification information. (For example, the *Meat Buyers Guide* produced by the National Association of Meat Producers can help with the development of specifications for meat purchases.)

❖ Institutional Meat Purchase Specifications (IMPS). These documents developed by the United States Department of Agriculture define quality grading standards and related information.

❖ Large national distributors of frozen and canned goods may have general quality information available for these products.

❖ Produce growers and distribution cooperatives may have information covering their products. Also, question local produce suppliers about available information. (Note: service and information provided by a supplier is valuable and should be considered in addition to product costs when supplier eligibility decisions are made.)

Assume a 10-lb top butt costs $6.50 per lb. Yield tests have concluded there is a 15% trim loss; it is cut into *10-oz* (EP) steaks for restaurant use. It takes 15 minutes to butcher steaks from the 10-lb top butt, and the cook is paid $8.50 per hour with an additional 15% fringe benefit. The item will also be used for an up-coming banquet for 400 persons; an *8-oz* (EP) steak will be needed; labor costs per butt are the same when it is used for banquets.

The manager wants to know the food cost for one 10-oz steak.

Step 1—Calculate cost per servable lb

$$\frac{\text{AP price}}{\text{Yield \%}} = \frac{\$6.50}{100\% - 15\%} = \frac{\$6.50}{85\%} = \$7.65$$

Step 2—Calculate cost per steak

$$\frac{\text{Cost per servable lb}}{\substack{\text{Number of servings} \\ \text{per lb}}} = \frac{\$7.65}{16 \text{ oz} \div 10 \text{ oz}} = \frac{\$7.65}{1.6} = \$4.78$$

The manager wants to know the direct labor cost for one 10-oz steak.

Step 1—Determine the number of steaks per top butt

$$\frac{\substack{\text{Number of} \\ \text{usable ozs/butt}}}{\substack{\text{Number of ozs} \\ \text{per steak}}} = \frac{10 \text{ lbs} \times 16 \text{ oz} \times 85\% \text{ yield}}{10 \text{ ozs}} =$$

$$\frac{135 \text{ ozs}}{10 \text{ ozs}} = 13 \text{ steaks (5 ozs of remaining top butt are left for another purpose)}$$

Step 2—Determine labor cost to butcher one top butt

$$\frac{\substack{\text{Hourly rate} + \text{(hourly} \\ \text{rate} \times \text{benefit \%)}}}{\text{Butchering time}} = \frac{\substack{\$8.50 + \\ (\$8.50 \times 15\%)}}{60 \text{ min} \div 15 \text{ min}} = \frac{\$9.78}{4} = \$2.45$$

Step 3—Calculate labor cost per steak

$$\frac{\text{Labor cost}}{\text{Number of steaks}} = \frac{\$2.45}{13} = \$.19$$

The manager wants to know the total prime (food and labor) cost for one steak.

Food cost	$4.78
Labor cost	.19
Total prime cost	$4.97

The manager wants to know how many 10-lb top butts are needed to feed 270 restaurant guests a 10-oz (EP) serving.

Step 1—Determine total ozs needed

$$\frac{\substack{\text{Number of guests} \times \\ \text{portion size (EP)}}}{\text{Yield \%}} = \frac{270 \times 10 \text{ oz}}{85\%} = 3176 \text{ oz}$$

Step 2—Determine total lbs needed

$$\frac{\text{Total ozs needed}}{16 \text{ ozs (lb)}} = \frac{3176 \text{ oz}}{16 \text{ oz}} = 199 \text{ lbs}$$

The manager wants to know the total purchase cost for top butt if 325 guests are to be served the steak item on the banquet menu (8 oz portion).

Step 1—Determine the total ozs needed

$$\frac{325 \text{ guests} \times 8 \text{ oz (EP)}}{\text{Yield \%}} = \frac{2600 \text{ oz}}{85\%} = 3059 \text{ oz}$$

Step 2—Determine the total lbs needed

$$\frac{3059 \text{ oz}}{16 \text{ oz}} = 191.19 \text{ lbs}$$

Step 3—Determine total top butt cost

$$191.19 \text{ lbs} \times \$6.50/\text{lb} = \$1242.75 \text{ (rounded)}$$

The manager wants to know the entrée cost for each banquet guest.

$$\underset{\text{(Total cost)}}{\$1242.75} \div \underset{\text{(Number of guests)}}{325} = \$3.82$$

The manager wants to know how many 10-lb top butts must be purchased for the banquet if there are three butts of correct quality already available in the refrigerator.

Step 1—Determine number of top butts needed

$$\frac{\text{Total lbs needed}}{\text{lbs per butt}} = \frac{191.19}{10} = 19.0 \text{ (rounded)}$$

Step 2—Determine number of top butts to purchase

$$\underset{\substack{\text{(Total top butts} \\ \text{needed)}}}{19} - \underset{\substack{\text{(Total top butts} \\ \text{available)}}}{3} = \underset{\substack{\text{(Number of} \\ \text{top butts to} \\ \text{purchase)}}}{16}$$

Figure 3. Sample Format for Food Purchase Specification.

Product Name: _____

Product Use: _____

Product Description
(Provide Details)

_____
_____
_____
_____
_____
_____
_____

Method of Test for Specification Compliance: _____
_____
_____
_____

Other Information: _____
_____
_____
_____

The Foodservice Operating Budget and the Control Process[4]

An operating budget should be at the heart of the management and control system for any foodservice operation. It establishes performance standards necessary for implementation of the control system. It provides the base of comparison against which financial—including "bottom line"—goals can be measured.

[4]Adapted from: Ninemeier, J. D. & Schmidgall, R. (1984). *Basic Accounting Standards*, Westport, CT: AVI Publishing Company, Inc. (See Chapter 8).

Sometimes, however, budgets are used because they are required by operating procedures and routines or because "the boss says so." Proforma operating budgets and other financial management tools might be developed only because a lending institution or the organization's investors require them rather than because management recognizes their critical need.

In contrast, consider a participative budget that (a) is developed because its importance is realized, (b) is constructed with collective input and "give-and-take" decision-making by all management levels, and (c) is used as an integral aspect of the ongoing management and control process. Managers responsible for specific aspects of the budget participate in its development. They have an opportunity to explain, defend, and justify initial budget proposals and to implement alternative plans as the budget development process evolves.

All foodservice operations need an operating budget, and careful thought must be given to its development and use. Actual (historical) accounting data is needed to construct this important profit plan. Used as a base of comparison with financial statements, the operating budget provides timely help to the manager desiring to know where, if at all, corrective action must be taken. Viewed with this priority, the budget is a foundation to help the property meet its economic goals.

Overview of Budget Process

An operating budget is used by a commercial operation to estimate how much revenue will be generated and how it should be spent to meet profit requirements. In non-commercial operations, it presents a plan for spending revenue in a manner that does not result in a loss (or in a greater deficiency than that which has been estimated).

The foodservice operation's primary need is for a short-term (one-year) operating budget which covers items affecting the income statement (also called profit and loss statement in a commercial operation and departmental operating statement in a not-for-profit operation). It is a constant reminder about the level of revenues and the amount of costs that are planned. If the estimated revenue is not generated and/or the cost limits are exceeded, budgeted profits decrease (or estimated deficits increase).

Once developed, managers know that when actual costs exceed budget limitations, there may be problems. The budget plan tells managers how much money remains to be spent in each cost category. Budgets are also used to develop new budgets. (Information from the current budget, along with actual accounting information, becomes the basis for developing the budget for the next fiscal year.)

Close Look at the Budget Control Process

The user of an accurately developed operating budget has access to a very effective control tool. It lays out the revenue and cost plan. In control terms, then, the operating budget defines standard (expected) revenue and costs. (Recall that this is the first step in the control process discussed earlier in this chapter.) The foodservice manager can compare the financial plan expressed in the budget with actual operating data detailed in the income statement. (This is the second step in the control process.) If actual revenues reported in the income statement are less than that estimated in the operating budget and/or if actual costs are greater than those anticipated in the operating budget, corrective action may be necessary. (This is the third step in the control process and its purpose is to bring revenue and costs to levels outlined in the budget.) The impact of the corrective action procedures which are taken will need to be evaluated by reviewing whether actual results expressed in later income statements more closely approximate those estimated in the operating budget plan. (This is the fourth and last step in the control process.)

Budget Development Procedures

The economic goals of a commercial property relate to generating a profit which meets the investment requirements of the owners. Financial goals of non-profit dietary services focus on minimizing costs. The ability of a property in either segment of the foodservice industry to attain economic goals rests on its ability to accurately estimate revenues, which are generated by sales to guests. (A non-profit operation may accrue additional revenues from deficits budgeted by

the facility). This first step in the budget development process sets the pace for planning allowable cost levels. If revenue levels can be accurately estimated and if profit requirements, if any, are planned, the levels of costs must be adjusted to match anticipated revenue levels.

When developing a budget, expected revenues are first determined; then the costs incurred to generate these revenues are calculated. One of the costs assessed is the profit requirement itself. (The concept of treating profit as a cost is explained below.)

In small foodservice operations, the owner/manager develops the budget. In larger operations, other staff members provide important assistance. Supervisors, who are expected to stay within budget limitations, might budget cost levels for their areas of responsibility in consultation with senior management personnel. In larger operations, a committee of managers may review departmental revenue and cost plans before a final property-wide budget is approved.

The budget is frequently developed by projecting revenue, profit, and cost information by month; this data is then combined for the year. As the budget year evolves, information for remaining months may need revision to reflect changes in revenues or cost levels. (A process called *reforecasting* which is beyond the scope of this discussion is used for this purpose.)[5]

Calculation of Projected Revenues

Food and beverage revenue forecasts should be prepared separately. Factors to consider when determining revenue estimates include the following:

❖ **Sales histories**. Identifying trends can help to project revenues for

---

[5]For more information about budget reforecasting see Schmidgall, R. (1997). *Hospitality Industry Managerial Accounting*, 4th ed. Orlando, FL: Educational Institute of American Hotel & Motel Association. (See Chapter 10).

the new budget period. For example, if food and/or beverage revenues have increased by 8% for the past five years, current revenues plus 8% might be the base for estimating revenues for the upcoming budget period.

❖ **Current factors**. Current factors such as increased competition, street improvement projects, and necessary remodeling projects may affect revenue levels.

❖ **Economic variables**. Inflation creates changes in the public's habits and lifestyles. Guests demand ever-increasing value for their eating and drinking dollars at the same time that costs increase.

Calculation of Profit Requirements

Projected revenue must be used for two purposes:

1. to pay for necessary costs
2. to yield required profit

Frequently, cost levels are assessed after revenue is estimated. Profit is what remains from revenue after deducting costs. However, it is also possible to calculate profit requirements so that, in effect, the property pays itself first. Funds remaining after profit is deducted from revenues are then used for costs. This approach treats profit as a cost. The foodservice manager is concerned about profit and wants to assure that sufficient revenue is generated to meet incurred costs without sacrificing the property's quality requirements.

Calculation of Costs

Many costs are directly related to revenue volume and vary as revenue changes. For example, food and beverage costs increase as revenues rise because more food and beverage products must be purchased. Once revenues are known, costs required to generate the projected revenues can be estimated. Two methods are most popular:

1. **Simple markup calculations**. The current cost level (base) is increased (or infrequently, decreased) to arrive at the cost level for the new budget. For example, if the current year's food cost is $135,000, and a 12% increase in food cost is anticipated, the food cost for the new budget period is:

$$\$135,000 + (\$135,000 \times 12\%) = \$151,200$$

A similar calculation for all other variable costs will yield estimated variable costs for the new budget period.

2. **Simple percentage calculations**. This method considers the current percentage of each cost relative to revenues (for example, beverage cost ÷ beverage revenues = beverage cost percentage) for the current budget period. This percent is used to revise cost forecasts. If the current beverage cost is 24% of beverage revenues when the new budget is developed, 24% of the estimated beverage revenue will be allocated for beverage costs.

Simple markup and simple percentage calculations are not effective ways to estimate fixed costs which stay the same regardless of revenue levels. Many fixed costs do not vary between budget periods; they may be constant for many years. (Examples may include rent as specified in long-term leases, interest on capital loans, and license fees.)

Use of Budget for Control Purposes

Once the budgeted food and beverage costs are calculated, managers in commercial operations can express them as a percentage of revenue (budgeted food or beverage costs ÷ by budgeted food or beverage revenue). Managers in non-commercial operations can express budgeted food costs as a percentage of total operating costs (budgeted food costs ÷ total budgeted operating costs. Non-profit operations do not generally offer alcoholic beverages and, therefore, would not generate beverage revenue or expenses.) This percentage can be compared with actual operating results to measure effectiveness of management plans. This simple process is very important and provides the basis for the subsequent operating control systems.

Managers have at least two special concerns as they establish revenue and expense standards in the operating budget. First, the standards must be attainable. Personnel will become frustrated if standards are impossible (or overly difficult) to attain. Second, standards must not compromise the property's established quality requirements. For example, while lower food expenses might be achieved by raising prices, reducing portion sizes, or purchasing lower quality products, these procedures are not likely to be accepted by guests.

The Budget and Menu Pricing

If the budget has been planned to incorporate profit requirements from the food and beverage operation, it can also help establish the base for menu pricing in commercial properties. Product (and all other) costs must remain within limitations imposed by the operating budget. Once budgeted food costs are known the menu planner can establish base selling prices for food items. The procedure to incorporate budget standards into selling prices is simple:

1. Use the food cost percentage established by the budget. (For example, assume a 35% budgeted food cost.)
2. Calculate the price multiplier:

$$\frac{100}{\text{Food cost \%}} = \text{Price multiplier}$$

With a 35% food cost, the calculation is:

$$\frac{100}{35} = 2.86$$

3. Multiply the price multiplier by the standard food cost calculated from precosting the standard recipe. If, for example, the standard food cost of an a la carte soup item is 0.85, the base selling price is:

$$\underset{\text{multiplier}}{2.85} \times \underset{\substack{\text{standard} \\ \text{food cost}}}{0.85} = \underset{\substack{\text{Base} \\ \text{Selling} \\ \text{Price}}}{\$2.42}$$

4. Adjust the base-selling price developed above by factors such as competition and the property's existing pricing structure.

Using this budget markup approach, the actual cost of producing the item should generally fall within the cost standards established by the operating budget. This is true because the manager "backs into" the selling price considering the budgeted costs. In the example cited, an item selling for approximately $2.45 with a food cost of $0.85 will yield a 35% food cost (which is that planned in the budget).

Example of the Budget as Control Tool

Look at Figure 4 (Budget Worksheet). It shows:

- in column 1—The revenue and type of cost
- in column 2—The percentage of revenue budgeted for each cost
- in columns 3 and 4—Budgeted dollars for the month and year for revenue and each cost
- in columns 5 and 6—Actual dollars for the month and year for revenue and each cost
- in columns 7 and 8—The dollars and percentage of monthly profit.

Information in the Budget Worksheet tells the food manager:

- what food revenues, costs, and profits should be; and
- what food revenues, costs, and profits actually are.

Important information is obvious in the Budget Worksheet:

Figure 4. Budget Worksheet.

FOODSERVICE OPERATING BUDGET

Month: January

Revenue/Cost	Budget %	Budget		Actual		Monthly Profit calculation	
		Month	Year	Month	Year[a]	Amount	%
1	2	3	4	5	6	7	8
Food Revenue	100%	$153,950	$1,947,240	$160,100	$160,100	$160,100	100%
Cost of goods sold:							
Food cost	35%	53,880	685,130	57,640	57,640	(57,640)	(36)%
Operating costs							
Payroll	24%	36,950	467,340	37,500	37,500	x[b]	x
Payroll tax/Benefits	2%	3,080	38,940	3,250	3,250	x	x
Direct operating costs	5%	7,700	97,360	8,700	8,700	x	x
Music/Entertainment	—	—	—	—	—	x	x
Advertising	2%	3,080	38,940	3,080	3,080	x	x
Utilities	5%	7,700	97,360	8,100	8,100	x	x
Administration/General	4%	6,160	77,890	5,500	5,500	x	x
Repairs/Maintenance	1%	1,540	19,470	1,100	1,100	x	x
Rent	7%	10,780	136,310	10,780	10,780	x	x
Real estate/Property taxes	1%	1,540	19,470	1,540	1,540	x	x
Insurance	2%	3,080	38,940	3,080	3,080	x	x
Interest cost	4%	6,160	77,890	6,160	6,160	x	x
Depreciation	3%	4,620	58,420	4,620	4,620	x	x
Other (specify)	—	—	—	—	—	x	x
Total Operating costs	60%	$ 92,390	$1,168,330	$ 93,410	$ (93,410)	$ (93,410)	(58)%
Profit (before tax)	5%	$ 7,680	$ 97,380	x	x	$ 9,050	6%

[a]The amounts in the year column are the same as the month (column 5) as the statement is for January, the first month of the year.
[b]Individual costs are included in total operating costs ($93,410) below.

1. The actual food revenue for January was greater than anticipated ($160,100 actual food revenue minus $153,950 planned food revenues represents an increase in revenues of $6,150.)

2. Food costs were $3,760 greater than planned ($57,640 actual food cost minus $53,880 budgeted food costs). Some additional food costs are expected since food revenues were greater than planned. However, the actual cost percentage of 36% (col. 8) is greater than the planned food cost percentage of 35% (col. 2). Since food cost is variable and should correlate directly with revenue, the actual food cost should approximate 35% regardless of revenue level. Since this is the first month in the budget year, the foodservice manager may choose to do nothing now and closely monitor food costs in the future.

3. Operating costs were $1,020 greater than planned—$93,410 actual operating costs minus $92,390 budgeted operating costs.

4. Profit was $1,370 more than planned—$9,050 actual profit minus $7,680 planned profit.

In reviewing these budget results, the manager should look at several operating costs to determine whether higher revenues can explain higher than budgeted costs. If higher costs cannot be explained, further analysis is in order.

The comparison of budgeted and actual costs suggests that some direct operating costs may be out of line. The cost review and control process should begin with these items. Also, since food costs were slightly greater than anticipated, some analysis may be appropriate. However, it is difficult to generalize about budget costs after only one month. More accurate and meaningful analysis becomes possible with data from several months. Information gained from this analysis may be helpful in revising budget projections for the remainder of the year. Likewise, recall that a separate budget process is used for the beverage profit center. Analysis of that program may indicate where, if at all, corrective action efforts can help to generate additional profit from the beverage program.

Principles of Product Control

Product control involves six activities: purchasing, receiving, storing, issuing, production, and service. Combined they create the product control cycle. Each of these activities is discussed in the remainder of the chapter.

Purchasing

Planning and control in food and beverage operations begin with the menu. While its impact on the control system might be obvious, effective product control also requires the skills, abilities, knowledge, and motivation of the purchasing personnel and others who develop purchase specifications. If inefficient and ineffective purchasing routines are used, no amount of planning and control will make the operation successful.

What is purchasing? It is much more than buying and ordering. Purchasing involves determining product needs and setting specifications necessary to meet these needs. It also involves selecting suppliers. Relevant issues to consider include products available, price, level of product and service quality, frequency of deliveries, cleanliness of facilities, and the general ability of the supplier to provide operational assistance. Also suppliers should provide information about product development, price trends, and other concerns.

Suppliers' services have nothing to do with holiday presents, small favors, gifts etc. Purchasers should not be put in the position of feeling indebted to a supplier. If one does not accept gifts and favors, there is no need to feel obligated. The relationship with the supplier should be such that all that is owed upon receipt of products or services is the pre-determined price.

Good food purchasing involves having the right product in the right amount at the right place at the right time at the right price. Purchasers forecast needs based upon menu and anticipated volume. If one under-purchases, stock-outs occur, customers and staff are dissatisfied, negative word of mouth is generated. If one overpurchases, excessive products become available leading to spoilage potential and loss of money. Money tied up in excess products should be put to use generating revenues or interest income. As discussed earlier, it is also necessary to consider the difference between AP (as purchased), EP (edible portion), and AS (as served) quantities. When preparing, cooking, or serving products one may experience product loss, which depends on the quality of the item prepared, the method and techniques of preparation, and the method of holding and service.

Purchasing Control Cycle

Purchasing control involves a series of eight inter-linked procedures and activities that must be considered. Each is identified in Figure 5 (The Purchasing Cycle). The first activity is the requisition. When a food or beverage product is needed, an authorized representative should complete a requisition form for the storeroom manager. As a second step, the required products are issued to the user's department. Thirdly, when the products' inventory levels reach a predetermined re-order point, a purchase requisition is forwarded to the purchasing official. A fourth step involves products ordered from the appropriate suppliers using a purchasing form. The fifth step requires purchasing personnel to

Figure 5. The Purchasing Cycle.

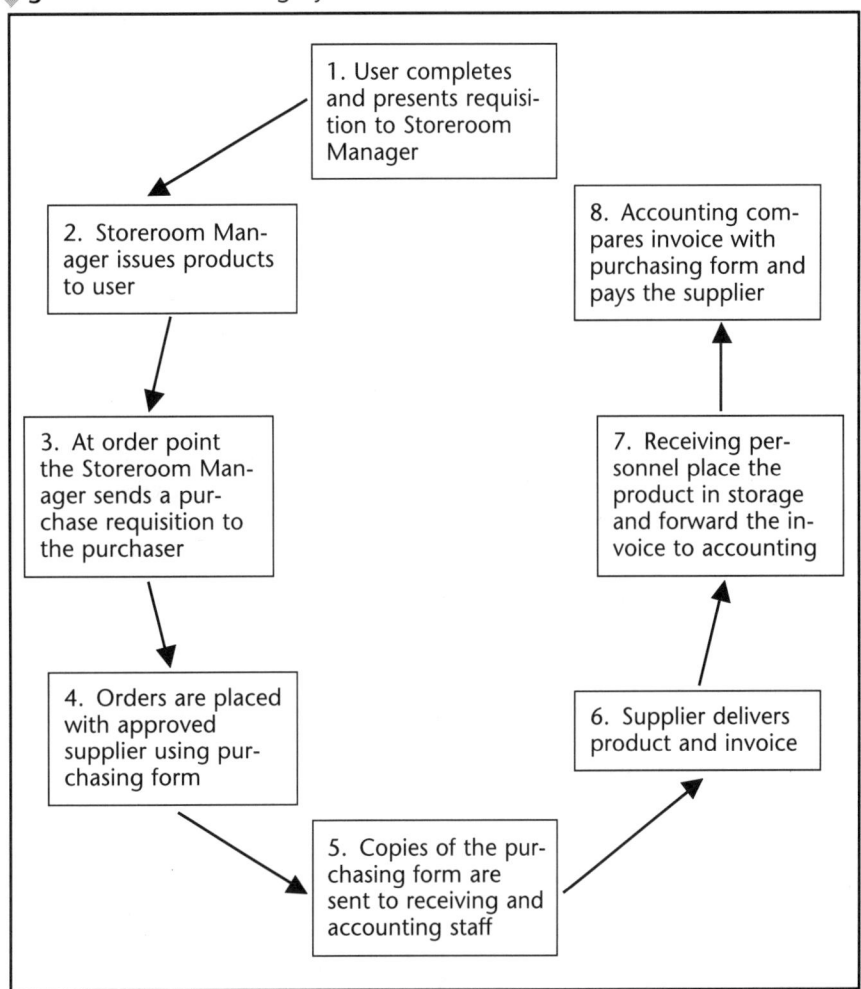

1. User completes and presents requisition to Storeroom Manager

2. Storeroom Manager issues products to user

3. At order point the Storeroom Manager sends a purchase requisition to the purchaser

4. Orders are placed with approved supplier using purchasing form

5. Copies of the purchasing form are sent to receiving and accounting staff

6. Supplier delivers product and invoice

7. Receiving personnel place the product in storage and forward the invoice to accounting

8. Accounting compares invoice with purchasing form and pays the supplier

send a copy of the purchasing form to receiving and the accounting department so it can keep track of incoming products and purchase commitments. The supplier delivers the product to the receiving department as the sixth step in the cycle. The seventh step requires the receiving department personnel to place the product in the proper storage and forward the invoice to the accounting department. (Sometimes food and beverage managers review the forms before they are sent to accounting.) The eighth step involves further processing of the document by accounting staff who send payment to the supplier and file copies of purchasing receiving forms for accounting and/or control purposes. The entire purchasing cycle is repeated whenever a purchase is made to help establish an audit trail by a series of records, documents, and reports to trace the flow of food, beverage, supplies, and equipment throughout the operation.

Who is responsible for purchasing? Responsibility can be delegated to one or a number of persons depending upon the organization's structure and the management system in place. In small properties the owner, manager, or chef may have the responsibility. In large properties, staff purchasing agents have the responsibility to perform these tasks.

As noted earlier in the chapter, purchase specifications are needed to accurately describe minimum quality requirements and to assure that (a) suppliers have no doubt about the requirements, and (b) receiving personnel can recognize the proper quality of products received.

In addition to purchase specifications developed by the individual hospitality property, the United States government has developed three additional standards that help with product control. These are:

❖ **Standard of identity.** The standard of identity for a covered product specifies that a product name may only be used when cer-

tain characteristics are satisfied. For example, "corned beef hash" must have at least 35% corned beef on a cooked basis and potatoes. Onions, garlic, other seasoning, fat, broth etc. are optional. The moisture content, however, must not exceed 72%. Note: Standards of identity establish minimum requirements and may specify a lesser quality product than desired by the purchaser.

❖ **Standard of fill.** The standard of fill refers to the quantity that must be in specific package types. For example, a barrel of cranberries must contain 100 pounds of cranberries.

❖ **Standard of quality.** The standard of quality or grading for covered products refers to standards for wholesomeness and for quality and yield grading.

Inspections for wholesomeness assess whether food is fit for human consumption; it is not an assessment of quality. (A food product may be wholesome, but of poor quality.) All meats are inspected for wholesomeness as required by federal law. Inspections of fresh seafood are NOT mandatory while processed seafood must be inspected. Shellfish can only be harvested from waters approved safe by the National Shellfish Sanitation Program. The Federal Government must inspect all meat and poultry transported and sold in interstate commerce; the box or package of meat must bear the plant's inspection number. State inspection is mandatory for meat and poultry being transported and sold within a state.

When a food product is graded for quality, factors such as marbling, texture, firmness, color, maturity, and general conformity with the norm are considered. Quality grading does not reflect the relative wholesomeness; it is an assessment of palatability. Grading for quality is voluntary and indicates that specified standards have been met. Buyers can request inspections of products that are not

required to be inspected and can likewise require that grading be performed. Buyers must cover the cost of requested inspections and grading. Yield grading relates to the fat to meat ratio, i.e., the degree of usable meat in proportion to fat and fat deposits.

Purchasing and Ordering

At least three basic purchasing decisions should be made by the chef and managers and should not be delegated. The first decision is what to purchase (i.e., what items are required by the menu and what are their purchase specifications). The second decision is how much to stock: what inventory level should be available? Thirdly, from whom should purchases be made? Once these three decisions are made restocking or reordering procedures can be delegated to other employees.

How Much to Order? Perishable products such as produce and dairy are typically purchased several times weekly for immediate use. Less perishables products, such as frozen items and grocery items, are typically purchased less frequently.

The quantity of perishable items to purchase is determined as follows: quantity needed less quantity already available. To determine the quantity needed one must:

❖ determine the typical usage rate for the order period
❖ establish safety levels, if any
❖ estimate the lead time usage, i.e., the amounts that will be used between the point of order and the point of delivery.

To summarize our discussion of purchasing perishables, assume the following:

❖ order for two days
❖ usage rate is 5 cases a day
❖ one day order time
❖ one case safety time
❖ one case available

Purchase Quantity = Quantity Needed + [Lead time usage + Safety level quantity] − Quantity Available

15 cases = 5 cases × 2 days + [(5 cases × 1 day) + 1 case] − 1 case

There is a difference between the quantity available at purchase and the quantity available after initial processing. Consider, for example, the difference between a whole onion and a peeled onion. These quantities are referred to as purchased (AP) and edible portion (EP) quantities, respectively. Recipes usually specify EP quantities. If a recipe specifies one pound (EP) of onions, the quantity needed is found by dividing the one pound needed by the expected yield. For example:

$$16 \text{ oz. EP} / \text{Yield \%} =$$
AP amount needed for recipe

The person responsible for purchasing perishables must take a daily inventory to establish the amount of product on hand. Then the usage rate (the amount of product typically used during the order period) must be determined. In addition, one may wish to establish a safety margin (such as 10% or 5 cases more than typically used during the order period). The quantity used between the time the order is placed and delivered must also be assessed. For example, if you are ordering on Monday and the delivery occurs on Wednesday there are two days of usage.

When determining order quantities, it is frequently necessary to round up quantities to fit available pack sizes. For example, assume you need 210 *eighty-count* potatoes. (Potato count is a measure of potato size based on the number of potatoes per 50 pounds. An 80-count potato weighs 10oz. [50 pounds × 16 oz. / 80]). If these were only available in 50-pound cartons, one would need to purchase three cartons (3 cases × 80 per case = 240 potatoes purchased). Suppliers willing to sell partial packs will typically charge more for the product.

When purchasing non-perishables one also needs to establish the daily usage rate and consider lead-time and safety-levels, using the same calculation as described above; however, ordering methods influence the quantity of product to order:

❖ **Par stock**—this method specifies a specific amount of stock to be kept on hand. For example, if par stock for applesauce is 10 cases, orders are placed to bring the quantity on hand to 10 cases. Par stocks are based upon a reasonable usage rate plus a safety factor.

❖ **Mini-Max**—this approach considers the minimum and the maximum quantities to be available. For example, the minimum level may be the safety level plus one day's usage. Typically products are only purchased when the minimum level is reached, and the quantity ordered will bring the amount on hand to the maximum quantity.

❖ **Standing Order**—this involves receiving a specific quantity every time a delivery is made. For example, one might know from experience that the gift shop sells about 25 city newspapers daily, so the standing order is for 30 newspapers.

Supplier Selection

Supplier selection is an important component in the product control process. With the proliferation of products, single suppliers cannot carry all possible products, and since quality of even seemingly identical products tend to vary, selecting the right supplier can have significant bottom line results.

There has been much consolidation among suppliers in recent years. In any given market there are likely to be several very large and a few small suppliers. Some suppliers offer *one-stop* service and indicate they offer low prices resulting from low margins compensated by large volume deliveries. Supplier consolidation has

typically been beneficial for large operations. For small-volume buyers, consolidation has meant more pressure because the supplier can dictate terms relative to frequency and size of deliveries, necessary lead-time, etc.

When selecting a supplier, look at the operation to assess needs, strengths, and weaknesses. For example, what is the product mix and nature of the menu? (It may limit who can serve the establishment.) What types of products are needed? Is a wide range of products needed or can a limited range of items meet needs? Does the establishment routinely need smaller orders? Is there a need for a great variety of products? Are specialty items needed? What kinds of payment terms are desired?

Consider quality needs. The quality needed must be clear. Wanting only the best is not consistent with always emphasizing price: Operators looking for the highest quality product will typically have to pay top dollar. In establishing necessary quality, the intended use of the product must be considered. For example, high quality tomatoes may be needed for a salad, but a lesser quality may be adequate for use in soup.

Consider frequency of deliveries that are expensive. One might be able to negotiate smaller margins if the numbers of deliveries are reduced or the size of deliveries is increased. Timing is also important: Accepting deliveries at times convenient for the supplier may also yield lower prices.

Consider the need for special deliveries. Most food service operations need a special delivery occasionally, but a frequent need indicates a problem with purchasing procedures.

Also consider suppliers' sales efforts. If product needs are known and orders are placed by phone, prices may be better than if a salesperson must make an on-site visit.

Buying Methods

Buying methods can be informal and formal. Informal methods are suitable for casual buying of smaller quantities and for speed and simplicity. Both price and supply may vary considerably. Formal methods are used for large contracts over a long period of time. They typically offer little price variation (the price may be guaranteed, for example) and a more stable supply.

Informal Buying Methods

Cash Buying. Cash buying occurs when the buyer pays cash on delivery or when picking up an order. Many small operations do this, especially if there are local markets available. The owner or chef may visit the markets to select produce, for example. Suppliers will often give a rebate for cash purchases.

◆ *Potential Advantages*

1. Freshness and high quality can often be assured.
2. The amount of money tied up in inventory may be reduced with daily purchases.
3. Waste may be reduced if one only purchases what is needed.
4. The middle person is eliminated and lower prices may result.
5. Cash rebates are often offered.
6. Bookkeeping is facilitated, as daily receipts are available.

◆ *Potential Disadvantages*

1. The buyer has fewer options about product availability and price.
2. It may be time consuming to travel to the market.
3. Menu planning may be difficult if there is inconsistent product availability.

Quotation Order Sheets. When using quotation order sheets, the purchaser calls approved suppliers and obtains price quotes for products of the specified quality and quantity. Approved suppliers need relevant purchase specifications to quote prices for the correct quality product. The purchaser should obtain quotes from at least three suppliers and will purchase from the supplier with the lowest quote.

◆ *Potential Advantages*

1. Price comparisons are available.
2. Vendors know that several suppliers are bidding.
3. Better prices may result.
4. The purchaser has current market information.

◆ *Potential Disadvantages*

1. It can be time consuming.
2. There is no written contract.
3. If the supplier does not have copies of purchase specifications problems can arise.

Cost-Plus Method. This method (also known as fixed markup method) can be used when the prices are not known and when the market is unstable. Suppliers like this method because they do not have to consider the risk of price fluctuation, and they are guaranteed a fixed profit. They can buy at the most favorable price and add the agreed-upon markup. Purchasers may also benefit because product availability is better assured. A typical component of this method allows the purchaser to audit the supplier.

Formal Buying Methods

Formal buying (also called competitive or bid buying) involves sending written invitations or bids to *identified* suppliers to solicit prices for products with detailed specifications. Generally, large quantities of products are involved. The purchaser then evaluates the bids that are received. Formal buying is more time consuming and complex than informal methods and is usually done by large organizations. Bid specifications must be very clear and leave no doubt about quality characteristics. The bid from the supplier is a binding contract. Advantages of formal methods are that they yield competition and promote fair purchasing policies and practices.

The Competitive Bid. This is the most common formal method. Suppliers submit bids based on written specifications and, sometimes, must also provide product samples for testing. (This is especially important when dealing with a new supplier and/or new product.) The bid covers a specified time period, and it should be solicited from at least three suppliers and should include specifications about quality, quantity, package size, etc. Also terms of payments, relevant discounts, method and frequency of delivery, ordering procedures, etc. are included.

Typically the purchaser sets a specific time for bid submission. The selected bidder is announced, and the bid price can be announced to ensure fair handling and no favoritism. The competition among suppliers often allows the purchaser to obtain the lowest price. This method may be expensive; however, depending on the frequency of bidding and the number of bids the purchasing staff must manage. Another concern arises when the purchaser changes suppliers and does not have a close relationship with the supplier.

Negotiated Buy. This method is typically used when suppliers are hesitant to bid due to time restrictions, fluctuating market prices, etc. It is best used when prices are stable, and there is little difference in the prices. Purchasers undertake informal negotiations with several suppliers and establish a written agreement with one of them. Performed on a weekly basis this method is similar to quotation order sheets discussed earlier. It allows for quick action and flexibility and can reduce paperwork.

Standing Order. The standing order typically involves products arriving at fixed intervals. The quantity may be fixed, or it can be a min/max amount. Sometimes the supplier replenishes the stock directly. (While not necessarily recommended, this can be convenient and timesaving for some items.)

Futures and Contract. Large businesses make contracts for future deliveries of commodities at an established bid price. This assures an adequate supply at an established price, but it is speculative and involves some risk. (If the prices fall, the purchaser still has to pay the contracted higher price.) Sometimes this arrangement is used for short periods for perishable items, while long-term contracts are more common for less perishable items.

Other Purchasing Methods

Some managers use one-stop shopping and group purchasing systems. With the former, all or most products are purchased from one supplier. This can be an excellent "bargaining chip," as most suppliers would like to be the sole supplier for a foodservice operation. Purchasers must compare the prices with prevailing market prices. This is a less serious concern if the one-stop shopping supplier is selected as a result of bids. Occasionally one-stop shopping is combined with the cost-plus method.

Smaller food and beverage operations may benefit if they join a group purchasing unit designed around (a) membership in a professional association or organization, (b) proximity to other small operators, (c) some common business, religious or other affiliation. Use of group purchasing can save money. A drawback is that the purchaser typically must use the products and supplier selected by the purchasing group.

Responsibility for Purchasing

The ultimate responsibility for purchasing rests with management. Larger firms may have a staff purchasing agent or department, while smaller operations use the general manager or other designated person.

It is recommended that, when practical, different people perform the purchasing, receiving, and storing functions. If the same individual is allowed to purchase and receive control problems arise. This problem is expanded if the same individual is also in charge of storage. When the individual is involved in production the loss of control is almost complete.

If separation of function is not possible, supervision becomes paramount. The manager should occasionally, and without warning, perform some functions to assure that all procedures are consistently followed.

It is important that only authorized personnel purchase or place orders. Ideally, each supplier is sent a list of approved individuals. An alternative to such control is "backdoor selling" (where anyone can commit on behalf of the organization and, perhaps, for personal gain.) It is also useful to limit the maximum dollar commitment per delivery without authorization.

Record Keeping for Purchases

Two forms are used in many food service operations: purchase orders (in large-volume business) and purchase records (in smaller operations). If purchase orders are required no order should be filled or received without a purchase order number. The purchase order should be sent to the supplier as authorization to fill an order. They can be closed (that is, they can deal with specific one-time purchases) or open-ended (so purchases can be made from the same suppliers throughout the entire year). Purchase orders are typically:

❖ tied with the supplier awarded the bid
❖ limited by time and dollar commitment
❖ detailed with information about specifications, quantities, warranties, guarantees, payment terms, and other contractual agreements.

A copy of the purchase order should be sent to receiving and accounting staff to indicate what and when deliveries are expected. Establishments that use purchase orders should reject deliveries not accompanied by a purchase order number.

Purchase records are used by smaller operations to summarize purchase commitments such as product quantities and delivery dates. While suppliers do not typically receive the purchase record, a copy is typically kept in purchasing and sent to receiving. If a delivery arrives and there is no purchase record, the delivery should be rejected.

Security Concerns and Ethical Issues

Managers have the responsibility of ensuring ethical practices for all activities including purchasing, receiving, and storage and expect and demand ethical practices of themselves and other employees and suppliers. When purchasing, consider the welfare and benefit of the company. Suggestions include:

❖ Place an emphasis on honesty and make it a clear policy that everyone—including the manager—will adhere to it. (If employees see the manager violating a rule they will often think, "if the manager can, why can't I?")
❖ If possible, assign specific and different people to purchasing, receiving, storing, and issuing activities.
❖ Do not allow anyone to accept gifts from suppliers.
❖ Make purchase specifications clear and concise.
❖ Do not over purchase.
❖ Check the credentials of suppliers, ask for references, and check with colleagues.
❖ Be on the lookout for "own use" purchases. (Employees of organizations may place orders for their personal use.) Make sure that all incoming products are consistent with what is needed and that there is proper documentation for each order.
❖ Check all invoices for accuracy and completion of extensions, quantities, etc.
❖ If a delivery does not contain all ordered products or if some/all

products are rejected, request a credit memo. (A credit memo is similar to a delivery notice but reverses the direction of the product; the receiver and the driver sign it.) Retain the original invoice until corrected or a credit invoice is issued. Never accept a non-complete delivery without written documentation that is was incomplete.

❖ Show no leniency if an employee engages in unethical practices or is stealing.

Receiving

Receiving is an important control point. Proper food specifications and use of other purchasing procedures will not help if receiving is neglected. Poor receiving leads to product waste, to poor quality, and disappearing products. If care is taken to establish control during purchasing and no attention is paid to receiving, all of the previous efforts have been wasted.

Ordering products in specified quantities and qualities does not guarantee that they will arrive. Wrong products may be delivered by accident or with intent. The supplier may deliver products in the wrong quantities, of the wrong qualities, and/or at the wrong prices.

The primary goal of receiving is to verify that the quantities, qualities, and prices conform to the orders placed. Some establishments delegate receiving to whomever is "closest to the back door." This is clearly a wrong practice unless this employee has been trained to properly receive. Other establishments use receiving clerks, while others may require that the manager do receiving. Whoever receives should be clearly designated and carefully trained. If possible, the individual that receives products should not be the person who also orders the products.

An invoice should accompany all deliveries. It is usually provided in duplicate or triplicate. The clerk may keep one copy, but additional copies should be forwarded to the accounting department.

Six steps in receiving are:

❖ Check incoming products against the purchase order or record to assure receipt of the proper order.

❖ Check incoming products against purchase specifications to ensure that products are of correct quality. (Check product temperatures; unwrap, unpack, and weigh items separately. Spot-check cases because top layers always look the best.)

❖ Check incoming products against the delivery invoice to ensure that products received are of proper quantity and cost. If the product is rejected or is not present, modify the invoice. Use a credit memo, signed by both the driver and receiver to note problems with the products.

❖ Accept the product by signing the delivery invoice. Never sign the invoice until all items are properly accepted. When signed, the products on the invoice have been officially accepted. It then becomes difficult to return a product. Sometimes drivers do not have time to wait while proper procedures are used. Do not be pressured into signing. If the operation has a good working relationship with the supplier the receiving employee may be able to accept products conditionally with problems resolved after the invoice has been signed. The signed invoice should be stamped with date, receiver's name, and verification of price and extension.

❖ Move the incoming products to storage as quickly as possible.

❖ Complete the daily receiving report that contains information about all deliveries received that day.

Blind Receiving

Rather than receive invoices at time of delivery some establishments use a blind receiving method. This involves the receiver using a blank invoice or purchase order to list the merchandise. The receiving clerk provides information about quantity, quality, weights, and prices on the invoice, which necessitates a serious check of incoming products. A separate invoice with detailed information is mailed to the accounting office and is checked against the clerk's blind copy. This can be an accurate method of checking products and verifying deliveries but it is time consuming and costly. Partial blind receiving is sometimes used as an alternative: The receiving clerk is given itemized receiving documents with only the quantities or some other data omitted, which must be listed in the space provided.

Storage

Effective procedures are needed to prevent any additional, unplanned, and unacceptable costs while the products are in storage. Managers must focus on minimizing loss, spoilage, contamination, and pilferage/theft. Key issues include conditions of the facilities, location of facilities, and security practices that are in use.

Condition of Facilities

Proper storage conditions consider temperature, storage containers, shelving, and cleanliness. Temperature is a key factor. In dry storage, for example, the ideal temperature range is usually 50–70°F; for fruits the ideal temperature is 34–50°F. Produce and eggs have a more narrow ideal range of 34–45°F. Dairy products should be held at 34–40°F; fresh meats should be held at 34–38°F; and poultry should be kept at 32–36°F. Fresh seafood is usually kept on crushed ice and should be near freezing temperatures. (The ideal temperature range is 28–34°F.) All frozen products should ideally be kept at 0–10°F. If temperatures are allowed to arise above these levels, shelf life will be shortened.

Most food and beverage operations do not have numerous storage areas that can be dedicated to specific storage needs. Rather, they have three types of storage available:

1. Dry storage at 50–70°F.
2. Refrigerated storage at 45°F or lower.
3. Frozen storage at 0°F or lower.

Storage containers must be insect-proof and airtight. Shelving for perishables should permit air circulation to facilitate cleaning and to reduce the risk of insect or rodent problems and accidents due to spills. Slotted or wire shelving is recommended. Non-perishable items can be put on solid shelves. Products should never be stored on the floor. Cleanliness is essential. The facilities need to be cleaned daily and treated against pests such as insects and rodents as needed.

Location

Food products should have a definite location in storage to facilitate control since it becomes easier to observe, count, and obtain the products when needed. Food products should be rotated using a FIFO (first-in, first-out) plan. Items that are most frequently used should be stored closest to the door. Ideally the storage room should be located between receiving and production to speed storage and issue tasks and to maximize security and reduce labor requirements.

Security During Storage

Storage areas should be clearly defined and access should be limited to authorized personnel only. Prioritize items to be controlled. Typically 20% of the items require 80% of the cost; these items should be kept under lock or in attended storerooms. Very expensive or theft-proof items that can be easily consumed or sold for cash can be kept in a secured room within the storage facilities.

Issuing

Issuing is the controlled process of transferring foods or other items from storage to production. The issuing control system has four primary objectives:

1. To limit access to storage areas to authorized personnel only.
2. To issue products only in relationship to actual production requirements.
3. To establish the quantity and costs of products removed from storage.
4. To update perpetual inventory records and to determine daily food or beverage costs.

Products in storage represent money and the use of requisitions for expensive items is a reasonable deterrent to theft. Requisitions should identify the types and amounts of each item necessary for production during a given shift or day, and they should include information such as the date, name of the item, weight, and the count of items along with their cost. When products are issued, the person authorized to receive the product signs the requisition. One copy is provided to the receiver, the issuer keeps one copy, and one copy is sent to accounting as part of the audit trail. If an operation does not limit accesses to storage areas or keep records of items removed from storage, it becomes difficult to control product costs.

Production

Production involves four components: preparing, cooking, holding, and portioning. Production planning is needed to get ready for production. Regardless of the size of the operation one needs to plan to assure that there will be no (or few) surprises during the work shift.

Careful production planning reduces leftovers by controlling production quantities. Estimating (forecasting) how much to produce is the first step. In food and beverage operations

with a pre-determined number of clients or guests, estimating can be straightforward, yet it is still dependent on the type of menu and patron choices.

Managers can forecast revenue (dollars) and the number of guests and/or sales (the number of the items to be served). These forecasts are inter-linked: The estimated number of guests multiplied by guest check average yields estimated revenue; the selling price multiplied by number of items sold yields revenue. Operators must keep sales records to use when forecasting future production needs. Maintaining these records is facilitated by point-of-sales computerized systems that tally sales mixes for specified time intervals. However, even if a manual system is used it is important to track sales and special events, as well as weather and other activities that might impact sales. (For example, a large festival during a weekend can bolster sales over an average weekend.)

Menu Types

The type of menu used may impact the forecasting activity. There are three types:

1. set (also known as non-selective)
2. free choice (also known as selective)
3. partial choice (also known as partially selective)

A set menu is typically used in an institutional setting and can be used for banquets where the host has predetermined the menu. When the number of patrons to be served is known it is relatively easy to produce the needed quantity. If standard recipes are used there should be minimal waste.

Free choice menus allow guests to make extensive or more limited choices. Their use requires accurate records for forecasting. It is essential to know past menu mix percentages by specific time intervals to determine the types of foods to produce.

Partial choice menus may be found in schools and other settings where patrons can make limited choices. For example, there may be a choice of two entrées and several vegetables. Historical records are also important to forecast production needs.

Menus can also be classified as static or cyclical. A static menu does not change. For example, a quick service restaurant has the same breakfast menu each day. The operator can develop historical records to predict demand relatively precisely. By contrast, a cycle menu is built around time blocks such as one, two, or six weeks, and the menu is repeated one time during that cycle. For example, with a two-week cycle the dinner menu will vary each day for two weeks and will then repeat (although there can be some variation for reasons of holidays, special events, etc.). Menus may also contain static and cycle variations. For example, a property may have a static menu and offer a one-week cycle of different "specials" each weekday.

Mise en place

This French term literally means "put in place." In a quality food operation it refers to a state of constant readiness. For example, when kitchen staff prepare for a particular day or shift, everything that is needed such as necessary tools, equipment, and ingredients must be available in the workstation. Having a well defined and prepared mise en place is essential for production of high quality products in a timely fashion.

Many quality food operators are faced with a food quality challenge: There is too much work to produce everything to order, and yet most foods are at their best quality immediately upon preparation. A solution is to look at each recipe and break it into stages of production. Carefully consider what can be done in advance without noticeable effect on quality. For many recipes, the first few steps can often be done ahead of time, as can parts of later steps. These steps

can then become part of the routine mise en place. Secondly, an operator should consider sanitation aspects of holding prepared items. The danger zone (40°F–145°F) is important and one must minimize the time foods are kept within this range. Unfortunately some products which should be served hot deteriorate rapidly when held above the danger zone. (Cream soup or steamed vegetables are examples.) Other products such as a consommé can be held above the danger zone and still maintain quality.

Managers must consider mise en place and holding times. For example, if extended meal service times are available, batch cookery or cooking to order will be used depending upon the item. If set meal service is used, quantity cookery practices can be applied, and the actual batch needed to serve all can be completed at once. This happens for banquets.

Portion Control Standards

The need for standard recipes and purchase specifications was discussed earlier. They are necessary to help assure quality at time of food production. Additionally, portion control is important.

Portion control tools such as accurate scales for weighing and scoops/ladles for measuring should always be used. Likewise, serving dishes, such as soup cups and salad bowls, that can contain a maximum sized serving should be available.

Standard portion costs allow the manager to determine the expected costs when items are prepared according to standard recipes with ingredients meeting purchase specifications. A standard portion cost is the sum of the recipe's total ingredient costs divided by the recipe's yield (number of portions). Computerized systems allow managers to compare expected costs with actual costs as part of the control process: the total number of all items sold multiplied by each item's portion cost can be compared with actual food cost calculations to

measure the impact of the property's food cost control system.

Service Controls

Service management is discussed in Chapter 11. Here, it will be considered from a control perspective. Personal aspects of service relate to the management and leadership styles prevalent in the organization. The manager should hire service employees that are friendly, personable, interested, and tactful. They need to be willing to serve guests and have a positive attitude about service. Servers should be inquiring, interested, and willing to discover and meet guests' needs.

Procedural aspects of service relate the method by which service is delivered. They deal with timeliness, efficiency, uniform and dress and, in general, how products and services are conveyed to the guests. The type of service offered is determined by the menu, skill and training of personnel, the ambiance, style and feel of the establishment, and by market needs.

There are three types of service: table service, buffet-service, and counter service. Each type meets the specific needs and requirements that are driven by the demands of different guests and different circumstances.

Photo © 1998 PhotoDisc, Inc.

Servers should be inquiring, interested, and willing to discover and meet guests' needs.

Table Service

There are four types of table service:

1. French service (sometimes called cart service or gueridon service)
2. Russian service (sometimes called platter service or silver service)
3. American service (sometimes called plate service)
4. English service (sometimes called family service)

French Service

French service involves final (finishing) cooking done tableside on a gueridon or cart. This service is considered to be most elaborate and elegant and offers the greatest personal attention to the guest. Service employees spend significant amounts of time tableside interacting with guests and preparing foods. They can tailor the food to exactly fit the guests' needs. French service is distinguished by use of two servers for each station. The primary server is called Chef de Rang; the secondary server is called Commis de Rang. The primary server typically takes the order and serves all the drinks and finishes the food preparation. The secondary server places the order with the kitchen and brings food to the tableside station and assists the primary server.

The characteristics of French service are that food and beverages are served and cleared from the right, that a cart or gueridon is used tableside and that there is high quality personalized attention and service. The menu price is typically higher because of the increased service components and the service time required.

Service employees must be well trained and highly skilled. French service requires a considerable investment in equipment, silver platters, tableside carts, and cookware. Fewer guests can be served, as more space is needed in the dining room per each guest.

Russian Service

With this service style food is finished in the kitchen, placed onto attractive silver platters and brought to the table for portioning tableside. Russian service is less showy than French service, and there is less opportunity to interact with the guests. However, it is still elegant. Speed replaces showmanship. Prior to portioning, the server presents the silver platter(s) to the guests so they can see the food presentation. The platter is presented on the guests' left side and the server transfers the food to the plate. Service staff needs to be well trained and experienced. Precise timing and organization are essential if the food is to reach the guest at its maximum quality. Disadvantages of Russian service include the necessary investment in service equipment, the staff must be skilled, and it is difficult for the tray to look appealing when the last guest is served.

American Service

With this service style food is finished and plated in the kitchen and served to the guest typically by a single server. It is inexpensive service since one server can serve many guests. It is also less complicated and can be handled by staff with less training. The service employee carries food on a large tray, which is placed on a tray stand. The plates of food are then served from the left with the left hand. Beverages are served from the right with the right hand. Food and beverages are both cleared from the right with the right hand. It is relatively quick, little equipment is needed, less space is required, portion and quality control can be closely monitored, service staff need less training, and lower menu prices can be maintained. Disadvantages include its less elaborate style, and that the service is less personal.

English Service

With this type of service food is prepared in the kitchen and the guests typically help themselves from platters or bowls placed on the table. The maître d' or the host may carve at the table and serve the main dinner item and then allow everyone to help themselves to other items from platters or bowls. This type of service is informal. Advantages include: (a) fast service, (b) less need for highly skilled personnel, (c) potential for lower menu prices, (d) fairly high turnover of guests, and (e) more guests served per service person. A disadvantage is that platters and dishes may accumulate on the table.

Buffet and Counter Service

Buffet Service

In addition to table service styles discussed above, meals can also be served on buffets or at service counters. With this type of service guests help themselves to food items which are presented attractively on a series of tables. Buffets are used to generate simple and fast service when a large number of people must be served in a short period of time. Guests generally pay a set price and help themselves as they pass from one food item to the next along the buffet line. Active portion control is possible if a server is positioned behind the buffet to assist guests with plating or carving. One must replenish food and assure that food displays are maintained and attractive. The menu can be preplanned; it can be very profitable, and limited additional equipment is needed. Service personnel need not be highly skilled, and quality control can be maintained if food is cooked in batches. A disadvantage of buffets is that food can become unappetizing if held to long or when many guests have helped themselves from the food. Food costs can be high if waste is excessive, and there is little personal service.

Counter Service

Counter service is typically associated with the quick service industry. It requires low labor costs and can be quick and efficient. It is most appealing to guests in a hurry. It allows for very limited personal service, and guest turnover is typically high. There is a potential for high profits and quality portion size can be readily controlled.

Beverage Control

Alcoholic beverages warrant special control. Many of the control strategies already noted apply to beverage production. Maintaining quality and cost standards are, for example, just as important as with food controls. There are, however, some specific cost-control procedures required for beverage production:

❖ Use portion control tools such as shots, glasses and jiggers or automated beverage systems. (These beverage systems dispense predetermined measures of alcoholic beverages. Many systems are tied to point of sales systems that require that a sale be entered to pour a beverage; other systems keep track of sales and dispensing quantities for reconciliation.)

❖ Supervise to assure that all beverage control procedures are consistently followed.

❖ Train beverage production as well as the service staff. They need to know how to produce drinks according to the established standards to meet the property's quality and cost requirements.

❖ Use updated job descriptions and specifications; this facilitates the hiring of personnel who can work quickly, who are knowledgeable about recipes and work procedures,

and who can produce beverages quickly and adequately.

❖ Require that all returned drinks and drink mistakes be saved for management's review to determine the causes of the errors.

❖ Managers should require that authorized personnel approve all free and complimentary drinks.

❖ Lock bar inventories when the bar is not in use.

❖ Standard costs should be compared with actual costs (preferably on a shift by shift basis to allow for tighter control).

❖ Hold the bartender responsible for cash collected and for bar inventory.

❖ Reconcile start-of-shift with end-of-shift inventories and revenues.

❖ Establish bar par levels. The daily par level in the bar is a key link in the control system. The par level should be based upon the amount of product needed for a busy day plus, perhaps, a safety margin.

❖ Issue beverages only in response to requisitions or use the "empty for full bottle replacement method."

❖ Provide adequate supplies to support beverage personnel. Mise en place is as important in the bar as in the kitchen.

Supervise to assure that all beverage control procedures are consistently followed.

Questions and Assignments

1. Discuss the importance of control systems and some of the advantages and disadvantages of such systems. Summarize the key points and be prepared for discussion with your team or classmates.

2. Discuss the role of controlling from the perspective of the management process.

3. List and describe the three major components of a control system. Develop an example application of the system.

4. List and discuss the issues that must be considered when designing a control system. Using your library resources or the web browser and search engine of your choice, identify an article that discusses controls or control systems in food and/or beverage operations. Summarize the key points and be prepared for discussion.

5. Discuss the issue of yield and the process of establishing yield ratios. Use an example of your choice to demonstrate the difference between AP, EP, and AS. Be prepared to share your discussion and example with your team or classmates.

6. Establish the potential benefits of using purchase specifications.

7. Using your library resources, develop a purchase specification for a food item of your choosing.

8. What role does the budget play in the control process? Identify key points and be prepared for discussion.

9. Identify the eight components of the purchasing cycle and discuss key issues for each component. Using your library resources or the web browser and search engine of your choice, identify an article in support of one or more of the key issues. Summarize the key points and be prepared for discussion with your team or classmates.

10. Choose two formal and two informal buying methods. Differentiate the methods, establishing when either method is most appropriate.

11. Using your library resources or the web browser and search engine of your choice, identify an article that discusses one-stop shopping or purchasing groups. Summarize the key points and be prepared for discussion.

12. Discuss the difference between active and passive portion control.

13. Define mise en place.

14. Choose two of the approaches to table service. Describe the approaches and discuss their advantages and disadvantages. Using your library resources or the web browser and search engine of your choice, identify an article that discusses table service. Summarize the key points and be prepared for discussion with your team or classmates.

Bibliography and Suggested Readings

Dittmer, P. R. & Griffin, G. G. (1989). *Principles of Food, Beverage and Labor Cost Controls for Hotels and Restaurants*, 4th ed. New York, NY: Van Nostrand Reinhold.

Keiser, J. & DeMicco, F. J. (1993). *Controlling and Analyzing Costs in Foodservice Operations*. New York, NY: Macmillan Publishing Co.

Knight, J. B. & Kotschevar, L. H. (1989). *Quantity Food Production, Planning, and Management*. Boston, MA: CBI Publishing Company.

Kotschevar, L. H. & Levinson, C. (1988). *Quantity Food Purchasing*. New York, NY: Macmillan Publishing.

Kotschevar, L. H. & Tanke, M. L. (1991). *Managing Bar and Beverage Operations*. East Lansing, MI: Educational Institute of the American Hotel & Motel Association.

Ninemeier, J. D. (1998). *Planning and Control for Food and Beverage Operations*, 4th ed. Orlando, FL: Educational Institute of the American Hotel & Motel Association.

Reed, L. (1993). SPECS: *The Comprehensive Foodservice Purchasing and Specification Manual*, 2nd ed. New York, NY: Van Nostrand Reinhold.

Sanders, E. E. & Hill, T. H. (1998). *Foodservice Profitability: A Control Approach*. Upper Saddle River, NJ: Prentice Hall.

The Human Resource Perspective

Robert W. Woods, *Department of Restaurant,
Hotel & Institutional Management*, PURDUE UNIVERSITY

ABSTRACT

This chapter will introduce and briefly discuss key human resource issues that affect the way hospitality companies are managed. There are many internal and external issues that dictate how we do business. In addition, hospitality managers need to choose approaches among the many that are available where human resource dictates do not exist. This chapter will provide some guidance as to the prevailing requirements, as well as the available options that may work best in particular situations.

OBJECTIVES

At the end of this chapter the student should be able to:

1. Outline and discuss the key principles of human resource management.

2. Understand and discuss the critical importance of job analysis, job design, job descriptions, and job specifications.

3. Describe key recruiting practices.

4. Discuss the process of selection and describe various selection approaches.

5. Demonstrate a familiarity with a variety of evaluation and appraisal approaches.

6. Establish the role that human resource management plays in overall business success.

7. Introduce and outline key legal issues that impact human resource management.

Introduction

Human resources is the management of people. Managers and supervisors at all organizational levels manage people. The number of people and the time frame for their decisions involving those people is determined by their position on the organizational chart. Supervisors manage small groups of staff members. Middle managers manage a larger number. One of the noticeable things about management is that as a manager advances up the corporate ladder, he or she is responsible for managing more and more people either directly or indirectly. For instance, the president or CEO of an organization is responsible for the management of all staff members. A second noticeable managerial fact is that as a manager advances, the time frame of his or her decisions expands as well.

Few hospitality management students will become human resource specialists or will manage human resources departments, but they all must become proficient at managing human resources at some level. As a result, all hospitality industry managers must develop human resource management skills.

Human resources is a continuous process. Each step builds on the other. The process is illustrated in Figure 2.

Job Analysis, Design, Description, and Specification

The first step in the human resource process is designing what work will be done in a job. To human resource specialists and managers this is known as job analysis. Job analysis is defined as identifying the elements or factors that go into a job, i.e., what a job consists of. Each job contains at least four factors: tasks, responsibilities, behaviors, and personal characteristics. Job analysis is the method managers use to determine what role each of these factors plays in a job. (See Figure 3.)

Job design, the second step in the continuous human resource process, involves determining how work is to be done. As we already noted, each job has specific tasks, responsibilities, behaviors, and personal characteristics associated with it. Each job also has specific ways in which it must be carried out. While managers sometimes like to blame employees for a job poorly done, most problems in

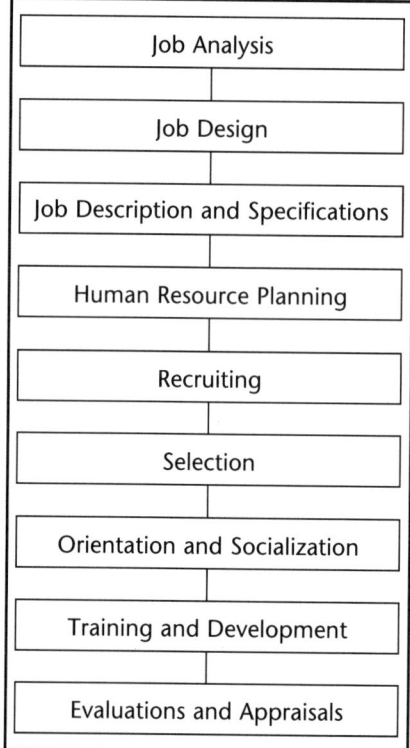

Figure 2. The Human Resource Process.

| Job Analysis |
| Job Design |
| Job Description and Specifications |
| Human Resource Planning |
| Recruiting |
| Selection |
| Orientation and Socialization |
| Training and Development |
| Evaluations and Appraisals |

hospitality organizations are not associated with the person doing the job, but rather with how the job itself is designed. When a job is well designed and completely understood, it is usually conducted thoroughly and effectively. However, a poorly designed job generally results in just the opposite. No matter how well intentioned the staff member, problems are more likely to occur when jobs are poorly designed.

There are four major approaches to job design:

1. **Job simplification**—breaking jobs down into their smallest part and then assessing how best to conduct that small task.
2. **Job enlargement**—horizontally broadening the components of a job by adding tasks that usually require similar skills.
3. **Job rotation**—cross-training employees to do more than one job.
4. **Job enrichment**—adding responsibilities to a job to vertically expand what it entails.

Figure 1. Time Frame for Management Decisions.

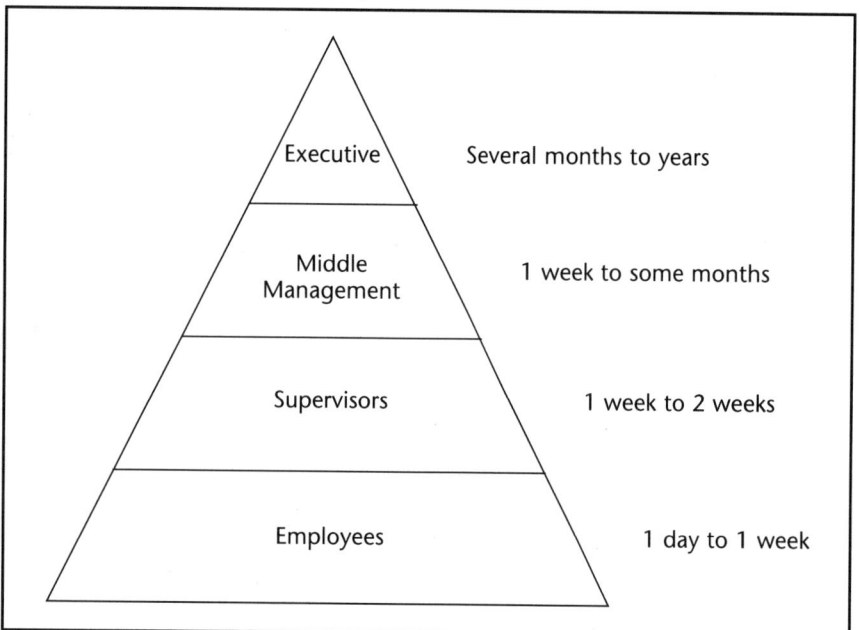

Executive — Several months to years

Middle Management — 1 week to some months

Supervisors — 1 week to 2 weeks

Employees — 1 day to 1 week

Figure 3. Steps in Job Analysis.

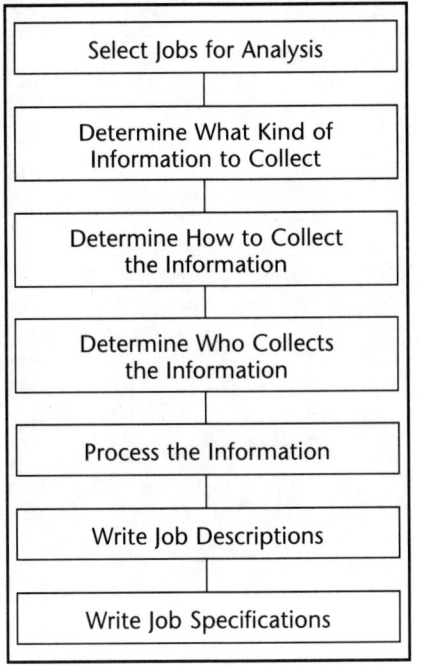

Select Jobs for Analysis

Determine What Kind of Information to Collect

Determine How to Collect the Information

Determine Who Collects the Information

Process the Information

Write Job Descriptions

Write Job Specifications

Source: Woods (1997).

Of these, only job enrichment is seen as a significant method of motivating employees to do a good job over a long period of time. In contrast, each of the other three methods typically results in adding more boring tasks to already existing boring tasks, or adding responsibility without control.

After managers conduct a job analysis and design the job, they must then write job descriptions and specifications for each position. This is the third step in the human resource process. While a simple step, many organizations fail to adequately complete this important aspect of the human resource cycle. As illustrated in Figure 4, job descriptions explain and summarize what the job entails. They identify the duties of the job, specific activities that must be conducted within the job, work conditions of the job, responsibilities, and expectations of performance on the job.

Job specifications delineate what types of skills, behaviors, knowledge, and abilities are required for the job. A properly written job specification serves as a filter which allows only qualified personnel to apply, while preventing the unqualified from wasting valuable management time.

Human Resource Planning

The fourth major step in the human resource process is planning. Effective planning of human resource needs is key to the delivery of quality goods and services. A simple example which illustrates this is the impact a manager has on a restaurant if he or she correctly anticipates the correct number, as well as the knowledge, skills, and abilities (KSAs) of personnel needed on a given shift. If correctly planned, the operation will run smoothly during that time. The opposite is true of improper planning. In a more macro sense, correctly planning the number as well as the KSAs that an organization must have over a longer period of time, for instance, a month or a year, will also more likely result in an effective operation. Therefore, effective human resource planning includes not only short-term anticipation of needs but long-term as well. Planning over the long-term includes anticipation of future needs, of course. As a result, this type of planning involves recruitment, the fourth key step in human resources.

Recruiting

Hiring the right people for the organization is critical. Too often managers are caught in the trap of filling positions with any available person. To borrow a phrase from computing, this "garbage-in, garbage-out" approach consistently leads to human resource problems on the job. Successful hospitality organizations consistently follow the same recruiting steps over and over to insure that the right number and types of personnel are recruited. The first of these steps is pre-recruitment planning.

Pre-recruitment planning consists of reviewing job analyses, job descriptions, and job specifications to ensure that one knows what KSAs are needed for the job. After this is done,

Figure 4. Job Description: Assistant Director of Human Resources.

Description of Work:

General Statement of Duties: Perform complex technical work in recruitment, examination, classification, wage and salary administration, training, and other functions of a personnel program.

Supervision: Reports directly to Director of Personnel. Exercises supervision over assigned personnel.

Work Performed:

	% TIME
Recruitment	20%
Examination administration	15%
Classification of jobs and employees	20%
Wage and salary administration	20%
Training	25%

Work Conditions: Work primarily in office setting. Recruitment conducted in out-of-house settings including schools, colleges and universities; churches and synagogues; apartment complexes; youth, senior citizen, and community group environments.

Source: Woods (1997).

managers must identify and review the applicable laws and regulations that cover each position to be filled and determine how the organization wants to advertise the positions. Since recruiting is a two-way process in which both the applicants and the organization learn, hospitality managers must also determine what message they wish to send to potential recruits, and what information they hope to gain about the recruits and the outside world in the process.

After these first pre-recruitment steps are complete, managers then turn their attention to the issue of where to recruit. Both internal recruitment (recruiting from among the existing staff) and external recruitment (recruiting from outside the organization) can be successful if appropriately applied. Both approaches offer considerable advantages and disadvantages. For instance, recruiting internally often improves the morale of employees who see opportunities that encourage them to remain with the organization. In addition, managers often have much better information on internal recruits than on external recruits. Since internal recruits already know the organizational system, this type of recruiting also costs less and can result in lowered training costs. Disadvantages include the promotion of inbreeding, in the sense that it is possible that internal recruiting may reduce the amount of collective information that an organization knows about its external environment. Internal recruiting can also cause potential political and morale problems for those not recruited. Finally, since every internally recruited person results in the need to fill another position, this approach can lead to causing critical gaps in one department by filling those of another.

External recruiting has the advantages of bringing new ideas into the organization and giving recruiters an opportunity to see how things are on the outside. It provides the opportunity and motivation for managers and recruiters to think about how others see their organization, and it serves as

a form of advertising about the company. On the other hand, external recruiting has the disadvantages of creating morale problems internally among employees who may want a posted job; it may cost more because of the need to identify the KSAs of applicants and because of the cost of advertising for recruits. With external recruiting it may be more difficult to find a good "fit" for the organization, and as external recruits typically require more training, productivity may be lower for a period of time.

The final steps in the recruitment process include identifying recruitment sources, or determining where to recruit. Some hospitality managers have success in recruiting at schools and colleges, others recruit better through job placement agencies, religious organizations, senior citizen groups, friends of current employees, or a variety of other resources. Each has its advantages and disadvantages, and managers must thoughtfully consider which is the best for their organization at that particular point in time.

Selection

The sixth major step in human resources is selecting applicants. Unwanted turnover can be reduced and productivity increased by selecting the right personnel for the job. However, even knowing this, many hospitality managers pay too little attention to this important aspect of the human resource process.

Selection contains several important human resource considerations for managers. Perhaps the first is determining the validity of the selection process. Validity refers to the measurement of what is designed to be measured. In terms of selection, managers must be concerned about both criterion-related validity (the extent to which their selection techniques accurate predict success on the job) and content validity (the extent to which their selection techniques consider what is needed to complete the whole job, not just part of it). To

Reduce unwanted turnover and increase productivity by selecting the right personnel for the job.

date, too few hospitality organizations have considered whether or not the predictors of success they use actually work. Instead, most rely primarily on the opinions of recruiters in face-to-face interviews and their interpretations of resumes or completed application blanks as the criterion which determines whether or not an applicant is likely to perform the job well.

Selection also includes determining whether managers will use a "multiple hurdles" approach to selection or a "compensatory" approach. The two differ greatly. The multiple hurdles approach allows applicants to be eliminated at any point during the selection process if they fail to display needed qualities or to "get over a hurdle." In effect, this approach requires applicants to be able to perform each of the qualifications and specifications of a job. A compensatory approach, in contrast, allows applicants to be very good at some responsibilities of a job and not as good at others, and still qualify for consideration.

Selection in some hospitality organizations might also include pre-employment tests used to determine whether or not applicants meet the criterion of the position. Pre-employment tests in use in hospitality include:

- Paper-and-pencil tests (tests of job knowledge)
- Honesty tests
- Physical and motor ability tests (to evaluate whether or not the applicant can physically perform the work)
- Body fluid tests (to determine drug and/or alcohol abuse problems)
- Work samples (to determine whether applicants can perform specific aspects of the job)
- Assessment centers (designed to evaluate overall performance in the job position).

Each of these pre-employment tests can serve to help managers identify potentially qualified applicants for a job. However, before performing any pre-employment tests, managers must consider the impact that they might have on applicants and their civil rights. Tests that discriminate against any applicant should never be used; there is potential for legal action by an applicant who is turned down for a job. Generally speaking, in order to use any pre-employment test, managers must use the same test for all applicants in order to avoid discrimination charges. For example, if body fluid tests are used to determine whether applicants are using drugs or alcohol which may impair their work on the job, managers must test all applicants. Testing some applicants while not testing others is discriminatory.

A second example involves physical and motor ability tests. The Americans with Disabilities Act (ADA), which went into effect in 1994, protects all Americans. According to this law, those with disabilities cannot be legally discriminated against if they can perform the "essential functions" of the job. In this case managers must determine whether or not applicants can perform the key elements of the job. For instance, a hearing-impaired cook is

still eligible for a cooking position, even though the food and beverage operation has used a system of "calling out" orders in the past. Because the ADA requires employers to make reasonable accommodations for the disabled on the job, foodservice operations may need to change their system from verbal ordering to written ordering in order to allow a hearing-impaired applicant to apply.

Interviewing is the final part of the selection process. Interviewing, while not totally reliable as a predictor of job success, is the most frequently used selection technique. While perhaps considered the easiest method of predicting job success, interviewing can be fraught with the potential for error. Because interviewing relies on the ability of one person to interpret the ability of another to perform on the job, a variety of personality-related errors can occur during the process. For instance, interviewing is subject to:

- Similarity errors (liking or disliking an applicant because he or she is similar in some ways to the recruiter or other employees)
- Contrast errors (liking or disliking an applicant because he or she is dissimilar to others)
- Focusing on negative information (it is common for interviewers to look for the reasons why an applicant will not fit in, rather than why they will fit in)
- First impression bias (basing opinions on first impressions)
- Race, sex, or age bias (allowing pre-existing opinions about races, sex, or age to influence interviewing decisions)
- Halo effect and devil's horns effect (seeing someone as "angelic" or "devilish" overall based on a single attribute or behavior)
- Poor listening (many managers are not good active listeners)
- Recency errors (relying more on immediately-past performance rather than on a string of performance)

- Leniency errors (being too lenient with everyone)
- Severity errors (being too severe with everyone)

Any of these errors can lead to making the wrong decision about an applicant, and all of them are quite common.

Another issue to consider in interviewing is the type of interviews used. For instance, managers may choose to use unstructured interviews (ask different applicants different sets of questions), structured interviews (ask each applicant exactly the same set of questions, in the same order, and if possible, with the same intent and emotion), semi-structured interviews (some structured, some unstructured), or even stress interviews (in which applicants are intentionally placed in stressful situations to see how they would perform). Each approach has advantages and disadvantages.

Before using any interviewing approach a manager should consider the legal implications of that method. For instance, if unstructured interviews are chosen, applicants can potentially complain that interviewers unfairly discriminated against one person or group by choosing to ask tougher interview questions than they did with another person or group. On the other hand, structured interviews may not allow the valuable diversity of an applicant to be exposed. Managers may also choose to ask questions that require only yes/no responses (direct approach), open-ended responses (indirect approach), or both (eclectic approach). Generally, asking open-ended questions leads to the collection of more information because this method allows the respondent to elaborate his or her responses.

Orientation and Socialization

The seventh major step in the human resource process is orientation and/or socialization. While finding the right personnel for the organization and the job are critical to eventual success, orienting and socializing these people to the company, department, and individual goals provides the basis for getting off on the right foot. Since unwanted turnover most often occurs in the first 30–60 days of employment, orientation and/or socialization are viewed as critical turnover-reduction strategies in many organizations.

Orientation of new employees to a job or organizational environment is designed to reduce the stress a new employee feels on the job. It is well known that crossing organizational boundaries, either entering or leaving an organization, can cause stress. Reducing that stress through orientation can allow new employees to perform at higher levels in shorter periods of time.

Two types of orientation are generally used. The first, general orientation informs new employees about the organization itself and about generic or general policies and procedures or guidelines used within the organization. General orientation can include such items as informing new employees about the organization's mission, its management philosophy, general policies and procedures, insurance, benefits, personnel forms used in the organization, and compensation. Specific job orientation defines exactly what employees do on the job, whom they report to and who reports to them, the location of equipment used on the job, the department's relationship with other departments, performance appraisals or evaluations used for the position, and the actual work environment. Many organizations provide an orientation kit to new employees which includes written job descriptions, organizational charts, information on compensation, benefits and insurance, and a variety of other useful information that employees can take home with them to study.

Socialization and orientation differ primarily in their intent. The intent of orientation is to provide new employees with accurate information about the job and the organization. In contrast, the intent of socialization

is to provide new employees with information about the unwritten rules, values, norms, acceptable behaviors associated with the job or the organization, and information about the organizational culture. While research has shown that new employees who are successfully socialized to their jobs generally perform at higher levels more quickly, many managers still do not take socialization seriously enough. In addition, managers not fully informed about socialization may choose the wrong socialization strategies or tactics. (See Figure 5.)

Training and Development

The eighth step in the human resource process really consists of two processes, training and development. A total of about $50 billion is spent on these two processes annually in the U.S. Some of this money is well spent and some is wasted. Training generally refers to teaching employees how to perform their jobs better or to acquire new job skills. Development, on the other hand, generally includes

such items as personal improvement, career development, and retirement planning.

As illustrated in Figure 6, training is a continuous cycle. It begins with conducting a needs analysis to determine if a discrepancy exits between wanted and delivered performances, behaviors, or outcomes.

This needs analysis can be conducted in a variety of ways. In some companies the manager alone determines the need for training. However, there are better ways. Needs analyses can be conducted by advisory committees, conducting work sampling through the examination of job performance measurements; through attitude surveys; or a variety of other methods.

The second stage in the training cycle is the identification of training objectives. Unless managers identify exactly what it is that they hope to accomplish by training, the process is likely to fail. By establishing training objectives or goals they expect trainees to reach after training, training is more effective.

Figure 5. Socialization Strategies.

1. *Formal vs. Informal.* In formal strategies, newcomers are segregated from other organizational members. In informal strategies, newcomers are included with members; much of the learning takes place in their natural environments.

2. *Individual vs. Collective.* Newcomers either go through socialization alone or as part of a group.

3. *Sequential vs. Non-sequential.* Newcomers either go through identifiably different stages or the process is one single transitional stage.

4. *Fixed vs. Variable.* Fixed strategies have specific timetables for certain types of training; variable strategies have no timetables.

5. *Tournament vs. Contest.* In tournaments, newcomers win to move on the next stage; in contests, newcomers are given multiple opportunities to succeed.

6. *Serial vs. Disjunctive.* Serial strategies involve current members teaching newcomers to "act as we act"; disjunctive strategies allow for new behaviors.

7. *Investiture vs. Divestiture.* In investiture, the process is one of "giving" information to newcomers; in divestiture, the process is one of taking old habits away.

Source: Adapted from John Van Maanen, "People Processing: Strategies of Organization Socialization," *Organizational Dynamics* (Summer 1978): 240–259.

Figure 6. The Training Cycle.

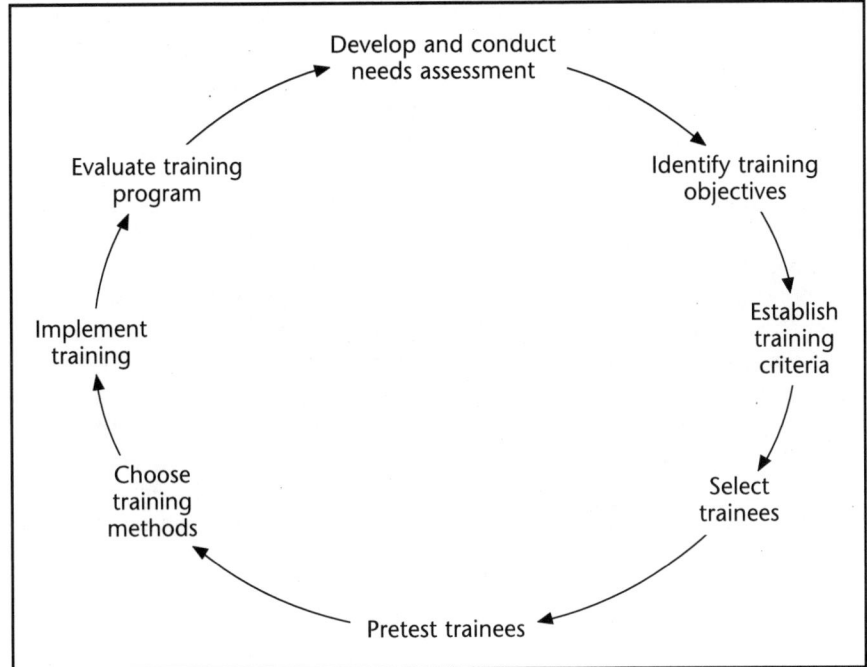

Develop and conduct needs assessment

Evaluate training program

Identify training objectives

Implement training

Establish training criteria

Choose training methods

Select trainees

Pretest trainees

Source: Woods (1997).

The third stage of the training cycle is the establishment of training criteria. Criteria are the benchmarks hospitality managers establish to measure the effectiveness of their training process. For example, a manager may establish complete knowledge of the menu as the training criteria for a program designed to teach employees to be more effective at presenting menu options to customers.

The fourth stage of the training cycle is the selection and pre-testing of trainees. Trainees can be either new or existing employees. Not all employees require training. Some already know the content information which is to be presented in a planned training process. If this is true, then these employees will likely consider training a waste of time. By measuring what employees already know, managers are able to effectively establish who should receive training. This pre-testing provides managers with the information they need to determine who should be trained. Many successful managers enhance this process by establishing two training groups—one group which will be pre-tested for

knowledge, trained and then re-tested for added knowledge, and a second group which receives only pre-and post-testing and no actual training. By measuring the performance in both groups before and after training implementation, managers can determine the effectiveness of their training process.

Managers must also choose the appropriate training methods. Many different methods are available to managers. Some methods are better with individuals and small groups, while others are better with larger groups. Some are better at training employees' technical skills and others are better at training behavioral skills. Which technique a manager chooses to use can often determine the overall effectiveness of training. No single technique is better than another. This is why many training specialists refer to training as "situational" in nature.

Training can consist of both off-the-job and on-the-job training. Off-the-job training is primarily concerned with teaching employees new processes, techniques, or behaviors—

all in environments other than the actual workplace. Lectures, case studies, programmed instruction (computer or paper-and-pencil training in which trainees generally teach themselves), role playing, and other techniques are effective in off-the-job training. On-the-job training, often called simply OJT and sometimes job-instruction training (or JIT), is concerned with training employees in their workplace or at their workstation.

The final step in the training cycle is evaluation. Unless managers evaluate their training process, they do not know whether or not their employees have prospered from the process. Four types of evaluation can be used:

1. Reaction evaluations to determine the views of trainees about the program.
2. Learning-acquired evaluations to test what trainees learned in the process.
3. On-the-job-behavior evaluations to determine whether behaviors have been affected.
4. Results-oriented evaluations used to determine the effect training has had on performance, production and so on.

Evaluations can be in the form of tests (oral, written, or performance), observations of work progress, or even observations of simulations of work. The ultimate test of training, of course, is the impact that is has on the organization or the department. Good programs have positive effects while poor programs have either negative or no effect.

Once evaluation is complete, the training cycle begins again. In fact, evaluation closely resembles the first step in the training cycle—needs analysis—in the sense that it measures what employees know or need to know.

Evaluations and Appraisals

The ninth step in the human resource process is staff evaluation or appraisal.

Many, perhaps most, employees begin a new job enthusiastically and excited about the prospects of long-term employment and growth. However, within months the honeymoon often fades and managers find it difficult to motivate their personnel. Several methods of encouraging and insuring long-term performance are available to managers in the form of performance evaluations or appraisals. While useful in motivating performance, this is not the only use for performance evaluations or appraisals. Performance evaluations or appraisals are useful in compensation, promotion, transfer, grievance, or discipline decisions as well.

Effective performance evaluation or appraisal procedures must meet specific criteria. For instance, they must:

❖ Measure what they claim to measure (construct validity)
❖ Measure the entire issue, not just a part of it (content validity)
❖ Be consistent (they must always measure the same thing)
❖ Have inter-rater reliability (or agreement between raters) because so many different people typically are involved in the evaluations or appraisals

Earlier we mentioned errors that occur in selection. These same errors, halo effect and devil's horns, recency, leniency and so on are also common with performance evaluations or appraisals.

Several choices must be made when deciding how to evaluate staff performance. The first is to decide which type of rating system to use. Managers can use either trait-based systems (in which personal characteristics are the focus), behavior-based systems (in which displayed behaviors are the focus), or they may use results-based systems (in which the focus is on more improved productivity results). In addition, managers must choose from a variety of approaches for evaluations. One approach is to

use peer appraisals (or evaluations by peers of their co-workers). Another is to use managerial appraisals (wherein managers evaluate employee performance), self-appraisals, guest appraisals, or even third-party appraisals (wherein external appraisal experts evaluate performance). Each method can be effective when used properly.

Managers must also choose how to rank performance. Among the choices are the simple ranking methods in which managers simply rank employees from best to worst on whatever dimension is being evaluated. The alternative evaluation method allows managers to choose first the best performer, then the worst, then the second best, then second worst, and so on until all employees have been chosen. Paired comparisons (Mary Sue vs. Jim, Mary Sue vs. April, April vs. Jim, and so on) can also be an effective method.

In addition to the previous choices managers must make about performance evaluations or appraisals they also must decide on exactly what method of evaluation is to be used. There are a variety of methods available. The most common method is the graphic rating scale in which the rater rates employees on 10–15 criteria using a 1–5 scale (from excellent to poor). While effective in some instances, this method often falls prey to leniency, severity, and central tendency (ranking everyone in the mid-range) errors. Behaviorally anchored rating scales, in which raters rate employees on dimensions inherent with the job, is a more effective method, yet it takes considerable time to develop. Other methods include the critical incidents approach, in which raters rate the performance of employees in comparison to critical incidents performed on the job; narrative essays, in which raters write narrative reports on the performance of employees; and management-by-objective, in which employees and raters determine in advance what they will accomplish and then are rated on their accomplishment of those goals.

Each method can be effectively used in different situations. The key to performance evaluations or appraisals lies in training raters how to conduct them effectively. Training raters about potential errors, different methods of evaluation, different techniques for appraisal, and the like, can all lead to greater reliability and consistency in the process.

Managers often wonder how often they should conduct evaluations or appraisals. There is no correct answer. Some companies conduct annual evaluations and appraisals effectively while for others this process does not work because too much emphasis is put on recent performance or behaviors. Others conduct evaluations or appraisals bi-annually, monthly, and so on. Some managers even conduct daily performance evaluations or appraisals by sitting down with the employee at the end of each shift and reviewing what went right, what went wrong, and planning for improvement, although this is rare because of the time involved. While an argument can be made that the more frequently evaluations or appraisals are conducted, the more likely desired performance and behaviors will result, we must also recognize that managers have a variety of duties in their positions, and that they may not have the time for such evaluations. On the other hand, some might argue that a manager's most important task is the constant improvement of employee performance and behaviors and therefore no amount of time would be considered a waste. How companies view this issue is determined by their management philosophy of what managers should do.

Conclusion

This chapter outlined the principal activities managers perform in the human resource process. Managers are often involved in other human resource-related activities as well. For instance, managers often are involved in compensation administration, incentive and benefit administration, labor union negotiation and collective bargaining, health, safety and employee assistance programs, social responsibility and ethics issues, and discipline issues. While there is much that managers should know about each issue, this is not the place for that discussion. Managers and students interested in information about these issues should consult the reading list provided at the end of this chapter for more information.

It is important to remember that human resources is an evolving process. Managers today are likely to have to develop new techniques and approaches for dealing with problems and issues in the future because of the rapidly changing nature of the hospitality workforce. The changing values of employees, the shrinking and changing demographics of the labor market, societal pressure to behave in a socially responsible manner, rapid consolidation of the hospitality industry through mergers and acquisitions, globalization, undesirable high turnover, and a variety of other modern ills all affect how hospitality personnel are managed today. For that reason, managers and students should hold the view that effective human resource management is something that they will continue to learn about and alter throughout their managerial lives. Resting on what you now know or believe to be true or effective will undoubtedly lead to failure at some point in the future. History has proven time and time again that the process of managing people changes with the time. For example, there was a time, not too many years ago in fact, when managers were faced with a glut of potential employees. Today there is a scarcity. There was also a time when the predominant managerial philosophy of the day emphasized motivating employees through threats and punishments. Today we empha-

size the use of positive reinforcements far more often than threats.

Laws and regulations that affect human resources will also undoubtedly change. Beginning with the Equal Employment Opportunity Act of 1963, which provided that men and women doing the same work should be paid the same amount, the federal and state governments in the U.S. have taken a more and more active role in determining how business is to be conducted. As operators know, these laws seem to progress in the degree to which they influence the daily operations of business. In the future, managers will likely spend more and more of their time on making sure that their organizations operate within the laws. While some managers believe that many of these laws are unfair, history has shown that the laws were enacted only because abuse by business was first observed. In other words, the argument can be made that if business had established ethical practices in the first place, these laws would not be necessary.

Laws That Affect the Human Resource Perspective

In 1964 the U.S. Civil Rights Law was passed. Title VII of that law prohibited workplace discrimination on the basis of race, color, religion, sex, or national origin. Because of its wide-sweeping nature, this law dramatically changed the relationship between employers and employees. Since 1964 several additional laws have been passed which affect the manner in which human resource management is conducted. These laws and their principal components are mentioned here because of their effect of the human resource perspective. Only the most significant laws are

mentioned. Several other laws and executive orders also affect human resource practices. It is important to remember that each of these laws affects the entire human resource process, from job analysis through performance evaluations and appraisals. Managers must abide by these laws throughout the human resource process.

❖ **Civil Rights Law–1964**—forbids workplace discrimination on the basis of race, color, religion, sex, or national origin. This law prohibited employers from taking any workplace action which discriminated against these "protected groups."

❖ **Age Discrimination in Employment Act (ADEA)–1967**—Prohibits discrimination on the basis of age for those over 40 years old.

❖ **Immigration Reform and Control Act (IRCA)–1986**—Prohibits recruiting and hiring of aliens not eligible for U.S. employment.

❖ **Pregnancy Discrimination Act–1978**—Prohibits employers from discriminating against pregnant women.

❖ **Americans with Disabilities Act (ADA)–1992**—Prohibits employers from discriminating against the disabled and provides that organizations must make reasonable accommodations to make the workplace accessible to disabled people.

❖ **Executive Order 11246** (Issued by President Lyndon Johnson in 1965)—Established affirmative action policies for U.S. government contractors (i.e., any business doing business with the government).

❖ **Family and Medical Leave Act–1993**—Provides for employees to take up to 12 weeks of unpaid leave for birth, adoption, care for elderly or ill parent, spouse, or child, or to undergo treatment.

Questions and Assignments

1. Define human resource management.

2. Describe briefly the first three steps of the human resource process. Using your library resources or the web browser and search engine of your choice, identify an article that discusses one or all of these steps. Summarize your response and bring your findings to class for discussion with your team or classmates.

3. Which of the four job design approaches do you favor? Justify your position.

4. Define recruiting, and discuss the various steps and approaches to the recruitment process. Using your library resources or the web browser and search engine of your choice, identify an article that discusses recruitment in hospitality. Summarize your findings and be prepared for class discussion.

5. Discuss validity and selection. What are the key issues?

6. Differentiate the "multiple hurdles approach" from the "compensatory approach" to selection. Which of the approaches do you favor? Justify your choice. Summarize your results and be prepared for class discussion.

7. List and describe the various pre-employment tests that are available in the selection process. Using your library resources or the web browser and search engine of your choice, identify an article that discusses pre-employment testing. Which of the approaches do you favor? Justify your choice. Summarize your results and be prepared for class discussion.

8. How can a pre-employment test be discriminatory?

9. List and describe the various personality-related errors that are a concern in the employment interview process. Using your library resources or the web browser and search engine of your choice, identify an article that discusses interviewing. Summarize your findings and be prepared for class discussion.

10. What is the role of orientation and socialization? How did orientation and socialization take place for you in your most recent job? Critique the process as you experienced it. Summarize your findings and be prepared for class discussion.

11. Discuss the key issues involved in training employees. Using your library resources or the web browser and search engine of your choice, identify an article that discusses training in hospitality. Summarize your findings and be prepared for class discussion.

12. Discuss the role of performance appraisals. When were you last appraised of your performance on the job? How was the appraisal conducted? Critique the process as you experienced it. Summarize your findings and be prepared for class discussion.

13. Using your library resources or the web browser and search engine of your choice, identify an article that discusses performance appraisal in hospitality. Summarize your findings and be prepared for class discussion.

14. Consider the paragraph on laws that affect the human resources perspective. Using your library resources or the web browser and search engine of your choice, identify a hospitality article that discusses one of these laws. Summarize your findings and be prepared for class discussion.

15. Perform an informational interview with a human resource professional. The procedure is discussed in Chapter One. Check with your instructor to see how the students are to avoid contacting the same HR professional repeatedly.

16. Do you find a career in hospitality human resources attractive? Provide your reasoning.

Bibliography and Suggested Readings

Bernardin, J. H. (1997). *Human Resource Management; An Experiential Approach*, 2nd ed. New York, NY: McGraw-Hill Companies.

Forrest, L. C., Jr. (1996). *Training for the Hospitality Industry*, 2nd ed. East Lansing, MI: Educational Institute of the American Hotel & Motel Association.

Milkovich, G. T. (1994). *Human Resources Management*, 7th ed. Burr Ridge, IL: Irwin Publications.

Mill, R. C. (1989). *Managing for Productivity in the Hospitality Industry*. New York, NY: Van Nostrand Reinhold.

Woods, R. H. (1992). *Managing Hospitality Human Resources*. East Lansing, MI: Educational Institute of the American Hotel & Motel Association.

Woods, R. H. (1997). *Managing Hospitality Human Resources*, 2nd ed. East Lansing, MI: Educational Institute of the American Hotel & Motel Association, 51.

Woods, R. H. & King, J. Z. (1996). *Managing for Quality in the Hospitality Industry*. East Lansing, MI: Educational Institute of the American Hotel & Motel Association.

Hospitality Perspectives on Technology

Michael L. Kasavana, *The School of Hospitality Business*, MICHIGAN STATE UNIVERSITY

ABSTRACT

This chapter will introduce and discuss computer-based technologies that have assisted greatly in hospitality management. Software applications for property management, front office management, revenue management, restaurant management, catering, night audit, and accounting will be introduced as concept, and discussed in functional terms. Hardware related technologies such as PMS interfaces, ECRs, POSs, and beverage control systems will also be discussed. The roles of the hospitality information system (HIS) and systems manager will be explained. The potential role of the Internet and the WWW will be briefly introduced.

OBJECTIVES

At the end of this chapter the student should be able to:

1. Discuss the potential benefits of hospitality technology.

2. Define and describe a number of hospitality software and hardware products in terms of functionality.

3. Explain the role of the systems manager and hospitality information systems.

4. Explain briefly the Internet and the WWW.

5. Discuss how the Internet and the WWW can benefit hospitality managers and employees.

Introduction

Nothing has enhanced the professionalism nor increased the productivity of the hospitality industry more than information technology. Computers have changed the way hotels, restaurants, clubs and casinos plan, coordinate, evaluate, and control operations. Recent technological developments in the management of computers in the lodging industry have significantly affected both front and back office procedures. Hotel staff is no longer dependent upon an assortment of metal racks, a collection of mechanical equipment, or a set of routine clerical tasks. From the moment potential guests contact a property for reservations to the settlement of their accounts, a computer system is capable of monitoring, charting, and recording all transactions between guests and the hotel. Likewise, computer systems technology has also significantly affected foodservice and management activities in food and beverage operations. Restaurateurs are no longer dependent upon mechanical cash registers, volumes of sales journals, and routine clerical procedures. Private clubs are better able to accommodate members' needs with improved operational efficiency. Casinos are capable of tracking "live-action" table games as well as slot machines and auxiliary operations. The dependence of the hospitality industry on computer processing is continuing to grow. In fact, nearly all aspects of the industry employ comprehensive computer-based information systems.

Property Management Systems

A computer-based lodging information system is commonly called a property management system (PMS). Although the components of a PMS may vary, the term "PMS" is generally used to describe the set of computer programs that directly relate to front office and back office activities. "Application software" is the term for computer programs that instruct the hardware of a computer system in what to do, when to do it, and how to do it.

Computerized front office applications consist of a series of software programs (or modules) including reservations, rooms management, and guest accounting functions. A variety of stand-alone applications may also be interfaced with an installed property management system. Popular interfaces include microcomputers, point-of-sale systems, call accounting systems, electronic locking systems, energy management systems, auxiliary guest service devices, and guest-operated devices. Computerized back office applications typically included in back office PMS packages contain modules covering accounting and internal-control functions.

Front Office Applications

While hotel property management systems differ, many of them offer front office application software in relation to reservations, rooms management, and guest accounting functions. A reservation module enables a hotel to rapidly process room requests and generate timely and accurate rooms, revenue, and forecasting reports. Reservations received at a central reservations site can be processed, confirmed, and communicated to the destination property before the reservationist finishes talking with the caller on the telephone. When the destination property uses a property management system, the reservation module receives data directly from the central (or global) reservation system, and in-house reservations records, files, and revenue forecasts are immediately updated. In addition, the reservations data can be automatically reformatted into pre-registration materials and an updated expected-arrivals list can be generated.

Although many other industries started computerization during the 1960s, the hotel industry did not actively pursue the possibilities of automation until the early 1970s. This relatively late start in computerization enabled the hotel industry to benefit from advances in computer technology. When other industries were struggling to upgrade their existing computer systems, hoteliers received greater value for dollars spent on newer computer hardware components and easier-to-operate software packages. This is especially true in regard to the first generation of computerized reservation systems. However, these reservation systems became outdated as technological advances linked reservations directly to comprehensive property management systems. Soon, second generation systems matured and were pushed to their processing capabilities. The implementation of next generation reservation systems has already begun. These global reservation systems more effectively link hotel reservations to systems developed for airlines, car rental agencies, travel agencies, and other travel-related businesses.

Global distribution systems are often formed as joint ventures linking a number of diverse businesses. By directly linking the reservation systems of hotel, airline, car rental, and travel agency companies on a worldwide basis through the Internet or private networks, global distribution systems provide access to travel and tourism inventories around the world. A global distribution system can represent a significant portion of reservations business for many airport and resort properties. Domestic competition for hotel reservation commissions is intense since other segments of the travel industry also operate reservation systems. Airline carriers, travel agencies, car rental companies, and chain hotels offer stiff competition to independent central reservation systems entering the reservations marketplace.

Since the early 1970s, the hospitality industry has seen many independent central reservation systems enter and leave the marketplace. The problems encountered by these systems are not related to difficulties in generating demand for their services. Rather, they are related to servicing demand at an acceptable level of profitability. Expensive computer equipment (hardware components and communication devices), high overhead, and extensive operating costs have made it difficult for many independent central reservation systems to succeed. Increased online interaction between hotel properties and a central reservation office (CRO) decentralizes the reservation function but centralizes marketing and sales efforts in relation to the reservations process. This results in greater control of reservations handling at the property level and increased sales efforts at the CRO on behalf of the participating properties. The goals of a central reservation system are to improve guest service while enhancing profitability and operating efficiency. A CRO accomplishes these goals by: providing access to special room rates and promotional packages, instantly confirming reservations, communicating with major airline, travel, and car rental agencies, and building extensive guest files. Basic services provided by most central reservation systems include automatic room availability updating and corporate-wide marketing.

The term *intersell agency* refers to a reservation network that handles more than one product line. Intersell agencies typically handle reservations for airline flights, car rentals, and hotel rooms. The spirit of an intersell promotion is captured by the expression "one call does it all." Although intersell agencies typically channel their reservation requests directly to individual hotels, some may also communicate with central reservation systems and, on occasion, to a global distribution system.

The proper handling of reservation information is critical to the success of hotel companies and individual properties. Reservations can be made for individuals, groups, tours, or conventions. Each request for accommodations creates a need for an accurate

response in relation to the room types and rates available at a given point in time.

A rooms management module is an important information and communications branch within a front office property management system. It is primarily designed to strengthen the communication links between the front office and the housekeeping department. Most rooms management modules perform the following functions: identify current room status, assist in assigning rooms to guests at check-in, provide information on in-house guests, organize housekeeping activities, provide auxiliary services, and generate useful reports for management.

A rooms management module alerts front desk employees of the status of each room, just as room racks do in non-automated operations. A front desk employee simply enters the room's number, and the current status of the room is displayed immediately on the terminal's screen. Once a room becomes clean and ready for occupancy, housekeeping staff change the rooms status through a terminal in their work area, and the information is immediately communicated to terminals at the front desk. Rooms status reports may also be printed at any time for use by management.

A rooms management module maintains up-to-date information regarding the status of rooms, assists in the assignment of rooms during registration, and helps coordinate many guest services. Since this module replaces most traditional front office equipment, it often becomes a major determinant in the selection of one PMS over another. This module alerts front desk employees of each room's status just as room and information racks do in non-automated environments. For example, with a room rack, an upside-down card without a folio covering it may signify that the previous night's guest has checked out, but that the room has not yet been cleaned for resale. This status will remain unchanged until house-

keeping notifies the front desk that the room is clean and ready for occupancy. In a computerized system, the front desk employee simply enters the room's number at a keyboard and the current status of the room appears immediately on a display screen. Once the room becomes clean and ready for occupancy, housekeeping changes the room's status through a terminal in the housekeeping work area, and the information is immediately communicated to the front desk.

A guest accounting module increases the hotel's control over guest accounts and significantly modifies the night audit routine. Guest accounts are maintained electronically, thereby eliminating the need for folio cards, trays, or posting machinery. The guest accounting module monitors predetermined guest credit limits and provides flexibility through multiple folio formats. When revenue centers are connected to the PMS, remote electronic cash registers or point-of-sale terminals communicate with the front desk, and guest charges are automatically posted to the appropriate folios. At checkout, outstanding account balances are transferred automatically to the city ledger (accounts receivable) for collection.

The guest accounting module is considered to be the most critical component of a front office system. The creation of electronic folios enables remote point-of-sale terminals to post charges directly to guest and non-guest accounts. The guest accounting module gives management considerable control over financial aspects of the hotel's guest cycle. This front office module is primarily responsible for online charge postings, automatic file updating (auditing) and maintenance, and folio display/printing upon demand. In addition, guest accounting modules may provide electronic controls over such areas as folio handling, account balances, cashier reconciliation, food and beverage guest check control, account auditing, and accounts receivable. Guest accounting modules take responsibility for creating and monitoring various types of guest accounts (referred to as folios), procedures for posting charges to folios, maintaining accurate accounts, managing account settlement, and producing managerial reports.

Revenue Management

Hotel sales office staff spend a great part of each day processing paperwork related to information collected through prospecting, selling, booking, and reporting. At many properties, much of this time consuming and costly effort is handled with technology. In a fully automated sales office, every salesperson with a computer terminal has immediate access to guestroom control information. Bookings and cancellations can be quickly processed as they occur—even as the salesperson is on the telephone with the client. This helps ensure that every salesperson has access to exactly the same information, and that "definite" and "tentative" bookings are clearly identified to prevent errors. Also, an automated sales office system can produce reports that provide information on accounts, bookings, market segments, sales staff productivity, average room rates, occupancy, revenue, service history, lost business, and important marketing data. Many of these reports would take several hours to produce manually.

Yield management, also called revenue management, is a set of demand forecasting techniques used to determine whether room rates should be adjusted (raised or lowered) and whether a reservation request should be accepted or rejected in order to maximize revenue. Yield management is based on supply and demand. Prices tend to rise when demand exceeds supply; prices tend to fall when supply exceeds demand. One of the principal computations involved in yield management is yield, which is the ratio of actual revenue to potential revenue. Actual revenue is the revenue generated by the number of rooms sold. Potential revenue is the amount of money that the property would receive if all of its rooms were sold at full rack rates.

There are many formulas used to implement yield management strategies. Although the individual computations involving yield management can be performed manually, doing so is very difficult and time consuming. The most efficient means of handling data and generating yield statistics is through a computer. Sophisticated yield management software can integrate room demand and room price statistics, and project the highest revenue-generating product mix.

Night Audit

In a non-automated property, the night auditor must post all room rates, taxes, and any departmental charges not posted earlier in the day. The night auditor also balances all guest, non-guest, and departmental accounts. In an automated property, the system update routine takes responsibility for completing these tasks. The ongoing nature of the property management system design has led to a simplification of the audit and enables hotels to perform auditing tasks much more rapidly than is possible in non-automated environments.

A system update performs many of the same functions as those performed by the night audit routine in non-automated properties. System updates are run daily to allow for report production, system file reorganization, system maintenance, and to provide an end-of-day time frame.

The update routine normally requires the user (auditor, systems manager, or another designated employee) to respond to brief system instructions and then monitor the computer's execution of a predetermined set of software applications. Employees no longer have to perform tedious auditing tasks during the slow early morning hours; an equivalent routine may be initiated at any time during the day.

As part of the system update, the guest accounting module automati-

cally posts charges for room rates and taxes to folios for every occupied guestroom. In addition, the module automatically balances departmental accounts by cashier shift and generates the equivalent of a traditional trial balance. Although postings from remote point-of-sale (POS) terminals are processed electronically (and in some instances automatically), managers can attach a voucher printer to each POS terminal. This creates a tangible cross-reference document. Guest accounting modules can also automatically transfer entries between two folios and perform multiple guest splits for any accounting transaction. Multiple guest splits involve charges that are to be divided among a group of guests. For example, the cost of a cocktail reception may be shared by several in-house guests.

A computer-based audit trail consists of cross-references from source document serial numbers, workshifts, cashiers, POS terminals, and departmental (control folio) accounts. Guest accounting modules generally use enough reference codes to enable cashiers to identify the origin (location) of entries and to verify amounts posted to folios with minimal cross-checking against charge vouchers or source documents. Well documented folios reduce the chance of error when charges are posted to accounts. Reducing posting errors may also minimize charges disputed by guests at checkout.

PMS Interfaces

PMS interface applications are stand-alone computer packages that may be linked to a hotel computer system. Although the number and kinds of software packages that may be linked to a hotel system are continuously growing, the most popular interfaces include those discussed in the following sections.

Technology interfaces to larger hotel computer systems have become a popular means of expanding data processing capabilities. Downloading (transferring) data from the hotel systems to another computer enables management to use data contained in the hotel system's software with software applications designed for additional applications. For example, the lodging system may maintain all of a hotel's accounting data. When designing next year's budget, management may wish to base projections on actual transactions of the current accounting period. If management is able to export the necessary accounting data from the PMS to an independent software package, the data can be used by supplemental software applications that may include word processing, electronic spreadsheets, database management, and communications programs.

Restaurant Management Systems

While a hotel property management system consists of modules, a restaurant management system (RMS) functions through a variety of computer hardware components and application software packages.

Food and beverage service applications vary considerably depending upon the type of operation (quick service, table service, or institutional service), kinds of meals offered (breakfast, lunch, dinner, banquets, etc.), and the degree of autonomy given to restaurant management officials (independent, franchise, or corporate).

The term "service applications" is used to refer to software programs used by restaurant management systems to process data related to front-of-the-house food service activities. Service-oriented applications of a restaurant management system rely upon electronic cash register (ECR) and point-of-sale (POS) technology to monitor service area transactions through cashier terminals, precheck terminals, remote workstation devices, and network controllers.

The term "cashier terminal" refers to a POS device that is connected to a cash drawer. A terminal without a cash drawer is commonly called a

precheck terminal. Since POS devices are generally sold as modular units, everything but the basic terminal is considered optional equipment. The cash drawer is no exception. Management may connect several cash drawers to a single cashier terminal. Multiple cash drawers may enhance management's cash control system when several cashiers work at the same cashier terminal during the same shift. Each cashier can be assigned a separate cash drawer so that, at the end of the shift, cash drawer receipts are individually reconciled.

Precheck terminals are used to enter orders, not to settle accounts. For example, a server can use a precheck terminal located in a dining room service station to relay orders to the appropriate kitchen and bar production areas, but cannot use the terminal to settle guest checks. Only cashier terminals can be used for cash settlement.

A POS device with a cash drawer can normally support both prechecking and cashiering functions. For example, an employee at a cashier stand in a hotel restaurant may serve as the cashier for the food service outlet and as an order taker for room service. When answering room service calls, the employee uses the cashier terminal as a precheck terminal. The cashier terminal relays the room service orders to the appropriate kitchen and bar production areas. Before delivering the room service order, a room service employee stops at the cashier station and picks up the printed guest check from the cashier. After delivering the order, the room service employee presents the settled or signed guest check to the cashier, who then uses the cashier terminal to close the guest check or transfer the folio charge within the system.

The term electronic cash register refers to an independent (stand-alone) computer system. The cash register frame houses the necessary three components of a computer system: an input/output device, a central processing unit, and storage (memory) capability. A point-of-sale

terminal, on the other hand, contains its own input/output device and may even possess a small storage (memory) capacity, but it does not contain its own central processing unit. In order for POS transactions to be processed, the terminal must be interfaced with (connected to) a central processing unit that is located outside of the terminal's housing. Some food service properties may reduce the cost of automation by interfacing several POS terminals with a large central processing unit. Other operations may find a series of electronic cash registers (ECRs) or POS terminals to be more effective.

ECRs and POS terminals are hardware components. The physical layout and interconnection of hardware components within an automated system is called a configuration. Like all computer hardware components, ECRs and POS terminals require software programs that direct operations, process data, and control output. Service-related application software programs include prechecking, check tracking, sales analysis, time and attendance monitoring, and inventory control packages.

Beverage Control Systems

Automated beverage systems reduce many of the time-consuming management tasks associated with controlling beverage operations. While automated beverage systems vary, most systems can dispense drinks according to the operation's standard drink recipes and count the number of drinks poured.

Automated beverage systems can be programmed to dispense both alcoholic and non-alcoholic drinks with different portion sizes. They can also generate expected sales information based on different pricing periods as defined by management. With many systems the station at which drinks are prepared can be connected to a guest check printer that records every sale as drinks are dispensed. As a control technique, some systems require that a guest check be inserted into the printer before a drink can be dispensed. Most equipment can, and should, be connected to the bar cash register to automatically record all sales generated through automated equipment.

Catering Software

Catering software monitors and controls the activities associated with each stage of catering service. Many of the files created through the use of catering software packages perform functions similar to restaurant management applications. In addition to containing data on all purchased food and beverage products, catering files include data on such nonfood items as labor, serving utensils, production equipment, rental equipment, disposable items, and entertainment options. The more complete this file, the easier it becomes for the caterer to assemble an entire catering service package.

Hospitality Accounting Applications

The number of accounting software modules provided by a back office software package may vary widely. A typical back office system contains application software designed to monitor and process accounts receivable and accounts payable transactions, payroll accounting, and financial reporting. The term "management applications" refers to application software used by restaurant management systems to process data related to back-of-the-house food service activities. Additional back office programs include inventory control and valuation, purchasing, and budgeting. The following sections present an overview of the applications typically included in a back office package.

An accounts receivable module monitors outstanding balances of guest accounts. An account receivable is a dollar amount representing charged purchases made by a guest who has deferred payment for the products and services rendered by

the hotel. Accounts receivable balances can be automatically transferred from front office software applications, or they can be manually posted directly into an accounts receivable program. Once entered into the back office system, account collection begins. Account billings and the aging of accounts receivable can also be monitored by back office software.

The accounts payable module tracks purchases, creditor positions, and the hotel's banking status. Accounts payable activities normally consist of posting purveyor invoices, determining amounts due, and printing checks for payment. Three major files maintained by an accounts payable module are: vendor master file, invoice register file, and check register file

The vendor master file contains an index of vendor names, addresses, telephone numbers and vendor code numbers, standard discount terms (time and percentage), and space for additional information. An invoice register file is a complete list of outstanding invoices cataloged by vendor, invoice date, invoice number, or invoice due date. This file becomes especially important when management wishes to take advantage of vendor discount rates. The calculation and printing of bank checks for payment to vendors is monitored through the check register file. Check production and distribution is summarized into an accounts payable report and reconciled with bank statements.

A payroll accounting module is an important part of a back office software package because of the complexities involved in properly processing time and attendance records, unique employee benefits, pay rates, withholdings, deductions, and required payroll reports. The payroll accounting module must be capable of handling job codes, employee meals, uniform credits, tips, taxes, and other data that affect the net pay of employees. The unique nature of payroll data dictates that special care be taken to maintain an accurate payroll register, to closely control the

issuing of payroll checks, and to protect the confidentiality and propriety of payroll data.

A back office inventory module automates several internal-control and accounting functions. Internal control is essential to efficient hospitality industry operations. By accessing inventory data maintained by an inventory master file, a back office inventory module is generally able to address three of the most common inventory concerns: inventory status, inventory variance, and inventory valuation. "Inventory status" refers to an account of how much of each item is in storage; "inventory variance" refers to differences between a physical count of an item and the balance maintained by the perpetual inventory system; and "inventory valuation" refers to the monetary or dollar value of items in inventory.

A back office purchasing module maintains a purchase order file and a bid specification file. This module enhances management's control over purchasing, ordering, and receiving practices. Using minimum/maximum inventory-level data transferred from the inventory module, the purchasing module generates purchase orders based on an order point established through usage rate and lead-time factors. A purchasing module may also use a zero-based inventory system and generate purchase orders based on projected sales volume.

The use of a financial reporting module, also called a general ledger module, involves the specification of a chart of accounts (a list of financial statement accounts and their account numbers) and a systematic approach to recording transactions. The design of the general ledger module is often crucial to an effective back office system. The financial reporting module is generally capable of tracking accounts receivable, accounts payable, cash, and adjusting entries. In addition, most financial reporting modules are capable of accessing data from front office and back office modules to prepare financial statements, which include the balance sheet, the statement of income (and supporting departmental schedules), and a variety of reports for use by management.

Hospitality Information Systems

A hospitality information system (HIS) can be defined as a collection of interrelated and interdependent subsystems dependent upon a coordinating network that supports the managerial decision-making process, helps monitor and control operations and is responsive to the dynamic needs of the firm.

Although hospitality information system design may vary throughout the industry, they usually incorporate the same basic underlying principles:

❖ Provide a means by which to achieve organizational objectives.

❖ Treat information as an important resource and takes responsibility for its proper handling and flow.

❖ Has comprehensive informational product that enables the integration of functional operations, communications, and overall organizational coordination.

❖ Interface people and systems in relationships designed to free personnel to fulfill jobs requiring the human capability (human engineering).

❖ Provide a collection of historical and/or transactional data to support corporate planning, decision-making, and evaluation.

Since a hospitality information system has such broad characteristics, its design configuration must mirror the firm's organizational structure to ensure that the objectives of the organization will be met. The design of an effective HIS is built around the information needs of departmental managers. As managers define and prioritize their specific information needs, an information system can be designed to organize computer applications so that they support decision-

making activities at all levels within the organization. The levels of decision-making supported typically include strategic planning, tactical decision-making, and operational decision-making. Strategic planning refers to decision-making activities through which future oriented goals and objectives of an organization are established. Tactical decisions relate to activities required to implement strategic planning decisions. Operational decisions address specific tasks that normally follow previously established rules and patterns.

Once the information needs of managers have been identified, an HIS can be designed to perform the following functions:

❖ Enable managers to better monitor and administer transactions and activities.

❖ Provide a high level of operation and internal control over business resources.

❖ Produce timely and comprehensive reports formatted to the specific needs of managers.

❖ Reduce managerial paperwork and operational expenses by eliminating unnecessary source documents and streamlining data transfer and recording procedures.

It is for these reasons that the hospitality information system framework has become modeled around the overall corporate management structure while enabling operating departments to pursue their own areas of interests. The management reporting system component of the system combines various departmental facts with company goals and objectives, and presents control, efficiency, and managerial effectiveness evaluations. The design of an information system, therefore, is an integration of several interrelated subsystems that support managerial decision-making, assist in the planning and control of operations, and is responsive to the changing requirements of the organization.

Systems Manager

The manager of hospitality information systems, often referred to simply as the systems manager or systems supervisor, has a wide scope of responsibilities requiring familiarity with a variety of technology applications as well as functional operations of a hospitality organization. The manager must be able to unify on-site and off-site EDP (electronic data processing) systems while providing a reliable and efficient information distribution system for management and staff.

A successful hospitality information systems manager is a generalist, rather than a specialist or a technician. He or she has to be concerned with budgeting, problem solving, training, maintenance, and optimization of overall organization goals. The manager must possess an understanding of the complexities and interrelations arising through the integration of diverse functions. A sound knowledge of computer technology, information processing techniques, and management and decision making principles are needed.

The manager is responsible for directing the information system that performs the data processing and information activities for all major functional departments. Duties of the manager of hospitality information systems typically include:

❖ Planning and control of information system activities.

❖ Evaluation and selection of computer hardware and software applications.

❖ Development of configuration and design alternatives.

❖ Selection of personnel and establishment of training programs.

❖ Identification of processing priorities within the system.

❖ Establishment and implementation of system security requirements.

❖ Definition and documentation of system operations.

The systems manager typically is an individual who assumes overall technology responsibility at the property level. The systems manager, who serves as the property expert, tends to be more effective when exposed to advanced training and participation in the evaluation, selection, design, and installation stages of system implementation. A systems manager should be cross-trained in a diversity of applications and be capable of troubleshooting any system application wherever and whenever necessary. The information systems manager serves as the on-premises primary support person. In addition to other responsibilities, systems managers also review and present requests for system modification to management. If approved, the property expert discusses desired changes with appropriate vendors. The systems manager should document system changes.

HIS Manager Responsibilities

Specific duties of a hospitality information systems manager may include: authorizing and training users, establishing and enforcing data handling policies and procedures, ensuring continuous system operations, performance of preventive and emergency maintenance, and monitoring of system component and data file security. The information systems manager should be knowledgeable about the operating system and hardware components of all installed systems and networks. While a computer programming background may not be necessary, a familiarity with application software is extremely valuable.

Certified Hospitality Technology Professional (CHTP)

The International Association of Hospitality Accountants (IAHA) and the Educational Institute of the American Hotel & Motel Association (EI of AH&MA) maintain a joint certification program for hospitality technology professionals. The Certified Hospitality Technology Professional (CHTP) Program is administered by the IAHA and has the following objectives:

❖ To provide professional recognition to hospitality technology professionals who have acquired the basic educational proficiencies and practical experience that signify successful career progression.

❖ To encourage the education and advancement of hospitality association members (e.g., IAHA, AH&MA, CMAA, NRA and CHRIE).

❖ To cultivate professional cooperation among individuals within the hospitality industry.

Internet and Hospitality

The Internet is a large and complex series of computer networks designed to provide universal access to information and communication services around the world. Often referred to as the "information superhighway," the Internet resembles the intricate traffic patterns of local and county roads with connections to state and interstate highways. The Internet was initially conceived at about the same time as the development of interstate highways. The design of the interstate highway system, linking major cities across the country, was based upon the need to maintain a continuous flow of supplies throughout the country. The roadways were designed with sufficient alternate routing so that a steady flow of materials to all parts of the nation could be assured.

Similar ideas were important in the creation of the Internet. Using the interstate highway system as a model, the government turned its attention to similarly securing its intelligence system. The focus shifted from protecting vehicular traffic patterns to ensuring a continuous movement of data between mainframe computers at various strategic locations from coast to coast. Internet planners sought to create a myriad of alternate communication routes across a wide range of computer platforms.

The Internet has created a communications and information explosion with the potential to affect virtually every aspect of the hospitality industry. In an office environment, most networks connect individual microcomputers to a separate computer called a server or file server. The file server controls the flow of information along the network. It can also be used to establish a gateway to other computer networks beyond the office environment. The Internet takes the concept of networks to its fullest application by connecting large numbers of very complex networks. The Internet is an affiliation of tens of thousands of private, commercial, educational, and government-supported networks around the world. When a user connects to the Internet, data and information can be shared with millions of other users.

World Wide Web

The World Wide Web (WWW), also known simply as the Web, is only one of the many different parts of the Internet. It is the best-known part because its user-friendly features have attracted millions of users. Unlike text-only sites found on much of the Internet, the Web offers an incredibly rich combination of text, images, sound, animation, and video. The visual options of the Web and the surging numbers of "surfers" have enticed thousands of businesses, organizations, educational institutions, government agencies, and individuals to create their own Web pages and participate in the dissemination of information along the Web. For information about the Web sites of specific hospitality organizations, visit the sites listed at the end of this chapter.

Much of the user-friendly nature of the Web stems from the *hypertext transfer protocol* (http) that structures information on the Web. This protocol is a set of file download commands embedded within the *hypertext markup language* (html) used to place text, graphics, video, and other information displays on the Web. The http indicates that the Web page can handle nonsequential links to other hypertext pages—a trait characteristic of all Web pages.

A *Uniform Resource Locator* (URL) designates the Internet address of a site, usually the site's homepage. A site's homepage is the first screen or Web page presented when a destination site is located. URLs are usually built into the hypertext of a Web document, enabling users to jump from site to site along the Web. The URL for an organization, hotel, restaurant, club, or individual consists of a series of letters and punctuation marks that may seem confusing, even intimidating, to a novice Web user. Each grouping of letters represents a section of the path that leads to a desired site.

The best way to find a Web site when you don't know its address is to use a search engine. Commonly used search engines include:

❖ Yahoo
www.yahoo.com

❖ Netscape
www.netscape.com

❖ Web Crawler
www.webcrawler.com

❖ Net Guide
www.netguide.com

❖ Lycos
www.lycos.com

❖ Excite
www.excite.com

A search engine is a software program that reads indexed Web sites and creates lists and links to sites that match a user's inquiry. Most search engines provide tips on how to efficiently search for information. Generally, the more specific your query, the more relevant the list of sites generated. However, even if the resulting list is long, you can usually scroll or page through the list and decide which sites are worth a look. Then it's simply a matter of clicking on the link or URL to go directly to the Web document.

Questions and Assignments

1. Discuss briefly the growth of technology in hospitality. Use your library resources or the web browser and search engine of your choice, and identify an article that discusses technology and hospitality. Summarize your findings, and bring your results to class for discussion.

2. What is a PMS?

3. Discuss the potential capabilities of a front office application.

4. Why is it beneficial that the hospitality industry was late in adopting computer technology?

5. Define and describe "global distribution system."

6. Summarize the tasks and activities that a rooms management module can assist in.

7. Why is the guest accounting module considered to be a critical part of a front office system?

8. How do yield management (revenue management) systems benefit a lodging company? Use your library resources or the web browser and search engine of your choice, and identify an article that discusses yield management (revenue management) systems. Summarize your findings, and bring your results to class for discussion.

9. How has technology changed the night auditor's job?

10. Describe the various components of a restaurant management system (RMS). Use your library resources or the web browser and search engine of your choice, and identify an article that discusses RMS. Summarize your findings, and bring your results to class for discussion.

11. Briefly summarize the capabilities of hospitality accounting applications.

12. Define and briefly describe an effective HIS.

13. What is the role of a hospitality systems manager?

14. What exactly is the Internet? Use your library resources or the web browser and search engine of your choice, and identify an article that discusses the Internet and hospitality. Summarize your findings.

15. Perform an informational interview with a hospitality systems manager or an employee of a hospitality supplier of technology. The procedures are outlined in Chapter One. Check with your instructor how to avoid contacting someone already interviewed.

Bibliography and Suggested Readings

Kasavana, M. L. (1997). *Untangling the Web*. Orlando, FL: The Educational Institute of the American Hotel & Motel Association.

Kasavana, M. L. & Borchgrevink, C. P. (1997). Taking a byte out of the Internet: The best of cyberfoodservice. *Journal of Hospitality & Tourism Education*, 9(1), 56–61.

Kasavana, M. L. & Brooks, R. M. (1998). *Managing Front Office Operations*, 5th ed. Orlando, FL: The Educational Institute of the American Hotel & Motel Association.

Kasavana, M. L. & Cahill, J. J. (1997). *Managing Computers in the Hospitality Industry*, 3rd ed. Orlando, FL: The Educational Institute of the American Hotel & Motel Association.

Perspective on Innovation and Creativity in Hospitality

Bonnie Knutson, *The School of Hospitality Business*, MICHIGAN STATE UNIVERSITY

ABSTRACT

Taking a creative risk in business is no longer an option in the hospitality industry. It is a necessity in order to break through the increasingly competitive clutter. The hospitality industry is at a breakpoint between the *logical* and the *creative* phases in its business thinking. Practitioners of the new creative believe that the creative process, not the logic of the past, is the dynamic force of the future. They also believe that change is driven by the pull of the future, not the predictive push from the past.

OBJECTIVES

At the end of this chapter the student should be able to:

1. Understand the potential of innovation and creativity.

2. Understand the key reasons why creativity and innovation are often stifled.

3. Demonstrate their own level of creativity and innovation.

Introduction

Once upon a time there were three jewelry stores that stood next to each other. Each had the same front door, the same front window, and the same brick facade. The owners. Mr. X, Mr. Y, and Mr. Z all carried similar merchandise and targeted the same customers. In short, there wasn't much to differentiate one from another.

One day, Mr. X, who owned the store on the left, hung a huge banner across his storefront. It boldly read "Sale." The banner had the desired effect and soon Mr. X had more customers and was selling more jewelry than either of his competitors.

Seeing the success of his neighbor, Mr. Y, who owned the store on the right, decided that he too would promote his wares. Not to be outdone, he hoisted a banner high above his front door, which boasted "Biggest Sale Ever." Again, the sign produced the hoped for results and Mr. Y soon enjoyed more sales than the other two stores.

Poor Mr. Z. sandwiched between a "Sale" and the "Biggest Sale Ever," was experiencing declining customers, dwindling sales, and shrinking profits. He was in trouble. But what to do? How was he to get customers in the door? Being a small, independent business, Mr. Z didn't have a big advertising budget. He couldn't afford a catchy radio jingle or a big newspaper ad, let along a slick television commercial. So he thought; he pondered; he brainstormed. Then "Eureka!"

And a few days later . . .

Hung high on the facade of his jewelry store, between the "Sale" and "Biggest Sale Ever" banners of his competition, Mr. Z placed a sign which merely said, "Main Entrance" (with an arrow pointing downward to his front door)!

Moral of the story: *In an increasingly competitive business environment, you have to be creative!*

Very few of you will work for a company that can go head to head with the marketing might of a McDonald's, the clout of a Disney, or the energy of a Pepsi Cola. But what your company might lack in dollars or other tangible resources, it can make up for in the imagination magic of its people.

Consider AsiaGraphics, a small print shop located in the atrium area of a Shanghai, China conference center. It printed a simple half-page flyer and slipped it under the hotel room doors of the 350 attendees of an international business meeting. The message? "Run out of manual copies? Need extra name cards today? 'Oh man, I don't have a Mac to work on!' Now you can relax. Come to . . . etc."

Cost? Minimal.

What was the effect? Well, I know of at least 20 people who had Asia-Graphics print overheads, additional copies of materials, or additional business cards with their Chinese translations.

In other words, this little independent print shop used a creative message to show it was the easy solution to the traveler's big far-away-from-home problem. And it worked.

Consider the owner of a Chicago area pharmacy who spends 35 cents a day in his creative marketing campaign. Each day, on his way into work, he goes through the tollgate when he exits the interstate near his store. Knowing that most people who take that exit work in the area, he hands the gate attendant the 35 cents for his fee and another 35 cents for the car in back of him. He then asks the attendant to give his business card to the following car and say that the driver ahead has paid the toll. Within the first month, he had seven new customers, in the second month, nine, and (to borrow from Linda Ellerby) so the story goes.

Consider the owner of a Minnesota hardware store who creatively markets to the moms and dads watching their children play soccer in the field across the street. Every Saturday morning in the spring and fall, he makes a big pot of coffee, and then he and a helper walk over, cups and cof-fee in hand, to a group of about 60 grateful parents. Where do you think these people go when they need a hammer or a box of nails?

Finally, consider the manager of a travel agency who reaped more than a quarter of a million dollars in sales from a creative $75 advertisement. On a crisp November Saturday in 1987, Michigan State University was on the verge of wrapping up its first trip to the Rose Bowl in 20 some years. Knowing that most travel agencies were not even open on Saturdays, and those who were would be closed by the time the game was over, the young manager placed a small ad on the *sports* (note the location) page of the local newspaper. The ad stated that "*when* (note the choice of wording) MSU wins today, we will be open to take your reservations to the Rose Bowl." Before the night was over, she had booked 170 air/hotel/game packages, and by the end of the weekend, she had more than 300 customers going to cheer their team in California. At an average of $815 per booking, that is not a bad return on investment. And this was before any of her competition got their first dollar. To round out this story, many of the first-time customers stayed on to become regular clients.

You get the point. It doesn't take a lot of dollars to develop and implement a successful business strategy. What it takes is creativity and the belief in that creativity. Somewhere, between childhood and adulthood, most of us bury our creative powers deep in our minds. We forget how to be Tom Hanks in the movie *Big!* We forget to look for opportunities by seeing the world from a top-of-the-desk perspective like Mr. Keating did in the film *Dead Poet's Society*. We forget what it's like to create.

Why have so many of us buried our innate creativity? For students and managers alike, the cause seems to lie in the tightly intertwined 3 Rs: *Rut, Risk, Reward.* The ruts are too deep; the risks are too high; the rewards are too rare.

Rut

A few years ago, there was a great television commercial for a car that starts out showing a young elementary school girl creatively scribbling in her coloring book. It's obvious that she is "beating to a different drummer." Standing over her, with the camera lens purposely distorting his face in a black and white shot, is her teacher, who admonishes, "Stay within the lines. The lines are our friends." Scene two, of course, shows the same girl, all grown up, driving the car's convertible model on an open back road. She is as happy as a lark. The message to you as a hospitality management student is clear: Don't get into a rut. Don't let anyone stifle your creativity.

In recent years, organizations have come under the gun for not creatively using creativity. One of the strongest critics has been Dr. W. Edwards Deming, often credited with helping to place Japan on its economic highroad. He believes "our prevailing system . . . has destroyed our people. The destruction starts with toddlers . . . and [goes] on up through the university" (Pope, 1992, p. 1). Harold J. Leavitt, one of the founders of managerial psychology agrees, adding that socialized learning is "such a pervasive problem that you can't say to someone, 'Don't be socialized,' We are just socialized as h- - -" (Ray & Meyers, 1986, p. xv). In other words, you have been socialized to color inside the lines.

As Pogo would say, "We have met the enemy and it is us." (sic)

Businesses have fallen into a routine of training knowledge, not imagination. Yet, as Albert Einstein has been quoted as saying, "Imagination is more important than knowledge." And herein lies the first problem. While this knowledge-approach to business in general, and hospitality business in particular, may have worked in the past, it can't work for the future. By the turn of the century, the environment in which you will be living and working, will be

unprecedented. None of your predecessors will have experienced anything close to what you will be confronting. There will be no clear road map on how to manage the incredibly challenging business opportunities that will come with a global economy, a culturally-diverse workforce, exponential growth in technology and communication, and a very, very demanding customer base. Therefore, how can you learn the way you learned in the past? How can you justify learning *just* things—*just* knowledge?

The best hospitality leaders will have vision and guts. They'll ask *what-if* questions, and try to answer them with creativity. They'll turn things upside-down and inside-out to get new perspectives. They won't hesitate to carve a new path rather than following the one well worn (Stevens, 1991). Said another way, tomorrow's leaders will be creative thinkers. But are you adequately preparing yourself to compete in this new creative business world?

In his longitudinal study on learning preferences, Stevens (1990) found that today's hospitality management students prefer both pedagogical (teacher directed) and andragogical (self-directed) teaching less than any of their predecessors. This doesn't mean that they don't want to learn per se, he maintains. What it does mean is that they don't respond well to the learning process as currently dictated in the vast majority of higher education.

As a member of the Millennium or Generation X generation, you value prosperity, an exciting life, pleasure, and friendship more than earlier generations. You are the MTV generation who grew up with remote controls, computers, and stimuli that stretch far beyond a textbook, lectures, exams, and term papers. Consequently, you value, and will respond positively to, "innovative instructional efficiency," i.e., "learn me quickly" and let me have fun stretching beyond the norm (Stevens, 1990). In other words, to prepare yourself

today to effectively manage tomorrow's hospitality environment, the best hospitality students will break out of their past routine and create a learning environment in which they enhance their imagination *as well as* their knowledge.

In her book, *The Social Psychology of Creativity*, Theresa Amabile gives a scientific definition of creativity: "A response will be judged as creative to the extent that it is both a novel and appropriate, useful, correct, or valuable response to the task at hand, and (b) the task is heuristic rather than algorithmic" (Ray & Meyers, 1986, p. 4). The "a" part of the definition is easy. Whatever you do is creative if it is new, different and helpful.

It's the "b" part where we can get stymied. A *heuristic* is an incomplete guideline or rule of thumb that can lead to learning or discovery. An algorithm is a complete mechanical rule for solving a problem or dealing with a situation. Thus, according to Amabile, if a task is algorithmic, it imposes its own tried and true solution; if a task is heuristic, it offers no such clear path. You must create one.

But since when is any business situation totally algorithmic? Isn't it far more likely that a task at hand becomes algorithmic only when it is approached algorithmically, i.e., when managers approach it from a tried and true perspective? When they stay in their routine? When they stay in their rut?

The word *heuristic* has the same Greek root as the exclamation word "Eureka!" which is sometimes said to signal the "WOW" of a new idea. According to legend, Archimedes was sitting in a bath when he discovered a way for identifying the purity of gold by applying the principle of specific gravity. He was so excited that he supposedly ran naked through the streets shouting "Eureka!" (I have found it).

But why do people find it more comfortable to stay in their routine? Why doesn't creativity appear more often in business? To a great degree, the answer lies in the other two R's, *Risk* and *Reward*.

 ## Risk

Every act of creativity is actually an act of destruction. It destroys the past, the comfortable, the known, and the accepted. Therefore, a show of creativity is seen as risky and risk is seen as expensive—expensive in terms of dollars, in terms of time, and in terms of one's own career. Do you ever wonder what happened to the person who broke through the advertising clutter with the *Herb* commercial for Burger King? How many students risk their limited time and energies doing something "off the wall" in the classroom?

Try taking a truly heuristic approach to a term project. The first time or two when you set out the project's *un-guidelines*, you will be apprehensive. "But what does the prof want?" you'll query with an anxious face. What you may want to do is stand on the desk, turn the problem inside out and upside down, ask what-if questions, and develop a really creative answer. But then the "rut" will take over, you'll be afraid of the "risk," and fear you won't be "rewarded" with a good grade. So chances are you will look at your prof and just ask, "What size margins do you want on the report?"

Reality Check!

If you were asked to rate yourself on a creativity scale, like many students, you would probably put yourself below average. After all, you're not a painter, or architect, or musician; besides, you are going into business. What you may fail to realize, however, is that creativity thrives at all levels and in all phases of business: housekeeping, servers, corporate heads and everyone in between.

You can't totally fault yourself, however. By the time you reach college, most of you have been socialized not to take risks in school. You have found it too expensive to color outside the lines. In general, all you want to do is to follow the rules, pass the course, and graduate. What you have to remember is that you will be graduating into a world that will desperately need the same creative powers that you have been quietly harboring for years.

Faced with an increasingly challenging business environment, today's hospitality industry is beginning to look at risk taking in a more positive light. In a 1992 survey, for example, food-service leaders agree that effective leaders encourage risk in their organizations (Cichy, Sciarini, & Patton, 1992). This sentiment was echoed by speakers at an international industry conference (Carlino, 1993). The reason is not altruistic, however; it is survivalistic! Change is beginning to be seen more as a competitive advantage instead of a drawback, as a way to prosper instead of merely survive. It is coming so rapidly today, and from so many sides, that it may seem like a random bombardment. In reality, however, these changes are manifestations of deep-seated shifts in fundamental values that mandate fundamental change (Land & Jarman, 1992; Popcorn, 1992; Tucker, 1991).

Taking a risk in business is no longer an option; it is a necessity to break through the competitive clutter that exists in the hospitality industry. If a hotel, restaurant, or attraction can't break through the competitive clutter, it can't get noticed; if it can't get noticed, it can't be profitable. It's as simple as that. Perhaps Michael Roux, the former president of Carillon Importers, says it best. Doing something different "always involves risk because it always involves change. If you think the tried and true approaches are the best road to success, you won't break through the clutter, you will just add to it." (Knutson, 1991). In other words, if it ain't broke, fix it anyway!

The key to taking a risk in business is being sure you take a *calculated* risk. In other words, you have to do your research, analyze what you find, then work on developing a unique solution for the opportunity you've discovered. Remember, you don't have to create something from nothing to be creative in the hospitality business. You can simply put a new twist on something that already exists. Futurist Faith Popcorn calls that either *Twisting the Familiar* or *TrendBending* (Popcorn, 1991).

When you Twist the Familiar, you take something comfortable and turn it into something new. It is a way to grow a new market by building on something that people already know and like. For example, Ritz Crackers developed Ritz Bitz. McDonald's took a favorite food (fried chicken) and came up with Chicken McNuggets. The original Martini now comes in green, blue, and orange and is attracting many Generation Xers. What are the opportunities for you? Can tacos be shaped like ice cream cones so they would be easier to eat in a car? Could vitamins be added to beer? Could a guest check in and out of a hotel just by voice command? The possibilities are endless for creative twisting of what already exists.

TrendBending involves wrapping your promotional strategy around emerging consumer trends. Picking up on the move towards healthier eating, the Pork Council adopted the new tagline, "the other white meat" to position pork closer to chicken. Many bread companies, like Wonder, are now printing "No Cholesterol" or "Fat Free" on their wrappers. Their breads never have had fat or cholesterol, but recognizing consumers' craze for anything low-fat, fat free, or Lite, these food companies have bent their advertising around the trend. Hotels now tout Bounce Back or Get-Away Weekends. The hotel rooms haven't changed; what has changed is how hotels have wrapped their promotion around the 99-Lives trend. (99 Lives is Popcorn's name for increasingly busy, hectic lives.)

So how can you nurture such creativity into your hospitality career?

You can be a role model for risk. You can demonstrate the power of risk, creative ideas, and inventive actions by your example. As a future hospitality manager, you can show others not to fear change, but to embrace the risk that comes with being the *first*. Think about the success of Cabbage Patch Kids, Hula Hoops, Trivial Pursuit, and more recently, Beenie Babies. In the hospitality industry, there's the first drive-thru, the first all-suite hotel, and the first "eatertainment" restaurant. What creative firsts lie ahead for you?

Reward

One of my favorite stories goes something like this: There was a farmer who wanted to breed his three female pigs, so he loaded them into the back of his pick-up truck and took them to visit some boars at the next farm. While the pigs were getting acquainted, the first farmer asked the second, "How will I know if my pigs are pregnant?"

"That's easy," said the other farmer. "They wallow in the grass when it takes and they wallow in the mud when it doesn't."

The next morning, when the farmer looked out of the window, he saw his pigs wallowing in the mud. So he loaded them back into the truck and took them to the boars again. The following morning, the pigs were still wallowing in the mud. Undaunted, the farmer once again loaded the pigs into his truck and took them back to the boars for a third time.

Now, as it happened, the farmer had to be away from his farm overnight. As soon as he awoke, he anxiously phoned his wife and asked, "Are the pigs wallowing in the grass or in the mud?"

"Neither," she replied, "two of them are in the back of the pick-up and the third one is in the driver's seat blowing the horn!"

Out of this story comes two lessons that psychologists and parents of toddlers learned long ago, but business leaders are just now beginning to really understand. First, every behavior has its consequences; second, future behavior is a result of the consequences of past behavior. Put another way, you get the behavior you reward (LeBoeuf, 1987).

Isn't this just all common business sense? Sure it is. But like Ralph Waldo Emerson said, "Society is always taken by surprise at any new example of common sense."

In most cases, the greatest obstacle to creative performance in organizations is the mismatch between what is said and what is rewarded. Corporate boards tell their executives to focus on creative, long-term results, but then pay them big bonuses based on this year's earnings. University administrators say that professors are to be creative dedicated teachers, but tenure, promotion and raises go to those who do the most research and publishing. Even voters tell their representatives in Washington to reduce the federal deficit, but reelect those who spend the most money on their district's special interests (LeBoeuf, 1987). If you ever wonder why people behave the way they do, just look at what is being rewarded.

Every organization has its reward system, formal and informal. Sooner or later, almost everyone figures it out and behaves the way the reward system teaches them to behave. When the heuristic approach is rewarded, employees will come to see that creative behavior is integral to business, because such behavior is resourceful, useful, profitable, and self-expressive. It is not being different just for the sake of being different. Managers don't get what they hope for, ask for, wish for, or beg for from their employees. They get what they reward. "Creative energy will flow consistent with the pressures or constraints of the control structures, with what people are rewarded for . . ." (Kiefer, 1985).

The Future and Beyond

Casey Stengel supposedly said, "The future ain't what it used to be." How right he was. For those of us in the hospitality industry who insist, and many will, on clinging to the traditional ways of how things work, the future will hold even more problems than the present. But for those who change their assumptions, the future offers unparalleled opportunities for growth and fulfillment. This is the message of George Land and Beth Jarman (1992). They believe that all of nature follows a three-phase paradigm and that this cycle experiences abrupt shifts or breakpoints between phases. At a breakpoint, the way things work changes dramatically, and disorder reigns until a new perspective is formulated and put into operation. And as with any breakpoint, people and organizations experience a great temptation to cling to the past and resist the change.

These authors draw the exciting conclusion that, after thousands of years, civilization is at the breakpoint between *logical* (Phase 2) and *creative* (Phase 3). To date, Phase 2 logic has served us well. It has helped make our business practices the envy of the world. But moving to the creative Phase 3 requires us to do more than experiment with a new method or a new technique. It requires us to change our basic assumptions on how our whole world works. If you thought it yesterday, if you're thinking it today, you won't think it tomorrow. If you want to reap the rewards of a creative Phase 3 business world, but insist on thinking like a logical Phase 2 manager, the growth and innovation you will seek for your company will be beyond your grasp.

Land and Jarman maintain that practitioners of the new creative truly believe that (1) the creative process, not the logic of the past, is the dynamic force of the future, and (2) change is driven by the pull of the future, not the predictive push from the past. These ideas are not new. More than a decade ago, Alvin Toffler (1980) mapped out the third wave. More recently, Peter Senge (1990) admonished organizations to move their thought processes into the creative realm. What is new is the urgency of the breakpoint, the survivalistic nature of the change.

Phase 3 hospitality companies value people for their unique creative potential. They also understand that creative people are guided by vision, not by past success. Said another way, they value people who color outside the lines. Freedom begets creativity and creativity begets productivity (Popcorn, 1991). In your companies, assignments need to be purposely sparse on specifics and long on what goal has to be reached or question needs to be answered. At first, your employees will find this unstructured structure disconcerting. So will you. *Good!* We are all too used to rules that dictate the process and product of a project. *Margins . . . number of pages, Section III-A-4-d-(2)-(c) . . . ad infinitum*. So where is it written that a report must be submitted on 8½" x 11" paper? There's e-mail, videotape, rap music, a child's tablet, a ribbon roll. You get the idea.

We are taught to have only one right answer. The problem is, that once we find it, we stop looking. And nothing is more dangerous than an idea when it is the only one you have. If you place a dot on a chalkboard, elementary kids see all kinds of shapes and things in it. It's a donut hole. It's the eye of an invisible snowman. Or it's a lonely snowflake. Show the same dot to a group of corporate executives and they will squirm and fidget, then show relief when one of them says that the chalk dot is exactly that—a chalk dot. Noted educator Neil Postman says, "Children enter school as question marks and leave as periods" (Gerkman, 1992). The role of hospitality business is to put the question mark back in its people. The role of hospitality managers, then, is to get out of their rut, take risks, and reward creative behavior.

The hospitality winners of the year 2000 and beyond will be creative thinkers, not necessarily big dollar spenders. It doesn't matter whether they get their creative juices going in the shower, while jogging, or while playing couch potato in front of the television. What does matter is that you dig up your creative talents, trust them, and soon, like Mr. Z, you will be attracting more customers in your "Main Entrance."

Questions and Assignments

1. What are the key elements in developing a successful business strategy? Find an article to support your statement. Use your library resources or the web browser and search engine of your choice. Summarize the key points and be prepared to discuss with your team or classmates.

2. List and describe briefly the 3 R's described in the chapter. Have they ever hindered you personally?

3. Using your library resources or the web browser and search engine of your choice, search for articles that deal with innovation and creativity. Summarize the key points, and be prepared for a discussion with your team or classmates.

4. How would you suggest that a hospitality manager go about harnessing and encouraging creativity among his staff? Justify your response.

5. Choose a hospitality organization of your choice. Develop a creative and innovative presentation of this company using factual data.

Bibliography and Suggested Readings

Carlino, B. (1993, March 15). COEX: Paving the road to change. *Nation's Restaurant News.* 3, 63.

Cichy, R. F., Sciarini, M. & Patton, M. E. (1992). Food-service leaders: Could Attila run a restaurant. *Cornell Hotel and Restaurant Administration Quarterly,* 33(1), 46–55.

Gerkman, B. (1992). *Creativity in the Hospitality Classroom.* Lecturer's written notes from a presentation to a senior marketing class, Michigan State University, fall term, 1992.

Kiefer, C. F. (1985). *Leadership in Metanoic Organizations.* Unpublished manuscript.

Knutson, B. J. (1991, June). Breaking through the clutter. *Greater Lansing Business Monthly,* 44–47.

Land, G. & Jarman, B. (1992). *Breakpoint and Beyond.* New York, NY: Harper Business.

LeBoeuf, M. (1987). *How to Win Customers and Keep Them for Life.* New York, NY: G.P. Putnam's Sons.

Popcorn, F. (1991). *The Popcorn Report.* New York, NY: Doubleday.

Pope, L. (1992). *Peter Senge on Schools as Learning Organizations.* Written synthesis of 1991 presentation to Douglas County Schools.

Ray, M. & Myers, R. (1986). *Creativity in Business.* New York, NY: Doubleday.

Senge, P. (1990). *The Fifth Discipline—The Art and Practice of the Learning Organization.* New York, NY: Doubleday.

Stevens, P. (1990). Should I juggle and tell jokes? *International Journal of Hospitality Management,* 9(2), 95–102.

Stevens, P. (1991). Future of the hospitality industry. In Robert A. Brymer (ed.) *Introduction to Hotel, Restaurant, and Institutional Management.* 6th ed. Dubuque, IA: Kendall-Hunt Publishing Company.

Toffler, A. (1980). *The Third Wave.* New York, NY: William Morrow and Company.

The Leadership Perspective

Ronald F. Cichy, *The School of Hospitality Business*, MICHIGAN STATE UNIVERSITY

ABSTRACT

This chapter will introduce the concept of leadership and discuss some leadership perspectives. Foundational leadership issues such as trust, communication, vision, and perseverance will be introduced and defined. The importance of leadership to hospitality establishments will be emphasized.

OBJECTIVES

At the end of this chapter the student should be able to:

1. Define and discuss several approaches to leadership.

2. Outline the potential benefits of leadership.

3. List and define the foundations of leadership.

4. Establish the importance of mentoring.

Introduction

The philosophies of leadership have changed over the past decades in American businesses, in general, and hospitality businesses, in particular. In the early days of American business history, leaders were often charismatic authoritarians who simply willed things to happen. These autocrats had little appreciation for the value that their staff members added to their companies and the products and services that were produced for customers. Similarly, in hospitality businesses staff members were viewed as simply "employees" who were to be tolerated and little more. There was always another person waiting for an open position as the result of turnover, so why care about the people who create and deliver the products and services for your guests?

Today and into the future, staff members are increasingly being viewed as essential to the success and long-term viability of the place of hospitality. These "internal customers" are to be selected, not simply hired; trained; and developed to become all they are capable of becoming. The leader's role has changed dramatically. The effective leader of today and tomorrow recognizes that the four foundations of leadership—vision, communication, trust, and perseverance—are essential to achieve leadership excellence.

Traditional Leadership

When you think about a traditional leader, what comes to mind? Perhaps, you envision a great political or social leader such as Winston Churchill or Abraham Lincoln or Martin Luther King, Jr. who inspired others to see a different future and make the necessary sacrifices to transform the dream into a reality. Perhaps, you think about a "captain of industry," such as John D. Rockefeller or Henry Ford or Bill Gates who, with their ideas, transformed the way that we live. Or perhaps, you may think about a sports hero or an actress or a teacher that

has touched your life in a special way and encouraged you to grow and explore all of your options in this journey called life.

If you were asked to list the traits of effective leaders whom you have read about or have personally known, what would they be? Traditional and modern-day leaders have many similarities and differences. In this chapter, we will explore their leadership trait similarities, specifically as they relate to hospitality business leadership.

A Decade of Leadership Discovery

Beginning in 1989, researchers in *The* School of Hospitality Business at Michigan State University have systematically studied leadership qualities of chief executive officers (CEOs) and presidents of hospitality organizations. The study began with a survey of CEOs and presidents of the fifty largest United States lodging organizations. We conducted the study to find out what lodging leaders "stood for" in terms of their leadership qualities, keys, and secrets.

In two additional separate research studies, CEOs and presidents of the U.S.-based noncommercial foodservice industry and commercial foodservice industry were surveyed. Two subsequent studies focused on the leadership qualities of Japanese lodging industry and Japanese commercial foodservice industry CEOs and presidents. Next, the leadership qualities of U.S. lodging chief financial executives were identified, followed by a survey of U.S. club industry controllers. Since 1994, the leadership qualities of club chief operating officers have been tracked. In 1997, we identified the leadership traits of U.S. foodservice industry chief financial officers. Results of these nine studies clearly identify common attributes present in effective hospitality leaders, both domestic as well as international. Those qualities most strongly identified were related to trust, communication, vision, and perseverance;

these four have been identified as the four foundations of leadership in the hospitality industry. The four foundations are presented in Figure 1.

Trust and Leadership

Pearl S. Buck, an American woman who won the Nobel Prize for Literature, has said: "Integrity is honesty carried through the fibers of the being and the whole mind, into thought as well as action so that the person is complete in honesty. That kind of integrity I put above all else as essential."

This definition of integrity is intimately related to one of the foundations of leadership that we have repeatedly discovered over the past decade in our research: trust.

On the top of the list of leadership qualities that we have discovered is a strong personal value or belief system. This leadership quality is related to trust and tied to a leader's ability to know personal strengths and constantly work to enhance them. The capacity to develop and improve upon their skills separates leaders from followers. Self-awareness and self-understanding lead to being self-directed toward a shared vision for the organization. Self-awareness is the leadership quality embodied in the statement that leadership is first, foremost, and always an inner quest. Leadership must start from within, with self-awareness and self-understanding. An analysis of self begins the leadership process and helps guide the leader to be more effective in the achievement of goals tied to the shared vision.

Self-awareness is improved when an individual continuously evaluates inner feelings, motivations, and desired outcomes. Self-improvement is fueled by a knowledge that drives leaders to commit to a vision and live it. Leaders internalize their vision and make desired outcomes tangible by example and by acting as role models.

The feelings and perceptions of others must be understood and taken into consideration in all relationships. This understanding leads to modifica-

Figure 1. The Foundations of Leadership in Hospitality Business.

Foundation	Some Qualities of the Foundation
Trust	Strong Personal Value or Belief System
	Credibility
	Integrity
	Empathy
Communication	Listening
	Provide Information
	Ask the Best Questions
	Informality Enhances Communication
Vision	Compelling Message
	Tangible Desired Outcomes
	Precise Desired Outcomes
	Create the Desired Circumstances
Perseverance	Ability to Adjust
	Best Judged in Extraordinary Circumstances
	Courage
	Tenacity

tions in the leader's qualities and interactions as relationships develop with others. A variety of inputs coming from staff members, guests, peers, and superiors permit leaders to be effective with different individuals and groups they are leading.

For the leader, self-awareness also extends to awareness of the organization. This includes an analysis of the organization's strengths and weaknesses, its shared vision, mission, culture, and value system. A leader must be aware of the desired outcomes while considering available resources, as well as the competition. Organizational self-awareness includes a marketing analysis, systems and operational analysis, financial analysis, and most importantly, a human resources analysis.

Trust is built and reinforced by supporting staff members and encouraging decision-making at all levels. Effective leaders understand their positions and responsibilities and those of their staff members by being sincere, open, and truthful.

Trust is not instant; it is built over time and must be nurtured. It begins with honesty and reaches fruition through realistic self-assessment and development of personal conviction.

Thus, true leaders understand themselves and their convictions before attempting to build trust in a personal relationship or organization.

All strong human relationships are built on trust. Leaders develop trust-based relationships with individuals on the staff. From self-esteem comes trust, from trust comes commitment, and from commitment comes performance. The relationship of trust to empowerment is best summed up by surrounding yourself with great people, giving them the tools to do their jobs, and keeping them challenged. Leaders encourage risk-taking and encourage their staff members to carry out their responsibilities and grow in their careers.

When it comes to trust, the respect of others is earned through example and hands-on efforts. Leaders set the ethical and moral standards for their staff members and organizations. Whether or not the leader believes so, the leader is on center stage at all times and the examples the leader displays, both good and bad, build or tear down trust. While maintaining integrity and self-esteem, the leader must be honest in thoughts, feelings, and actions. Leaders trust people, as they would want to be trusted. They

develop a high level of personal and professional ethics and values. By basing leadership on those values, the staff members will personally grow to trust and respect others including the leader. A leader empowers and takes care of the staff; they in turn take care of the guests of the hospitality business. Leaders with integrity create trust in their organizations. This trust instills confidence in individuals and in organizations.

If a leader is consistent in the dealings with others (both staff and guests), trust and mutual respect develops. All staff members need to believe and feel that they are important to the success of the organization. A leader cannot expect that staff members will go all out if the staff members think that the leader does not believe in them. By keeping a focus on strong personal values as a leader, integrity and trust are built.

Communication: Interpersonal and Organizational

Leaders listen as well as, if not better than, they speak. Leaders listen carefully to others at all levels in the organization. Listening is the most important skill of communication, and listening patiently is critical to a leader's success and the long-term success of the organization.

Leaders listen and act on what they hear primarily from three sources: guests, staff members, and investors. Once information is obtained from these three sources, leaders focus all of their organization's efforts on supporting these three groups. The only way to recognize divergence and the modifications needed to rectify it is by listening. Leaders build teams through candor, communication, and commitment.

Successful leaders communicate the big picture or overall desired result to their people. Everyone wants to know where the organization is going—the vision for the organization—and how to get there—the goals and the strategic plan. By listening to suggestions from others in the organization, leaders become sensitive to better ways of doing business.

Leaders listen carefully to all others in the organization. Listening opens up new pathways of information for the leader. Leaders listen, then think, then act. A leader can enhance the hospitality business team's effectiveness by using listening skills to build commitment. New knowledge must be shared with members of the organization's team. Leaders enjoy and distribute knowledge and not ever waste it or hoard it. Look, listen, learn, and communicate is sound advice.

The process of learning is particularly important as it relates to communication. Communication skills are among the most important a leader can continue to build. Listening to others at all levels is essential. Actions speak louder than words. A leader lets her or his actions speak for themselves. Trust is built and reinforced by supporting others in the organization and encouraging decision making. There is a need for leaders to have a high degree of integrity, empathy, and trust, as well as the ability to communicate these qualities both verbally and non-verbally.

Leaders listen to others. They express their opinions explicitly. Leaders keep their supervisors well informed and maintain good communications with those surrounding them. An organization's climate can become vital and robust through better communications. Leaders who are good communicators develop strong listening skills. Leaders realize that they have nothing more valuable than their word and actions.

It is important to keep the lines of communication open at all times. Patience with others helps leaders become better listeners. Almost all hospitality businesses would be better if communications among the staff were better, and this starts with the leader. While traditional leaders bark out orders, effective leaders listen to the wonderful free feedback from their staff and guests. Effective leaders

are always good listeners. They pay attention and act in a timely manner based on what others are saying. Leaders solicit input from all levels of their staff and listen to the feedback with interest, empathy, understanding, and patience. Then these leaders try to facilitate the staff's suggestions and ideas that will help the hospitality business accomplish its mission.

Leaders are great listeners, first, and communicators, second. Leaders ask questions and then listen to what is spoken and unspoken. Listening to people, showing confidence, and using good sense when making decisions assist in the considerations of how decisions will affect all involved. Listening more than talking will help a leader understand the motives of an individual before prematurely judging that person's actions.

Leader-Member Exchange

Although there is no shortage of leadership theories, one way to explain leadership is through leader-member exchange. Simply stated, a leader does not act the same way with all others in the organization. Rather, the leader acts and behaves differently with different "members" (i.e., staff members) of the organization. In contrast to many traditional leadership theories, this one says that a leader interacts differently with different people in the hospitality business.

These interactions between the leader and individual staff members are related to a number of concerns that have traditionally faced hospitality businesses, namely burnout, job satisfaction, performance, and turnover. Burnout is a pervasive concern in many industries, including hospitality businesses. Burnout negatively affects both the individual and the organization. The individual is likely to experience burnout in ways that include physical and psychological effects, lowered job satisfaction, and negative behaviors including abuse of alcohol and illegal drugs. The hospitality business may suffer the consequences of staff member burnout

through dissatisfaction of other staff members, increased turnover as staff members leave for other employment opportunities, negative attitudes of those staff who remain, poor service quality, dissatisfied guests, and reduced profitability. A possible chain of these consequences is presented in Figure 2.

Job satisfaction is affected by the quality of the leader-member exchange. Additional relationships have been discovered between job satisfaction and performance, and job satisfaction and staff turnover. Job satisfaction is affected by other variables including the quality of communication between the leader and others in the organization. When leaders engage staff members in conversation about both work-related and non-work-related issues, the quality of the exchange improves. These conversations take place one-on-one with the leader and the staff member, not communication from the leader to

Figure 2. Possible Consequences of Burnout in a Hospitality Business.

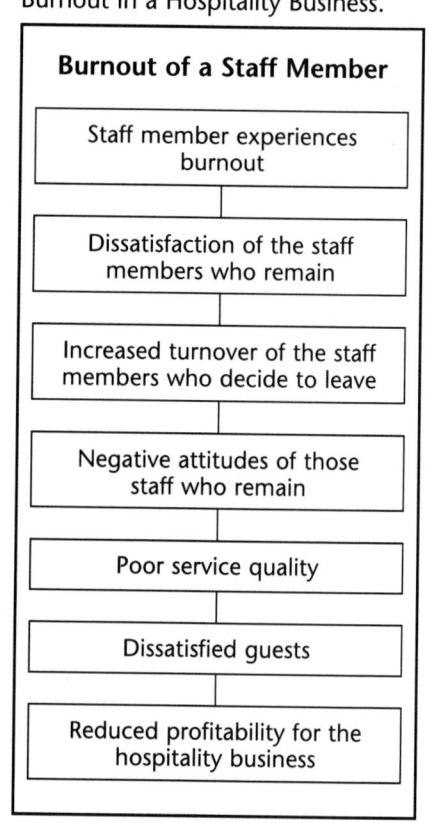

Burnout of a Staff Member

Staff member experiences burnout

Dissatisfaction of the staff members who remain

Increased turnover of the staff members who decide to leave

Negative attitudes of those staff who remain

Poor service quality

Dissatisfied guests

Reduced profitability for the hospitality business

all staff members at one time. When leaders spend time interacting with individual staff members, these individual relationships are enhanced and the quality of the leader-member exchange improves. Using this information, you realize the critical importance of mentor programs in which more experienced individuals help less experienced individuals understand the written and unwritten traditions, ways, and rules of the particular hospitality business.

The Tale of Mentor

The story of Mentor came from Homer's Odyssey. When Odysseus, King of Ithaca, went to fight in the Trojan War, he entrusted the care of his kingdom to Mentor who served as the teacher and overseer of Odysseus's son, Telemachus.

After the war and many years later, Telemachus, now grown, went in search for his father. Telemachus was accompanied in his search by Athena, Goddess of War and patroness of the arts and industry, who assumed the role of Mentor.

Father and son were reunited and together they cast down those desiring Odysseus's throne and Telemachus's birthright. Athena's role as Mentor for Telemachus was not only to raise him, but to develop him for responsibilities he was to assume in his lifetime. In time, the word Mentor became synonymous with trusted friend, advisor, teacher, and wise person.

—From *The* School of Hospitality Business World Wide Web Spartan Sponsors Mentor Program page. You can access this through *The* School's website at: www.bus.msu.edu/shb. Click on the Spartan Sponsors Mentor Program icon.

The modern-day application of the story is the link that occurs between a hospitality business leader and an individual who aspires to become like the leader. The mentor provides a source of knowledge about the dynamics of the industry as well as specific career opportunities. The opportunity for the person being mentored is to enhance her or his knowledge and learn the written and unwritten rules of the hospitality business. Think about the mentors that you have had in your life so far. Perhaps they were parents, relatives,

teachers, coaches, religious leaders, scout leaders, employers, supervisors, and others. What benefits did you realize from this leader-member exchange mentor relationship?

Most great leaders have been mentors to others. Choose carefully your mentors and learn from their experiences. Once you are in a position to mentor others, do so as a trusted friend, advisor, teacher, and wise person.

◆ Conclusion

To be a leader, fundamentally, means that you accept the great responsibilities associated with leadership. Since all leadership is relationship-based, a primary responsibility is to build trusting relationships based on integrity. Since leaders recognize the critical nature of communication, they listen as well as, if not better than, they speak. In your journey to becoming a leader in hospitality business, enlist the support of mentors along the way. Try to benefit from the leader-member exchanges in which you participate. Keep your focus on the end results and never give up. Model leadership behaviors and one day you will count yourself among the great leaders of this global $4 trillion hospitality industry.

◆ Questions and Assignments

1. Discuss the changes that have taken place in leadership philosophies over the years.

2. Using your library resources or the web browser and search engine of your choice, identify a current article that deals with leadership. Summarize the key points, and come to class prepared for a discussion.

3. List and define the four foundations of effective leadership.

4. Using your library resources or the web browser and search engine of your choice, identify a current article that deals with one or more of the foundations of effective leadership. Summarize the key points, and come to class prepared for a discussion.

5. Discuss the role of employee training and development from the leadership perspective.

6. Define "internal customers." How can "internal customers" impact the profitability of a hospitality business?

7. Using your library resources or the web browser and search engine of your choice, identify a current article that deals with "internal customers." Summarize the key points, and come to class prepared for a discussion.

8. Discuss the role of listening from the leadership perspective.

9. Using your library resources or the web browser and search engine of your choice, identify a current article that deals with listening. Summarize the key points, and come to class prepared to discuss the articles as it relates to hospitality management.

10. Using your library resources or the web browser and search engine of your choice, identify a current article that deals with leader-member exchange or mentoring. Summarize the key points, and come to class prepared to discuss the article as it relates to hospitality management.

◆ Bibliography and Suggested Readings

Borchgrevink, C. P., Cichy, R. F. & Susskind, A. M. (1997). Lean and mean do not equal profitable and hospitable. *FIU Hospitality Review*, 15(2), 17–25.

Borchgrevink, C. P. (1997). Paying attention to your immediate subordinate pays off. *FIU Hospitality Review*, 15(1), 97–102.

Cichy, R. F. (1998). Blueprint for leadership. *Michigan Lodging*, 13(6), 15.

Cichy, R. F. & Sciarini, M. P. (1990). Do you fit this profile of a hospitality leader? *Lodging*, 15(10), 40–42.

Cichy, R. F., Sciarini, M. P., Cook, C. L. & Patton, M. E. (1991). Leadership in the lodging and non-commercial food service industries. *FIU Hospitality Review*, 9(1), 1–10.

Cichy, R. F. & Cook, C. L. (1991). Leadership qualities: The non-commercial foodservice industry. *Restaurant Personnel Management.*, 4(8), 6–7.

Cichy, R. F., Sciarini, M. P. & Patton., M. E. (1992). Food-Service leadership: Could attila run a restaurant? *The Cornell Hotel and Restaurant Quarterly*, 33(1), 46–55.

Cichy, R. F., Aoki, T., Patton, M. E. & Sciarini, M. P. (1992). Five foundations of leadership in Japan's lodging industry. *FIU Hospitality Review*, 10(2), 65–77.

Cichy, R. F., Aoki, T., Patton, M. E. & Hwang, K. Y. (1993). Shido-sei: Leadership in Japan's commercial foodservice industry. *The Cornell H.R.A. Quarterly*, 34(1), 88–95.

Cichy, R. F. & Schmidgall, R. S. (1996). Leadership qualities of financial executives in the U.S. lodging industry. *The Cornell H.R.A. Quarterly*, 37(3), 56–62.

Cichy, R. F. & Singerling, J. B. (1997). Club COO leadership: A comparative study of leadership qualities of club industry chief operating officers. *FIU Hospitality Review*, 15(1), 25–36.

Cichy, R. F. (1997). Hospitality industry leadership: What do you stand for? *Lodging Unlimited Quarterly*, April 1997, 1–3.

Cichy, R. F. & Schmidgall, R. S. (1997). Financial executives in U.S. clubs: Foundations of leadership. *The Cornell H.R.A. Quarterly*, 38(5), 67–73.

Schmidgall, R. S. & Cichy, R. F. (1996). Historian versus visionary: Leadership traits of lodging financial executives. *The Bottomline*, 11(5), 9–13, 28.

Perspectives on the Hospitality Industry

INSTRUCTIONAL DISK

The computer disk included with this book contains the executive summaries of the chapters, and reviews the chapters in terms of primary topic areas. It also contains study questions, many of which require you to explore the WWW/Internet.

The disk is written in html (hyper text markup language) and can be read with any browser, such as Netscape or Internet Explorer. Because the disk is written in html, you can enter the Internet directly as you read the questions (provided you are logged on to the Internet).

Some questions have specified Internet sites. In those cases, you can simply click on the sites and the browser will take you there.